Magna Carta of Space

by William A. Hyman, A.B., LL.B., D.H.L.

New York City

Original Edition
First Printing

Magna Carta of Space

by William A. Hyman, A.B., LL.B., D.H.L.

PRINTED AND PUBLISHED IN THE UNITED STATES OF AMERICA BY

AMHERST PRESS
Amherst, Wisconsin

DEDICATION

To the Champions of Human Rights the whole world over.

"Then let us pray that come it may
(As come it will for a' that),
That Sense and Worth, o'er a' the earth,
Shall bear the gree, an' a' that.
For a' that, an' a' that,
It's coming yet for a' that,
The Man to Man, the world o'er,
Shall brothers be for a' that."
Robert Burns

ACKNOWLEDGMENTS

It is impractical to name specifically all those distinguished men and women to whom I feel a debt of gratitude for their dedicated and sacrificial service to the world of space, since to do so would make this acknowledgment burdensome and subject to charges of omissions for which due penance could never be done. Nevertheless, certain of these heroes in the new world beyond the horizons must be mentioned for special accreditation because they worked more closely with me or contributed much material for thought and action by their own comments, activities and writings.

Some of these warriors for peace through science and law serving in the great cause of human rights, who have given the author special inspiration and cooperation, are listed here alphabetically: (Note---All persons mentioned herein are in nowise responsible for, nor endorsers of, any statements in this book, all of which are solely the opinions and convictions of the author).

DR. ARTURO A. ALAFRIZ
Solicitor General of the Republic of the Philippines

DR. WERNHER von BRAUN
Director, George C. Marshall Space Flight Center, National Aeronautics and Space Administration, Huntsville, Alabama

PAUL DEMBLING
Lawyer, Lecturer General Counsel for NASA

MADELINE C. DINU
Member of the Section on Interplanetary Space Law, Inter-American Bar Association

LEON DRESKIN

Esquire, Member of the Section on Interplanetary Space Law, Inter-American Bar Association

DR. C. A. DUNSHEE de ABRANCHES

Lawyer, Educator, Author of "Espaca Exterior e Responsabilidade Internacional", Commentator on the Magna Carta of Space in Brazil and at Geneva

DR. ERNST FASAN

President of the Hermann Oberth Society (formerly the Austrian Rocket Society), of Austria

His Excellency
GEORGE J. FELDMAN

Formerly Director and Chief Counsel to the Committee on Astronautics and Space Exploration of the United States House of Representatives, formerly Member of the United States Delegation to the United Nations, now Ambassador from the United States to Malta

DR. JULIO FORCADE

Lawyer, Economist and Political Scientist

DR. LUIS E. GUILLEN

Member of the Section on Inter-Planetary Space Law, of the Charter, American Bar Association

DR. ANDREW G. HALEY

Author, Lawyer, General Counsel of the International Astronautical Federation

MELVILLE HARRIS

Lawyer, Specialist in Aviation and Insurance Law

His Excellency
MIHAIL HASEGUNA

Vice-Chairman, Committee on the Peaceful Uses of Outer-Space, United Nations; Romania

INTER-AMERICAN BAR ASSOCIATION
Section on Interplanetary Space Law

COL. MORTON S. JAFFE
Lawyer, Author, Legal Advisor to the Allied Forces Southern Europe

ROY W. JOHNS
Lawyer, Member of the Council, Inter-American Bar Association

His Excellency
PROFESSOR MANFRED LACHS
Author and Science Editor of The Saturday Review Lawyer, Member of the United States House of Representatives from the State of New York

S. HOUSTON LAY
Lawyer, Research Expert, Director of the International Law Program of the American Bar Foundation

JOHN LEAR
Author and Science Editor of The Saturday Review

HON. JOHN V. LINDSAY
Lawyer, formerly Member of the United States House of Representatives from the State of New York, Mayor of the City of New York.

His Excellency
DR. FRANZ MATSCH
Chairman, Committee on the Peaceful Uses of Outer-Space, United Nations; Austria

DR. MAURICIO A. OTTOLENGHI
Lawyer, Author, Banker; Argentine

JOSEPH A. OSTER

Lawyer, Insurance Department of the State of New York

RICHARD C. PEET
Lawyer; Washington, D.C.

PROFESSOR EUGENE PEPIN
Lawyer, Author, Educator, Professeur, de Droit de L'Espace a L'Institut International D'Etudes, President of International Institute of Space Law, 1965; Paris

HON. CLAUDE PEPPER
Lawyer, Author, Lecturer, Member of the United States House of Representatives from the State of Florida

DR. NICHOLAS LLINAS PIMIENTA
Lawyer, Educator; Colombia, South America

DR. JOSE ANTONIO RIVERA, hijo
Lawyer, Banker; Republic of El Salvador, Central America

DR. MICHEL SMIRNOFF
Lawyer, Author, Director of the Institute of Law and Science of Yugoslavia

WALTER SOIHER
Lawyer, General Council for NASA

JOHN E. STEPHEN
Lawyer, Author, and General Counsel to the Air Transport Association, Washington D.C.

DR. MARTIN SUMMERFIELD
Author, Educator, Forrestal Research Center, Princeton University

CONSTANTINE G. VAICOUSIS
Lawyer, Legal Advisor of Civil Aviation Administration; Greece

HON. LEO D. WELCH

Banker, Industrialist, Chairman and Chief Executive Officer of "COMSAT" (Communications Satellite Corporation)

DR. EDWARD C. WELSH

Scientist, Executive Secretary of the Executive Office of the National Council on Aeronautics and Space, President Johnson's personal scientific advisor

And finally, my dear wife, Marjorie, for her critical co-operation during the preparation of this book, without which this book would have been written in half the time it actually took.

CONTENTS

LIST OF ILLUSTRATIONS

FOREWORD

1

Space technology has progressed with an astonishing speed in the few years that have elapsed since the Russians orbited the first artificial satellite. Statesmen, diplomats, lawyers, scientists, moralists and other scholars have devoted a great amount of time and effort to developing rules for the control and guidance of activities in space and a very substantial amount of progress has been accomplished as reflected in the nuclear test ban treaty and the various United Nations resolutions setting forth recommendations for the conduct of nations and their activities in space. That the conduct of mankind organized into or subordinate to national governments is far from ideal is not in doubt.

William A. Hyman, author of this book and originator of the Magna Carta of Space is an angry, provoked idealist. He is provoked and angry that world leaders have not more promptly arrived at agreements which would assure mankind that activities in outer space would be conducted with an international harmony not yet found on the earth's surface. The author recognizes that activities in space constitute only one phase of man's activities which need regulating but he concentrates on the space aspects of human conduct, an area to which he has devoted much time and thought over the last several years. He acknowledges that the rules he proposes would be broken from time to time but points out that no one proposes repealing the Ten Commandments because of violations. He is also displeased with United States space efforts and places blame on government officials, industry leaders, labor unions and the general public with numerous illustrations of the shortcomings.

The author offers as a constitution or basic law for space activities the idealistic Magna Carta of Space which he has developed over a period of years. Mr. Hyman, a successful practitioner of various aspects of air law and other law presents a popularized and colorful argument attesting to the urgent need for agreement on broad rules of conduct of nations in space. His presentation has many of the attributes of an impatient plea to a jury in a case where everyone of conscience must agree with his ideals but where hard practical agreements to support the action demanded are difficult to come by. He deplores the inability of the United Nations to make faster progress.

Mr. Hyman poses most of the basic questions which are proving to be major stumbling blocks. Where is outer space? Where does air space end? How may the accident victim of activities in space be compensated? How can nuclear activity be controlled? What is peace? What is a peaceful and what is an aggressive use of space? Where does national sovereignty end and how is sovereignty acquired? How should space communications be organized and controlled? The author delves into history, morality, religion and current occurrences in pointing out the necessity, urgency and feasibility of agreement along broad guidelines for conduct in space. He indicates that agreements once adopted would not be static but would be subject to modification and interpretation consistent with advancing technology.

In his efforts to impress on the readers the urgency for political and legal agreements, advocate Hyman has deliberately inserted some minor inconsistencies and overstatements. For example, he refers repeatedly to the legal vacuum in space but when referring to the International Geophysical Year on page 78, he says, "Thus practically at the very commencement of the space age at least minimum essential rules and regulations were in existence to furnish some degree of cooperation and coordination." But later in his book on page 168, humanist Hyman states that his "long battle to bring the issue of space law before the world's conscience has not been for the sake of man in space but for the sake of man on earth, . . ." (See Footnote, page 20)

Mr. Hyman displays a far ranging knowledge of information about and related to space. He has deliberately written in a controversial manner in his determination to stir up concern about the conduct of mankind in space. There will be many who read this book who will disagree vigorously with some of the statements contained in it. I count myself among that group. Mr. Hyman will be delighted provided the reader feels strongly enough about the problem to lend his assistance to getting something done about it.

S. Houston Lay
Director, International Law Program
American Bar Foundation

(Footnote): In reference to the statement by Mr. S. Houston Lay, on page 19, lines 26 to 36, the International Geophysical Year agreement was primarily an agreement for scientific investigation that was limited specifically in time so as to run only from July 1, 1957 to December 31, 1958. Further, it was specifically understood that it was not to be the basis for the claims of any new legal rights by any nation. While it is true that subsequently the late Ambassador Adlai Stephenson did contend that the basic provisions of the International Geophysical Year agreement established a new mores for the world and therefore constituted a basis for a new "common law" which would hold after the expiration of the agreement, his views were not accepted. - William A. Hyman.

2

Few reasonable men doubt today that building a peaceful world is the most important job we have to do. We have learned that peace cannot be built by arms, conventional or unconventional; it can only be built by law, conventional and unconventional. And the leading architects of that effort must be the lawyers of the world.

Notable among these architects is William A. Hyman. His vigorous writings, speeches and debates, over the past decade especially, have contributed significantly to awakening the public and the Bar, in many nations, to the challenging problems confronting us in the space and thermonuclear age. His sensitive appreciation of the yearning of all mankind for peace, and the need to subordinate power to the hope of peace, mark all his work. He seeks what President Woodrow Wilson identified well as "The reign of law based upon the consent of the governed and sustained by the organized opinion of mankind." As did President Franklin Roosevelt, he understands that "all people must be as one in rejecting the thesis that any ruler, or any people, possess the right to achieve their ends or objectives through the taking of action which will plunge countless millions of people into war and which will bring distress and suffering to every nation of the world, belligerent and neutral, when such ends and objectives, so far as they are just and reasonable, can be satisfied through processes of peaceful negotiation and resort to judicial arbitration."

What is new and supplementary to these appreciations in Hyman's work is their amplification and application to space. His purpose is "to continue to alert all people, irrespective of their economic, ideological, political and educational status, to the threat to peace from unregulated space activities."

He is not content, and never has been, to be merely a listener or spectator. He is the able advocate whose clients' needs, as he sees them, require him to shape, think out, and state opinions and be responsible for them. In this he is fulfilling the advocate's office, which he cannot abdicate for reasons of apathy, inertia or timidity without forswearing his duty to his profession and the people he serves.

That is why he has written this book and that is why it should be greeted as a contribution to peace and an aid to those who work toward the realization of that goal.

I think he has done well to describe his work as "Magna Carta of Space". Dr. Helen Cam, in her Seldon Society Lecture in July of this 750th anniversary, reminds us that "The event, without precedent, set a precedent." Called "a stumbling block in English constitutional development" and "a charter, not of liberty, but of liberties - of privileges for privileged class", it has nurtured the rule of law. Pope Innocent, III, reacting to the event, described John as being "forced to accept an agreement that was shameful, illegal and unjust, impairing his royal rights and dignity. Therefore, we utterly reject and condemn this settlement, ordering under threat of excommunication, that the King should not dare to observe it nor the Barons require it to be observed, and we declare the charter, with all the undertakings arising from it, to be null and void for ever".

The declaration did not take. Rather, and notwithstanding John's repudiation of the charter of 19 June 1215, as Dr. Cam relates, it was revised and reissued three times through 1225. "This Charter of 1225 . . . was to become the first statute on the statute roll, not yet in existence in 1225. This, and not the Runneymede Charter, was the one enforced in the courts, revised and confirmed at least sixty times between 1216 and 1422; expounded clause by clause by Coke in the second Institute; the Charter of which nine clauses are still the law of the land; cited as recently as 1920 . . . 1951 . . . and 1955". Moreover today in the United States, it lives and thrives in the concept of due process of law.

Magna Carta has never been a finite or universally accepted concept. Nor is it to be expected that Magna Carta of Space will be. Rather it is to be hoped that it will serve as a working statement of principles to promote our understanding of the world in relation to space, the development of relevant law, and the achievement of the international legal order on which the hopes for mankind's survival largely depend.

From his independent position, and rich practical experience, and while acknowledging the impossibility of offering answers to all the legal questions relevant to space activity, Mr. Hyman has succeeded in proposing some viable solutions to the most vexing problems currently confronting us. He appreciates that "International law may be most realistically observed, and fruitfully conceived, as a process of authoritative decision transcending state lines by which the peoples of the world seek to clarify and implement their common interests in both minimum order, in the sense of the prevention of unauthorized coercion, and optimum order, in the sense of the promotion of the greater production and wider distribution of all values."

There are those who will both agree and disagree with Hyman's convictions, apprehensions and positions. Some will be awed by the feeling of unreality that one still experiences when discussing the law of space. Others, neutralists or of practical bent, will continue to view insouciantly matters remote from their daily work. Many will argue that preoccupation with the transnational and domestic legal, economic, social and political problems here on earth, preludes their concern with law for space. Some will wish for additional technical and scientific experience, for more preparatory work, even for controversies before essaying principles for space law.

For all of these and others, Mr. Hyman has written this book, but especially for the interested lay reader as well as for the lawyer of the future, aware, as Mr. Justice Frankfurter admonished, "that law is not a system of abstract logic, but the web of arrangements, rooted in history but also in hopes, for promoting to the maximum the full use of a nation's resources and talents." They will be rewarded by its persual.

Morton S. Jaffe
Colonel, US Army

INTRODUCTION

MAN BREAKS HIS earthbound shackles! Science opens up new worlds across the horizons and into the regions far beyond the old dreams and hopes of mankind.

A missile whirls through space at a fantastic speed of 18,000 miles an hour, circling the earth in an hour and one-half. That is science today.

A bullock pulls a cart slowly down a road deeply gutted with ruts made by preceding carts, practically at a standstill and unable to reach the market place to deliver its farm products a few miles down the road---before the missile has completed its world orbit. This is law for space today.

Global science is moving fast. Global space law is little past a standstill. Space incidents which threaten peace occur more and more frequently.

Research rockets of one nation can drop in foreign lands. Missiles sent by one nation traverse the airways, and the spaceways which belong jointly to all nations. A bitter missile race continues between certain nations foremost in this new science. The weapons of war are developing faster than the weapons for peace. Alarm over surprise attack through the area of spaceways fills the world with fear and brings us nearer to the danger of a suicidal war. The law alone, the weapon of civilized man, can save the situation.

Yet the law now stands still!

Why has this book been entitled *The Magna Carta of Space?*

Seven hundred and fifty years ago, the original Magna Carta was signed at Runnymede, England. It exacted from sovereign King John certain rights deemed necessary by the feudal barons for their own survival. The book's proposed law, set forth in *The Magna Carta* is directed to the survival of all Mankind. The establishment of the fundamental principles embodied in *The Magna Carta of Space* provides the protection for every human being in this world (or any other) against exploitation, destruction of human rights and dignity, and perhaps extinction, and provides the foundation from which there must evolve subsequently further specific regulations which will make the maintenance of those human and civil rights invulnerable to attack.

It is conceded by the vast majority of scholars and scientists that space will be the avenue to war or peace. International control of space, as provided in this *Magna Carta* will be a powerful force to compel the proper use of space---for peace---and thus avoid murderous conflict.

The author, in this book, will not usurp the function of the scientist, of the engineer, of the technologist, of the astronomer, of the nuclear physicist, of the chemist; although he will advert to these areas insofar as they are correlated with legal and sociological problems in space activities affecting the rights and obligations of mankind, as well as the survival of man. Nor will he undertake a detailed analysis of the tremendous scientific, technological and engineering research and results achieved in the realm of space.

Furthermore, the author has not cluttered this book with a great number of references and footnotes, although some references have been given in the appendix, since this work is intended for the layman as well as for the lawyer, the scholar and the diplomat. Some would have found the reading more difficult, the comprehension more delayed, and the burden intolerable, by voluminous citations and references such as are ordinarily incorporated in a brief or textbook.

With the removal of the psychological barriers---footnotes and interrupting citations---a book is more easily readable. Furthermore, effort has been made to avoid the "gobbledegook" and "gobbledegawk" resorted to by some writers in this field who have gone so far as to create their own terminology and to attempt to secure for themselves a monopoly of same, which could achieve no other objective than to create a dubious reputation for learning---if the readers ever completed reading such books.

This is a "fast" age. Outside of those initiated scholars and scientists dedicated to the analysis, anticipation and solution of the new problems confronting the world today, in the field of space, there are comparatively few who can and will patiently study and meditate on such problems. To reach not only the select group of specially trained men in this field, but also to reach the interested lay reader, the "common man" everywhere, this book has been written so that "he who runs, may read."

The author also, has given heed to the urgent request made by Muriel Beadle, to her husband, Nobel Prize Laureate George W. Beadle, in connection with a certain book he was writing and which contained technical terminology, making difficult the comprehension of his work:

"But, please George, write it in English."

The purpose here is to continue to alert all people, irrespective of their economic, ideological, political and educational status, to the threat to peace from unregulated space activities, and to the necessity for meeting such threat. To this end, although all problems cannot be set forth and fully discussed, reference to the most important critical issues are made and some answers are posed for thought and action.

It is not possible, of course, to offer solutions for all the complex legal, sociological and international political problems now present and also those which will arise in the accelerated use of outer-space. As of today, problems are created by the tremendous increase of activity by scientists, engineers and all others in the space field, yet without control and regulation by law and without protection of those greater rights of all mankind---human rights.

The Magna Carta of Space may be summed up as a humanitarian "bill of rights" for the world. If properly accepted and approved implemented and enforced, it will be a long step forward to the attainment of the goal of lasting peace through law, through offering an immediate palliative, if not a complete remedy to control these basic threats to human welfare.

Back in 1845, Urbaine Leverrier of France was first given full and sole credit for the discovery of the planet

Neptune's telescopic position---until it came out that John Couch Adams of England had preceded him by many months in making the same calculations predicting where the invisible new world could be viewed by telescope.

Many other such cases of "mistaken identity" as to the true discoverer, or the original author of a new concept, abound in history.

It is the author's belief that he has experienced the same mischance. The basic space-law principles contained in *The Magna Carta of Space* were officially recognized in February of 1961. Its basic tenets he had worked out many years before.

To his knowledge, and according to all search made, no one preceded him in stating this skeletal code and formulating this precise declaration of principles for space-law. Yet, time and again, his ideas---often his verbatim words---have been quoted or reference was made thereto in articles, books and speeches, but without any acknowledgement to the author. This may be complimentary to him but it is not helpful if any scholar, teacher, student, or any other member of the public, should raise a question as to the intent, definition or connotation of a particular principle, or a clause, or a sentence in *The Magna Carta of Space* and seek the answer from the author---if he is unacknowledged.

Accreditation to the author would help to overcome this difficulty by readily indicating to the inquirer to whom such inquiry should be directed.

While a few others in the field of space-law and allied areas early proclaimed, quite properly, "that law must precede man into space,"---notably that enterprising and able pioneer, Dr. Andrew G. Haley, of Washington---and while a few did proclaim some principles applicable to certain limited activities such as meteorology and telemetry, nevertheless, generally, there was silence, and even fear, disguised as caution, concerning the declaration of a set of legal principles relating to the problems of law and sociology in space ---the objective, this author aimed for in *The Magna Carta* from the beginning.

Some scholars in the field opposed any such short, concise declaration of principles, even though these were intended to serve only as guidelines. They urged that nothing should be done in this direction until the passage of time had produced many experiences and problems to go by, thus furnishing, according to them, the basis for an extensive and intensive code of regulations, including many minutiae as well as the larger issues.

They disregarded, however, the accelerated action of scientific achievements in space and the promise of still greater performances in the future---an increase in the threat to mankind and even to nature which might prevent the successful pursuit of such a dilatory course.

Fortunately, this last mentioned philosophy has been rejected. The philosophy advocated by the author has been generally accepted. A short statement of principles relating to all aspects of the use of space has been given preference to the dangerous alternative of waiting too long.

The fundamental philosophy of *The Magna Carta* is predicated on the principle that a reasonable man has the obligation to guard against foreseeable conflicts which a reasonable man should anticipate. No better way to accomplish this purpose exists than to adopt firm guidelines such as set forth in the writer's document.

This book establishes, therefore, that *The Magna Carta* is the first complete statement of the principles of space law in skeletal form to appear anywhere in the world, before they were presented by others in any definitive form. John Couch Adams made sure that he did not go down in historical obscurity for the discovery of a new planet. The largely unspecified "discovery" of a new world in the legal heavens is *The Magna Carta of Space.*

Space is the most vulnerable spot in the armor of every nation today, since the uncontested control of space would enable an aggressor to devastate the earth. Retaliatory power is of minimal value and potentiality in such a catastrophic situation. The nation which controls space will control the world. If this control comes into the hands of a ruthless, dictatorial nation, it may mark the end of freedom for all mankind. Public opinion, the determination of the common man throughout the world, backed by united action of the governments through an international law such as

The Magna Carta can prevent such a captured world.

The seriousness of the threat is well emphasized in the brilliant words of that far-seeing diplomat, Mr. Dean Acheson, in his book "Power and Diplomacy":

> "Our Promethean punishment for having stolen the nuclear fire of the gods is not only to live with the horror of our achievement but to live with the achievements and decisions of others."

The importance of international space law as the means of maintaining future peace cannot be overestimated.

Space science, plunging ahead in spite of the numerous sensational goals already attained, will produce still greater achievements in the future. This will make mandatory a change in the course of life everywhere---not merely on earth, but also in space and on the planets some day---and affect our relationships on an international and interplanetary basis.

President Lyndon B. Johnson, at the time that he was Chairman of the Subcommittee on Space and Astronautics of the United States Senate, stated in November, 1958:

> "Space has implications for virtually all of human activity. Space, as a dimension, enlarges the field of all our various earthly enterprises from commerce and trade to education and communication. The material of the Space Age may well reshape the structure of basic industry. The technology of space will have incredible impact upon our consumer goods.
>
> "Our leisure and luxuries, as well as our essentials, will be affected. The size of our economy and its financial values will be influenced and altered. So also will be where we live, what jobs we hold, what products we sell, what foods we eat, what land we farm, what medicines are prescribed for us. At present our vision in this realm could scarcely be more myopic."

Emphasizing again the dominating force of space on the world of today and tomorrow, President Johnson, in his Inaugural Address on January 20, 1965, pointed out:

> "For every generation, there is a destiny. For some, history decides. For this generation, the choice must be our own.

"Even now, a rocket moves toward Mars (Mariner-4). It reminds us that the world will not be the same for our children, or even for ourselves in a short span of years. The next man to stand here will look out on a scene different from our own.

"Ours is a time of change---rapid and fantastic change---baring the secrets of nature---multiplying the nations---placing in uncertain hands new weapons for mastery and destruction---shaking old values and uprooting old ways."

Do we dare wait any longer to establish the legal guidelines in regulation of space?

William A. Hyman
January 1, 1966

LIST OF PAPERS BY WM. A. HYMAN

The material in this book has in part been excerpted from and in part based upon the following papers presented by William A. Hyman before various organizations, American and foreign:

February 20, 1958
REPORT ON SPACE, American Bar Association, Committee on Aeronautical Law; Mid-Year Meeting, Atlanta Georgia

November 12, 1958
OUTER SPACE - SOME PROBLEMS AND SOLUTIONS, New York State Bar Association; Symposium on Outer Space, New York City

February 23, 1959
REPORT OF SUBCOMMITTEE ON SPACE LAW, American Bar Association, Standing Committee on Aeronautical Law; Mid-Year Meeting

April 10-19, 1959
REPORT AND RESOLUTION, Inter-American Bar Association, Committee on Interplanetary Space; Convention at Miami, Florida

April 1959
RESOLUTION, Federal Bar Association of New York, New Jersey, and Connecticut

November 16-20, 1959
WORLD PEACE THROUGH SPACE LAW, American Rocket Society; 14th Annual Meeting, Washington D.C.

December 28, 1959

WORLD PEACE THROUGH SPACE LAW, Philippine Lawyers' Association; Manila, Republic of the Philippines

August 16, 1960

SOVEREIGNTY OVER SPACE, XIth International Astronautical Congress, Third Colloquium on the Law of Outer Space; Stockholm, Sweden

October 10, 1960

SOME TERRESTRIAL AND CELESTIAL MEDICAL PROBLEMS, IMPACT OF THE SPACE AGE, Society of Medical Jurisprudence, New York Academy of Medicine; New York City

December 5-8, 1960

SPACE SOVEREIGNTY - ANALYSIS OF CONFLICTING THEORIES AND A SUGGESTION, American Rocket Society; 15th Annual Meeting, Washington, D.C.

February 1, 1961

MAGNA CARTA OF SPACE, Inter-American Bar Association; General Assembly of the 12th Conference, Bogota, Columbia

October 9-15, 1961

SPACE - THE LAWLESS REALM OF SCIENCE --IS MAGNA CARTA OF SPACE THE WAY TO PEACE? American Rocket Society; Space Flight Report to the Nation, New York City

April 24, 1962

WANTED-A POLICEMAN FOR OUTER SPACE American Rocket Society; Space Law and Sociology Conference, New York City

May 25, 1962

UNITED STATES COMMUNICATIONS SATELLITE ACT OF 1962, Federal Bar Association of New York, New Jersey, and Connecticut, Committee on Aeronautics; New

York City

September 25, 1962

THE MAGNA CARTA OF SPACE, XIIIth International Astronautical Congress & International Institute of Space Law; Fifth Colloquium on the Law of Outer Space, Varna, Bulgaria

April 22, 1963

THE MAGNA CARTA OF SPACE - THE LEGAL LODE-STAR, Inter-American Bar Association; Thirteenth Conference, Panama City, Panama

September 9, 1964

WILL EARTHLY CORRUPTION, COWARDICE, AND CONTENTMENT BE BARRED FROM THE INTERPLANETARY HEAVENS BY THE MAGNA CARTA OF SPACE? International Astronautical Federation, International Institute of Space Law; Seventh Colloquium of Space Law, Warsaw, Poland

May 22-29, 1965

MAGNA CARTA OF SPACE - A REVIEW OF SOME PROBLEMS, Congress of the Inter-American Bar Association, San Juan, Puerto Rico

September 15, 1965

THE COMMUNICATIONS SATELLITE CORPORATION, THE BEGINNING OF A COMMERCIAL ERA IN SPACE, Sixteenth International Astronautical Congress, VIIIth Colloquium of Space Law of the International Institute of Space Law; Athens, Greece

BIOGRAPHY

WILLIAM A. HYMAN, A.B., LLB, DHL (Hon.)
Pertinent Biography

Originally a native of Tampa, Florida.

Graduate of Washington & Lee University, Lexington, Virginia - A.B.

Graduate of Columbia University Law School - L.L.B.

Formerly Special Deputy Attorney General of the State of New York.

Formerly Assistant to the late Judge Charles B. Parkhill of the Supreme Court of Florida.

Member of the Bar of the State of New York, Federal Courts, and Supreme Court of the United States.

Trial Lawyer specializing in Insurance, Negligence, Aeronautical, Space, and International Law.

Formerly President, and formerly Chairman, of the Board of Governors of the Brooklyn-Manhattan Trial Counsel Association.

Inter-American Bar Association

President of the Committee on Interplanetary Space Law. Delegate of American Bar Association and New York County Lawyers' Association to the XIIth Conference of this Association at Bogota, Colombia, January 27th to February 4th, 1961.

American Rocket Society

Member Space Law and Sociology Committee.
Delegate-at-large to Congress of International Astronautical Federation, Stockholm, Sweden, August, 1960.

New York Academy of Sciences - Member.

The Explorers Club - Member.

Federal Bar Association of New York, New Jersey and Connecticut. Chairman of Committee on Aeronautics.
Chairman of Committee to Promote the Ideals of Democracy.

New York County Lawyers' Association (of New York City)
Chairman of Committee on Law of Space.
Member of Committee on Aeronautical Law.

American Bar Association
Member of Advisory Committee to Standing Committee on Aeronautical Law.
Member of Subcommittee on International Agreements of the Standing Committee on Aeronautical Law.
First Chairman of the Subcommittee on Space Law of the Standing Committee on Aeronautical Law.

International Law Association - Member.

International Bar Association - Patron.

American Society of International Law - Member.

International Association of Insurance Counsel - Member and one of the founders.

New York State Bar Association
Formerly Chairman of the Subcommittee on Air Space Law.
Formerly member of the Committee on Aeronautical Law.

Presided as Chairman at various colloquia on Aviation and on Space.

Lecturer at Law School of Kyoto University, Kyoto, Japan.

Lecturer at Law School of Cornell University, Ithaca, New York.

Lecturer at Law School of Washington & Lee University, Lexington, Virginia.

Lecturer before various bar associations, state, national and international and also at various conventions of other associations.

Pioneer in the fields of Aeronautical and Space Law.

Formerly associated with Professor Raphael Lemkin on the Committee to accomplish a Convention to Outlaw Genocide at the United Nations.

American Institute of Aeronautics and Astronautics
Section of Space Law and Sociology - Sometime Chairman of various Symposia on Space problems.
Delegate-at-large to Congress of International Astronautical Federation, Stockholm, Sweden. August, 1960.
Delegate to Congress of International Astronautical Federation, Athens, Greece, Sept. 1965.

Author of:
"The Magna Carta of Space"
"Space - The Lawless Realm of Science"
"Wanted - A Policeman for Outer Space"
"World Peace Through Space Law"
"Space Sovereignty - Analysis of Conflicting Theories and Suggestion"
"Some Terrestrial and Celestial Medical Problems - Impact of the Space Age"
"Sovereignty Over Space"
"Outer Space - Some Problems and Solutions"
"The Magna Carta of Space - The Legal Lodestar"
"Wanted - Law and a Policeman in Space with the Magna Carta of Space"
"Magna Carta of Space - A Review of Some Problems"

"The Communications Satellite Corporation"
"The Beginning of a Commercial Era In Space"

Delegate to International Bar Association Conventions in Madrid, Spain, and Oslo, Norway.

Addressed the Convention of the I.B.A. at Madrid on "Inadequacy of Liability Limits under the Warsaw Convention."

Address entitled "Sovereignty Over Space" delivered at the Congress of the I.A.F. at Stockholm, 1960, was the only paper accepted for reprint and redistribution in the Scandinavian Law Journal known as "Juristnytt".

Mr. Hyman contributed articles on the subject of Space Sovereignty and other Space Problems to numerous publications and also, he has discussed these problems over the radio and television in the United States and in other parts of the world.

Mr. Hyman is also recognized as a pioneer in the efforts to establish an international statement of principles regulating the peaceful uses of outer-space for the purpose of establishing law instead of lawlessness in this new field. He is still very active in pursuing this goal.

His address "World Peace through Space Law" delivered before the National Lawyers Association of The Philippines of December 28, 1959 was selected as one of two principal articles in the centennary edition of the Ateneo Law Journal of Ateneo University of Manila.

A winner in 1964 of the award for the most significant contribution to the field of the law of space; also, winner of the humanitarian award in New York City for the year 1964; sole champion in the courts of New York State in the famous "human guinea pigs" case stopping the use of elderly human beings in hospitals as guinea pigs in the live cancer injection experients; winner of various awards for his fight for human rights.

1

SCIENCE AND LAW

ON OCTOBER 4, 1957, the launching of the first Sputnik blasted upon us the opening of the Space Age. Then followed the numerous ventures into space. Missiles, rockets, satellites became household words in the language of the young as well as the old.

Progress has been astoundingly rapid through the years since then. First, the unmanned instrumented satellites, then the launchings of animals, followed by manned flights culminating by 1965 in "walks in space" by both American and Soviet astronauts.

Future history books will forever record that the first man in space was Major (now Colonel) Yuri Gagarin of Russia, first human being to enter the "space hall of fame" for his pioneering space flight.

On April 12, 1961, the most important stage in this new era was opened up when Major Yuri Gagarin of Russia orbited the earth---the first manned spacecraft. Then followed the flight of Soviet Major Gherman S. Titov, who orbited the earth seventeen times in twenty-five hours on August 7, 1961. In between came the short flights of Commander Alan B. Shepard, Jr. and Captain Virgil I. Grissom, American astronauts, eventually followed by long orbital flights of the Mercury astronauts from Col. John H. Glenn Jr. to Major L. Gordon Cooper Jr. In that time, the Soviets also placed several of their cosmonauts into orbit for extended periods. Russian two and three-man flights and our own two-man Gemini schedule have introduced the advent of spaceship "crews".

The crescendo of thundering space rockets has risen to fantastic proportions today. In the first eight years of the Space Age no less than 450 vehicles (USA and USSR) have been hurled into space, out of which some 200 earth-satellites are orbiting over our heads at this moment. Altogether, including such "hardware" as empty rocket-shells, spent retropacks, spin-weights, and the like, over 1,500 such pieces of "space junk" also orbit with those working satellites. Their "decay" or fall from orbit occurs at the rate of some 300 per year, or almost one every day. Some are gigantic third-stage rocketshells weighing tons, and at least one such man-made "meteor" (Sputnik IV) did not burn up completely in September, 1962, and showered a trail of debris on earth through Minnesota and Wisconsin, fortunately not striking any people though some had narrow escapes and saw pieces land at frightful speed and still smoking hot.

SPACE TRAFFIC JAM

It is estimated that by the end of 1970, there will be over 1000 satellites and space stations orbiting earth, along with a staggering 15,000 pieces of rocket debris --- a "space traffic" problem that is already worrying the National Aeronautics and Space Administration (NASA) and no doubt the Soviet leadership of their space program also.

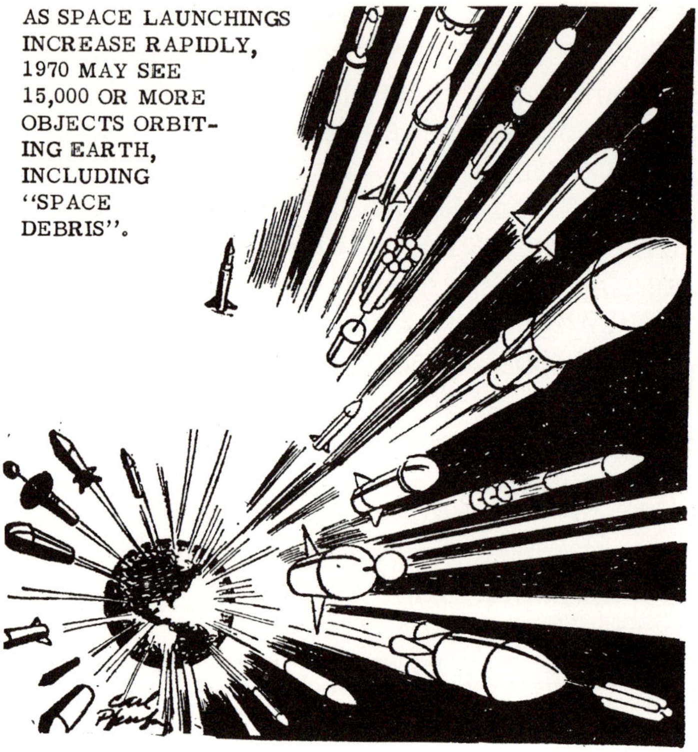

As a blurb in Pageant magazine (July, 1965, We Need Space Law Now! by William A. Hyman) puts it:

> "Traffic jamming the heavens is becoming a politically explosive issue, warns this expert in international law. And unless the United Nations devises a workable code for outer-space, the historical pattern of earthly chaos will be repeated in the sky."

To give other sensational developments in science:

Plans have already been discussed in this country to effectuate a mail service by rockets and missiles that would permit delivery of a letter mailed from New York to be received in Tokyo in an hour.

Polaris missiles fired from submarines beneath the sea surface can strike a target almost 3,500 miles distant. The development of the first true amplification of light might soon lead to the capacity to generate a fine light beam which could develop sufficient intensity to illuminate parts of the moon's surface and to vaporize materials in its path, notwithstanding that the moon is 240,000 miles from earth. It could also be used to devastate parts of earth.

New orbiting laboratories, as yet unmanned, are being sent to probe the magnetic field in outer-space. This will all too soon help science to measure the influence of powerful magnetic fields on such tiny particles as electrons, protons and neutrons and lead to the discovery of new surprises in the cosmic system, bringing to light the vast reaches of outer-space including the bombardment of earth by cosmic rays.

World meteorological projects, not only for weather forecasting, but even weather control, are in the area of attainment. Eventually this will lead perhaps to the dispersion of fog and to such control of weather so as to stop hurricanes and typhoons while they are being formed. Likewise, the possible effects on agriculture are most apparent.

Suppose one nation succeeds in controlling rainfall. Then through this control it diverts rain necessary for agriculture from some other country. By so doing, the controlling nation might be able to convert a fertile land, rich in fruits, grains and vegetables, into an arid and desolate wasteland. What can the victim nation do to prevent this danger? What can the devastated country do to bring the wrongdoer to account?

CURRENT TIROS AND NIMBUS WEATHER SATELLITES MAY LEAD TO CONTROL OF RAINFALL SOMEDAY BY MEANS OF HEAT-MANIPULATING (INFRA-RED) SUN-POWER SATELLITES.

The use of space for such purposes, as well as for other numerous purposes such as communications, surveillance, transportation and the like, need not be amplified at this time. They are well known to scholars in this field. They all present problems for which at the present time there is no adequate legal answer.

THE LEGAL VACUUM IN SPACE

The Age of Rocketry has moved ahead at such a speed as hardly to permit the ink to dry on one rocket plan before another plan has been formulated. The speed is incomprehensible and it is still increasing in the accomplishments of space exploration.

It poses the question: should we not take steps to guard against foreseeable damage, danger, dispute? We cannot wait any longer for slowly evolving case law to determine the minimum standards of conduct. We must anticipate and we must take steps to meet the crises which we anticipate before crises develop.

In February, 1958, at the time this writer was the Chairman of the Subcommittee on the Law of Space (of the Committee on Aeronautics of the American Bar Association, the first committee in that Association to undertake the duty of analyzing the requirements of legal regulations of space) he urged that the President of the United States consider the legal problems relating to space and, impliedly, take steps to meet these problems. Some effort was made but nothing much came of it.

One of the principal dangers against which we must guard is the lack of a sense of urgency. The Vostok and Voskhod, the nuclear tests in space, the recent triumphs of the Soviet, have corrected this to some extent. Undoubtedly, they did prod our Government intc still greater and more determined scientific efforts and perhaps take the mind of our lethargic public momentarily away from television murders, westerns and deodorant advestisements. But not enough. The situation is urgent, perhaps critical.

Global science has advanced at a pace far beyond the wildest dreams of man. Law has remained static! Diplomacy has retrogressed!

Of course, there have been and will be difficulties in solving the procedural and substantive problems involved in the creation of an adequate International Declaration of Law on Outer-Space. There will be conflicting questions of sovereignty. There will be individuals in a position to influence opinion and events who may consider the problems solely from nationalistic viewpoints. Nevertheless, we must realize that we must pass from the era of the nation-state to the era of the embryo world-state. As members of the community of world-states, we must settle our differences peaceably and without resort to combat.

Be it quickly noted that this does not mean that the United States should not be at all times fully prepared to meet any contingency which might be precipitated by a breach of international law. The author's proposal does not imply a policy of unpreparedness. On the contrary, the greater our military and economic strength, the better is our position for enforcement of international law.

Let's not forget Munich and its false peace. Let's not forget the second Munich---the surrender of Suez and its false peace and fateful consequences. Let's not forget those countries whose conquest was preceded by co-existence agreements and by abandonment of preparedness. Let there be not third Munich---in space. Let there be peace based upon law and preparedness. In this manner can we secure world peace through space law.

This theme has been urged constantly by sagacious men who foresee the dangers of lawless space, too long continued like a festering sore. A look back through mankind's long history does not ease our worries, for unfortunately, since Cain killed Abel, man has sought to destroy man. The sixth Commandment, "Thou shalt not kill", has been broken not only by individual murderers but by murdering nations as well. Man has visited upon his fellow-man the most horrible sufferings and tortures.

In fact, he has even sought to destroy whole races of people for no other reason than that their peoples belong to ethnic groups other than those of the conquering madmen. The explanation may be over-simplified but it is found in a simple fact: reason is not always the master of emotion. Unfortunately, emotion, too often, is the master of reason. The result has been world crime and chaos for suffering humanity.

As members of the community of world-wide nation-states, we must find a way to live together peacefully, under law. In this regard I believe that the statement by former President Harry S. Truman, in Kansas City in 1945, after he had come East from San Francisco following the birth of the United Nations, is most fitting:

> "It would be just as easy for nations to get along in a republic of the world as it is for you to get along in the republic of the United States. Now when Kansas and Colorado have a quarrel over the water in the Arkansas River, they don't call out the National Guard in each state and go to war over it. They bring a suit in the Supreme Court of the United States and abide by the decision. There isn't a reason in the world why we cannot do that internationally."

This republic of the world may well be aborning in the United Nations.

There is no perfect solution because no system invented by imperfect man can ever be perfect. The creation of an international space law for the world will provide the surest means of achieving the goal of all human beings---World Peace.

In a speech delivered before the American Rocket Society on December 7, 1960, at the 15th Annual ARS Meeting in Washington, D.C., the author ended with the following statement:

> "And what if we fail to fill the law vacuum? Some scholar in an age yet unborn, writing in a script yet unknown, may tersely comment: 'That's the way it was when the world went out, not with a whimper but with a bang'."

A nuclear bang, that is.

If space remains lawless, the threat of nuclear bombs delivered from orbit will haunt the world.

NEED FOR SPACE LAW

Formerly United States Senator Hon. Kenneth B. Keating now judge of the Court of Appeals of the State of New York, and (then Congressman from New York State) urged at the Convention of the International Astronautical Federation at The Hague in August, 1958, that a Space Code be drafted immediately. He stated: "It is too risky to wait for slowly evolving laws to develop for the control of outer-space." He called for a world conference within a year or two to ratify such a code. This was not done.

Honorable Earl Warren, Chief Justice of the United States, in his address before the Georgia Institute of Technology in Atlanta, Georgia, on February 12, 1963, stated: "A society that is governed by law will not permit these great (scientific) discoveries to be used for destructive purposes. A world without law is hell-bent for destruction with or without scientific discoveries".

The four billion dollar anti-missile radar screen of North America gives only thirty minutes' warning of nuclear attack. Thus, "life expectancy" is thirty minutes. This is the status of the continuity of the world today.

The controversial "Needles" project of the U.S. Air Force placed in orbit a cloud of copper needles as part of a military communications experiment---described by Sir Bernard Lovell of the Jodrell Bank Laboratory in England as "an act of extraterrestrial contamination". The blast of H-bombs high over the Pacific (Operation Dominic, Project Hardtack, July, 1962) in the lower reaches of aerospace, interfered with the existing radiation belt and created a man-made radiation belt, described by this same leading scientist as "one of the most clumsy and dangerous experiments ever devised". The high-energy radiation thus created also seriously damaged five American satellites. Suppose they had been satellites of another country!

Complaints came, as early as March 1947, from Japanese tuna-fishermen whose health and catches of fish had been damaged by fallout from the Marshall Island thermonuclear test explosions in the Pacific.

Was there any law under which they could be given compensation? There was none. However, the United States, recognizing the moral obligation and responsibility, in spite of the absence of any regulation of space, undertook to make satisfactory arrangements for the victims of these experiments.

The Russian launching of space-booster rockets over a distance of 8,500 miles, and pinpointed to a small impact area near the U.S.'s Johnston Island in the Pacific, has occurred every year since 1960. Presumably, more powerful launch vehicles were tested each time, the latest rumored to be perhaps twice as powerful as our Saturn-1 vehicle with 1,500,000 pounds thrust.

In the first of such long-range tests in 1960, one of the shots by accident almost come in contact with a Qantas airplane carrying over one hundred passengers. That Soviet test rocket penetrated through an area of earth that belonged to everyone, and in which every nation has equal rights of free passage for its airliners and ocean liners.

Also, a Soviet nose-cone---probably jettisoned after one of its satellite launchings---landed in Alaska. And rocket fragments from a Soviet launch landed in South Africa in September of 1960.

The United States is not guiltless. As early as December 5, 1956 (prior to Sputnik) a Snark guided-missile left Cape Canaveral on a test-flight and went out of control. It was lost in the Brazilian interior, somewhere in the Amazon, fortunately without striking any isolated Indian villages there.

Then, in 1961, a launch from Cape Canaveral reportedly "showered debris" from the empty first-stage casing down on Cuba, killing a cow and endangering nearby people.

But what about test rockets and the possibility of striking a ship or plane with loss of lives? Will there be any solution to inevitably conflicting claims, except by force ultimately?

The possible dangers of acting too soon are outweighed by the certain dangers of waiting too long for the enactment of regulations governing the use of outer-space. Not only in the United States but in other parts of the world, the urgency for establishment of law to regulate the peaceful uses of space has been emphasized.

Outer-space is now being explored by an increasing number of individual nations and will soon be put to extensive use. Shall we sit idly by or shall we do what we can to insure that the use of outer-space be devoted to the common benefit of all mankind?

The apathy towards legal protection and regulation of outer-space still remains, with only little indication of an awakening. To avert the catastrophic threats which will be multiplied by the increase in scientific developments and further victories in space---whether a landing on the moon, the launching of a platform, the control of the cosmic ray, nuclear testing in space with disastrous fallout, or other overwhelming scientific accomplishments---in whether it is now necessary that the people of the world be protected by establishment of law rather than be exposed to a continuance of lawlessness in the new world so recklessly exploited by science.

Catastrophic threats through space will be multiplied tremendously as these scientific developments occur, in- now that we anticipate as much as we can these future that we now anticipate as much as we can these future problems and provide for reduction of their disastrous consequences internationally, through the establishment of regulation of space by an international skeletal code.

It would make this treatise too extended to envisage and describe the invasions of the interplanetary world which could result in conflict, unless the restraint of law were first imposed upon the space explorers. The favorable reaction on the part of some scientists to the necessity for correcting this vacuum in space is reflected in the comment made by Dr. Wernher von Braun, when he stated in a letter to the author:

> "I read your enclosed piece 'Wanted - A Policeman for Outer Space' with much interest and was impressed with the statement 'Let us now terminate the legal vacuum in space. Let us now unite on the fundamental principles

for the protection of all--- *The Magna Carta of Space* and the establishment of the United Nations as the policeman in space'."

"LET US NOW UNITE ON...THE ESTABLISHMENT OF THE U. N. AS THE POLICEMAN IN SPACE"...FROM A PAPER BY WILLIAM A. HYMAN AS QUOTED AY DR. WERHNER von BRAUN.

In a speech delivered on June 14, 1917, President Theodore Roosevelt said: "Nine-tenths of wisdom is being wise in time".

INVOLVEMENT - OR APATHY?

"Help me! Help me!" pierced the midnight air of a well-to-do middle-class neighborhood, Kew Gardens, New York City, in March, 1964. But there was no help.

Lights went on, windows opened up, "good neighbors" put their heads out of the windows. The assailant jumped into his car and fled away. Lying on the sidewalk, stabbed several times, the young victim staggered up to go to her home, only three doors away. The windows closed, the lights went out.

Again screams: "Help me! I am dying. Won't somebody please help me?" The assailant had returned and resumed his attack.

Again the lights went on in the apartments of the "good neighbors", and the windows opened. People looked, but no one went to help this agonized young woman who lay dying on the sidewalk. Again the lights went out.

Once more the assailant, who had fled a second time, returned to attack his victim again. In the vestibule of her own home, she died.

Eleven times she had been stabbed. Not one person had given her help. The police interrogated these "good neighbors", middle-class, comfortable and well-to-do. "Why did you not call the police?---Why?" And the answer came from each: "I didn't want to get involved."

While a cheerful sun was shining, in the month of May, 1964, a young lady, an office worker in a working-people's section of the Bronx, was assaulted, beaten, raped---while forty people heard her screams and saw the attack. Yet, not one raised a finger to help her; not one called a policeman. Accidentally, a patrolman was passing the scene and rushed to her help, but all too late. The witnesses scattered, but several were finally identified and questioned: "Why did you not call the police?" Again the answer: "I didn't want to get involved."

Another case in point: In July, 1963, twenty-two helpless, friendless, penniless, chronic invalid patients in the Jewish Chronic Disease Hospital in Brooklyn, New York, were offered up by the Medical Director to experimenters from the Sloan-Kettering Memorial Hospital in New York to serve as human guinea pigs to receive injections of live cancer cells, for the purpose of determining whether such cancer cells could be induced or be rejected in patients who are non-cancerous but were suffering from other diseases.

These human guinea pigs never gave consent, nor were they informed that live cancer cells were to be injected into them. Some patients died. Three young doctors in the Jewish Chronic Disease Hospital, acting as Medical Coordinators, were requested by the Medical Director to conduct these experiments secretly. They refused. These doctors, demonstrating the highest degree of loyalty to medical ethics and to honorable conduct in their profession, openly proclaimed their dedication to the Code of Ethics on Human Experimentation that evolved from the Nazi medical prosecutions at Nuremberg.

Behind the experimenters from Memorial Hospital stood institutions with millions of dollars and tremendous political support and protection. On the Board of Directors of the hospital in Brooklyn were political office-holders of great power.

A vain protest was made by one Director against these Nazi-like practices, which violated the Nuremburg Code, and which invaded the human and civil rights of the helpless captive patients.

The Board of Directors of the Jewish Chronic Disease Hospital refused to discipline the offenders or to take any action to stop the assault of experimenters on patients incapable of understanding or giving consent. They offered the same excuse: "We do not want to get involved. In fact, they did nothing to stop these practices, but voted to continue these outrages on condition that consent should be obtained---consent from patients incapable of giving consent.

Some directors stated "the Hospital gets 20% of the moneys received by the medical director and his doctors for these experiments and we can use the money for administration expenses"---paralleling the acts of the negro tribal chieftains in the fifteenth century who sold members of their tribes to the white slave-traders for use in the Caribbean.

Here this hospital, through some of these directors, was selling the human rights of innocent, uninformed, helpless patients to get money for the hospital---a practice found to be quite common in many hospitals in the State of New York and in the United States. This supplemented the moneys retained by the experimenters themselves.

When one Director dared go into court to obtain access to the medical records of the patients on whom these experiments were imposed, to determine the results of these experiments in order to deter these practices which brought Dachau to America, everyone ran to cover.

For their protection against exposure certain parties in the hospital obtained the aid of powerful politicians who brought their capacity for obstruction and concealment, in vain, to the aid of the hospital. In this instance the political cesspool proved a failure.

Thereupon, the Commissioner of Hospitals in the City of New York issued rules to the staff of every hospital under his jurisdiction, requiring that they first ascertain a patient's competency and ability to understand what was proposed to be done to him; that the patient's consent be obtained; and that the screening of such prospective guinea pigs be done by a Medical Committee; and that the consent be obtained in writing.

Numerous offers of cooperation were made to this Director by important people and associations, but at the last moment, practically all of them withheld open support.

The reason for this desertion? "We do not want to get involved!

But the lone director who had been denied access to the hospital records "of the human guinea pigs", which records he had sought to prove the invasion of their human rights, won the final decision in the Court of Appeals in the State of New York on his application as director to see the hospital records and the experimental records of these human guinea pigs.

In addition, the two medical experimenters in charge of this inhuman work had been brought up on charges of practicing fraud and deceit on these helpless invalid patients, the human guinea pigs, following the request for an investigation into their conduct made by the lone director who brought the action at law.

In a disciplinary proceeding the two head experimenters were found guilty on June 10, 1965, of practicing fraud and deceit in that they had failed to inform these helpless and friendless patients that they were being injected with live cancer cells and without disclosing to them what they were doing to them and without getting their informed consent in advance.

This one director mentioned above, fighting alone and disdaining the current false philosophy of "non-involovement", forced disclosure of the horrible invasion of human rights of helpless invalids. By so doing he re-established recognition of the supremacy of human rights.

Because it has happened many times before in human history and the history of slow, halting progress toward human rights, the author quotes from an article by the renowned science editor and author John Lear, in the Saturday Review (June 26, 1965, The Patient's Right to Know) in which, after reviewing the pertinent facts of the case, he states:

> "Mr. Hyman had to fight all the way up to the Court of Appeals of the State of New York, with no help from medical organizations or institutions. He won his case on March 18, 1965, as a lone lay petitioner..."

The writer of this book did not mind the fight. He is used to it in the legal profession. But that he was forced to fight his way alone to preserve a sacred façet of human rights---that is what makes the author fear for the future of civilized society. If everyone "does not get involved" in these matters soon, they will inexorably get involved in something else they won't like at all---denial or abrogation of the human rights that brave people fought for through the last five centuries, and which this generation seems willing to drop in a few short years.

SPACE AND THE PEOPLE

Now we pass from the local scene---undoubtedly duplicated in many parts of the world as to public apathy, the cowardice of some individuals, the corruption of political machines, and the content in many parts of the world to abide by the status quo---to the international stage.

"Help me!" is the cry now heard from the small underprivileged new nations---many of them weak, helpless, oppressed, poverty-stricken and hungry---to the powerful nations of the world. Their appeals cannot be answered by the selfish and stupid philosophy---"we cannot become involved."

We have passed from the era of the isolated Nation State to the era of the World State. All must become involved in the preservation of humanity---in the preservation of earth man---in the preservation of peace. This can only be done by establishment of law and order in the celestial arena---without waiting for landings, settlements and habitation on the planets beyond the earthly horizons of old.

To quote the great Albert Einstein, from his letter of August 2, 1939 concerning the nuclear bomb, to President Franklin D. Roosevelt:

> "Our defense is not in armament, nor in science nor in going underground. Our defense is in law and order."

The apathy of the public is cause for grave concern since governments will often not act until made to act by the aroused will of the people. This callous indifference may be due to failure on the part of leaders of nations to correctly, fully and properly inform and alert the common man as to the implications of the impact on life caused by uncontrolled and lawless science.

Furthermore, the political "machine" in control of government, in various places of the world, so dominates the common man that he is intimidated and fears to protest the actions of "the establishment," thus permitting the destruction of human rights to proceed in an unchecked and unrestrained manner.

It is the author's sincere belief that support by all of *The Magna Carta of Space* ---scientists, lawyers, diplomats, people in every walk of life of all nations---is a decisive method to awaken the world to the ever-increasing threat to survival, and to provide necessary restraint and avoidance of the inevitably fatal effects of lawlessness in outer-space.

After years of persistent effort by the writer in various parts of the world, the breakthrough was effectively made in Bogota, Colombia, in February, 1961, when *The Magna Carta of Space* was approved by the Inter-American Bar Association. This was followed by action through the United Nations, through scientists, diplomats, governmental and non-governmental leaders the world over, from the vast majority of whom came commendation and support.

To summarize, there is no security or protection for mankind in the refusal of anyone to "become involved" in a cause that is clearly just and cries for help from courageous, sincere and thinking people. There is no place for neutrality in the fight for the protection of human rights.

Involved people, all over earth, face many grave issues in the present and in the near future. Undoubtedly the landings of crews of American and Russian astronauts on the moon will create problems of sovereignty and of conflicting claims. This is only a few years ahead of us--- 1970 or sooner.

Will planets be deemed "terra nullius" (subject to appropriation under certain conditions) or will they be deemed "res communis" (that is, not subject to appropriation, but free for exploration or use by all) like the high seas and with equal obligations and rights for all mankind?

WITHOUT "MAGNA CARTA OF SPACE", WOULD INHABITANTS OF ANOTHER WORLD BE SUBJECTED TO CONQUESTS AND COLONIZATION PRACTICES OF 14TH AND 15TH CENTURIES?

What about life on other planets? If there is life in any form of culture, civilization or biological development, will the inhabitants of such other planets be subjected to the colonial invasions and conquests of the fourteenth and later centuries, which afflicted the earth and led to numerous wars?

Will the nations of the earth fight to get such control of outer-space so as to give to any conquering, dominant nation the same rights of sovereignty as were asserted in the earlier centuries by those who held sway over the oceans by their armadas and temporarily invincible fleets?

"Colonialism" in the interplanetary regions, in any disguised form, must be prevented!

Service to our nation and to the world can be rendered by the solution of these questions in only one effective manner---not by combat, but by an international law regulating the use of outer-space for peaceful purposes.

A skeletal code is desperately needed---now. And that is precisely what *The Magna Carta of Space* is designed to be.

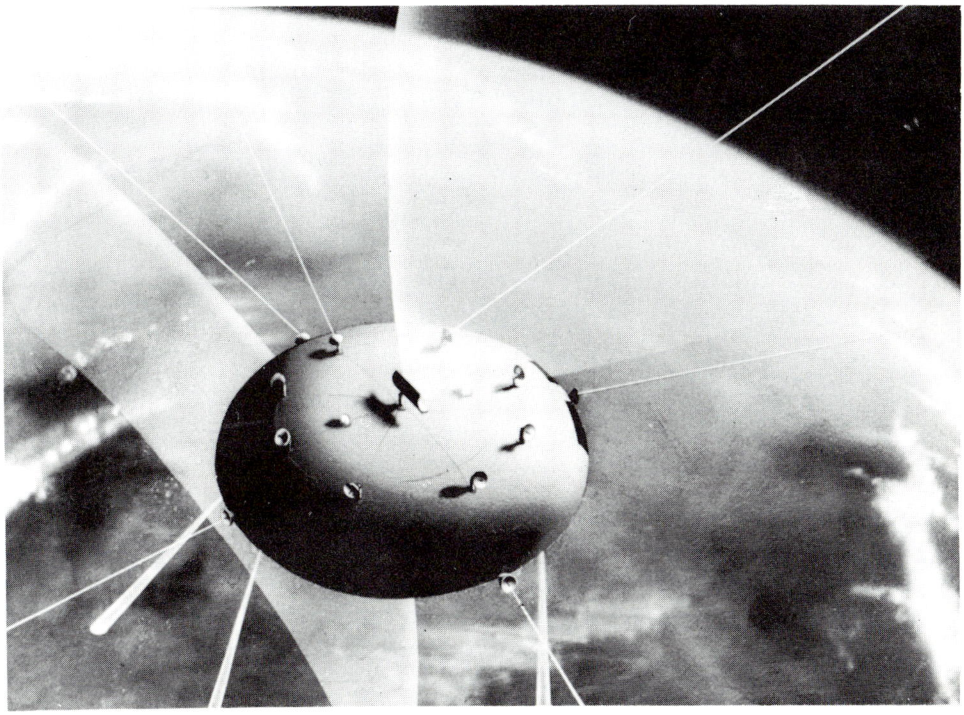

Without space law, this space engineer's "orbiting patrol craft" may someday prowl through the vacuum, equipped to detect and destroy enemy ICBMs or spacecraft.

2

LAW - CIVILIZATION'S ANCHOR

For purposes of orientation it might be forgivable to give a few elementary, fundamental definitions at the outset. What do we mean by "law"? What is "law"?

> "Law is the process and the art by which a society compels its members and the sub-groups within it to observe those purposes, principles and standards considered essential by the society or by its Government. Observance of law is never absolute . . . the law constitutes a valid description, not only of the society's ideals and values, but also of the actual behavior of its members. In a satisfactorily functioning system of law, 'ought' and 'is' are united . . .
> "Law has two aspects - essentialness and effectiveness. Law consists of those rules which a society believes are so essential that they ought to be enforced, and which at the same time are so effectively enforced that they can be relied on."

What is meant by "international law"?

This has been defined in broad terms as "the body of general principles and specific rules which are binding upon the members of the international community in their mutual relations . . ."

It has also been stated: "International law consists of certain rules of conduct which modern civilized States regard as being binding on them in their relations with one another, with a force comparable in nature and degree to that binding the conscientious person to obey the laws of his country; and which they also regard as being enforceable by appropriate means in case of infringement."

The fundamental principle also has been stated as follows:

> "It is the body of principles and rules which civilized

> States consider as binding upon them in their mutual relations. It rests upon the consent of the sovereign States."

International Law has been defined as the sum total of the limitations of rights of powers exercisable by the State. These rights of power remaining to the State are its sovereignty.

A broader definition has been given as follows:

> "We must expand our interpretation of the term 'international law'. We must cease to think of it as merely a set of principles to be applied by courts of law, and understand that it includes the whole legal organization of international life on the basis of peace and order. Such an organization must provide for peaceful and orderly use of political, as well as judicial, methods of adjustment."

What is meant by "space law"?

There has been no agreement among any of the nations in the first place, as to what constitutes outer-space. For the purpose of this book, it is suggested that "space law" might be deemed that law which shall be applicable to the area above the stratosphere (the analysis of airspace and outer-space, and the differences in the rights and obligations obtained therein, will be given in greater detail in Chapter VII).

Why do we limit this discussion to peace through "space law"? Why "space law"? Because it is generally conceded that space will soon---too soon perhaps---be the avenue to peace or war; that control of the use of space will impose restrictions on the unrestricted use of that avenue to war. The importance, therefore, of space law as the means to establishing peace cannot be overestimated.

WHAT IS "PEACE"?

Now we go to another attempted definition which, while simple in its connotation to the ordinary man, is in itself possessed of certain complexities and different interpretations in different parts of the world and in various social systems.

What is meant by "peace"?

This concept must be divided into the two fields of social systems now occupying the attention and causing the concern to the world, to the Soviet and to the Western Democracies.

The Soviet and Communist view of peace is one of co-existence and they have popularized the term "peaceful co-existence." Lenin, Stalin and Khrushchev all used the term reflecting a certain degree of continuity in the Communist vocabulary. Stalin speaking to the 14th Congress of the Communist Party on Dec. 18, 1925, said:

> "....The Capitalist world is being corroded by a whole series of internal contradictions which are enfeebling; on the other hand, our world, the world of Socialism, is becoming more and more closely welded, more united; . . . because of this, on precisely this basis, there arose that temporary equilibrium of force that put an end to war against us, that ushered in the period of 'peaceful co-existence' between the Soviet States and the Capitalist States."

The ingredients of the term "peaceful co-existence" are enunciated in a treaty between India and the Peoples Republic of China, signed on April 29, 1954, in Peiping. The treaty called for mutual respect for each other's territorial integrity and sovereignty, mutual non-aggression, mutual non-interferance in internal affairs, and equality and mutual benefit.

The Afro-Asian Conference of twenty-nine countries meeting in Bandung, Indonesia from April 18 to April 24, 1955, used the phrase "live together in peace" in place of the controversial term "peaceful co-existence". It is reported that it was Chou En-lai himself who proposed the substitution in order to influence colleagues skeptical of the term "peaceful co-existence."

Chou later told the Standing Committee of the International Peoples Congress in Peiping on May 13, 1955, that:

> "In actual fact, for countries of different social systems to live together in peace is the same as peaceful co-existence."

Khrushchev said on November 6, 1958, the 41st Anniversary of the Bolshevik Revolution, that:

> "Socialism and Capitalism exist on one planet and therefore, co-existence is an historic inevitability . . . peaceful co-existence should be built on life without war on the basis of peaceful competition".

SPACE CO-EXISTENCE?

The New York Times, Saturday, November 7, 1964; as made available in English, excerpts from a report delivered by Leonid I. Brezhnev, First Secretary of the Communist Party, at the celebration meeting in Moscow on the eve of the 47th Anniversary of the Bolshevik Revolution:

> "The Soviet Union has been pursuing and continues to pursue the Leninist policy of peaceful co-existence of states with different social systems.
> "The purpose of this policy is to prevent a world thermonuclear war, to settle disputes between states by negotiations, to respect the rights of each nation to select for itself the social and state system it desires, and to settle in its own way the problems of the internal development of the country."

As for America's attitude in this matter, Ambassador Henry Cabot Lodge told the General Committee of the General Assembly of the United Nations on Sept. 30, 1957, in discussing the principles of co-existence, that:

> "These principles stated in another way are what we are all committed to by our adherence to the Charter of the United Nations. All men of good will approve such ideas."

The usual Western view of the content of peace is expressed in the Teheran declaration by the United States, England and Russia on Dec. 1, 1943, following the Teheran Big Three Conference, as reported in the New York Post of Dec. 6, 1943:

"We fully recognize the supreme responsibility resting upon us and all the United Nations to make a peace which will command the good will of the overwhelming masses of the people of the world and banish the scourge and terror of war for many generations.
"We shall seek the cooperation and active participation of all nations, large and small, whose peoples in heart and mind are dedicated . . . to the elimination of tyranny, slavery, oppression and intolerance."

Speaking on the subject of peace Charles Evans Hughes (in Pathways of Peace, 1925) in his address before the Canadian Bar Association, Montreal Sept. 4, 1923, started with another man's quote:

" 'War,' said Sir Henry Maine, 'appears to be as old as mankind, but peace is a modern invention.' It is hardly that; it would seem to be an occasional experience rather than an achievement. To one who reviews the history of strife from the 'universal belligerency of primitive mankind' peace appears merely the lull between inevitable storms always gathering in some quarter with the fateful recurrence of the operation of nature.
"Great powers, well armed and having the vivid sense of opportunity, supported by popular clamor for vindication of national interests, are disposed to seize what they believe to be within their grasp. Resistance by force means war. Fear of opposing forces may stay the hand, but this does not mean peace---rather renewed preparation and the waiting for the day. There is only one way to make peace secure and that is the difficult but necessary effort to translate particular controversies into voluntary reasonable agreements . . .
"We have to take account of both the advantages and disadvantages of democratization. It is generally thought that Democracies are disposed to peace, but this is yet to be demonstrated, where there is deep feeling and a national sense of injury. Great wars, involving vast populations, cannot be fought without public support, but the most serious causes of war are precisely those which carry popular appeal. The peoples of the warring nations were never so united as during the last war, and this was generally true of both sides. A sense of injury is easily created and confused with a sense of justice. A despot may be as indisposed to war as any people, and Democracies never lack leaders to inflame popular passion.

> ". . . Conferences are often treated as though they provided an actual solution of all difficulties, but for most countries they accomplish nothing unless the conclusions are ratified by a popular assembly. Democracies may be loathe to go to war, but they are extremely difficult agencies of international compromise in the interest of peace."

What do we really mean by "peace"? Does it involve the cessation of the cold war? We think so. Do others agree with this thought? Does it involve abstention from efforts at subversion? Does it include the abandonment of propaganda and espionage? Does it mean that no one nation or group of nations should attempt to impose their social system upon another nation or group of nations who are living under another social system?

Does it mean that Communism shall refrain from attempting to impose its way of life upon the Western Democracies in the same manner as the Western Democracies shall be restrained from attempting to impose their way of life upon the Soviet, its satellites and other social systems existing in other parts of the world?

Does not true peace mean that each nation and each group of nations shall be free to choose their own legal system, their own social system and their own modus vivendi?

Cynicism and doubt, of course, cannot solve any problem. To quote President John F. Kennedy:

> "On both sides . . . civility is not a sign of weakness and sincerity is always subject to proof."

Does true peace mean that the United States and its allies shall desist from attempting to create its standard of life for those nations who are the recipients of aid as well as those nations who are not the recipients of aid from the United States? This simple word "peace" contains many connotations of an economic, political, scientific, sociological and legal nature which could well be defined within the scope of a skeleton outline of an international law relating to outer-space, and thus help to avoid conflict and misunderstanding.

Bear in mind that the realistic development in the practice of a theory does not follow the theoretical statement. Within its Communist framework, "peaceful co-existence" by no means indicates the end of the strife between the Communist States led by the Soviet Union and the Western alignment led by the United States. Sir Roger Makins, former British Ambassador in Washington, has aptly said:

> "For the Russians it (peaceful co-existence) signifies a temporary detente during which they can build up Communist strength and sap the will of the Free World, the state of what has been called provisional 'non-belligerency'."

Mr. Makins suggested that a more appropriate term would be "modus vivendi" implying peace through balancing strength.

THE RUSSIAN POSITION ON OUTER SPACE

In September, 1959, Lunik II launched by the Soviet hit the moon. American correspondents asked Mr. Nikita S. Khrushchev (then Premier) whether the landing of a Soviet pennant on the moon gave his country any grounds for making property claims on the moon. Mr. Khrushchev replied:

> "We regard the launching of a space rocket and the delivery of our pennant to the moon as our achievement, and when we say 'our' we imply all the countries of the world, that is, we imply that it is also your achievement and the achievement of all people living on earth."

The Soviet Union was among twenty-four signatories to a resolution of the United Nations A/Res/1721 (XVI) which was unanimously approved in the Political Committee of the General Assembly on December 11, 1961. The second part of paragraph B, Article 1 of this resolution declares that outer-space and celestial bodies are not subject to "national appropriation". Commenting on this resolution, Y. A. Korovin, member of the Academy of Sciences of the USSR, stated:

> "Any attempt by a power to establish its right of ownership of the boundless expanses of the cosmos would indeed be comical."

Similarly, I. E. Kovin, editor of International Affairs, Moscow, stated:

> "On the basis of this material, it must be concluded that national sovereignty does not extend to cosmic space. However, it does not follow that space is to be considered as some kind of 'legal vacuum' where no restrictions on freedom of action prevail. All universally accepted rules of international law apply to the cosmos as well. The presence or absence of separate specialized legal systems corresponding, for example, to international maritime control, cannot abolish the generally recognized principles of law prevailing in our time wherever people are acting on land, sea, air or space."

However, acceptance of or acquiescence to this statement has not been officially made by the Soviet nor given by other interested nations who find that existing law relating to land, sea and air do not cover sufficiently and properly the many legal problems arising in space.

The Russian distinction, furthermore, between peaceful and military uses of outer-space is inextricably intertwined with the Russian position on disarmament.

In "No Arms-No Wars", the memorandum of the Soviet government on the disarmament negotiations in the Committee of eighteen nations, states:

> "Control over rocket launchings for peaceful purposes.
> 1. The launchings of rockets and space devices shall be carried out for peaceful purposes only.
> 2. The International Disarmament Organization shall exercise control over the observance of the provisions of paragraph 1 of this article by establishing inspection teams

on the sites of peaceful rocket launchings, which shall be present at the launchings and shall thoroughly examine every rocket or satellite before it is launched.''

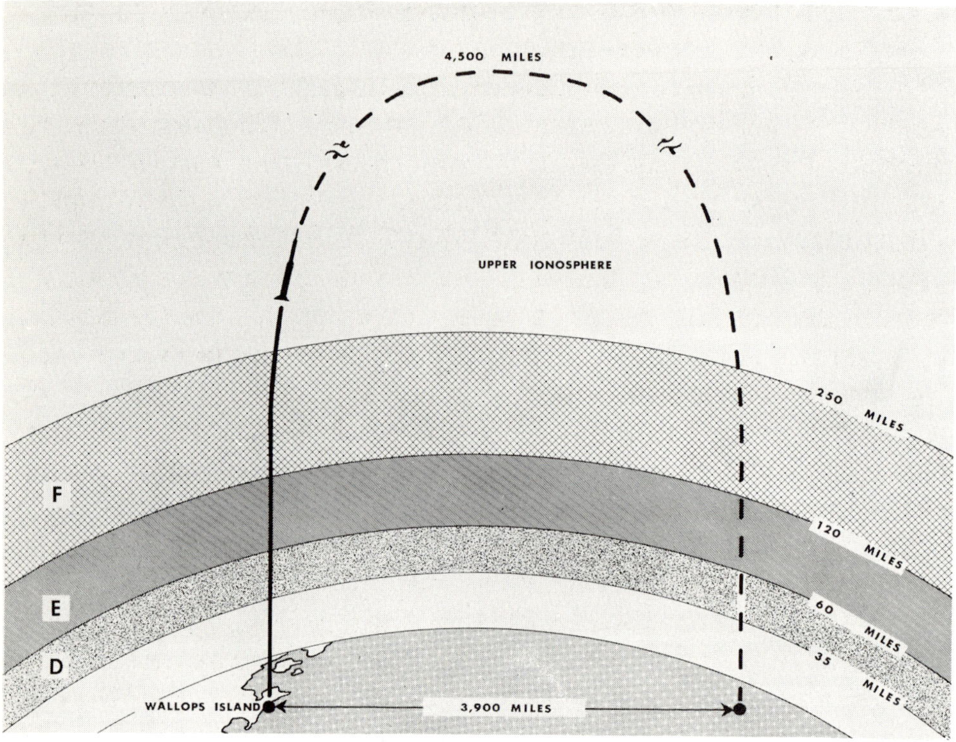

Today, no law chart exists dividing airspace from outer-space by international agreement.

The important question, however, as to the dividing line between airspace, where there is jurisdiction in the nation of the subjacent land, and on the other hand outer-space, where there is no such national exclusive sovereignty, is raised by Y. A. Korovin who stated:

> ''Like most Soviet scholars, I am not a protagonist of state sovereignty in space, but at the same time I consider it impossible to discover a rejection of the principle of the extension of sovereignty to outer-space in the United Nations resolutions. Indeed, none of the articles of the resolution say anything about where the boundary should pass between airspace, over which state sovereignty extends, and outer-space. The frontier of outer-space thus remains an open question.''

Obviously, there is presented as one of the most urgent questions before governments and lawyers of the world, the necessity for agreement on the important question as to where sovereignty over airspace ends and where non-sovereignty over outer-space begins.

In July, 1960, the Soviet Premier threatened with destruction Austria, a sovereign power, if missiles were launched from Italy which traversed the space above Austrian territory, notwithstanding the fact that Austria would have no basis for control of such passage nor even be in a position to prevent it, even if knowing about it. When a threat is made to send rockets from the Soviet to the United States, this implies that such rockets would pass over areas of outer-space and also airspace of intervening countries. Would there be responsibility on such intervening country for missiles launched over it by another country?

The problem is well stated in the National Space Program report of the Select Committee on Aeronautics and Space Exploration (United States) (1958), pp. 22 - 23: "A major legal problem raised by space flight concerns the upper limit of sovereignty over space above national territory."

This emphasizes the necessity of agreeing upon the principle of separation of these two areas and the determination of such boundary line, and the establishment of the zone of "Neutralia" referred to in *The Magna Carta of Space*. (See Chapter VIII).

3

FEAR BETWEEN GIANTS

THE fear in a new-born nation still possesses the Soviet. This is true notwithstanding the fact that it is today recognized as one of the great and powerful nations of the world and is an adult member of the family of nations. Full recognition of its status was given in the United Nations of which it became a member at birth in 1945.

But since Russia has passed its infancy and adolescence, and has now attained full and complete maturity in the international world, this fear should be replaced by friendship. Suspicion should be replaced by confidence. Doubts should be replaced by good faith. Thus, the pressing problems that disturb the world would follow the course of history and be substantially resolved to help establish peace.

The comparative study of early America and Russia should be helpful.

What was the experience of America as a new nation? What is the experience of Russia as a new nation? What are the fundamental attitudes which prevent or direct the course to a peaceful relationship? In this area the histories of both countries have a strange parallel.

THE AMERICAN REVOLUTION

In the American Revolution which was engendered not only by antagonism against England but which also involved friction within its own ranks, separating brother from brother (note the Randolphs of Virginia, the Morrises of New York and the Starks of Vermont), father from son (note the Franklins), cousin from cousin (note Nathan Hale and Samuel Hale), there was thrown across the world a new concept of life---American Democracy---government with the consent of the governed, a government of the people, by the people, and for the people and equality of all.

The victory of the Americans was followed by the bitterness of the British whose Tories sought the destruction of America. They could not accept America's new challenge to their world of privilege.

For the working class, America's experiment in this new democracy was revolutionary in spirit and in practice. A travel book of those days states: "A republican finds here A Republic, and the only Republic on the face of the earth that ever deserved the name; where all are under the protection of equal laws; of laws made by themselves."

Then there developed the War of 1812, a Second War of Independence---and a war of international importance. The British Tories thought they had an opportunity to smash the American "democratic system".

Coincident with the declaration of war by the United States against Great Britain, Napoleon was launching his campaign against Russia whose only ally was Great Britain. At that time, there was lucrative trade between the United States and Russia. Czar Alexander I offered to mediate a settlement between the two countries. President James Madison quickly accepted the offer, but the British Viscount Castlereagh rejected the Czar's formal offer and then proposed direct negotiations with Washington.

The Treaty of Ghent of December 24, 1814, brought relations between the two countries to a peaceful status even though the questions of acquisition of additional territory and abandonment of seamen's impressment provided some stumbling blocks.

Nevertheless, bitterness on both sides of the ocean still continued.

Henry Clay in 1816---Congressman from Kentucky, then Senator, and later Secretary of State under President John Quincy Adams---predicted "that man must be blind to the indications of the future who cannot see that we are destined to have war after war with Great Britain."

Although Great Britain and the United States have had their disagreements and more than once have come close to renewal of conflict, the peace concluded at Ghent has prevailed to this day. Trade expanded, the relationship became intertwined in the welfare of the world, and all problems arising between them have been resolved at the peace table.

Of course, resentment against the Americans was evident in the attitudes of a large segment of the English People as late as 1860. The English aristocracy carried the Tory sentiment, seeing in the conflict between the States a chance to weaken the potential threat to their social and economic system inherent in the success of American democracy.

This English aristocracy sought in the American civil conflict a chance to humiliate an upstart nation "whose democratic and equalitarian practices they detested."

Today it would be incomprehensible to think that England, the country whose Tories in the years during and after the Revolutionary War sought to destroy America because they feared this image of democracy which was destructive of their aristocracy, would ever resort to active war with the United States to settle any of their differences.

THE RUSSIAN REVOLUTION

In 1917 an extraordinary change of orientation appeared in Russia. It was nothing less than a collapse of the modern western civilization as far as Russia was concerned. Though comprising probably not more than 800,000 adherents before the Revolution, the Bolsheviks were able to establish themselves as a controlling force because there was nothing else honest or resolute, competent and devoted to stand against the force of deterioration. Following the capitulation to Germany at Brest-Litovsk in 1918, Russia's path separated from that of the Western Allies.

The Western Powers did not have a full understanding of Russian realities in the year of the Revolution of 1917. The Western diplomats were ignorant of Russia; their attentions were directed to the Russian Court rather than to Russia itself. Their concept of the Russian peasant as simple and unquestioningly loyal was a pre-reformation attitude.

With the overthrow of the Romanovs, a provisional government under Alexander Feodorovitch Kerensky came temporarily into power. Money was loaned to this government by the United States and then suspended. In the November Revolution, the American Ambassador, Mr. David Francis, thought that its leaders, Lenin and Trotsky, were "reckless adventurers".

Washington in general was bewildered, confused and angered by the Bolshevik coup. By mid-summer 1918 American troops were intervening against the Bolsheviks in Northern Russia and Siberia. This intervention was probably the collateral effect of a world at war whose military impact reached all areas.

President Woodrow Wilson's instructions to General William S. Graves directed him "not to interfere in Russian affairs." General Graves in his book says explicitly that the State Department of the United States advocated and initiated acts which could not be reconciled with the United States principles of non-interference with the internal affairs of the Russian people. He furthermore cites statements made by Dr. Schuman in his "American Policy Towards Russia Since 1917":

> "War had been waged under the pretext of showing the Russian people the path to peace and Democracy. An attempt had been made to overthrow the Soviet Republic under the appearance of guarding railways and extending economic assistance to Siberia."

Secretary of War Newton D. Baker summed up General Graves' attitude towards the Siberian adventure:

> "The Siberian situation will always illustrate the eccentricities of a remote and irrational emanation from the central madness of a warring world."

English, French and Japanese troops had by far a larger part in this Siberian intervention. It is unnecessary to go into their reasons for participating in this invasion except to state it was their own fear of loss of survival against a newborn philosophy and a threat to established institutions arising from this rebirth of a nation. However, after 1920, hostility against the Bolsheviks in Western Europe and

America was slowly giving way to saner conceptions. All foreign troops were withdrawn. By the end of 1920 a sort of uncivil peace existed between Russia and most of the rest of the world.

Early in 1921, both Great Britain and Italy made trade agreements with Russia---thus establishing a basis for amity and understanding of the need for peaceful cooperation. America showed its inevitable humane attitude and the generosity of its people, when Russia was afflicted with a great drought in 1921, by pouring generous supplies into Russia. By this time also Finland, Latvia, Estonia, Lithuania and the Far Eastern Republic of Siberia exchanged diplomats with the USSR.

In 1922 under the Treaty of Rapallo, Germany gave Russia de jure recognition. Fearful of a German monopoly on trade with Russia---trade again being the palliative---European states began to adopt a more docile policy. This was followed by the first international gathering attended by the Soviets in Genoa, Italy, in April, 1922 (International Economic Conference). Russia was anxious for full de jure recognition and offered Soviet acknowledgement of the debts of previous Russian governments.

Although England had made a trade convention with Russia on March 16, 1921, and the Labor Party of England on February 1, 1924, had voted English recognition of the Soviets, still on May 27, 1925, the Conservatives severed relations because the Communists were disseminating propaganda in England which was disclosed by a raid made on May 12, 1925, on the headquarters of the Soviet Trading Company, Acros, Ltd. The situation was then cleared up on October 3, 1929.

On September 18, 1934, France and Czechoslovakia succeeded in obtaining enough affirmative votes to extend to the Soviet Union an invitation to join the League of Nations.

It is, therefore, apparent that the trials and tribulations suffered by the rebirth of Russia, followed by trade with those who were antagonistic to it at its rebirth, constitute the parallel with the birth of America---in the attempts to destroy it in its infancy and adolescence, followed by trade which brought a peaceful relationship that is invulnerable to the forces of war.

The birth of a new nation---and particularly one projecting into the world of the old nations a new system of life, a new form of government, a new ideology---inevitably results in conflict. The bitterness of such a conflict is ameliorated with the establishment of tradé, the recognition of mutual rights and standards, and with the passing of time. Fear instilled by these conflicts is the barrier which must be overcome, and can be, by understanding.

This understanding today constitutes the basis of justification for the Soviet to eliminate fear, suspicion, distrust and doubt of the United States and the rest of the world. With the elimination of these evil forces certainly much could be achieved in the way of avoiding the expenditure of billions of dollars and rubles to create greater and more efficient weapons of world destruction. Much of the billions so saved could be the important objective of saving life.

This conclusion also must be taken in the light of the traditional policy of America that each nation has the right to determine its own economic system and its own government.

Thomas Jefferson, who drafted the Declaration of Independence and was the Third President of the United States, one of the early great champions of true democracy, stated:

> " . . . every nation has the right to govern itself internally under whatever form it pleases and to change these forms at its own will, and externally to transact business with other nations through whatever organ it chooses, whether that be a king, convention, committee, president, or whatever it be."

Henry Clay, a great statesman and Secretary of State in the Cabinet of President John Quincy Adams, urged:

> "Whatever form of government any society of people adopts, whomever they acknowledge as their sovereign, we consider that government or that sovereignty as the one to be acknowledged by us."

Andrew Jackson, the seventh President of the United States insisted:

> "The uniform practices and policy of the United States is to avoid all interference in the disputes which mainly relate to the internal government of other nations and to recognize the prevailing party eventually without reference to our own particular interests and views or the merits of the original controversy."

James Buchanan, the fifteenth President of the United States, emphasized:

> "We recognize the right of all nations to create and reform their political institutions according to their own will and pleasure. We do not go behind the existing government to involve ourselves in the question of legitimacy."

Bainbridge Colby, Secretary of State in the Cabinet of President Woodrow Wilson, however, formulated the reasons for the official American policy of non-recognition on August 10, 1920, because as he declared:

> "The Bolsheviks repudiated every principle of harmonious and trustful relations whether of nations or of individuals. Bolshevist Russia is based on the negation of honor and good faith and every usage and convention underlying the whole structure of international law."

In a note to the Ambassador from Italy on August 10, 1920, relating to the Russo-Polish situation, Bainbridge Colby stated:

> "The United States had sincere friendship for the Russians, but the very existence of Bolshevism in Russia, the maintenance of their own rule, depends and must continue to depend, upon the occurrence of revolutions in all other great civilized nations, including the United States, which will overthrow and destroy their governments and set up Bolshevist rule in their stead."

On December 6, 1923, President Calvin Coolidge indicated the basis for what appeared to be a departure from the principles enunciated by Jefferson, Clay, Jackson, and Buchanan in his statement:

"Whenever there appears any disposition to compensate our citizens who were despoiled, and to recognize that debt contracted with our government, not by the Tsar but by the newly formed Republic of Russia; whenever the active spirit of enmity to our institutions is abated; . . . our country ought to be the first to go to the economic and moral rescue of Russia."

The Kellogg-Briand Pact of 1928, which Russia was invited to sign and join, still did not give recognition to Russia.

Then there came the change of attitude towards Russia with the advent of the depression of the thirties and the election of Franklin D. Roosevelt as President, and the entry of the Democrats into national government. The feeling prevailed that the recognition of Russia would have a direct bearing upon the restoration of trade and the improvement of economic attitudes.

Accordingly, on November 16, 1933, recognition of the Soviets by the United States was declared and diplomatic relationships were established. The Soviet pledged itself to abandon its Russian Communist Party doctrine of world-revolution in the United States. The matter of questions of claims and counterclaims were left largely to future negotiations.

Thus, it is again established that the resolution of differences in a peaceful manner, and the establishment of international relationships on a friendly basis, become necessary for the preservation of peace and for the welfare and prosperity of mankind. This, of course, by no means requires the abandonment of protective measures, cautions, and preparatory defense tactics which the experience of the interested nation deems necessary.

It does dictate, however, the absurdity of the mad race for space control, the struggle for arms supremacy, the impairment of health and threat to life and destruction of property inherent in various activities in space, which could now be resolved and must be resolved through the agency of an impartial world tribunal, the United Nations. In its hands should be left the enforcement, the policing and the determination of all issues affecting the welfare of mankind.

The question is asked, will the Soviet abide by any agreement relating to the international regulation and use of outer-space? The answer may be found in the fact that the Soviet did sign the Convention to outlaw Genocide (among 70 nations) although two of the leading Western powers failed to do so.

No one can give absolute assurance against any breach. The amassing of public opinion behind those nations seeking to avoid conflict through international law would be a great factor for peace since recent years have shown that in their psychological warfare the Communists have given much time, effort and service to bring public opinion to support their views and conduct in connection with the alleged purpose of achieving peace.

What more fitting example can we have of the trend towards international cooperation than that demonstrated by the action of the nations who participated in the International Geophysical Year of 1957-58? The importance of this great event is recognized by all.

The International Geophysical Year which commenced on July 1, 1957 and continued to December 31, 1958 comprised the efforts of 66 nations including the major powers of the world, and the enthusiastic activities of over 30,000 scientists. This group of scientific experts devoted themselves to an intensive and co-ordinated observation and study of the planetary problems of the earth, ranging from outer-space down to the unfathomed depths of the oceans. The exploration of outer-space brought forth revelations by both the Soviet and the United States in regard to the launching of satellites. There was co-ordinated effort by both these nations and their representatives in connection with the following.

1. In Stockholm, the co-ordination of Arctic research plans including photographic ice surveys;
2. At Brussels and subsequently at Barcelona, studies of fallout and nuclear radiation;
3. At Utrecht, study for a network of collection stations and standardization for fallout data.

Launch of USA's Explorer-IV on July 28, 1958. Like Soviet Sputniks, it was part of IGY Program and discovered the famous Van Allen Belts.

Three world data centers were set up, each to use a complete set of International Geophysical Year data so as to insure against destruction of any one center and to make for general convenience. World Data Center (A) in the United States; World Data Center (B) in the Soviet Union and World Data Center (C) in Western Europe, with substations in Australia and Japan. The purpose was to complete and collect all data by the end of 1960.

The IGY program, in its proposed study of outer-space, devoted itself to the development of rules and regulations concerning the launching of satellites, which would require each launching country to submit to the World Data Centers information concerning the launching sites, firing schedules, announcement of launchings and tracking information.

It was during these activities that the Soviet Union on October 4, 1957, announced the launching of its satellite, Sputnik I. Thus, practically at the very commencement of the Space Age, at least minimum essential rules and regulations were in existence to furnish some degree of cooperation and co-ordination.

Whether sincere or not and taking the Soviet gesture at its face value, an advance towards cooperation was indicated by the proposal of the Soviet Union made in the United Nations on October 6, 1959, that the following year a conference of scientists be held to discuss the problems of space, and that such scientific conference be modeled on the scientific conferences on peaceful uses of atomic energy which were held at Geneva in 1955 and 1958.

Because the IGY cooperative effort in world science worked so well, the idea was born for following it up and President Johnson recently endorsed United States participation in this new venture---the IQSY*, the "Year of the Quiet Sun", meaning its period of lowest sunspot activity.

---

*Footnote---The acronym IQSY, though the letters somehow became disarranged, officially stands for the "International Year of the Quiet Sun".

There is no question that the IQSY as well as the IGY program will be a good step forward in cementing international relations in the science field. This same sort of "get together" spirit can, and must, be extended into the political and legal fields and bring about the "year of the quiet earth" someday.

In recent years, Russia has entered into other co-operative ventures in space with the United States, notably in weather-satellite data, with further negotiations under way for Soviet participation in our comsat (communications satellite) system, and possibly in the geophysical satellite area which studies earth as a physical body.

These, at least, are steps toward cooperation and indicate that there is a likelihood that the Soviet might join in an international code to regulate outer-space, to be established in a geopolitical-legal convention.

This optimism is held notwithstanding the fact that the Soviet and four other nations at first did abstain from participation in the conferences and discussions of the Ad Hoc Committee of the United Nations on the Peaceful Uses of Outer-Space.

Thus, it is seen that there has been cooperation, and that nations of the world are impressed with the necessity for cooperation. They have undertaken this even though it means the surrender of a part of each nation's sovereignty or sovereign-control. The fact that certain agreements were made during the International Geophysical Year is construed by some to mean that there was no intent to surrender any degree of sovereignty.

Mutual agreements under international law, however, always imply some such surrender.

NOW - OR TOMORROW?

There is a school of thought which opposed any short concise declaration of rights and obligations relating to the use of space, their numbers and influence have depreciated badly since the earlier days in the Space Age when they first declaimed vociferously in favor of their philosophy, since found untenable. They urged that we should

FUTURE "IGY" COOPERATION COULD RESULT IN PEACEFUL USES OF OUTER-SPACE, SUCH AS A PROPOSED "SPACEWARN" SYSTEM OF SATELLITES TO DETECT NATURAL DISASTERS ON EARTH.

FOREST FIRE

FLOOD

VOLCANIC·ERUPTION

await the development of incidents, the manifestation of problems and the detailed analysis of the professional analyst, before undertaking any legal guidelines.

Disregarding the fundamental fact that science in space was outdistancing law on land or in the interplanetary world, and that the time had come for action instead of verbose endless discussions, they proved at the outset a serious obstacle to the acceptance of any declaration of basic principles.

The second school of thought, of which the author is a member, realized that guidelines were necessary for control of the use of space so as to prevent international conflicts; and that the reduction of time and space to zero made it imperative that the best available legal protection should be adopted even though not perfect. Thus, the law would get a proper foothold and assert control over all the adventurers in the new world in the heavens.

Reliance was had on the stern lessons of history which justify this course.

Let us use the guidelines of the past.

a) The Ten Commandments---the monumental proscriptions set forth in the two tablets for over three thousand years have proven the basis for many millions of laws subsequently made by men. They formed the foundation of monotheistic religions, and the standards of ethical, moral and even political conduct throughout the greater part of the world.

b) The British Magna Carta in 1215 A.D. at Runnymede became the cornerstone of the common law and the democratic system.

c) The Articles of Confederation of the American colonies as planned at the Continental Congress in July 1776 and adopted in July 1778.

d) The Declaration of Independence of the U.S. signed on July 4, 1776.

e) The Constitution of the United States signed in 1787.

f) The Bill of Rights, comprising only about one hundred and twenty-three words, remains a cornerstone of our democratic political system and of the ethical and moral forces in our government and in our society. Though attacked time and again and amplified by many decisions, the basic principles were not set forth as an extensive code. Yet they have survived in their short, compact form.

All the foregoing pronouncements are in themselves short, concise and "bare bones" statements whose efficacy and influence cannot be questioned. They have proven to be the basis of security and progress.

The objection made by some critics, that any agreement for the regulation of space will be violated by the Soviet, even if accepted is insufficient to deter efforts to create legal regulations by international treaties dedicated to peace.

First of all, there is admittedly no absolute guarantee against violation of any law or treaty by any individual or by any nation. It requires no elaboration historically to point out the instances when treaties have been violated for purposes of survival, or for expediency, or to maintain the balance of power, or even selfishly to attempt to secure world domination.

No one ever claims that such conduct is justifiable. However, the violation, threatened, possible or even probable, does not constitute the basis for rejection of any such sincere international guidelines as proposed herein.

For example, the Sixth Commandment states unequivocally, "Thou shalt not kill". Laws have been enacted in every age and country prohibiting murder. Yet individuals as well as nations have consistently and constantly violated this proscription. In fact, war has been stated to be a "normal" routine of earthman and that peace itself is an "artificial creation."

Should the Ten Commandments then be set aside because of violations of the Sixth Commandment; also the homicide laws, and the other Commandments? Would anyone seriously argue that the Bill of Rights should be set aside or disregarded in this country because it is alleged that in certain sections of the United States civil rights have been denied to members of a certain minority of the people? The Government of the United States has made correction of these deficiences a primary gaol in the last few years and diligently seeks to promote their enjoyment.

Are not our courts full of litigation arising from violations of civil laws and criminal laws? Yet would anyone urge that because such laws are violated, they should be regarded as useless?

Another answer to the cynics and doubters is found in the status quo as to Soviet relations with the United States and the world. Attention is called to the fact that there are a number of bilateral American treaties in effect to which the Soviet is a party (see Appendix). In addition, there are numerous multilateral treaties among nations to which the Soviet is a party (see Appendix).

TREATY EXCHANGES

An outstanding example that there is sufficient faith on both sides to justify the making of treaties, is the bilateral agreement between the Soviets and the United States entitled "Cultural Relations" relating to exchanges in the scientific, technical, educational, cultural and other fields, signed at Moscow, February 22, 1964.

Entry into these treaties by the U.S. and other Western nations was not prevented by the thought or accusation that there would be no adherence to them by their signatories, meaning especially the Soviet Union.

Furthermore, if there is such doubt, then the question is posed as to why are the Western Powers seeking an agreement on the Berlin situation? Why did they seek (and obtain) an agreement to ban nuclear tests?

It is elementary, of course, to state firmly that there will be no surrender of vigilance and caution on the part of the U.S. defense forces.

The plain and perhaps unappreciated fact is that the Soviet Union is following the West in the matter of international law. May I also quote here an important observation:

> "Present Communist View. The present communist view of international law still vacillates to a degree. But generally it can be said that the Soviet Union accepts the traditional rules of international law as understood by the Western world, and considers them the legal basis of peaceful coexistence between communism and capitalism."

It seems indisputable that such an agreement as *The Magna Carta of Space* will amass behind it world-wide public opinion if adopted. It is in this area that the forces for proper behavior on the part of all nations are to be found.

Peace is the avowed desire of all people and all nations. The Communist countries have proclaimed their support of the doctrine of peaceful coexistence. The West likewise has indicated support of not merely peaceful but continued existence with all nations permitted to select their form of government and their own ideology, and that this selection be determined through peaceful means.

Time and patience and not combat will provide the final solutions---by the will of the people.

This is all the more probable because certain differences existing between the two ideologies appear to have been narrowed.

For example, Professor Leonid V. Kantorovich, the Soviet Union's leading mathematical economist, proposed certain reformations that amount to abandonment in part, if not entirely, of the labor theory formulated by Karl Marx. The capitalism which existed in the days of Karl Marx, with its monopolies and exploitations, no longer exists in the West. The transition has been definitely away from the extreme right towards the partial adoption of paternalistic principles and even towards some pseudo-socialistic views.

Ambassador Henry Cabot Lodge, in a speech delivered before the Economics Club in New York on September 17, 1959, said:

> "We live in a welfare state which seeks to put a floor below which no one sinks but builds no ceiling to prevent man from rising".

This is a far cry from the old capitalism which was the subject of so much socialistic attack. The merits of each system in the controversy between East and West must be decided in a peaceful competition and not by a war.

Not only is there no merit to the argument that treaties

should not be made with the Soviet because they will be broken, but also the history of our relationship in this field has been as good as that with the vast majority of other nations.

Furthermore, the trend of the Soviet to the position and attitude of the West in international law gives greater assurances that such treaties will be upheld, bringing greater trust and confidence on the part of each in the pledges of the other, and thus, help smooth the way towards a true peace.

4

SOVEREIGNTY – AND STRIFE

Having previously reviewed in simplified form the definitions of "law", of "international law", of "space law", and of "world peace", let us now give detailed attention to the ever-present threat to peace---the problem of "sovereignty".

What was contemplated by the use of this term, which has been relied upon in international conflicts, international conferences, diplomatic discussions and deliberations preliminary to the entrance into international agreements?

Fenwick in his "International Law" (3rd Ed. 1948) at p. 29 states:

> "The extent to which the doctrine of the sovereignty of States operated as a standing obstacle to the development of an organized community of nations cannot be exaggerated. In its extreme form, the doctrine implied the complete freedom of the State from the control of any higher power claiming authority to regulate its acts. It was a doctrine of legal anarchy. . .
>
> "The doctrine of sovereignty began as a principle of national unity. Kings were seeking to develop strong national states and to bring under their centralized control the various elements of local authority . . . It was part of the same political process that, in asserting their supremacy within the State, princes should assert that they were independent of control by any higher authority outside the State; that under the conditions of the times any higher authority would have meant the authority of some other emperor or king. Thus sovereignty became synonymous with independence. . .
>
> "In time, when the individual sovereign lost his personal rights as a ruler, 'the sovereign people' took over his authority, and 'the sovereign state' asserted its independent position in the international community."

Supreme Court Justice Joseph Story, in his famous work on the Constitution at Sec. 207, calls sovereignty:

> "the power to do everything in a State without accountability ---to make laws, to execute and to apply them, to impose and collect taxes and to levy contributions, to make war or peace, to form treaties of alliances or of commerce with foreign nations, and the like."

The claims of sovereignty, carrying with it claims of national ownership and control, have weighed heavily on the world. And today, more than ever, the question is acutely posed because of the advent of missiles and space rockets, violating national airspace under current law.

It is worth repeating that the nation which controls space will control the world. If that nation is the United States, the world may expect the same generously tolerant, friendly and cooperative attitude which on the balance sheet has mainly characterized the conduct of this country ---and including the day when the atom bomb was developed and Hiroshima indicated the commencement of the atomic age. If this control had come into the hands of a ruthless, uncompromising, dictatorial nation or group of nations, it might have marked the end of freedom and equality for mankind.

It, therefore, becomes necessary to answer the question as to what are the legal and political implications of the planting of the Soviet or American flag on the moon by her astronauts. Although Mr. Khrushchev, the former head of the Soviet Union, on his visit to the United States in 1959, stated that no claim would be made of ownership of the moon for Lunik II, a reversal of this attitude on the part of the Soviet is not inconceivable since, on some occasions, there has been an absolute reversal of position from that taken previously and unitalerally. For this reason it is necessary to analyze the validity of such a claim and to be prepared to meet it if it is asserted.

In days gone by, such an act (planting a flag on the moon) would have constituted the basis for a claim of extension of sovereignty for the nation whose subject or citizen had effected the alleged discovery.

SPACE MUST NOT SEE FOLLY OF HISTORY'S OUT-MODED "RIGHT OF DISCOVERY"---CLAIMING A WORLD BY MERELY PLANTING A FLAG.

Roman law stated that in order to obtain the right of possession of an immovable place, "a bodily attitude and mental attitude" were required. It was necessary that there be an intention to possess, and an act of seizure necessary to obtain mastery, with the power to retain mastery as a sine qua non.

This idea was set forth by the eminent Swiss Jurist, Dr. Max Huber, acting as arbitrator in the Island of Palmas case. Palmas is located 48 miles southeast of Mindanao in the Philippines. The Island of Palmas Case involved the United States and the Netherlands. The Permanent Court of Arbitration of the Hague held:

> "The growing insistence with which international law, ever since the middle of the 18th century, has demanded that the occupation shall be effective would be inconceivable, if effectiveness were required only for the act of acquisition and not equally for the maintenance of the right. . .
> "The title of discovery, ...under the most favorable and most extensive interpretation, exists only as an inchoate title, as a claim to establish sovereignty by effective occupation."

DISCOVERY "RIGHTS" - OR WRONGS?

With the beginning of the era of discovery in the Fifteenth Century, there was gross ignorance of the shape and location of areas newly ascertained. The existing legal solutions were abandoned. The path of least resistance was chosen. The creation of rights of sovereignty by a process, which did not call for maintenance of control over areas that ceased to be "res nullius", made its appeal when the Western Hemisphere could not be controlled by European occupation or other known devices; and when formalities served as useful and necessary instrumentalities in the scheme of perfecting and validating monarchial pretensions.

The rights of sovereignty by symbolic acts was the accepted basis in the period of approximately 1400 to 1800 A.D. "

The question develops as to just how the early explorers did actually take their formal possession for the sovereigns. The past explorer who today still evokes most interest is Columbus.

"MAGNA CARTA OF SPACE" SPECIFIES THAT FIRST "COLUMBUSES" TO REACH THE MOON CAN' ONLY CLAIM IT IN THE NAME OF ALL MANKIND.

How Columbus took possession on October 12, 1492, in the island group now known as the Bahamas, is known from the journal of his voyage:

"The Admiral took the royal standard and the captains went with two banners of the green cross which the Admiral took in all the ships as a sign, with an F and a Y and the crown over each letter, one on one side of the cross and the other on the other. Having landed, they saw trees very green, and much water, and fruits of diverse kinds. The Admiral called to the two captains and to the others who leaped on shore and to Rodrigo Escovedo, secretary of the whole fleet, and to Rodrigo Sanchez of Segovia and said that they should bear faithful testimony that he, in the presence of all, had taken, as he now took, possession of the said island for the King and for the Queen, his Lords..."

When Columbus sought a new route to India, going east by going west, he was subjected to much ridicule. In those days, not only the average person but also leaders of government and science contended the world was flat. Columbus urged that it was round. (Today, of course, in the light of space science, earth is known to be neither flat nor round but "a pear-shaped obloid lopsided through its transverse axes; namely, a geo-monstrosity". Translation; "in a hell of a shape".)

Columbus spent eight years beseeching King Ferdinand and Queen Isabella of Spain for financial help to send an expedition across the oceans to explore the world beyond. Queen Isabella finally responded to the supplications of Columbus (after King Ferdinand at first had denied his appeal) and personally advanced to him for his first three voyages a total of about $300,000 (calculated on the depreciated dollar of today) to outfit the Nina, the Pinta and the Santa Maria, and to meet all expected expenses.

Incidentally, Columbus was not lacking entirely in business ability. The contract which Christopher Columbus made with Their Royal Highnesses provided:

"April 17, 1492, Capitulations:

1. Their Highnesses appoint Christopher Columbus their Admiral in and over all islands and mainlands 'which shall be discovered or acquired by his labor and industry' and that title with all rights and prerogatives appertaining thereunto shall be enjoyed by his heirs and successors perpetually.

2. Christopher Columbus is appointed Viceroy and Governor-General over all such mainlands and islands as he shall discover or acquire in the said seas, and he may nominate three candidates for each office, from whom the Sovereigns will select one.
3. He shall take and keep a tenth of all gold, silver, pearls, gems and spices and other merchandise produced or obtained by barter and mining within the limits of these domains, free of all taxes.
4. Any case involving such merchandise or products will be adjudicated by him or his deputy, as Admiral.
5. He is given the option of paying an eighth part of the total expense of any ship sailing to these new possessions, and taking an eighth of the profits."

"Titulo (or Title) of April 30, 1492: After discovery and acquisition of the said islands and mainlands, (Christopher Columbus) 'shall be our Admiral of the said islands and mainland which he may thus discover and acquire, and shall be our Admiral and Viceroy and Governor therein, and shall be empowered henceforward to call and entitle himself Don Cristobal Colon, and his heirs and successors forever may be so entitled, and enjoy the offices of Admiral of the Ocean Sea, Viceroy and Governor of the said Islands and mainland.'"

Regrettably, the Royal backers ultimately forgot some of their obligations and left poor Don Cristobal Colon in the lurch. Upon his third voyage he was put in chains by the Spanish Governor at Santo Domingo and returned to Spain in disgrace. He was compelled to arrange his own financing for the fourth and dismal last voyage.

Another great explorer was John Cabot. By letters-patent granted by Henry VII, dated March 1496, Cabot was authorized "to set up our banners and ensignes in euery village, towne, castel, yle or maine lande, of them newely founde."

Between the end of the Middle Ages and the end of the Nineteenth Century it was accepted as sufficient that there was a landing accompanied by some symbolic taking of possession.

In 1624 and 1667 the English protested to the French that they claimed Canada and the countries adjacent because the discoveries were made by Cabot, an English national. In 1687 the English Hudson Bay Company made "proof" by such references as those to Cabot, the sailing of Henry Hudson, the erection of a cross at Port Nelson, Northern Manitoba, and the naming of the Rupert River in Western Quebec along with the customary symbolic acts. This was felt to justify the later granting of letters-patent to settlers in disputed areas.

Spain, Holland and France did not dispute the legal principle---only the historical question as to who had first actually made the discoveries and taken symbolic possession.

Settlement by any nation on any planet gives no right to ownership since that planet is "res communis"---belongs to all nations.

But beginning about 1790, in a controversy between England and Spain over Nootka Sound in British Columbia, the element of occupation was introduced into diplomatic correspondence.

SPACE "ANTARCTICA"?

The Nootka Sound problem involved the "usual forms of taking possession," by Spain. Russian vessels sailing in that area were informed by their own government that Spain owned the region by its acts. Englishmen, subsequently, purchased some land from the local Indians, and erected a house with flag. The Spanish claimed the territory and seized British vessels navigating and fishing the neighboring waters.

After two years of diplomatic exchanges, a convention between England and Spain guaranteed that:

> "their respective subjects shall not be disturbed or molested, either in navigating or carrying on their fisheries in the Pacific Ocean, in the South Seas, or in landing on the coasts of those seas in places not already occupied..."

The present view requiring occupation for legal title came forth more strongly as a result of the Northwest Territory controversy which continued for a half century after the American Revolution.

In the three-way contest between England, the United States and Russia, discovery and symbolic taking of possession was considered not sufficient to vest any legal title, and occupation in the succeeding periods was regarded as essential to the acquisition of newly discovered lands.

The United States' natural position was to oppose discovery without occupation as a legal basis for exercising sovereignty. Lord Stowell then adopted this viewpoint in aid of the British claim against the Russians in the same area---Northwest Territory. In a letter to Lord Melville on Dec. 25, 1821, he expressed the view that in case of islands, discovery alone has usually been held sufficient to constitute a title. Not so in the case of "continents".

The United States by its Minister to Russia then took a similiar position of 1823 in his correspondence there. Russia finally yielded to these principles. But United States correspondence with England seemed a confusing mixture of Stowell's view and the older view based on Lewis and Clark's discoveries.

Thereafter, occupation was developed as the test of legal title to "terra nullius" and was incorporated into articles 34 and 35 of the Berlin Convention of 1885, which dealt with new discoveries in Africa.

Territorial sovereignty through discovery and occupation today requires the right to exclude other states from a region and the duty to display therein the activities of a state.

There remains the problem of present views regarding the few remaining unexplored regions of the globe, principally the Arctic and the Antarctic areas. The United States' position has been consistently opposed to any nation's taking over sovereignty of these regions as a result of discovery.

The United States has been reluctant to claim sovereignty over Polar regions discovered by its citizens. It has not made claim to Wrangel Island located off Northeast Siberia, or Wilkes Island in Antarctica bordering the Indian Ocean, or the areas explored by Peary, Byrd or Ellsworth. Likewise, it has opposed claims made by other countries.

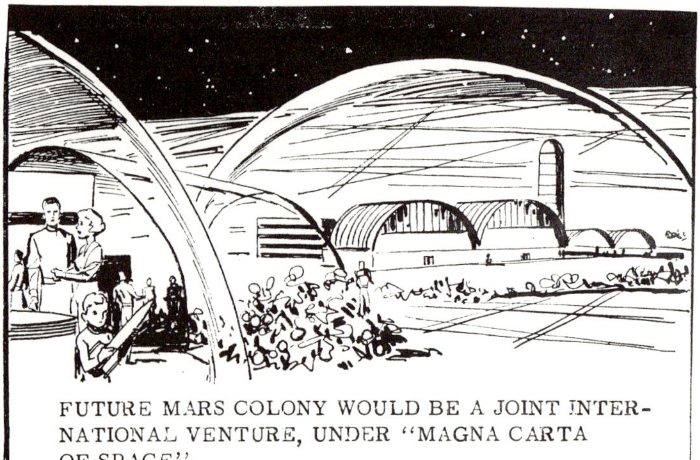

FUTURE MARS COLONY WOULD BE A JOINT INTERNATIONAL VENTURE, UNDER "MAGNA CARTA OF SPACE".

The United States' stand against Norway's claims following Amundsen's explorations was expressed by Secretary of State Charles Evans Hughes in a letter to A. W. Prescott on May 13, 1924:

> "It is the opinion of the Department that the discovery of lands unknown to civilization, even when coupled with a formal taking of possession, does not support a valid claim of sovereignty unless the discovery is followed by an actual settlement of the discovered country."

To the Norwegian Minister, H. H. Bryn, Secretary Hughes wrote on April 2,1924:

> "In my opinion rights similar to those which in earlier centuries were based upon the acts of a discoverer followed by occupation or settlement consummated at long and uncertain periods thereafter, are not capable of being acquired at the present time. Today, if an explorer is able to ascertain the existence of lands still unknown to civilization, his act of so-called discovery, coupled with a formal taking of possession, would have no significance, save as he might herald the advent of the settler; and where for climatic or other reason actual settlement would be an impossibility, as in the case of the Polar regions, such conduct on his part would afford frail support for a reasonable claim."

The rationale behind our position at the North Pole is expressed in this dispatch appearing via the Associated Press in the New York Times of May 22, 1937, at page 2:

> "State Department officials said today that no question of sovereignty over the area about the North Pole has ever arisen because there is no land there. For hundreds of miles in every direction from the Pole, geographers said, there is nothing but open sea, filled most of the time with ice floes."

The State Department took the same view about the airspace above Polar regions in its pronouncement of January 1, 1939, when it advised that American rights were reserved "with respect to the question of aerial navigation in the Antarctic and to the underlying questions of territorial sovereignty."

While maintaining its earlier position of no sovereign rights in the Arctic and none at the present in the Antarctic, the U.S. State Department, with the increased interest in scientific studies in the post-World War II period, suggested that nations give some thought to internationalization. Representative of these thoughts is the statement in 19 State Dept. Bull. 301, dated Aug. 28, 1948:

> "It is the viewpoint of the Department of State that the solution should be such as to promote scientific investigation and research in the area. The Department of State has suggested that this can perhaps be done most effectively and the problem of conflicting claims at the same time solved through agreement upon some form of internationalization.' '

This statement was made in regard to the British, Argentine and Chilean claims in the Antarctic and the Falkland Islands.

The Soviet Union indicated agreement with the United States that national territorial claims should not be recognized unless a nation can effectively occupy the area claimed. Nevertheless, seven nations have claimed sovereign territorial rights to slices of Antarctica. On Dec-

On December 1, 1959, a treaty was signed by twelve nations, including the United States and the Soviet Union, "freezing" the national territorial claims to Antarctica. This Antarctic Treaty provides that the claims by the seven nations are not to be affected in any way by the Treaty, but that no new claims can be made while the Treaty is in force.

This Treaty is a great historical event. It indicates the ability of nations to subordinate conflicting claims of national sovereignty to international cooperation for the benefit of all mankind. It is a splendid precedent for a similar treaty with regard to outer-space.

In 1825 Chief Justice John Marshall expressed the opinion of the United States Supreme Court on the question of what is State sovereignty:

> "the jurisdiction of the nation within its own territory is necessarily exclusive and absolute. It is susceptible to no limitation not imposed by itself . . . All exceptions to the full and complete power of a nation within its own territories must be traced up to the consent of the nation itself. It can flow from no other legitimate source."

If the State is truly "susceptible to no limitation not imposed by itself" to what extent, if any, can a sovereign state existing in an international community be motivated by principles of international law?

History provides the answer. International law in the form of international agreements or treaties has long been an area of conflict between national sovereignty and international order. Wolfgang Friedmann, Professor of International Law at Columbia University, points out, with reference to the U.S.S.R., specific treaties of non-aggression which have been violated and obligations under the UN Charter which have been ignored. Such instances include the attack by the Soviet Union on Finland in 1939, which violated the Soviet-Finnish non-aggression treaty of 1932, and the suppression of the Hungarian revolution by the armed intervention of Soviet troops in 1956, in violation of the UN Charter.

The Soviet Union is not alone in its defiance of its international obligations. The United States involvement in the Cuban exile invasion of 1961 as well as the armed action by England and France over the Suez Canal in 1956, are further examples of violations of the obligations these nations undertook in the UN Charter.

Friedmann further points out that the rules of restraint which were drafted at the Hague Conventions of 1907 (concerning laws of warfare on land) and the Declaration of Paris of 1856 (concerning rules of sea warfare) were practically obliterated during the Second World War. The extensive use of modern weapons during the Second

World War had destroyed established customs. "Military occupation took on totalitarian forms in keeping with the political principles of the occupant."

The distinction between military and non-military objectives disappeared. Germany's bombardment of Warsaw and other Polish cities in 1939 was followed by the bombardment of Rotterdam (a neutral city) and then London. British and American air power began equally indiscriminate bombings of German cities which resulted in the almost complete destruction of Berlin, Munich, Hamburg and numerous other German cities. The war in the Far East witnessed so many violations of the laws of war by Japan that the United States did not seriously consider the question of the legality of the use of the atomic bomb against Hiroshima and Nagasaki.

Charles Fenwick points out that governments assert their "right of national existence" in terms of the practical situations which confront them.

It becomes increasingly evident that where principles of international law conflict with the needs of national security, the nations invariably revert to their "right of self-preservation, to which all other laws are subordinate," as the "first law of nature"

Although since the end of the Second World War the world States have become increasingly cognizant of the need for co-existence by accepting rules for international order, nevertheless, Friedmann points out that "None is free from the propensity to violate international law if overriding interests of national policies so require." He further states that:

> "(Nations) whose philosophies and policies are imbued with strong nationalism are apt to reject the restraints of international law more easily and more frequently than satisfied States, or States that are too weak to assert a dominant role in international politics."

Friedmann looks to the imperialist philosophy as an example of a political ideology which . . . "by its very essence and definition (is) incompatible with respect for international law". Therefore, he concludes:

"the philosophy and policy of National Socialism was ...basically incompatible with any recognition of international law. It is aimed at an imposition of a governing caste, composed mainly of a German elite and of the leading strata of other Nordic nations, over other people."

CRIPPLED WORLD LAWS

Freidmann finds the Communist theory equally incompatible with the principles of international law. "In the pure theory of Marxism, which formed at least the theoretical point of departure for Soviet Communism---international law, in the sense in which it has developed since Gentili and Grotius, can have no place." However, the evolution of Communism in contemporary Soviet Russia has brought that country closer to traditional attitudes toward international law.

It has become clearer now, that the extent to which a sovereign State is motivated by the principles of international law is governed primarily by the political philosophy of that State. Friedmann concludes that:

"(the) threat to the universality of international law is posed by conflicts of political ideology, and most particularly by the conflicting ideologies of the Western and Communist groups of States."

The violations of international law mentioned earlier justify this conclusion.

If international law is to be a successful means of regulating the relations between individual states, it must recognize to a greater degree the existence of the divergence of political philosophies among the nations of the world.

And if international order is to prevail in a community of sovereign nations, some form of international adjudication must exist, for conflicts between the various political sovereigns is inevitable. The extent to which international courts have been successful in the past has been limited, partly because of the reluctance of any

State to submit to compulsory arbitration in international courts.

An example is provided by the International Court of Justice. Marek St. Korowicz observes that "in their declarations of acceptance of compulsory jurisdiction of the Court, the States generally include some reservations which are commonly called 'conditions of acceptance'." - He points out that Canada, New Zealand and the United Kingdom exclude from the compulsory jurisdiction of the Court "disputes with regard to questions which by international law fall exclusively within the jurisdiction of the (these nations)."

Furthermore, the United States, followed by Pakistan, the Union of South Africa, India and France reserved for themselves "disputes relating to matters which are essentially within the national jurisdiction" as determined by the government of that nation.

Korowicz cites a study by Professor C.H.M. Waldock printed in the British Yearbook of International Law, 1954, in which "he considers the U.S. form of reservation as incompatible with the Statute of the Court. He believes, in general, that the doctrine of the reserved domain as a limit upon the jurisdiction of legal tribunals, is both artificial and destructive of the avowed object of the acceptance of their jurisdiction. For it confuses jurisdiction with substantive rights and obligations."

Korowicz seems to agree with this position, for he maintains:

> "Whatever the political aspects of the reservation of domestic jurisdiction, as worded in the declaration of the U.S.A., France, Pakistan, India and South Africa, may be, it seems obvious...that such a reservation virtually contradicts the purpose for which a declaration of acceptance of compulsory jurisdiction of the court is made and deposited with the court. Indeed, it is difficult for any jurist to speak about a 'compulsory' jurisdiction in a legal situation in which it totally depends on the will of the defendant practically to withdraw his previously given consent to submit his legal disputes with another State to the Court's jurisdiction."

The reluctance to entrust the settlement of international disputes to an international court is a further example of each State's preoccupation with its individual sovereignty as a nation - that same cause of the violations of international agreements previously discussed.

Richard A. Falk, Professor of International Law at Princeton, observes that:

> "most governments and their populations continue to deem it improper to guide national conduct by deference to supra-national decision-making in critical areas; therefore, States are reluctant to entrust international tribunals with any dispute of which the outcome is perceived as vital to national power, wealth, or prestige."

As was stated earlier, international law must become more cognizant of the divergence of political philosophies among the nations in order to promulgate effective rules for international cooperation. Similarly, if a body for international adjudication is to be successful, it must be provided with political, as well as judicial authority. In connection with this, Falk maintains that:

> "an increase in the authority of central institutions without a corresponding acquisition of political power is likely to weaken the prospects of the growth of world law by emphasizing the disjunction between an authority to declare the law and an impotence to enforce it.
>
> "Power of enforcement must be granted to the agency entrusted with the final decision or to an affiliated authority, if law is to be given its full value in our society."

5

THE RACE INTO SPACE

On October 4, 1957, the complacency of the Western world was shattered. Sputnik I had been successfully launched by the Russians. The previously unknown realm of outer-space was pierced. Additional Russian accomplishments in exploring the space frontier have followed steadily.

In January, 1959, Lunik I was launched by the Soviet, sent past the moon and into orbit around the sun. On September 13, 1959, again the Soviet achieved a sensational advance in rocketry---they hit the moon with their rocket and allegedly dropped on the moon the flag of the Soviet encapsulated so as to survive the impact.

The "space spectaculars" achieved by the Soviet since then have continued and include:

-The first photos of the moon's other side.

-The first manned spaceflight in orbit.

-The first double launch of two manned craft.

-The first attempt at "rendezvous" in orbit.

-The first woman astronaut in space.

-The first 3-man spacecraft in orbit.

-The first "walk in space" outside of a spacecraft.

Their space feats to come, by the time you read this book, may include any of the following:

-First orbital docking between two spacecraft.

-Long duration flight of two or more weeks by cosmonauts.

-A manned flight around the moon without landing.

-Landing an unmanned vehicle on the moon for TV observations.

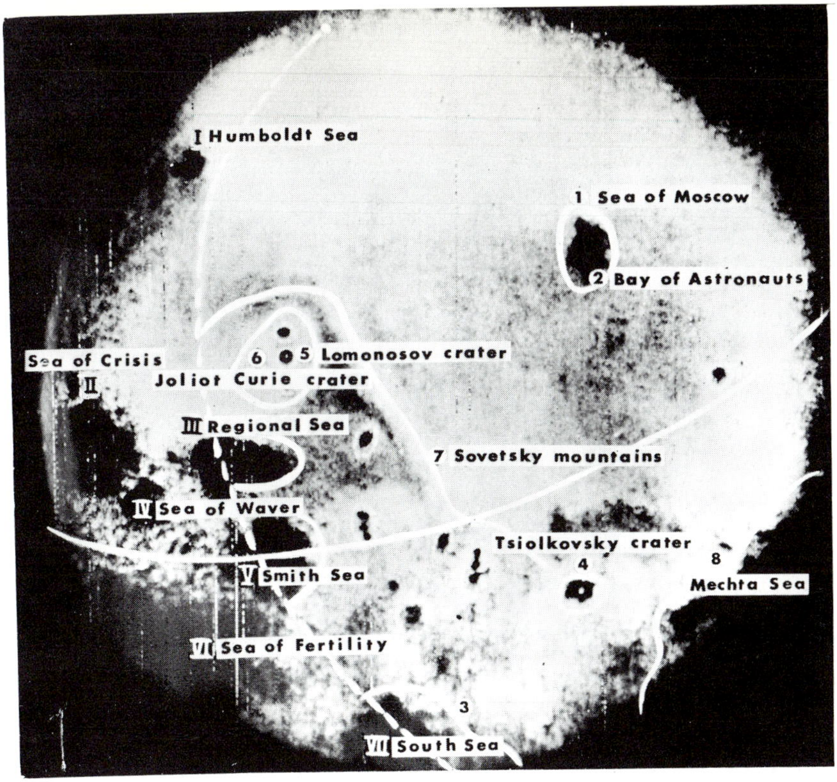

Unquestioned is right of USSR to name lunar features their photos "discovered", but not to "claim" any as "Soviet territory".

To balance the record and indicate they are not "space Supermen", it is also known that Soviet launches have failed at least ten times in the attempt to send probes to Mars and Venus. In contrast, the U.S. has superbly succeeded with its 1962 Venus-Mariner and 1965 Mars-Mariner.

However, the picture becomes less encouraging when we look at total payloads, wherein the Russians have a 4 to1 advantage in weight; in the size and tonnage of their manned spacecraft, about twice ours; and in estimated booster power where their giant launchers may have doubled the thrust of our space rockets.

There is little question but that in general, the Soviet is ahead of the United States in the above categories, even if they now stood still in their scientific work. But to believe they would stand still would be a false assumption in the light of the tremendous scientific progress they have been making in this new science.

Soviet's Lunik-III in October 1959 swung around and photographed moon's hidden side.

SPACE SHOT HEARD 'ROUND THE WORLD

Let us explode a space-age myth, once and for all. It has often been stated---quite mistakenly---that Soviet Russia did not announce the forthcoming launching of Sputnik I, as they were required to do at that time under the IGY rulings.

This false statement is probably still believed by the American public, simply because the press and government agencies never took the trouble to set the record straight.

This is the record (from A Chronology of Missile & Astronautic Events, compiled by the Committee on Science & Astronautics of the U.S. Senate):

> June 1, 1957---A. N. Nesmeyanoc of the Soviet Academy of Sciences stated in Pravda that "As the result of many years' work by Soviet scientists and engineers...rockets and all the necessary equipment and apparatus have been created by means of which the problem of an artificial Earth satellite...can be solved."
>
> June 9, 1957---Nesmeyanoc stated flatly that "....soon, literally within the next few months, our planet Earth will acquire another satellite (beside the moon)..."
>
> June 10. 1957---Officially submitted to the international IGY headquarters by Academician I. P. Bardin was the report that "the launching of the satellites (evidently meaning both Sputnik I and Sputnik II) will be made from the USSR at a small angle to the meridian...and will be consequently observed in all areas of the Earth except the Arctic and Antarctic."
>
> Late June, 1957---Appearing in a widespread amateur "ham" radio bulletin of the Soviet was an announcement of the wavelengths to tune in for the telemetry of the first artificial Earth satellite---two short-wave channels at 20 and 40 megacycles (which actually were used with minute variations from those round figures by Sputnik I).
>
> June 20, 1957---Chairman Fedorov of the Soviet IGY National Committee said that Russia's first satellite would be orbited before the end of 1957, and would orbit between 120 and 300 miles high.

June 22, 1957---The approximate dimensions of the first Soviet satellite were revealed as about 18 inches in diameter, with a weight of perhaps 110 pounds (actually, it was greater, 184 pounds).

July and August, 1957---The Soviet magazine Radio and other publications gave detailed information as to telemetry signals, tracking, planned orbit, and even alerted the U.S. Minitrack system how to follow their predicted satellite.

August 27, 1957---One day after their first successful ICBM shot into the Pacific, as a test of the booster for Sputnik, Russia announced their space rocket was ready for its great scientific task of orbiting a satellite.

September 1, 1957---The Soviet Government announced it planned two types of Earth satellites, not just one.

October 1, 1957---In a well-publicized release around the world, the wavelengths of their satellite were again specifically given as 20 and 40 mc. Along with this went the qualification that only a successful launching would be reported as "live" news, when and if it happened. Also, frankly, that a military rocket had been adapted as the booster for the space vehicle.

On that same day, October 1, the National Security Council of the U. S. met to digest Soviet reports and decide whether to inform the American public if this startling space coup did happen. The verdict---Keep the public in the dark; meaning, let's hope the Russians flop.

October 4, 1957---The world's first satellite, Sputnik I, was launched by the Soviet Union, marking the start of the Space Age, as will be recorded in all history books for all future time.

October 5 through 10, 1957---Certain officials in the U.S. government tried to establish that the Soviet had violated IGY rules by not announcing their forthcoming satellite ---until informed that several dozen announcements similar to the above had been duly submitted to IGY World HQ. Professor Marcel Nicolet of France, Secretary General of the IGY, angrily told the U.S. when complaints of that pitiful sort came in, that the Soviet had met IGY rules to the letter.

The truth of the matter is that, smitten by their own guilt feelings for having ignored Soviet warnings that they would beat the U.S. into space, a great many of our very high officials with very low diplomatic morals tried desperately to "save face" and somehow twist the great Soviet triumph into an evil dark deed of some nameless kind.

SPACE "SABOTAGE."

In a reverse parody of Winston Churchill's famed statement during World War II---"This is England's finest hour"---the reaction among American officialdom to the technological clobbering we took, and asked for, on October 4, 1957, can be termed "America's Most Degrading Hour".

Instead of admitting we had been honestly and fairly licked at our own game (technology), and congratulating the Soviet scientists on what can only be called history's greatest pioneering feat, we resorted to downright shameful public remarks.

Some of America's highest government leaders and authorities, unfortunately, were guilty of incredibly shortsighted comments, typified by (then) Secretary of State, Charles Wilson - "a scientific trick;" Clarence B. Randall, Presidential Advisor - "silly bauble"; and Percival Brundage, Budget Director, who predicted Sputnik would be forgotten in six months.

It is not so much that they churlishly withheld from the Soviet scientists and engineers their rightful accolade, but their crime is that this same "anti-space" spirit had prevailed for many prior years, a blockade to progress.

In 1963, before a meeting of the Institute of Electrical and Electronics Engineers, M. J. Mulhern of the Western Electric Co. reviewed events back in 1956, when in September, a modified Redstone missile soared 700 miles into space and arched down into the Atlantic 3000 miles from Cape Canaveral.

"Had the last rocket stage been loaded, the spinning payload could have been placed in orbit around the earth," he stated.

This was the very same "hardware" that Wernher von Braun and the Army experts were finally given permission to use to orbit America's first satellite---three months after Sputnik I, when it was too late. Wernher von Braun, who had unsuccessfully pleaded for a chance to orbit a payload with that 1956 shot, was finally ordered to do so, in desperation, by a Sputnik-stung government.

Model of Explorer-I, first American satellite, launched into orbit on January 31, 1958.

Since the United States had all the necessary rocket equipment to beat the Russians into space by a full year, why was it not done? The blame lay with a backward-thinking administration which had to be dragged screaming into the Space Age and will rate in history as a new low in unenlightened leadership. And so, the United States lost forever by default the chance to be first in the battle for space glory, handing the honor to the Russians on a silver platter.

It was perhaps the irony of fate that during this era of golden opportunity, America's president Dwight D. Eisenhower was totally unenthused about space.

The failure to comprehend the significance of space exploration and a spaceflight to the moon was clearly indicated by several incidents during the administration of President Dwight D. Eisenhower.

During Eisenhower administration's low-key space effort, Vanguard boosters failed to launch satellites, after Sputnik-I and before Explorer-I.

After Sputnik I was launched in October 1957, Mr. Sherman Adams, the Presidential assistant and advisor, was asked by certain congressmen to get President Eisenhower to make a strong statement that would restore the people's trust and confidence. Eisenhower, he said, preferred to play the whole thing down. But when asked as to what he, Sherman Adams, thought about it, he replied that "the Administration was not intent on making a high score in any outer-space basketball game." It is unbelievable that heads of government should construe such tremendously important scientific ventures as a form of a "basketball game," or any kind of a game!

When pressed for his support of a lunar flight, Mr. Eisenhower said: "What difference does it make who gets to the moon first? We have no enemies there."

Our salvation lay in the farsightedness, genius and dedication of a handful of great men during this distressing period---notably General Bernard Schriever, Dr. Wernher von Braun, Dr. William S. Pickering, Dr. S. Fred Singer, Dr. Fred L. Whipple, and a few others---who kept working away quietly and mainly undercover for fear of being reprimanded for "wasting time and money with that science-fiction nonsense."

Only through their self-sacrificing efforts, intelligent foresight, and incomparable talents did America miraculously recoup part of its staggering loss in world prestige and finally fire a satellite to share Sputnik's lonely splendor.

RACING ROCKETS

The United States launched its first satellite, Explorer I on January 31, 1958. To date it has completed the successful launching of 300-plus space vehicles (NASA and USAF combined). Over 150 of these are in orbit today, with about 45 still transmitting telemetry signals.

Though starting slowly in space, the United States has also accomplished its own "space firsts" of great significance---the Echo I radio-relay satellite of balloon size; the Transit satellite for guiding ships at sea and containing the first workable "atomic battery" units to supply electrical power; the Tiros vehicles for better weather forecasting; the sensational Telstar that first linked continents by radio, television, and telephone circuits; the OSO (Orbiting Solar Observatory) for measuring the sun's radiant energy; the OGO (Orbiting Geophysical Observatory) for "mapping" the earth's geographical dimensions and physical shape; and the 30-plus Explorer satellites that

Blast-off of Jupiter-C that carried Explorer-I into orbit, achieved by Army rocket team under Dr. Wernher von Braun.

have tabulated the Van Allen Belts and other mysterious radiations surrounding this ball we call earth.

The Ranger probe pictures of the moon in 1964 and 1965 also represent an area in which America has so far pulled ahead of Russia decisively.

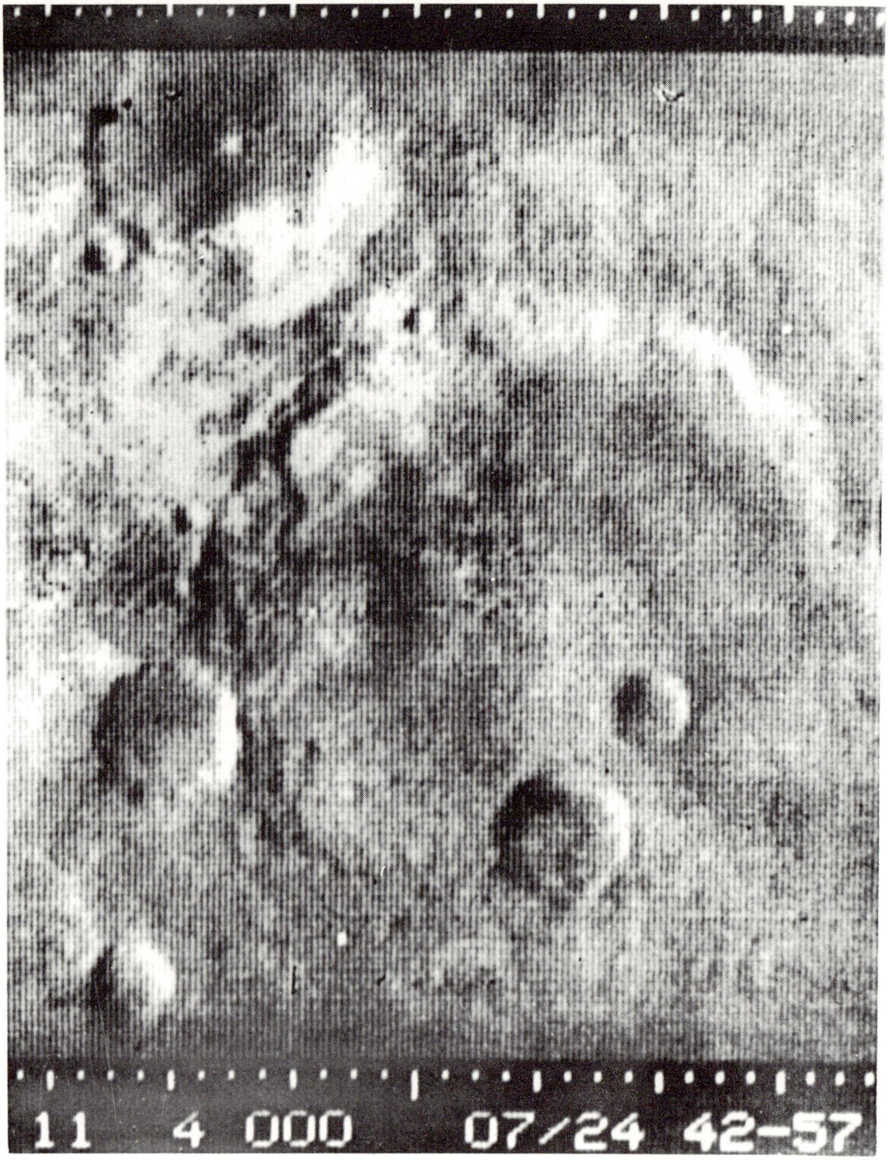

Moonlike Mars with craters, revealed by Mariner-IV, world's first successful Mars probe.

Perhaps most spectacular of all were the Mars series of close-ups of July, 1965, which stunned astronomers by revealing that Mars was more moon-like than earth-like, being pockmarked with innumerable craters. Preliminary estimates indicate that there may be over 70,000 craters in all, ranging up to 75 miles in diameter.

This upsets much previous theory regarding Mars, indicating that it may never have had large seas of water like earth in ancient times, which practically eliminates any possibility of the famed "canals" existing, and reduces the chances of Martian life considerably.

The large number of craters also means that Mars probably never had an extensive atmosphere, even in its earliest days, hence allowing giant meteors and asteroids to crash to the surface.

Much as "romantic" theory about Mars is shattered, NASA could well be jubilant over the great technical triumph that Mariner-4 represented, taking 21 close-range photos from within 6000 miles of the planet and faithfully transmitting them via telemetry across some 150,000,000 miles of space---a record far outstripping anything the Russians have done in the interplanetary sphere of space exploration.

However, the Soviet did achieve another feat in August, 1965, sending Lunik-6 to swing around the moon's hidden side and taking excellent photos of this unknown region, far clearer than the first crude pictures obtained by their Lunik-3 back in 1959.

Another rather puzzling mystery arose, this time regarding the moon---why is its other side more uniform in general than the side seen from earth, with far fewer mountain ranges and virtually no large smooth "seas" or flat areas? One theory is that the earth's enormous gravitational pull acting on the lunar hemisphere facing earthward has tended, through tidal action, to "roughen up" that side and leave the other side relatively undisturbed.

But getting back to Mariner-4, its sensational flight has accelerated NASA's plans to send further interplanetary probes of sophisticated designs to not only bypass and photograph but land on or orbit Mars, Venus, Mercury, even Jupiter. The United States has definitely taken the lead in such unmanned investigations of the solar system, as well as in scientific earth satellites.

Also the recent giant Nimbus weather-satellite, the OAO astronomical vehicles, the varied IMP, Pioneer, Pegasus, and other research "hardware"---all of these are a tribute to the United States and its technology of tomorrow.

Still, any hard-headed analyst of the "Space Olympics" will concede that the Soviet gold-medals far exceed our silver and bronze awards in space ventures. Space complacency was our worst enemy and by being rampant in high officials as well as in the public, it constantly eroded our chances to catch up in the field of pioneering astronautics and space exploration. We started out behind in the "space race" when Sputnik I startled the world, and it is questionable whether we have really "gained" since then, despite all the confident (and propagandistic) public declarations that we are either "catching up" or even "pulling ahead".

Helicopter pulls "Freedom 7" craft from sea.

Recovery of Alan Shepard, USA's first man in space (suborbital flight), May 5, 1961.

The last phrase is applicable perhaps only to our unmanned scientific vehicles, hardly to manned spaceflight. To mention one major factor, the Soviets can bring down manned craft weighing 5 to 7 tons on land, requiring techniques of aerodynamics during re-entry which we are only today researching. NASA reiterates constantly that it will stick to sea-landings for all Gemini craft into 1967, and perhaps even with the Apollo craft thereafter, requiring the participation of sizeable naval forces plus the risk of losing men to the treacherous sea. The plain truth is that the U.S has not yet solved the special problems of ground landings for manned spacecraft, which the Soviet has performed since its first flight in 1961.

Why is dryland re-entry from space important? Because we are almost certain that few if any planets have any seas or even lakes on their surface. What good then the sea-landing technique, especially without a convenient navy around? Having practiced terra firma landings on earth, Russian cosmonauts will be already trained for solid-ground landings on all other planets in our solar system.

We may win the scientific race into space, and lose the manned race to other worlds. Hardly a way of "pulling ahead" of the Soviet space program, or even "catching up."

The "space gap" has been, and still is, in the category of a real "defeat" in our competition versus Russia. For a nation with twice the vaunted industrial capacity and scientific manpower that Russia has, it is a sorry excuse indeed for the U.S. to keep whining that it can't catch up because the USSR had a big start on us.

After almost a decade, is that lame excuse still valid? Our space-lag we have inflicted on ourselves, if we are to be honest about it.

It is unnecessary to go into all the reasons for this critical and important defeat. However, brief reference to the principal causes will serve as a guide for our conduct and planning for the future.

This unfortunate second-place position, besides being due to indecision and lack of government foresight in the 1950's, can also be blamed on a policy of preference for a balanced budget instead of balanced science security, which appealed to the voters on a basis of economy at the sacrifice of national welfare. Again, the disdain for the psychological value of world prestige, to be achieved by the nation victorious in the space race, was a widespread factor in the American scene.

It is also indisputable that we were thrown three years or more behind in the race for space by the wave of "McCarthyism" which swept the nation into hysteria in 1952 and 1953 and caused many scientists to leave the service of our country or to be denied the opportunity to serve by reason of unjust and reckless character assassination committed by the demagogue from Wisconsin and his henchmen, whose rumblings can still be heard throughout the countryside.

No need to repeat the many instances of tragic destruction of lives and careers wrought by these vicious witch-hunters some of whom still are obtaining profit through the vulnerable victims of their emotional attacks. The era when there was guilt by association, guilt by inheritance, guilt by suspected thought, did an irreparable injury to our scientific development and concentration and seriously impaired the progress of our research in this most important field, the field of space, missiles and rockets, the field of defense and of security.

Let's make certain that this shall never happen again.

Notwithstanding the warning given by the outstanding Russian successes in space after 1957, the United States had deliberately curtailed in 1960 the production and development of its super rocket known as project Saturn,which might have evened the score with the Russians in the space race if started early enough. It appeared in 1960 that there was much concern on the part of the government for a balanced budget.

It requires no argument to establish that a balanced budget will mean nothing if our security is impaired as a result thereof. Also the conflict concerning civilian or military control of the space program afflicted us for some years.

Major General John B. Medaris, Commander of the Army Ordinance Missile Command (AOMC) stated in the press on October 12, 1959:

> "At present, plans based on the present budget plus what appears to be the probable budget for next year do not support the Saturn program at the speed at which it could be developed. We are not talking billions of dollars, either. We are talking millions."

Continuing, General Medaris stated:

> "The basic problem is simple. There must be a positive decision. Are we or are we not going to compete with the Russians? If we are, there has to be a solid, well-financed program. Right now we are straddling the issue."

Maj. Gen. John B. Medaris, testifying about Saturn Project before Senate Preparedness Committee (1958) whose chairman was Senator Lyndon B. Johnson, now President.

In addition to the comments of this highly respected and efficient expert, there was the comment of Dr. Wernher von Braun, another great expert, now Director of NASA's Marshall Space Flight Center at Huntsville, Alabama, who likewise stated in the press of Oct. 12, 1959:

"We are given almost exactly half of what we asked for to build Saturn. We are losing time and that is one thing we can't buy back."

Dr. Wernher von Braun, chief of Saturn Project and its most ardent supporter, during 1958 Senate investigation.

President (then Senator) Lyndon B. Johnson of Texas, in a press release from Washington dated Oct. 11, 1959, stated that there was no doubt that the Soviet Union had gotten a head start in intercontinental rocket missiles and in space exploration. He added:

"We are falling short. We ought to spend the money, time and effort to surpass the Russian effort.
"We must raise our sights, we must provide a better overall program. We must appeal to our people and warn them of the dangers that they face. We must take all steps possible that we do not remain second best."

SPACE SLOWDOWN

But even worse was another scandalous situation that came to light---the self-seeking policies of labor unions doing space work.

Some of the incidents showing their unpatriotic, selfish and non-cooperative attitude affecting our national security were elicited in the hearings of the Senate Committee before United States Senator John L. McClellan. The following are some of the incidents reported in Work Stoppage at Missile Bases, Hearings before the Permanent Sub-committee on Investigations of the Committee on Government Operations, U. S. Senate, 87th Congress, 1st Session, held in April, May and June, 1961. Testimony of Major General William J. Thurman:

> "From the commencement of the construction program in 1956 up to March 31, 1961, 327 work stoppages have occurred at the 19 Air Force operational sites and 3 test sites, resulting in a total loss of 162,872 man-days . . . due to strikes!"

Senator John L. McClellan:

> "Our missile and space programs, upon which our survival in the struggle with world Communism depends, have been deliberately and callously delayed during the last 4-1/2 years by some who have placed greed and profit ahead of their devotion to and the safety of our country."

B. G. McNabb, Base Operations Manager in Charge of Convair Astronautics at Cape Canaveral:

> "If we could place a man in orbital flight within six months after the Russians, it means that we could well have been

first in this achievement if there had been no work stoppages at our missile bases, and if everyone had been working at full productive capacity, instead of only forty percent of their capacity.

"Wildcat strikes, jurisdictional disputes, and work stoppages...have cost this country a lost of more than 162,000 man-days of work."

Other comments from the report were as follows:

"At Cape Canaveral, (now Cape Kennedy) a small general contractor was forced to keep his crew on the payroll even though they remained idle while awaiting completion of earlier stages of work---so he could follow in sequence. This cost was charged to the government on a cost-reimbursable contract. It should be noted that the first contractor's project had been placed on an overtime basis due to previous walkouts on other projects."

"Craft electrical unions insisted on completing wire terminations in the field... result... 2 to 4 per hour... while in the factory 24 to 26 could be done".

"Unions attempted to prolong contractual work to obtain additional but necessary employment, i. e. at Lowry Air Force Base, Colorado, the craft electricians walked out because of a jurisdictional dispute with the industrial electricians as to which union would operate the powerhouse after the completion of the project - clearly not 'construction work' within the terms of the Davis-Bacon Act".

Senator Karl E. Mundt:

"Two journeyman electricians at Cape Canaveral received extradordinarily high wages, mostly on overtime basis... one collected $21,432.00 in 52 weeks and the other $26,843.00 in 50 weeks. The overtime, caused by work stoppages at preceding jobs, caused their entire jobs to be classified as overtime jobs.

Paul J. Tierney, Counsel on Subcommittee:

"Craft unions have been and still are entering into discriminatory agreements fixing hourly wage rates on dams, powerhouses, air bases and missile bases at higher levels than elsewhere.

a- International Brotherhood of Electrical Workers and

the Montana Line Contractors Association provided that foremen and cable splicers would receive $4.35 per hour, receiving $3.75 elsewhere.''

Robert Palmer, Business Manager for IBEW Local 756, Florida, testified that his brother-in-law was on the IBEW payroll in June, 1956, as an apprentice and that he became a journeyman in January, 1959---serving as a foreman during this period at $145.00 per week---although the collective bargaining agreement stated that an apprentice was not to perform work except under the supervision of a journeyman. Another brother-in-law earned $9,000.00 in nine months although a coal miner by trade.

Local 295 of the Plumbers and Pipefitters of America, up to August, 1960, caused 24 work stoppages, according to Subcommittee Reports. The workers stayed away from their work when other crafts initiated their own walkouts, in most instances.

Charles Tebbe, Business Manager of Local 295 above, in January, 1957, would not agree to a proposal by a non-union sub-contractor to reactivate a dormant company and then to do a $95,000.00 water and sewer installation with hired union employees . . . his reason . . . the subcontractor was operating an open shop at Orlando, Florida, at the same time. This contract was then cancelled. In June, 1956, another open-shop subcontractor agreed to pay union wages to pipelayers even though their degree of skill need not be as great as for a plumber. The purpose was to avoid a plumbers' walkout elsewhere on the Cape; he testified that some of the walkouts were unjustifiable.

Raymond Belcher, Willie Kitchens (past and present officials of Local 402 Ironworkers at West Palm Beach, Florida) testified that a small non-union contractor was employed at Cape Canaveral in December, 1960 on a $26,500.00 camera platform fabrication project. He refused to yield to union pressure; the resultant walkout and shutdown lasted one week---a loss of 2,688 man-days. Both officials testified that they were ashamed of this walkout.

Local 402 refused to go on three 8-hour shifts a day, insisting on two 10-hour shifts a day.

Major General William T. Thurman stated that despite Florida's Right-to-Work Statute, there were twenty-three work stoppages and 9,045 man-days lost because of the presence of non-union workmen on Cape Canaveral.

(Unsigned letter to Senator Mundt):

> "The National Electrical Contractors Association have as members the Local Brotherhood of Electrical Contractors who collaborate to establish unreasonable wage rates, feather-bedding practices, fringe benefits and working conditions in exchange for 'national' support in applying economic pressure on any outside contractor who would perform work in that area".

A spot check of a contractor's payroll during a single week showed ninety pipefitters and electricians at Vandenberg Air Force Base were each paid more than the $365.00 received weekly by the Commanding General there.

Pipefitters at Vandenberg refused to install a manifold on grounds that all pipe under two inches should be assembled by them on the site under their contract. When told that this might harm the equipment they finally agreed to "bless the manifold". By blessing the manifold they put a scratch on the equipment and the men then sat around and did absolutely nothing, at full pay, for the time they estimated it would take to tear the manifold down and reassemble it.

Evidence revealed that the International Brotherhood of Electrical Workers was collecting a three percent assessment for workers' wages. This money was deducted by the employers and forwarded to the IBEW local. This work assessment was collected even from those who are not union members. A serious question in this connection---violation of the Copeland Anti-Kickback Act.

Joseph W. Morgan (A Teamster business agent) stated that a typical example of union irresponsibility was an organizational strike by the Teamsters that stopped all work at Cape Canaveral for a month. Rather than cooperate with the committee, he invoked the Fifth Amendment, thus demonstrating that we do have some "Fifth Amendment patriots'' calling the shots in some areas of our missile program.

Senator John L. McClellan indicated that the government had been ''bilked'' by the imposition of higher wages on missile sites. Overtime at Canaveral was higher than at non-government installations nearby. Contractors testified that because of a low labor productivity at the Cape, they doubled the normal labor costs in bidding on jobs, costing the government twice as much as it should have paid.

To quote Senator John L. McClellan's decisive expression in his opening remarks to the aforementioned Committee:

> ''Further progress and success in the missile and space exploration programs are imperative to our national defense and survival. It is admittedly of vital importance that these programs be expedited with all possible speed. No hampering, hindrance, or interruption from any avoidable causes should be permitted to occur, nor should any be tolerated where they may now exist.''

RETARDED ROCKETS

Information about the rash of work stoppages at missile sites was given to Washington Report in Sept. 1965, by Eugene Adams Keeney, Labor Counsel and Manager of the Chamber's Labor Relations Department. According to Mr. Keeney, federal officials opposed to the ''common situs'' bill gave two reasons for the union strikes. They were:

1. Construction unions decided after exposure of the ''missile gap'' myth that the U.S. missile program had lost much of its urgency, and
2. The President's Missile Sites Labor Commission, under the Chairmanship of Mr. Wirtz, has been given missile base strikes less publicity than they received under the Chairmanship of former Labor Secretary Arthur J. Goldberg, now a Supreme Court Justice. The Commission was set up four years ago to deal with an earlier disastrous strike outbreak.

Mr. Keeney said that spokesmen for the National Aeronautics and Space Administration concede privately that the latest series of strikes "seriously have impaired the nation's space program."

According to data from the President's Missile Sites Commission, he said, more than 1,000 man-days a week were being lost at space and missile sites. Mr. Keeney added that the data also showed this record of work stoppages:

	Number of Strikes	Man Days Lost
June 1961-May 1962	160	14,343
June 1962-May 1963	62	10,315
June 1963-May 1964	70	29,600
June 1964-May 1965	76	54,217

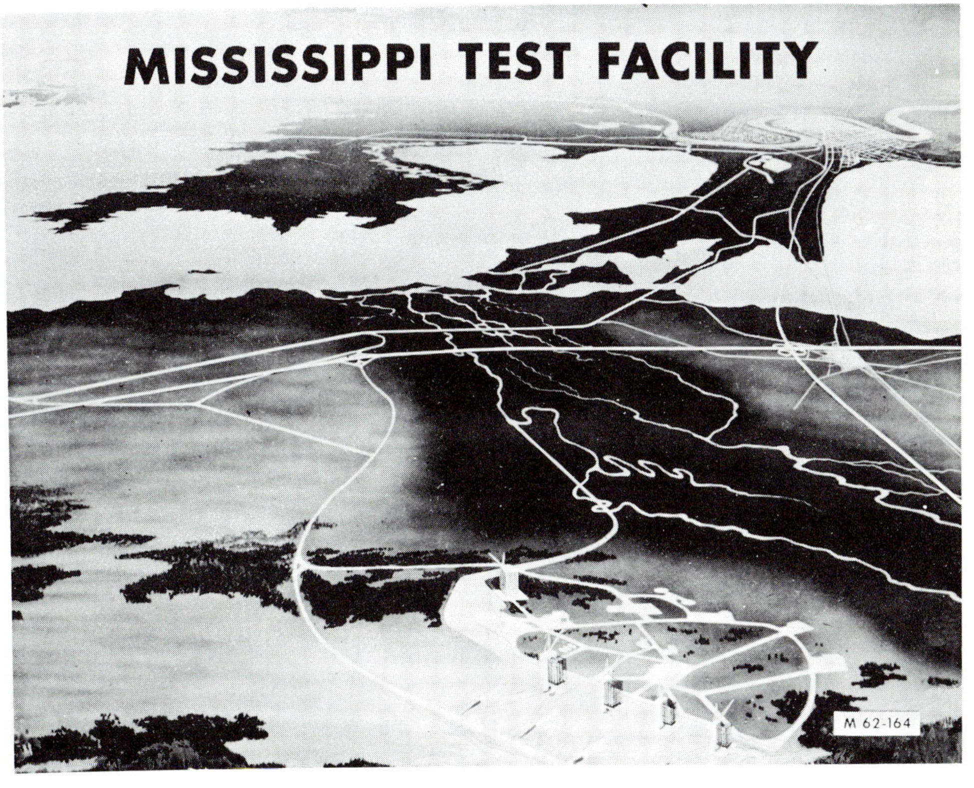

Besides Cape Kennedy, NASA's Mississippi Test Facility was most plagued by labor strikes in recent years.

Mr. Keeney also said the week-long strike in June 1965, that shut down half of Cape Kennedy was the worst since 1960. He added:

> "Despite union no-strike pledges at Cape Kennedy and the Mississippi Test Facility, where our future missile program is being worked out, most of the strikes of the past two years have been at these sites."

Reference to the above-mentioned abuses is not intended to indicate that the author is opposed to organized labor---far from it. It was inevitable that such a movement succeed in order to eliminate the abuses imposed upon labor by certain sections of industry around the turn of the century. But still, the present situation where the pendulum has swung far in the other direction, reflects the indefensible conduct of the unions as above indicated in a time of crisis in defense work and in matters involving our national security and even survival. Likewise, of course, the conduct of certain sections of industry in regulating prices, raising the cost of essentials to the government and to the country, is inexcusable. This too is not intended as an attack on industry in general, but only as an unbiased criticism of abuses in that part of our economy so vital to our ability to meet the present threat to our existence.

The special political considerations given to the demands of the labor unions promised new improvement in industrial/labor relations, which then permitted the practice of the abuses at the missile sites mentioned herein above.

The administration at Washington in May, 1965, undertook to destroy the "right to work" laws of 19 states of the Union, said states having barred compulsory membership in unions. This meant, of course, that the labor unions ---which already enjoyed and enjoy special privileges such as certain tax exemptions, and freedom from certain controls by the courts---would under such changes be able to exact dues from or deny employment to any working man, irrespective of the wishes of that working man. At the same time, the government would get no tax benefits from the funds obtained by these labor unions and would always be faced with the threat of domination by an organized minority of workers whose chief "product" for the politicians was the sale of votes.

And therein, in part, lies the story of why we are still today "first on earth" but "second in space". These instances illustrate the exploitation of the unorganized public, and its government, by organized labor minorities who place their own immediate unilateral gains ahead of the welfare and security of the nation. Hardly a worthy deed by those who once nobly fought the "robber barons" of industry because they had first selfishly sought unilateral gains at everyone else's expense.

A democratic society, a "democracy" is based on the principle of Government of the people, for the people, and by the people. The surrender of the rights of the people and the rights of the majority to any organized minority through the purchase of votes of that minority by politicians for special privileges and exemptions to repudiation of true democracy. History has shown that such tactics are the forerunner of decadence of a nation and of people. The results in impairment of national security and welfare through such practices are indisputable and unforgivable.

6

PEARL HARBOR OF SPACE?

Unfortunately, war has always prodded scientific progress. Peace, especially if compounded with prosperity, has ordinarily created apathy, indifference and complacency. The threat of war thunders across our land from afar and from near. To procrastinate in preparation for survival and defense is to encourage disaster and destruction.

All experts---scientific, military, economic, legal and diplomatic---agree that in space lies control of the destiny of the world.

FUTURE ATTACK BY AN AGGRESSOR WOULD COME NOT BY LAND, SEA OR AIR---BUT FROM SPACE.

Future attack on a nation would not be by land or sea, or even air only - but through space, via ICBM missiles if not orbital weapons, manned or unmanned. Acquisition of new fundamental knowledge concerning factors of life and life-control will be found in that far-away region. Perhaps new life, other forms of extraterrestrial life, said by some scientists to exist on various other planets, will bring to us additional knowledge and experience and help us solve some of our own problems on earth.

However critical the situation may have been through the years, there are many who said "Wait; let's see; let's not make any agreements." One of the exponents of this policy is the competent analyst, Rear Admiral Chester Ward, U.S.N. retired. In his article in the JAG Journal of February, 1959, he indicated several reasons for the United States withholding any participation in any international agreement on space, such as is advocated in this book. The principal reason given by this distinguished writer was the assumption that the United States possessed a nuclear advantage over the Soviet.

With the removal of this assumption, his thesis must necessarily fall and then we are faced with the reality of being too late in taking steps to guard against the threatened domination by a ruthless competitor.

The entry of Communist China into the family of nuclear and space nations and the acquisition of knowledge in that field by smaller powers make the threat greater and more critical. The urgency for immediate adoption of an international code such as *The Magna Carta of Space* to control the conduct of all, no longer can be questioned.

Recognition of the imminence of this treat of nuclear proliferation was indicated in the press on Oct. 12, 1965, when Senator Robert Kennedy of New York proposed that Red China be invited to join the Geneva disarmament talks among the big powers, scheduled for January of 1966. Speaking in the U.S. Senate, Robert Kennedy called for accelerated United States efforts to:

> "enlist the help of the United Nations and all other nations---including Communist China---in the effort to pre-

vent nuclear catastrophe....The rulers of China may be persuaded that their long-run interest, like that of the United States and all other nations, lies not in the spread of nuclear weapons but in their strict control....We should, at the outset, invite the Chinese to participate in the disarmament talks at Geneva....If they accept, the negotiations will be more meaningful---for they will then include all the nuclear powers.

"If the Chinese refuse, we will have lost nothing. We will have opened another door to peace, and the Chinese will show to the world that they are not interested.

"I think no one, looking at United States foreign policy since 1961, will interpret our civility as a sign-of weakness."

Let us remember that of the nuclear powers, Red China is not a signatory to the Nuclear Test Ban of 1963. Hence, they could if they wished hold tests of nuclear devices in outer-space in the near future, without violating any signed agreement with other nations. This might then be the signal for other nations to begin space nuclear tests so that China would not "get ahead" of them---and that would be the end of the Nuclear Test Ban.

Yet, even if the U.S. were in unquestioned first place in space exploration, it would not ease the burden of having to think ahead to space law---in fact, the problem would be brought up more sharply. Landing on the moon, domination of earth-orbit space, world communications systems, rendezvous accidents in space, or any activities suspected of not being devoted to peaceful purposes---all these would bring greater awareness for space law if they were "space firsts" for America.

Neither the current, and perhaps changing, winners and losers in the space competition, can for one moment ignore what their very pioneering is doing---opening up a new frontier for which there is not a shred of law, regulation, code, not even a "gentlemen's agreement".

Did blazing guns make the West, or the coming of law and order? Seemingly, our space leadership has not absorbed the lessons of history and are willing to let guns precede law into space.

AIRFLIGHTS - OR SPACEFLIGHTS?

Soviet orbits man - recovers him alive'' screamed the headlines of the press on April 12th, 1961---a memorable day in space history. This spaceship weighing over five tons, carrying a cosmonaut called Yuri Gagarin, was successfully launched and orbited around the earth, completing such revolution in 89.1 minutes. It was brought back to a predetermined area for landing, and in the landing a braking process was controlled by its occupant. Throughout its entire orbiting Vostok I was in constant radio contact with earth.

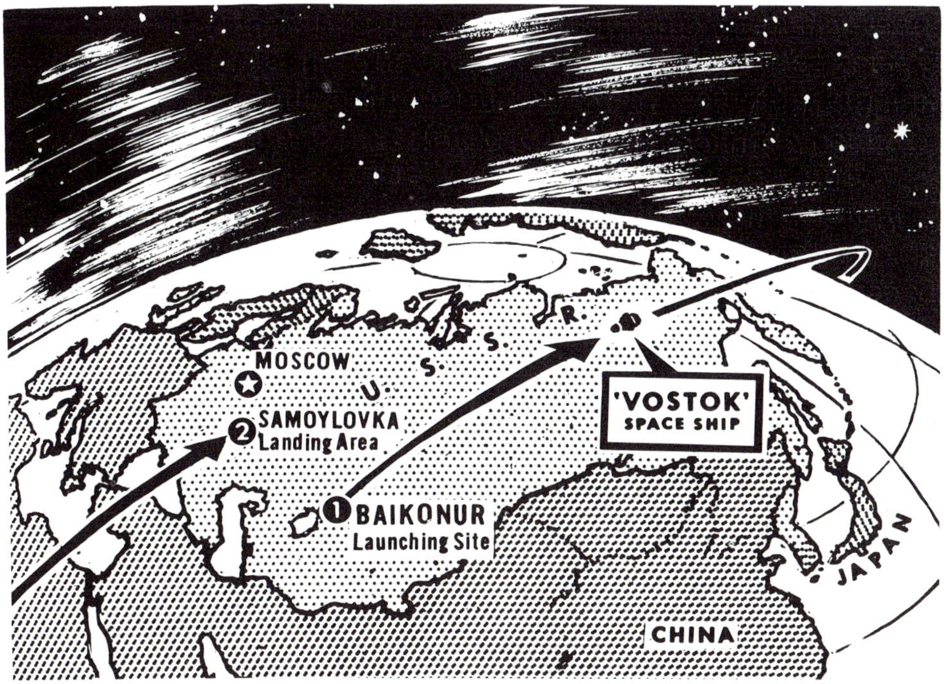

Second only in magnitude to Sputnik-I was another stunning ''space first'' by Russia---the manned orbital flight by Cosmonaut Yuri Gagarin on April 12, 1961.

It is significant that the minimum distance of the spaceship from the earth (at perigee or low point) was 112.5 miles, and the maximum (apogee) was 203 miles.

Gagarin's Vostok-I spaceship weighing more than 5 tons (compared to Mercury capsule of 2 tons).

down to a predetermined area in Vostok II. Perigee and apogee were 113.1 and 151.7 miles, respectively.

Lt. Col. John Glenn, U. S. Marine Corps, before successful 3-orbital spaceflight.

Mercury-Atlas launcher leaves the pad, carrying Astronaut John Glenn into space for America's first orbital flight on February 20, 1962.

Again on August 7, 1961, Gherman Titov, the second Soviet cosmonaut, completed seventeen orbits around the earth in twenty-five hours and eighteen minutes, covering about four hundred and thirty-five thousand miles, coming

And again, the achievement of Lt.Col. John H. Glenn, Jr., in his triple orbit of the earth in "Friendship 7" on February 20, 1962---a wholly disclosed, unconcealed sensational flight in which no details were suppressed or withheld from beginning to end---established a perigee or lowest altitude over subjacent countries during the flight of 100.3 miles above the surface of the earth.

On Saturday, August 11, 1962, Vostok III with Major

Andrian G. Nikolayev aboard, was launched into orbit (112.3 to 145.8 miles above the earth). This was followed on Sunday, August 12, 1962 by Vostok IV with Lt. Col. Pavel Popovich aboard (111.7 to 147.1 miles above the earth). Practically alongside of each other and at one point only three miles apart, they continued in orbit around the earth, coming down safely without external assistance.

Major Nikolayev had completed sixty-four orbits around the earth and traversed more than 1,663,000 miles in four days. Lt. Col. Popovich had completed forty-eight orbits and covered approximately 1,240,000 miles in three days. They communicated with earth. They were seen on television. They spoke to each other in space and they sang songs of good cheer.

June 14 and 16, 1963, saw the double launching of Cosmonaut Valery Bykovsky and "Cosmonautess" Valentina Tereshkova---the first woman in space. Their flights in Vostoks V and VI lasted 81 orbits (over 5 days) and 48 orbits, respectively.

The girl astronaut of Russia spent some 70 hours in space---more than twice the total time of all the four astronauts in America's Mercury Program, before Project Gemini and its 2-man flights began.

Again, taking note of their perigees, the Russian pair skimmed as low as 99 and 108 miles above earth---no more than the distance between Philadelphia and New York City. It was estimated by a tracking official at Goddard Space Flight Center, Greenbelt, Maryland, that Bykovsky overpassed the city of Washinton, D.C., four times at zenith positions, and crossed directly over every major city in the United States at least once. When queried, Khrushchev denied that Vostok V carried any bombs but "it could have," he said blandly.

1964 featured another Soviet space feat on October 12, when a crew of three men orbited for 24 hours in a new and larger craft called Voskhod I. Only one of them was a trained cosmonaut (astronaut) while the other two were scientists---a doctor and an engineer. This 3-man test flight corresponds to our Apollo 3-man craft, which isn't scheduled in our program until 1967 at the earliest---a rather plain sign of the fact that we are still behind the Soviets, at least in manned space flights.

On March 23, 1965, two cosmonauts---Pavel Belyayev and Alexei Leonov---went aloft and the latter took the first "walk in space", sallying free altogether from his craft Further Soviet "space firsts" around the corner will continue to startle us, but the common demoninator in all of their flights still remains the most significant factor---how low and how many times they flew over America.

America's first "walk in space" by Astronaut Edward White in the GT-4 flight with James McDivitt (June 3 to 7, 1965) for 97 hours, 58 minutes was featured by what can only be called sensational movies in color of his extra-vehicular antics, No one viewing those awesomely clear views down to earth, only 103 miles below, could help but think that the whole world lay as an open book beneath him.

At the Congress of the International Astronautical Federation at Athens on September 16, 1965, Soviet Cosmonauts Belyayev and Leonov showed their remarkably fine movies of the first "space walk" and revealed numerous details of earth and atmosphere and the landing in a forest---without hundreds of ships to help them---and then their departure on skis from their space craft.

The crowning proof of visual acuity in space came with the magnificent record-breaking GT-5 flight for 8 days---August 21, 1965, to August 29---by Gordon Cooper and Charles Conrad of the USA. This flight captured the long-duration ribbon from the USSR and also, for the first time, put us ahead of them in total man-hours of spaceflight.

But highly significent was the fact that Cooper, in his confirmed his startling report that he could see amazing details below on earth at times. Among them, from the GT-5 flight, were:

---Detecting a patterned "code" of aluminum squares placed over the ground near Laredo, Texas.

---Seeing the blast of a supersonic rocket-sled during space-medicine tests of high acceleration loads, at Holloman AFB, New Mexico.

---Observing a Minuteman ICBM launching from Vandenberg AFB, California.

---Watching the U.S. Carrier Lake Champlain cruising in the South Atlantic.

Also the streets of various cities, smoke from forest fires, the wakes of several ships at sea, railroad tracks, and turnpikes.

Biologists are hastily revising their outmoded theories of the power of human eyesight. From space, for reasons not yet defined, a man in orbit has the vision of a hawk and is able to see incredibly tiny details on the earth's surface, far more than anyone ever suspected before spaceflight.

SPACEMEN OF NATION X MAY SOMEDAY BE USING SPACE BOMBSIGHTS, IF SPACE WAR IS NOT OFFICIALLY OUTLAWED BY EARTHLY NATIONS.

No remotest land, no mountain fastness, no camouflaged desert hideaway, could escape the direct gaze or sharp camera lens of the two men floating weightlessly during their daily overpasses of every major dryland area on earth, bar none save perhaps New Zealand.

The whole world was conveniently turning under them, like a roast on a spit, and exposing every vulnerable area of every nation, large or small, secretive or open, peaceful of militaristic.

What if the spacemen of Nation X someday were given missions of orbital espionage? Or practicing with space bombsights? Or destruction of an enemy nation's launch-pads and missile sites at zero-hour---just when his own nation's salvo of space-crossing missiles had been secretly launched?

From a vantage-point in space, like an all-seeing eye, any crew of military astronauts would make the bombing of another nation's key military installations and industrial targets as easy as shooting clay ducks.

All the Vostoks, Voskhods, and other manned Soviet craft went into semi-polar (crosswise) orbit. All the cosmonauts thus passed low over America in four or five paths each day that sliced north and south in a slantwise direction. Almost every big city or military installation was within their visual, or instrumental, range during those cross-overs.

And let us remember that the Gemini flights also pass over large and important areas of Russia---and Red China---at low altitudes between 100 and 200 miles.

Now, we might ponder, do these USSR cosmonauts and USA astronauts "violate" the sovereignty of the subjacent lands by coming down so close to them? If so, was there violation of sovereignty, and with that a potential threat to security? The legal vacuum in space has no present solution since the demarcation between airspace, subject to sovereign control of the subjacent country, and outer-space, which is res communis (the land of all) has not been established. Yet it is in this most important area---invasion of sovereignty---where history has taught us devastating wars have been born.

ESPIONAGE - PEACEFUL?

Article 19 of *The Magna Carta of Space* provides:

Undefined extent of "space sovereignty" could unleash the dogs of space warfare sooner than we think ---within a decade or two.

"War in, by and through space is hereby barred forever."

"WAR IN, BY AND THROUGH SPACE IS HEREBY BARRED FOREVER": MAGNA CARTA OF SPACE, ARTICLE 19.

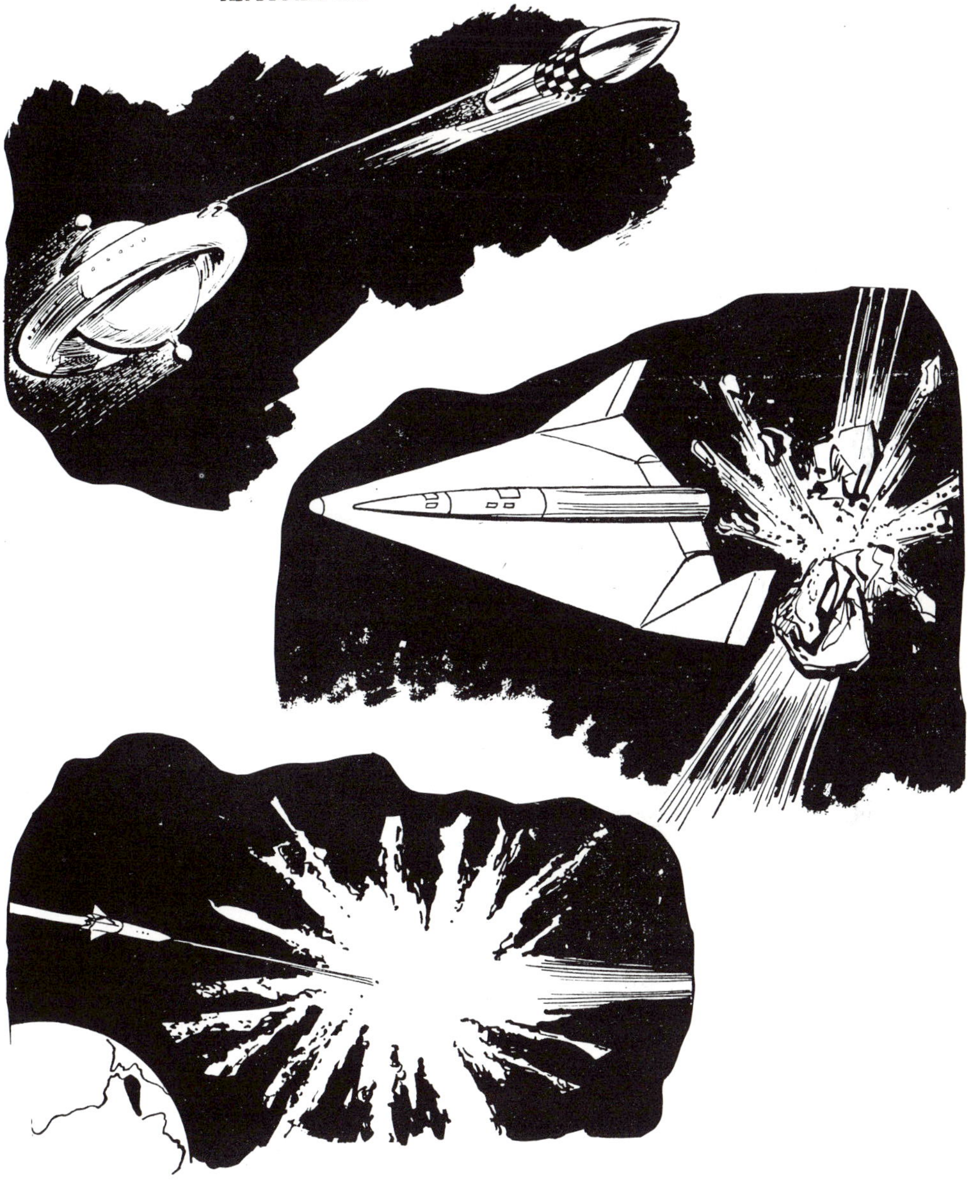

While we cannot now discuss all acts relating to war, one facet warrants comment.

The question now arises whether in the use of space by unmanned instrumented spacecraft as well as by manned vehicles, any acts are permissible which might be deemed within the category of espionage conducted in airspace.

While it is indisputable that law itself would never prevent violations---as shown by the continuous disregard of the Sixth Commandment, "Thou Shall Not Kill" ---nevertheless, the establishment of law regulating those responsible for such conduct proved a great deterrent. ("Thou shalt not kill" is designated as the Fifth Commandment in the Roman Catholic and Lutheran versions of the Ten Commandments. The Russian Orthodox, Hebrew and Protestant---except Lutheran---versions state this to be the Sixth Commandment.)

In this connection the laws against espionage of the country whose sovereignty is invaded should be the basis of such regulation and enforcement.

Previously, to subject a foreign agent to the espionage laws of a country, that foreign agent had to be within the sovereign limits of the victim country against whom espionage was being conducted. In this advanced age of science and long-range sensors, a foreign agent need not be within the territorial limits to secure information of that country.

We have had instances of ships represented as fishing trawlers proceeding in an area in the ocean just barely out of the three-mile limit, off the coast of the United States. Nevertheless, with powerful photographic equipment, electronic impulses, and other means, it is comparatively easy and feasible for an agent on such trawler to take photographs of naval maneuvers, of physical qualities of coastline, and to even send electric impulses so as to interfere with the scientific work of the country against whom these actions are directed.

When our nuclear sub George Washington shot the first Polaris underwater missile off the Atlantic Coast, it was a "secret" to all the world except Russia. Her electronics spy-ship Vega, a sea-going U-2, was at the spot---and we could do nothing about it due to maritime laws permitting "freedom of the seas for espionage", which they do by implication if not in words.

Based at Cuba and supported by all that island's facilities, the Vega and its sister craft can cruise close to American shores with impunity, using ingenious electronic probes and silent sensors to watch our military missile tests and space launches.

At least a dozen ships similar to the Vega hang behind the "espionage curtain" at sea, tabulating military data about U.S. defensive and offensive equipment. These ships are all transparently disguised as "fishing trawlers" to give the Soviets their usual bland excuse for being there---to get fish. What they are really fishing for is all the secrets they can possibly learn about our modern missile and rocket operations.

The Vega and the other "fishing trawlers" all carefully and correctly keep outside the 3-mile limit from U.S. shores. Why should they go closer? They have radars and other superb ray-sensors that can "see" and "hear" for fifty miles. And so, they keep tossing their fake nets overboard and dropping their baitless hooks---whenever the coast-guard or U.S. warships cruise by---but we know their true purpose. They know we know it. And we know they know that we know it. Yet we can't, under any international or maritime law, chase them away like the intelligence jackals they are, nibbling at our exposed flanks bordering the sea.

The U.S. does not, adapt such tactics as eavesdropping by sea. We eavesdrop by air. Everything the fishless trawlers of Russia do, our planes do in flights around the rim of the Soviet empire, from the bitter Arctics down to the warm Black Sea. And so we shamelessly spy on each other and never admit it (with the sole and astounding exception when President Eisenhower publicly confessed in 1960 to the world that our U-2 over-flights of the Soviet Union were espionage missions.)

Not merely the use of the place from which espionage is conducted should be subject to criticism but also the original motive and conduct of the venture should be critically analyzed to determine whetjer espionage was or was not involved in that undertaking.

May an astronaut engaged in a 'peaceful' flight in outer space be prosecuted for espionage if captured within the area of outer space, or in the area of air space, or on land or on sea, in the same manner as if he had conducted his venture in air space and if he had by so doing violated the sovereign authority of the subjacent country? And if he had completed his mission in outer space, and then had descended into air space and then was recovered in the area of the sovereign power whose territory he had invaded even unintentionally, should he still not be liable to prosecution as a spy even though the origin of his acts was in outer space? As yet, the law is silent on this question.

Why should such offenders be permitted to urge as a "defense" that they were not within the territorial limits of the victim country? It is not the location of the agent but rather the location of the impulses which he initiated outside of the territorial limits, and which trespassed across the territorial boundaries of the victims, which constitutes the real basis of objection and creates offense.

Of course, there will be no immediate unanimity of agreement on this suggestion since it is practically conceded that all nations engage in this practice.

ORBITING "EYES"

The legality of the conduct of reconnaissance satellites is largely dependent on the answer to the question whether or not the physical and electronic impulses transmitted by the satellite orbiting in outer space constitute an invasion of sovereignty of the nation invaded by these impulses. As indicated herein, the theory is advanced now that the location of the agent is not important---it is the act of invasion through scientific means, obtaining secret information and creating interference in the sovereign territory of another nation, which is definitely objectionable and should be prohibited.

In support of space reconnaissance, Dr. Gyula Gal of Hungary in his paper presented to the Fifth Colloquium on the Law of Outer-Space. International Institute of Space Law of the International Astronautical Federation, points out

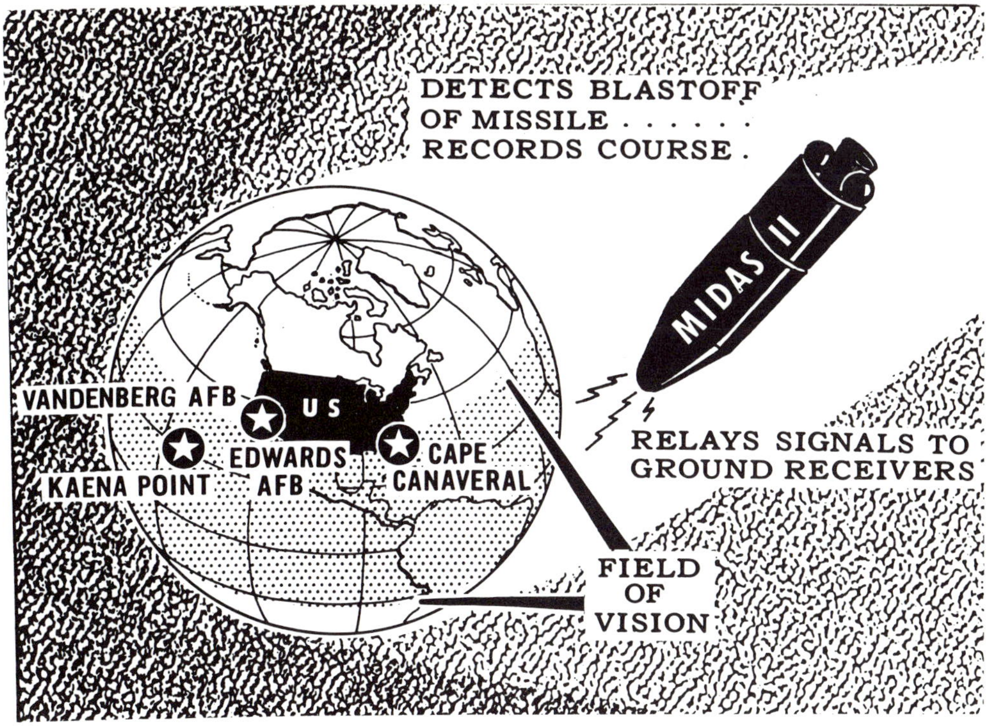

Midas satellite of U. S. Air Force "spies" electronically from orbital space.

that some space lawyers maintain "reconnaissance satellites are arching above the sphere of sovereignty of the subjacent states." Thus, they hold that these devices are in a certain sense "above the law" and can therefore operate "free from legal prohibitions."

On the other hand, authorities who maintain that espionage satellites are a violation of law point out that "according to the universally recognized rule of international law, States possess full and exclusive sovereignty over the airspace above their territories." This theory is silent as to outer-space. Furthermore, Todor Gabrowski of Bulgaria writes in his paper presented to the same Fifth Colloquium on the Law of Outer-Space that "at the end of my reflections over outer-space law, I still support my theory about the limit of the earth sovereignty, that it spreads as far as the economic interest and security of the underlying nation extend."

The present status of international treaties merely adds to the confusion.

Article 1 of the International Convention for Air Navigation, concluded in Paris on October 13, 1919, acknowledged the right of absolute and exclusive sovereignty over the airspace of each of the contracting nations. However, the airspace convention in 1926 between Spain and the United States, and a later convention in commercial airspace navigation in Havana signed on November 18, 1928, did not support the Paris Convention in respect to the exclusive sovereignty of nations. But, later at the Chicago Convention in 1944, Article 1 confirmed the earlier Article 1 of the Paris Convention.

Furthermore, resolution 1721 A/XVI/ of the United Nations adopted on December 20, 1961, provides that:

> "outer-space and celestial bodies are free for exploration and use by all States in conformity with international law and are not subject to national appropriation."

Perhaps the problem is best summed up by the Committee on Foreign Relations of the United States Senate, which stated that the U-2 incident "has pointed up the need for international agreement on the question of how high sovereignty extends skyward" (Legal Problems of Space Exploration. A Symposium. U.S. Government Printing Office, 1961, p.797).

Dr. Jerzy Sztucki of Poland, answering this question in his work presented to the aforesaid Fifth Colloquium on the Law of Outer-Space, points out that:

> "(e)xisting law, recognizing full and exclusive sovereignty of States in the airspace above their territories, does not provide for any definition of airspace and, consequently, for any fixed and defined upper territorial limit of national sovereignty . . . Accordingly, under existing law in force there is no upper territorial limit of national sovereignty."

Although espionage violates only national law and is not considered a crime under international law, photographic reconnaissance, for example, is as much of an invasion of sovereignty when accomplished by means of satellite higher up as when accomplished by aeroplane lower down.

Espionage is a criminal act. Some of its essential elements comprise the acquisition by the agent of one country of information respecting the national defense of another country, with intent or reason to believe that the information will be used to the injury of the country concerning whom information is obtained, or to the advantage of the foreign power obtaining this information (18 U.S.C.A., 793, 794).

This Espionage Act provides that whosoever uses or permits the use of an aircraft or any contrivance used or designed for navigation or flight in the air for the purpose of making a photograph, sketch, picture, drawing, map or geographical representation of vital military installations in violation of Section 795, is guilty of the crime of espionage (18 U.S.C.A. 796).

While such a law would apply clearly to the conduct of the U-2 jetplane over Russia, if the same acts were done over the United States by the Soviet, clearly the United States statute here cited did not contemplate space satellites. It is doubtful whether or not the law could be extended into the area of outer-space. Under our strict construction of penal statutes rule, it would probably not reach Soviet espionage from Space.

The author does not raise here the question of implementation and enforcement of any such restriction against the use of space for purposes of espionage. That subject requires full expert analysis for which there is no place at present in this book.

With the advancement of reconnaissance instruments, it would be ineffectual for a nation to merely bar the overflight of espionage aircraft, for the same end can be accomplished by espionage satellite. This is evidenced by the fact that the U-2 aircraft has become "obsolete" and has been replaced by such advanced systems as MIDAS (Missile Defense Alarm System) and SAMOS (Surveillance and Missile Observation Satellite) of the United States---systems which are capable of carrying out 24-hour surveillance of large parts of the earth. The Soviet has made such practices routine also with their recent series of Cosmos satellites, whose missions were never announced at all.

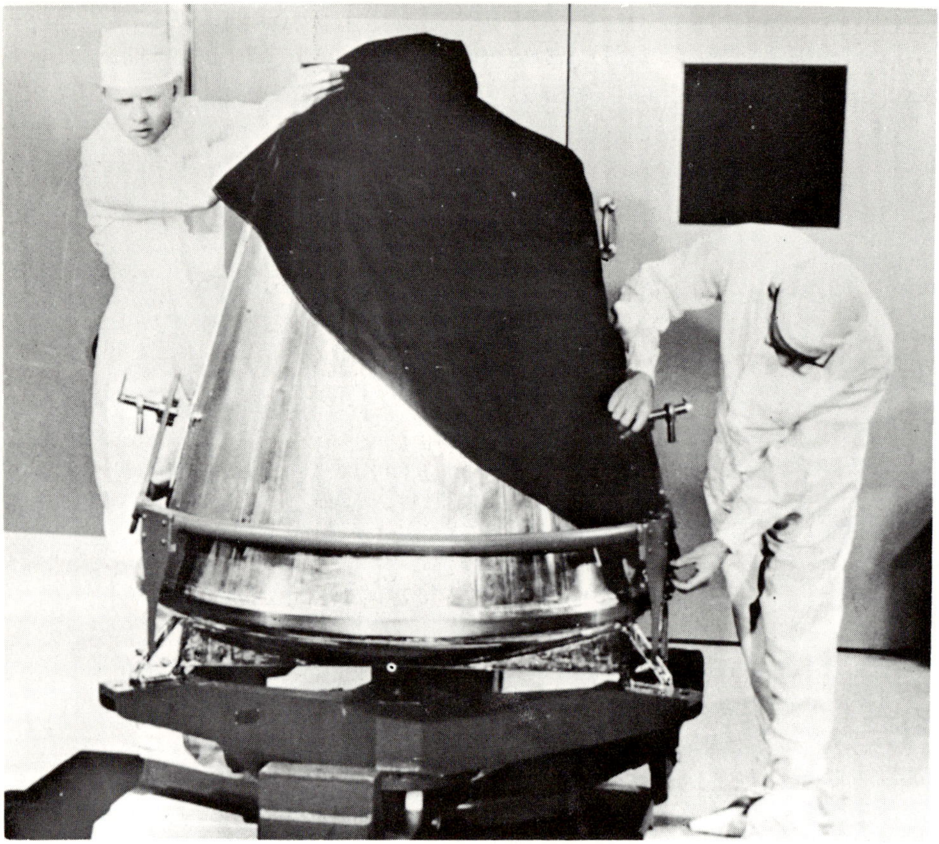

USA's Samos satellite, or ''spy in the sky'', photographs Communist territory and releases recoverable capsule containing film to be developed on earth. (Soviet has sent up over 100 ''Cosmos'' satellites, of which at least 50% are suspected to be their form of ''Samos''.

Security restrictions, both in the USA and USSR, do not permit firm data to be publicized as to the resolving power of orbiting cameras today. But sufficient "leakage" has come through technical channels to indicate truly awesome capabilities of spaceborne photographic equipment.

It is reputed, for instance, that from a height of 150 miles, structures no more than 6 to 10 feet wide can be discerned. This would easily include tanks, trucks, missile launchers, even automobiles. Furthermore, the art of night photography by "dark light" (infra-red heat waves) can outline the streets of cities below and detect the mass movement of any army by the heat of the human bodies given off.

Other and more "exotic" methods of even sharper photography or television-scanning pictures are in the offing, such as utilizing ultra-violet light and radar-waves to penetrate the best camouflage and reveal secret installations below in the nation being reconnoitered from space.

RADAR, INFRA-RED, ULTRA-VIOLET, LASER AND OTHER "EXOTIC" RADIATIONS WILL BE APPLIED TO SPACE ESPIONAGE VEHICLES OF THE FUTURE.

Finally, the sensational new LASER device, which operates via fine-beam "coherent" light-waves, holds promise of "illuminating" target objects below the orbiting "spy satellite" so brightly that snapshots taken 150 miles high will be as sharp as our family cameras taking snaps of subjects 150 inches away under a bright sun.

Quite obviously, with advancing technology, the "orbiting eye" satellites used for espionage purposes cannot be passed off as "too far away" to be effective, and may in fact produce photos far better than the best of old-time aerial reconnaissance days of the U-2 back in 1960.

Science has placed an eagle's eye in space, advancing the so-called art of espionage a thousand-fold. Make no mistake about that. It is the first indication of how space may be used for military purposes. That there will be other military applications for manned and unmanned space vehicles, in time, is as certain as the rising of the sun each morning.

History has overtaken the preparation of this book. On August 25, 1965, President Johnson announced his decision to instruct the Department of Defense to carry out Project MOL ---Manned Orbiting Laboratory.

The MOL will be a hooked-up combination of the Gemini spacecraft and a roomier "laboratory" 41 feet long and 10 feet in diameter, the total weighing some 20,000 pounds. The launch vehicle will be the Titan-3C with two strap-on solid-fuel boosters, recently successfully flight-tested.

Newly authorized MOL will be launched by Titan-III-C booster (MOL payload circled).

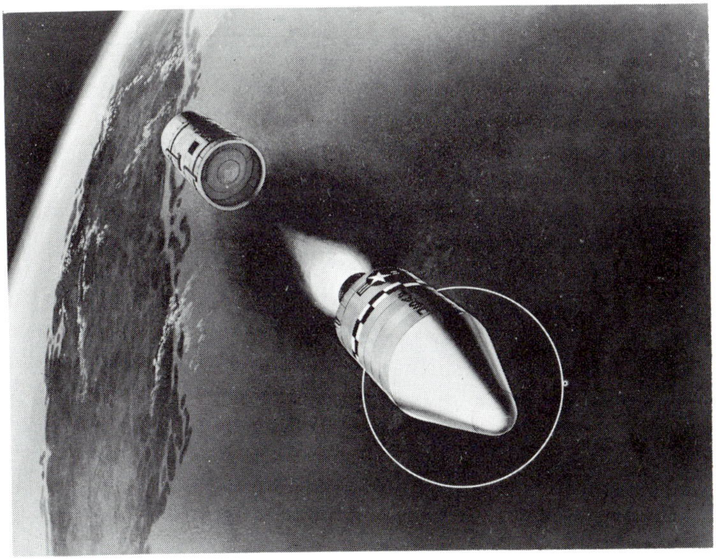

Separation of second stage, plus manned payload, from first stage of Titan (MOL circled).

Though the stated purpose of these MOL vehicles, in orbital flights of at least 30 days at a stretch, will be "space research", it is in fact the first MILITARY manned spaceflight program of the U.S. All personnel will be strictly under DOD/USAF orders, and the astronauts will come from the USAF's Aerospace Pilot Training School at Edwards AFB, California, where flights in the X-15 rocket-plane are part of their training.

At the start, five MOL's have been authorized, with the first manned flight scheduled in late 1967 or early 1968. The two-man crews will carry our extensive reconnassance and electromagnetic missions in polar orbits---which pass over all parts of Soviet Russia and Communist China daily.

The word "espionage" is carefully avoided, of course, but this will in effect be one of the main missions of the MOL astronauts.

The saddest part of it all is that this is apparently in

reaction to the strong possibility that the USSR is planning soon to establish manned "space stations" in orbit, whose transparent purpose will be espionage despite whatever propaganda smoke-screens are thrown up by the Soviet.

Space has turned the corner---into a new military arena. certainly the open announcement of President Johnson, and the secretive preparations of the USSR, should convince us all that the space handwriting is on the wall.

Today, manned recon orbiters. Tomorrow, orbital bombing platforms, rocketing warplanes, and armed space outposts. And not one internationally recognized law or restriction against this build-up of space might. It is time for a "space test ban" against experimental war machines in orbit. Today. Tomorrow may be too late.

SOMETIMES LAUNCHING 5 SATELLITES AT ONCE, SOVIET UNION'S COSMOS SERIES OF SATELLITES ARE ALSO KNOWN TO BE "ORBITING SPIES" OF SPACE.

SECRET SATELLITES

Illuminating comments on this aspect occur in letters written to the author in 1965, from Mr. S. Houston Lay, the celebrated Director of the International Law Program of the American Bar Association, who said:

> "...I know that the Soviets have endeavored to attach the term espionage to all intelligence gathering operations by Western nations, although they engage in the same type of activity to an even greater extent. It is much easier for intelligence gathering activities to be observed and identified within the closed Soviet society than it is for the same type of act to be identified within the open society of the Western world...
>
> "Is it espionage for a plane over the high seas to approach

foreign ships closely enough to take good pictures of them?

"...If, as both the United States and Russia claim, it is permissible for space vehicles to orbit the earth at elevations of 100 miles or more, without requesting the permission of the subjacent States, is the situation different than a ship on the high seas or an airplane flying in international air-space?

"I assume you are acquainted with the fact that within about the last year or so, the Russians have revised their thinking about the legality or lack of legality of satellites capable of taking pictures. The Russians have obviously been engaged in this practice themselves to a very considerable extent and have voiced almost no criticism of the U.S. for doing so within the last year."

Of course, espionage is controversial. Great weight must accordingly be given to the views of Dr. Edward C. Welsh, Secretary of the National Aeronautics and Space Council, and the President's personal advisor on science and space matters. Dr. Welsh, a dynamic scientific explorer and organizer whose exceptional ability and professional integrity are widely recognized, stated in a letter to the author:

"Thank you for sending me a copy of the December issue of Space World Magazine, which contains your article, 'Law and a Policeman in Space.'

"I found your article stimulating and informative. With much of your reasoning, I am in accord. Here and there I noted a point which I would debate. For example, you would seem to prohibit photography of the earth from space on the grounds that it is unwarranted or undesirable espionage. I believe that this practice, just as does the practice of checking in space for evidence of nuclear explosions, discourages surprise attack. Also, it helps break down artificial barriers and walls of secrecy---both of which encourage hostility. Moreover, a prohibition against such practice would deliver a death blow to meteorological satellites...."

In respectful rebuttal, the writer might briefly point out that the great espionage services of the major powers prior to both World War I and World War II did not, obviously, discourage attack and the outbreak of warfare. It seems dubious to expect a new kind of espionage---from space---to be in any significant way a peace-promoting factor in international affairs.

At least, let us say that the final answer is not yet in on that moot question, and that to play safe it is best to keep any and all military systems, of offense or defense, under strict supervision.

A grim mystery, about which there is only stony silence, has come up recently---why are both the USA and USSR deliberately destroying certain of their satellites in orbit?

On February 28, 1965, the Soviet Cosmos-57 suddenly burst into nearly 100 pieces according to the U.S. tracking network, which could only result from a violent explosion of the satellite. The Russians have released no information but it is suspected that Cosmos-57 was one of their series of reconnaissance vehicles. A ground radio-command signal could have touched off prepackaged explosions inside the vehicle.

Did Cosmos-57 stray off its course, with the possibility of re-entering into the hands of the U.S.? Did it contain new "spy instrumention" of such important nature that the Soviets could not afford to give us even a glimmer of it?

Other speculations are even more alarming---that it was an abortive atomic test; that it was a test for a "killer satellite" sent deliberately to destroy this target in space, which targets might someday be U.S. satellites; or that it was a test of remote-control signals being devised for forthcoming nuclear bombs in orbit.

U.S. experts believe that at least one other Soviet satellite, Cosmos-50 on October 28, 1964, was destroyed on purpose.

And the rumors are that several of our own satellites---those launched under security silence by the U.S. Air Force---were blown up by ground command. The tracking evidence again supported the belief of a sudden disruption of vehicles into dozens of pieces. The USAF is just as silent as Russia over these presumed "destructs".

Again, we can only speculate that for some reason---either as a test of a space-weapon system, or to prevent wrong-orbit vehicles from falling into Soviet hands---space was filled with this buckshot debris.

Another hazard arises if this practice is to continue and escalate. Most of the pieces are reported to fall out of orbit within months and burn up in the atmosphere. But like Sputnik-IV and others, it is not impossible for certain chunks to survive and strike earth. (On August 21, 1965, for the first time, part of a space booster fell back to earth virtually intact. It was the 1st stage tankage of the GT-5's Titan-2 launch vehicle, 23.5 feet long, 10 feet in diameter, weighing 1,500 pounds. This may be an ominous sign of the rain of rocket debris, of giant proportions, which might in the future occur when space launchings multiply. And it certainly indicates that any satellites blown up in orbit can be a meteor-like hazard to the inhabited world below).

What if dozens of such man-made meteorites came down someday in a populated area? What responsibility does either the USA or USSR bear in that case? For purposes of military "security", will they steadfastly deny knowledge of the rain of steel they caused? Where does that leave the unlucky people below who sustain property-damage, perhaps personal injury, or even loss of life?

NO SPACE LAW TODAY COVERS MAN-MADE "METEORITES" RAINING STEEL DOWN ON POPULOUS AREAS, AS HUGE SPACE VEHICLES FAIL TO BURN UP DURING RE-ENTRY.

From this single aspect, it can be seen how many tangled legal problems space can bring up, while a code of space law to cover such emergencies remains unborn.

If we are to maintain peace and order in outer-space, where we have failed to do so on earth, we must be realistic. It is without merit to hold that espionage in space is "above the law" and not an invasion of the sovereignty of the subjacent State, merely because the vehicle operates above an undefinable boundary between outer-space and airspace.

Espionage as an end result should not be justified by its means of achievement.

It is untenable to argue that radio waves, electronic impulses, or photographic radars are not capable of piercing a nation's sovereignty. Modern science has become dependent upon radio waves as a means of communication and control of space vehicles. Non-manual satellites depend entirely upon radio impulses from earth. And, just recently, nation's have destroyed "pirate television" stations based outside of their territorial marine jurisdiction, the only basis of justification being that the television signals were invading their sovereignty from offshore locations.

The question, however, cannot be readily answered now. It is subject to much dispute and will require further intensive study in order to determine what is proper regulation of activities in space which reach into the sovereign jurisdiction of other nations---activities not for peaceful purposes, but for military purposes. Men of considerable experience and learning, and leading scholars in the field, are not yet prepared at this moment to give adequate answers. The question, however, must be solved immediately to avoid provocations between nations.

SPACE A BATTLEGROUND?

We are faced with the tremendous preparations for launching of space laboratories in the near future containing as many as fifteen to twenty members, the placing of platforms in orbit, lunar landings and beyond. And someday will come explorations into the faraway galaxies of stars where such scientists as Dr. Harlow Shapley of

Harvard and Sir Bernard Lovell of Jodrell Bank Laboratory in Great Britain, believe "there may be hundreds of millions of heavenly bodies capable of supporting life".

These world-shaking accomplishments demonstrate unequivocally that the mind and body of man have broken through the barriers of radiation, weightlessness and space hazards, making it a foregone conclusion that man's progress towards heavier and commercialized traffic in space is attainable. It also marks the progress of the plan for a flight to the moon and for travel in the interplanetary regions.

Again, we cannot elaborate in detail all the problems and their solutions in the field of astronautics, physics, astronomy, electronics and communications. In the field of law, there is the need to supplement these great scientific results---to assure the establishment of an orderly society, to avoid chaos and confusion in our lives in the new space era, and to prevent destruction of all human values by the crushing weight of fast-moving science.

It is relevant here to call specific attention to the orbital voyages in space of all the astronauts, and the fact that at various times in their flights, they invaded the upper area of airspace, that portion of the atmosphere conceded to be within the domain of the sovereign jurisdiction of the subjacent land. At the present time, the sensational and magnetic appeal of their scientific achievements thrusts aside consideration of the legal problems presented by their orbiting "invasions" of this sovereign territory. The question of invasion of sovereignty, of course, must be resolved before the problems become further complicated and aggravated by acceleration of activities in space.

What is the significance of these history-making events? Do they portend more danger in the world---and to the world? Will it make the champions of an opposing ideology bolder in their determination and in their conduct? Does it mean a callous and indifferent invasion of the sovereign territory of subjacent nations through whose upper regions of airspace or through whose claimed areas of sovereignty these satellites orbit? Does it threaten to evolve into dynamic military demonstrations? Can this be limited

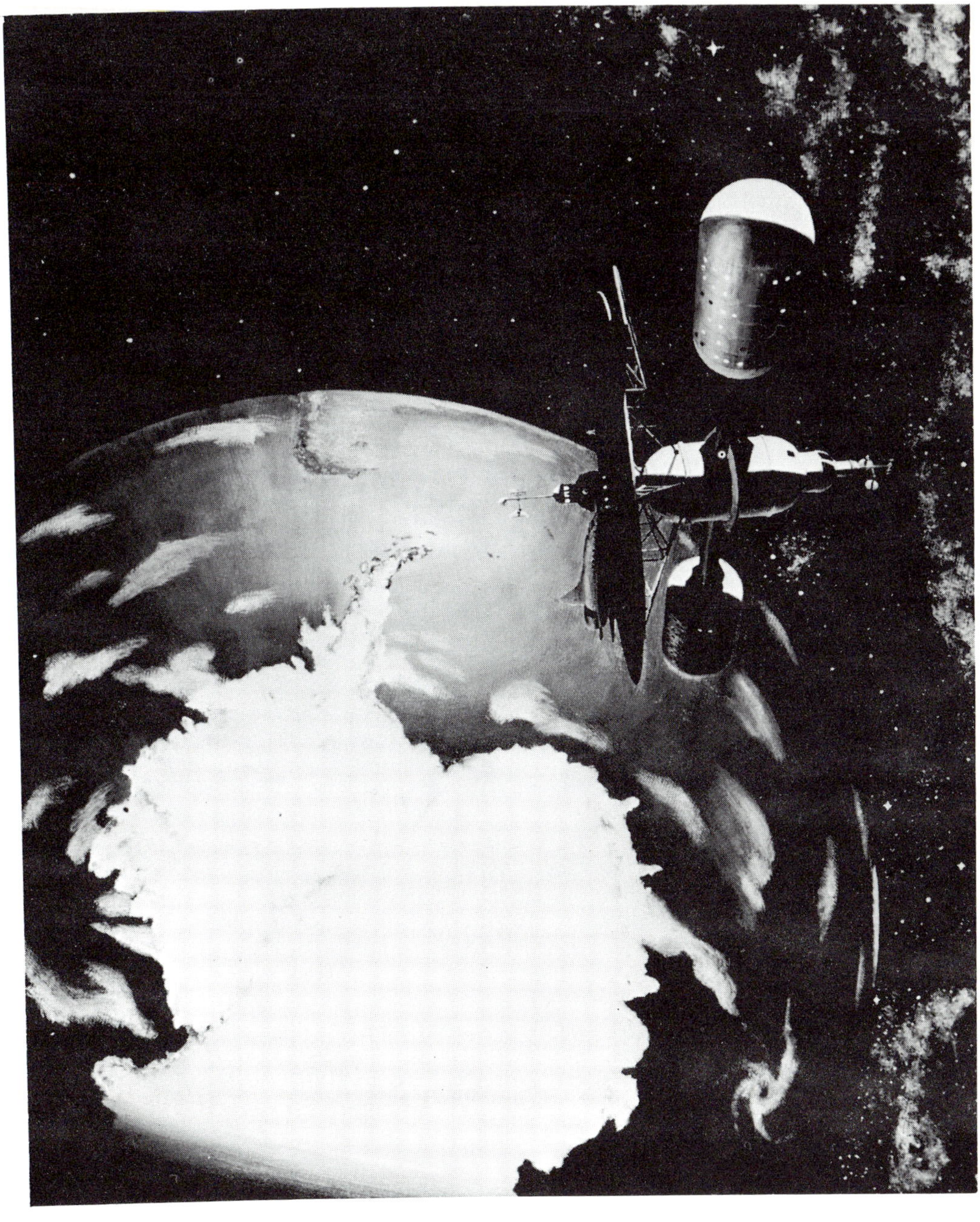

Future space stations and orbiting laboratories will be gigantic, with crews of 20 or more astronauts.

solely to peaceful purposes?

If a Vostok or Voskhod furthermore had landed not at a predetermined area but in the City of New York, striking the Empire State Building and killing thousands of people, what recourse would there be for the injured and the families of the dead, and for the Government of the United States against the launching nation?

LIKE JETPLANES, FUTURE MANNED SPACECRAFT MAY CRASH IN CROWDED CITIES LIKE A CELESTIAL "BOMB", FOR WHICH "SPACE INDEMNITY" LAWS SHOULD BE WORKED OUT NOW.

Or, in reverse if a space craft of the United States crashed into Moscow destroying the University of Moscow, doing great property damage, injuring and killing people, what legal redress would be available to the injured citizens and the Government of the Soviet?

Will these manned space flights in an orbit so near to the surface of the earth constitute a basis of accusation by some nation that its sovereign territory has been deliberately invaded? Will some nation claim that its air-space, its admitted sovereign territory, extends higher than 100 miles from the surface of the earth and that accordingly its upper regions were invaded by the orbiting spacecraft?

Will these problems be precipitated by the fact that there is no agreement between the nations of the world as to where airspace shall be deemed to end?

TOMORROW, THE MOON

At least twenty and perhaps forty billion dollars are being and will be spent by the United States of America in the race with the Soviet to place a man on the moon.

Apollo, the spaceship which is to carry three men aboard, is now beyond the dream stage and in the hardware stage. Gigantic projects go swiftly into shops and factories. Tremendous manpower drawn from the world of science is being amassed. The purpose is philosophical, military and psychological. Undoubtedly, it will create national prestige if successful.

Mercury, Gemini, and Apollo, sponsored by the National Aeronautics and Space Administration of the United States, will make this a reality. The "lunar rendezvous" and landing may be attained within this decade.

As we all know, on September 13, 1959, the Russian Lunik II hit the moon,dropping on its surface the encapsulated flag of the USSR, the first such incident in the new world of outer-space. Immediately the question arose as to whether this would constitute the basis of a claim of extension of Soviet sovereignty to the moon. The Soviet, through Nikita Khrushchev, then premier, sought to calm world anxiety by asserting that no claim to ownership would be made and that the moon belonged to the world---recognizing the principle urged by the United States that ownership to such "new lands" could not be asserted on the basis of mere implantation of a flag, nor even on the basis of discovery.

This second factor, of course, could not be alleged because all the world knows the moon was discovered by the earliest astronomers and carried forward as a known fact in the romantic songs of lovers to the somber statements of diplomats, astronomers and other scientists.

LUNAR INDUSTRIES

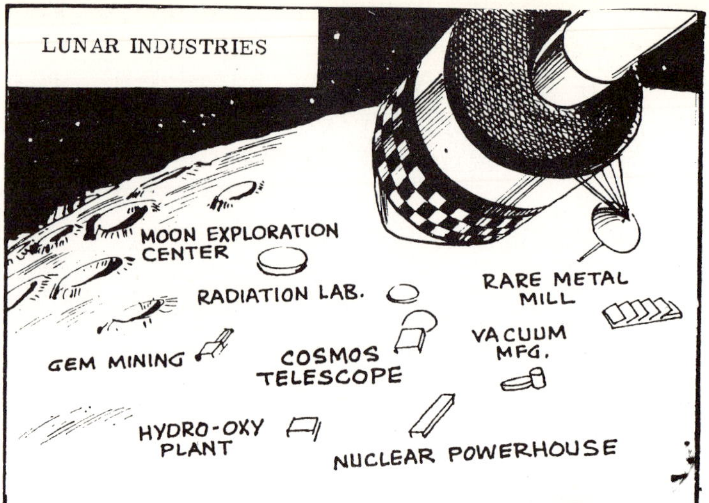

SOVIET ALREADY PLANS "INDUSTRIAL UNDERTAKINGS" ON THE MOON. FROM 1970 ON, THE MOON MAY GRADUALLY PAY OFF IN MANY WAYS...BONANZAS OF RARE METALS...EXOTIC MANUFACTURED PRODUCTS... PRECIOUS GEMS...NUCLEAR POWER! "MOON STOCKS" WORTH $100 BILLION MAY SELL HIGH ON WALL STREET AS "MOON MILLIONAIRES" ARE CREATED!

MOON MINING

LUNAR MINING CAMP. FROM THE MOON MINING CAMP, PROSPECTING VEHICLES MAY ROAM FORTH AND SEEK VALUABLE MINERALS, AND MOON MOBILES LOADED WITH ORES WILL RETURN TO PROCESS OUT GOLD, PLATINUM, SILVER AND SUCH RARE METALS AS GERMANIUM, BERYLLIUM, CESIUM, INDIUM, RADIUM, AND A DOZEN OTHERS!

However, on January 20, 1962, the press carried the story of Soviet plans to set up "an industrial undertaking" on the moon in the next few years to tap its resources. Tass, the official Soviet press agency, quoted their scientists as stating, "Man will visit the moon. The establishment on the moon of a permanent scientific station and subsequently an industrial undertaking will permit us to tap the yet undeveloped resources of this perpetual satellite of the earth." Does this indicate a change of their attitude on the question of ownership and sovereignty?

On April 2, 1963, the Soviet launched Lunik IV probably for the purpose of placing a robot on the moon preparatory to placing a man there but it missed the moon entirely. Of course, if it should be asserted that the placing of a man, and then a settlement and the establishment of an "industrial undertaking" on the moon, give a valid basis for its claim, this will bring to the fore the question of sovereign control and ownership, notwithstanding the earlier denials of any such intention.

The United States, on the 23rd day of April, 1962, established contact with the moon when Ranger IV impacted the lunar surface. There is nothing said about dropping any encapsulated flag on the moon. There is much said about placing a man on the moon, and later, a permanent station will be established there. It is not uncommon for nations to change their claims in accord with the rule of expediency for political and commercial advantages, even though the original declaration of position is made in good faith.

The probes to Mars launched in 1964 (arriving in 1965) by both the USA and USSR bring up those same reflections as to "claiming" Mars that are unresolved as yet about the much nearer moon. A half-dozen further planets, plus some 30 moons and several large asteroids---fifty new worlds at least awaiting mankind---all multiply the unsettled problem for the next generation, if not taken care of by us today.

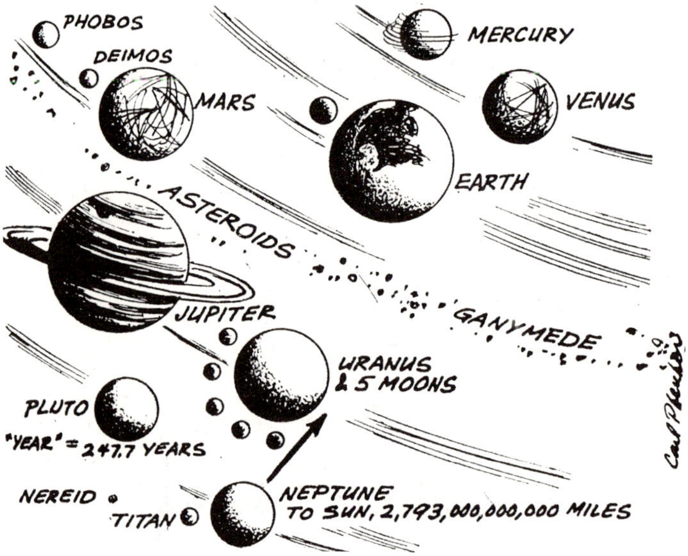

FIFTY WORLDS TO "CONQUER" IN OUR SOLAR SYSTEM!

That the landings on other worlds will be highly significant is emphasized by the quotes of eminent men. Wernher von Braun has always been in their forefront and has stated:

> "It is entirely conceivable that within our lifetimes rocketships will be transporting people to vacations in space, and that some of the famous European spas will be competing with new spas on Venus."

DR. WERNHER von BRAUN PROPHESIES THAT WITHIN OUR LIFETIME PEOPLE WILL VACATION AT VENUS SPAS OR MOONTELS.

Von Braun recently elaborated on this in the Bulletin of the American College of Surgeons (Volume 50, #2, March-April 1965) under the title "Space---The New Challenge":

Dr. Wernher von Braun, Director of NASA's Marshall Space Flight Center, compares space exploration to Renaissance Era of 14th century.

"One of the most significant milestones in space exploration, whether or not it is accomplished first by us, will be a manned lunar landing. I think none of us today can really imagine just how significant that day will be in the eyes of future generations. The nation with the vision, the capability, and the determination to achieve it will be recognized for its leadership as long as the history of man is recorded. And the implications on current international prestige and influence cannot be minimized.

"Success in space is equated in the eyes of many people with excellence in science and technology, economic strength, and determination of spirit. And this comparison, though oversimplified, is not too far afield...

"I firmly believe that we shall go on after Project Apollo is completed to explore the solar system. If we are to capture the reality of space, come to know it, and really use it, we must expose more people to space travel, for extended periods of time, and then apply what these people learn first hand in their new environment...

"Our position today brings to my mind an earlier period in the history of the Western World, the period when man first laid the great foundation, both in thought and achievement, for the better world we enjoy today. I speak of the Renaissance, the era of Michelangelo, da Vinci, and Shakespeare. It was in this period, beginning in the fourteenth century, that man took terrific strides to emancipate himself from his environment. In this period he undertook in earnest the conquest of his home planet as a place of human habitat. This was the age when men summoned their courage and set out on the high seas to explore the earth. It was the age of Columbus, da Gama, Sir Francis Drake, and Magellan.

"The Renaissance is often called the Age of Discovery. I believe we are entering the second great age of discovery, the exploration of outer space. To take part in that exploration is to take part in history during one of its great forward leaps."

SPACE COLUMBUSES WILL SOON LAUNCH ANOTHER GREAT AGE OF DISCOVERY UNPARALLELED IN PREVIOUS HISTORY.

Will this exploration of all the solar system happen? Will there be a migration to planets where human life may be sustained? Will earthman transfer his environment there or will he adjust himself to the environment he will find there?

In the Fifteenth Century, it was not thought that some day there would be jet planes flying across the oceans. Several decades ago not many people thought we would have X-15 rocket ships piercing the heavens at four or five thousand miles an hour. Just ten years ago---more than five centuries after the ventures of Columbus---it was not thought that there would be space-vehicles going at twenty-five thousand miles an hour, striking the moon, going around the moon, circling the sun, venturing in the regions of Venus and Mars, and invading the interplanetary area.

Scientists today plan for a trip to the moon taking two and one-half days to go and two and one-half days to come back---a round-trip total distance of about 500,000 miles. Compare this with the first voyage of Columbus from Palos, Spain, to Watling Island in the Bahamas (then called San Salvador) which took about ten weeks to cover a distance of approximately 3,000 miles.

Will the next conquest, in which America takes second place by past precedent, be the landing on the moon by the Soviet? What about launching platforms and the talk of orbital bombs to devastate a continent? Worried scientists allege that in this grim race the Soviet is still far ahead of us.

There is no doubt that the problems of the Space Age in the international world between nations, and between individuals and nations, have been tremendously increased. The urgency is greater with each passing hour. The demand for action to establish law must now be met.

The tremendous achievements of the astronauts open up the second new Age of Space---manned space flight. It is a fitting climax to the preceding unregulated achievements in this new world. It establishes more strongly the domination of the lawless realm of space by science that is unrestrained and unrestricted---after it is taken over by political forces that have not seen fit to impose any laws for the betterment of mankind.

Where is the Policeman in Space to regulate all these ventures? Will there be law in the face of the present anarchy? Or will the future see the evil old principle of colonization applied to space, simply because no Magna Carta has been ratified to extend law and order into the zone lying 500,000 feet above our heads?

The Space Age and its problems today are real. No longer is this important subject in the realm of fantasy fiction. The constant reference to space activities of the various nations, the acceleration in space programs, the aroused interest and deep concern of the common man everywhere, demand immediate attention to the necessity of resolving international conflict.

Where does the control of sovereignty over airspace end? Where shall there be a dividing line between the area of sovereign jurisdiction and the area of free international passage? If a missile or rocket is launched in Italy and passes through the area above Austria, has sovereign jurisdiction been invaded? If a vehicle is lost in the area of upper airspace, which is subject to the regulation of the sovereign power subjacent to this area, can this vehicle be attacked and destroyed by any other sovereign power on the assumption that there has been a trespass of its sovereign jurisdiction? Important questions such as these must be solved and resolved as speedily as possible if provocations to war and international bitterness are to be avoided.

Much thought has been given to this question and various conflicting concepts of space regulation have been suggested.

It is incumbent upon us in the next chapter to examine these conflicting theories and attempt out of this analysis to offer a guiding principle which, while still inadequate, may help fill the void of law to a satisfactory degree for the present and until such time as a better solution may be found.

But like Nature, Law abhors a vacuum.

7

WHO OWNS SPACE?

Do any of the present guide-posts relied upon by some experts provide us with a satisfactory basis for the definition of any proposed regulation of space? The answer is no.

The convention relating to the law of the sea in connection with which there was failure to attain complete agreement at Geneva in June, 1960, likewise does not provide sufficient and satisfactory guidance. Although this body of law suggests possible avenues of approach for international control it still presents decided weaknesses.

In the first place the framework of facts is quite different at sea and in the air:

> "i) At sea, the territorial belt and the High Sea have the same medium: water. In space, the air stratum and the outer layers are fundamentally different.
> "ii) At sea, the instrument enjoying innocent passage through the territorial waters is the ship. Entering into and egressing from the coastal zones are part of the uniform, non-distinguished shipping activity. In space, the vehicle crossing the supposedly marginal atmospheric belt is not the proper instrument of air navigation but a different artifact, built to navigate in another medium."

How far will this fundamental difference exert an influence on legal regulation?

Secondly, freedom of the seas is a qualified freedom. Although many countries are committed to a three-mile limit for their territorial seas, they may claim jurisdiction beyond this limit for varying distances, and some claim extra jurisdiction for customs purposes. Moreover, the theory upon which such jurisdiction is based rests upon the effect of these activities outside national boundaries.

In this manner, jurisdiction on the seas is often determined neither territorially nor spatially, but by arbitrarily changing the limit by whim or convenience.

This is hardly a reliable or concrete basis for the regulation of outer-space.

FREEDOM OF SPACE?

The various pre-space international conventions on the law of airspace do not provide us with sufficient support because the pertinent sections of these conventions did not contemplate or relate to space vehicles and space traffic, then non-existent.

It is generally agreed that the ad coelum pronouncements of these conventions refer to airspace---not to outer-space.

The "aircraft" mentioned in these conventions never included the new and then unforeseen vehicles for space flight.

This criticism of the ad coelum theory is also based upon the premise that if a cone were projected from the surface of the earth to infinity, within which cone the subjacent nation claimed possession, the contents within said cone would be ever-changing and impossible of definition. What is the air above one man's land one moment is the air above another man's land seconds later.

Since 1955 there has been a great deal written as to the means which should be utilized for control of air travel by missile, rocket, and other instrumentalities which do not in actuality require a reaction of the air for support. These new theories have in many instances come into conflict with preexisting theories advocated in centuries past.

A. The earliest theory advocated for control of the air was the ad coelum theory. This theory was predicated on the belief that a nation and even an individual land-owner controlled all of the space directly above its or his land, ad infinitum. The earliest advocate of this theory was the famous legal historian Blackstone who, in his Commentaries, Book 2, Chapter 2, Page 18, states:

> "Land hath also in its legal signification an indefinite extent upwards as well as outwards...so that the word 'land' includes not only the face of the earth but everything underneath."

The true absurdity of the ad coelum concept today is perhaps best reflected in the words of the poet, William Empson:

> "Your rights extend under and above your claim
> Without bound; you own land in Heaven and Hell;
> Your part of earth's surface and mass the same
> Of all cosmos volume and all stars as well."

Earlier proceedings indicate that space had a limited

connotation by no means commensurate with its scope as viewed today. The earliest Convention called to determine rules and regulations for air travel was the Paris Convention of 1910, at which it was decided that:

> "a. Each state possessed full sovereignty in the then usable space over its national lands and waters.
> b. There was no general right of international transit existing for aircraft of other states in the absence of international convention; and
> c. The only legal method of regulating international flight was by agreement which would provide for the grant of privileges of flight through such national space."

At no time was this Convention concerned with defining the words "air" or "aircraft". However, the Convention did refer to "usable space". These words in the light of that age could only mean the troposphere and possibly, though in all probability not, the stratosphere. This was the age of the beginning of airplane travel and the Convention at that time could not have been expected to think in terms of space beyond the stratosphere.

In 1919 a second Convention was called in Paris, generally referred to as the Paris Convention of 1919. This was the first major convention of world powers which had ever been called to ponder the problems of air travel.

The words "espace atmospherique" and "espazio atmosferico", used in the original French and Italian drafts of the Convention, were translated into the English version as "airspace" and without question must be equivalent to "atmospheric space". It was agreed at this Convention that each Nation possessed absolute sovereignty over the "airspace" above it. (The United States signed but never ratified this agreement.)

In this Convention, intended for the regulation of aerial navigation, it was stated that:

> "The High Contracting parties recognize that every Power has complete and exclusive sovereignty over the airspace above its territory."

It was agreed at this same Convention that "the word 'aircraft' shall comprise all machines which can derive support in the atmosphere from reactions of the air."

Again it can be seen that this Convention was primarily concerned with the earth's atmosphere as a source of travel, rather than with outer space; and again, in the light of the age, the word "atmosphere" must have meant to these statesmen an area comprising at the most the stratosphere because air travel beyond the limits of the stratosphere was not visualized.

The Civil Aeronautics Act of 1938 and its predecessor the Civil Aeronautics Act of 1926 were the first major efforts to codify a law relating to air travel for the United States. At no place in this statute is the word "airspace" defined, but the word "aircraft" is defined in both of these statutes as "...any contrivance now known or hereafter invented, used or designated for navigation of or flight in the air."

Previous Air Law never considered then-unborn X-15 rocketplane able to travel much higher than air-breathing flying machines.

In view of the fact that the phrase "any contrivance now known or hereafter invented" was used in the definition of the word "aircraft", it is difficult to determine exactly whether or not the legislators had in mind travel outside of the earth's atmosphere. However, owing to the presence of the word "air" in the definition and in view of its general meaning at that time, it is most probable that the legislators were concerning themselves only with atmospheric space and more likely with the area which at that time was used for air travel (to wit, the troposphere and possibly the stratosphere).

In the years between 1919 and 1944 there were various international conventions, such as the Warsaw Convention and the Rome Convention, which dealt with air travel, but nowhere in the agreements stemming from these Conventions does there appear to be any definitions of the words "airspace" or "air travel". This would lead one to believe that the statesmen were concerning themselves with nothing other than the troposphere and stratosphere.

Not until the Chicago Convention of 1944 (referred to at times as the International Civil Aviation Organization Conference) was a definition of the word "aircraft" given in an international agreement. Aircraft was defined as "any machine that can derive support in the atmosphere from reactions of the air."

It takes just a cursory comparison of the Chicago Convention's 1944 definition with the Paris Convention's 1919 definition to see that the definition in each case is exactly the same, and thus one can only conclude that there was no change of meaning of the word "aircraft" between 1919 and 1944.

One is led to believe, therefore, that the statesmen in 1944 had no greater outlook as to those areas in which air travel might be carried on than did the statesmen of 1919. It should be pointed out, however, that no definition of the word "airspace" was given in this Convention.

The most recent statute of any nation amongst the great powers dealing with the question of air travel is the British Air Navigation Order of 1949. Here again, there are no definitions of the words "airspace", "air travel" or "air commerce". The "aircraft" is defined as "including all balloons whether (captive or free) kites, gliders, airships and flying machines."

In 1949 there were no planes or ships of any sort which could travel higher than the stratosphere and most craft were limited to travel in the troposphere. Therefore, it must be concluded that the British Parliament was not concerned with travel beyond the stratosphere. On the other hand, satellites and rockets use the area above 100 miles for flight because they do not require "reactions of air for support". A flight below the 100 mile limit would create too much drag or heating for satellites to survive.

SPACE ANARCHY

The principles controlling or prohibiting claims of extension of sovereignty on the part of any one nation, the rules for internationalization of outer-space and the interplanetary system, the adoption of the principle superior to that of freedom of the seas, might well be a subject calling for the immediate agreement of the nations of the world before a crisis on this subject is created by any adverse claimant.

To some, it may appear that the possibility of adverse claims in regard to the use or control of outer-space is too remote to cause any present concern. In this connection, your attention is called to the switch of positions taken by the United States and Russia in regard to the extension of sovereignty into space.

In 1956, the United States, Great Britain, Turkey and West Germany were conducting meteorological studies. These studies necessitated the flights of unmanned scientific balloons through the stratosphere at a level of 80,000 to 90,000 feet. Though most of these balloons flew their predetermined course, some of them landed on Soviet and Soviet-dominated soil. Many of these that did not so land were forced, nevertheless, to fly over Soviet territory in the course of their flight. The Soviet Union, as well as most of the East European states allied with the Soviet Union, lodged protests with our country on the theory that we had trespassed on their sovereign territory.

When pre-Space Age balloons went 90,000 feet, higher than planes, "sovereignty" was simply extended upward that far.

On February 7, 1956, John Foster Dulles, then our Secretary of State, maintained "that although there was no clear rule of international law on the subject," the United States felt it had the right to send up these balloons. He said:

> "We would be disposed to be respectful of the strong views of any country which was opposed to it...We would do this, not as a matter of their right but as a matter of decent friendly relations".

The following points were made by Mr. Dulles in the course of his press interview concerning the flight of these balloons:

> "The question of the ownership of the upper air is a disputable question, and also the ether above the air...a legal position is quite obscure...what the legal position is I would not feel in a position to answer because I do not believe the legal position has even been clarified... There is no clear international law on the subject."

Thus, if we adhere to Mr. Dulles' conception of state sovereignty, airspace flight of any nation's balloons over another nation's territory at heights of 80,000 feet and above are presumably legal and cannot be objected to by any subjacent State. Since this view had been espoused by our Secretary of State who spoke with the authority of the executive branch of our government, we must assume that this was the United States policy on the subject in 1956.

Soviet policy on this point was in direct conflict with the United States policy and was in fact the antithesis of it. Article 1 of the Air Code of the USSR of August 7, 1935, states that "to the USSR belongs the complete and exclusive sovereignty in the airspace above the USSR."

The Soviet position was based on statements from other nations. As long ago as 1913, the French lawyer, Clunet, wrote "the right of sovereignty of each country to its territorial atmosphere must theoretically extend 'usque ad coelum,' as they used to say in olden times." Contemporary British lawyers interpreting the expression "complete and exclusive sovereignty over airspace" point out that "complete" signifies "without limit", that is, there is "no limit to height". Thus, the Soviet Air Code in 1935 recognized no distinction between "airspace" and what lay beyond, and their interpretation of "airspace" included everything above the earth's surface, ad infinitum.

Subsequently, however, in September, 1958 (and due to the launching of the Sputniks) a leading Soviet legal expert, Miss A. Galina, urged that no government should be permitted to incorporate any portion of interplanetary space under its jurisdiction. This leading legal writer, evidently speaking with the approval of her government, argued that since there is no international law covering space, any government may indefinitely launch rockets or satellites into interplanetary space without asking the permission of any other government. In this manner, this Soviet writer urged that even after the end of the International Geophysical Year (1957-58) all countries should continue to experiment by sending satellites or other apparatus over other countries' territories.

Was this an anticipatory defense to protests against Russia's contempleted launchings?

Since the Soviet government had protested in 1956 against the passage over its territory of American balloons equipped with instruments for gathering meteorological information, this new Soviet position indicated that she intended to send satellites over the United States and other countries.

Even as late as 1962 the Soviet Union, despite interim unofficial statements to the contrary, adhered officially to the principles in the original Air Code. An excerpt from the USSR Air Code, effective Jan. 1, 1962 states:

"Article 1---To the USSR belongs the full and exclusive sovereignty over the airspace of the USSR. By 'airspace of the USSR' is meant the airspace above the land and water territories of the USSR, including (the airspace) above territorial waters as defined in legislation of the USSR and international agreements concluded by the USSR."

On the other hand, in March, 1958, Mr. Loftus Becker, the Legal Adviser to the U.S. State Department, appearing before a Senate Committee, stated that the United States could still claim and defend all space above its territory.

The theory advanced by Mr. Becker, which is the ad coelum theory originally urged by the Soviet, is not recognized as a controlling principle by leading jurists, scientists and military men as sound today. (This limitation does not apply to military applications.) It therefore becomes necessary for the guidance of layman as well as lawyer to establish some basic elementary classifications even though they be tentative.

AEROSPACE DEFINITIONS

An attempt has been made to demonstrate that the great need for regulation of outer-space, the upward limitation of national sovereignty, and the establishment of rights and obligations, cannot be guided satisfactorily by reliance on the classic bodies of international law. We must recognize that there are difficulties in establishing a recognized boundary between airspace and outer-space.

Should the division be defined in terms of the physical characteristics of the air? Or should it be based on the purpose of flight or on the physical characteristics of flightcraft? What laws of physics, astronautics and scientific controls appply to these questions?

It is, therefore, desirable to analyze some samples of thought of authors and experts on the question of sovereignty. Three groups have emerged in this new but now crowded field on the law of outer-space. Fundamentally, they may be described as follows:

a) One group consists of those who refuse to set present limits of sovereignty though admitting that present law does not adequately cover existing circumstances.
b) The second group comprises those whose views have constantly fluctuated at different periods without formulating any final conclusions. This vacillation, however sincere, provides provocation for further delay but does not constitute a contribution on which great reliance can be placed.
c) The third group comprises those who offer specific, consistent and logical solutions, even though these solutions are not complete and even though the need for further action and thought is undeniable. It comprises those who believe that a skeletal outline of an international code should be established to provide a basis for a minimum of understanding and cooperation, in the effort to reduce provocations for dissension which inactivity would not cor-

rect. This group too may be subdivided into two further groups, to wit:

1. Those who propose limitations of sovereignty based on mechanical measurements, and
2. Those whose proposals of such limitations are predicated on non-mechanical criteria.

The first group mentioned (a) believes it is undesirable to set any present limits of sovereignty, whether unilateral or international, because they allege there is insufficient information and knowledge of outer-space to guide them. They argue moreover that crucial problems of domestic and international law relate to airspace and not to outer-space, and that proposed agreements would limit both national sovereignty and national security.

The weaknesses of these arguments are apparent on analysis. Although our knowledge of the physical properties of space is still incomplete, events nevertheless are moving so rapidly that no nation can wait for evolution of law based upon experience, as in the case of the development of law of the automobile. Events are moving so rapidly in outer-space that the problems and questions must be anticipated and steps taken to guard against catastrophe. The "stand-patters" do not furnish a satisfactory argument against the establishment of a line of demarcation between airspace and outer-space so necessary for the purpose of limiting sovereignty.

Such a line will have to be designed for legal significance. It is not necessarily dependent on complete knowledge of the physical characteristics of outer-space.

While it is also true that there are a great number of unsolved problems relating to airspace, and even to conflicts between the law of the subjacent land and the law relating to navigable airspace, these problems have not heretofore prevented the creation of various agreements and conventions and laws for the guidance and development of the use of airways used by aircraft.

How much more important is the need for solving the legal problems of outer-space, which are potentially much more serious and, if not properly solved, may prove cataclysmic.

Agreements limiting sovereign control of nations are hardly new. On the issue of national security it may be effectively argued that the greatest step toward national and international security would be to place the areas of space and the interplanetary system beyond the whim, caprice or ambition of a sovereign power or a potential aggressor against the world, now or in the future.

Mutual agreement on the classification of outer-space as "res communis" and airspace as part of sovereign territory, would be a great contribution to the avoidance of conflicts arising over the question of exercise of sovereign power.

THE SPACE OCEAN

The second group (b) while conceding that there is no satisfactorily applicable law, has offered conflicting and fluctuating views that provide no meaningful solution. They have offered, in contrast to the ad coelum theory, many new theories, including the following:

Mr. Bin Cheng, a leading lecturer of laws at University College in London believes that the following, developed by custom and usage rather than by international agreement and legislation, fits the present theory of state sovereignty over airspace: "Free flight space represents such portions of flight space as are not subject to national sovereignty and today includes airspace above the high seas, airspace above terra nullius and extra-terrestrial airspace."[5] Terra nullius is defined by the author as the airspace above land not yet under the sovereign control of any nation, such as Antarctica. Unfortunately, he fails to recognize "res communis."

It is important, however, to note at this time that there have been claims made over Antarctica as well as over the Arctic by various nations, including Argentina, the United States, Great Britain, Canada and the Soviet Union. Extra-terrestrial space is defined by the author as that area above the exosphere's outer limits estimated at about 600 miles above the surface of the earth.

If this theory is accepted, as the author asserts most people today do, then there would remain but one question for solution. What right have nations to fly machines over another nation's territory within the earth's atmosphere? We would be limited to this one question, since flight beyond the exosphere, flight over terra nullius, and flight over the high seas, are deemed free to all nations, and flight within the troposphere is deemed controlled by the subjacent State.

In the early 1950's and the latter part of the 1940's, Mr. John Cobb Cooper, Professor of International Law, expounded the theory of sovereignty of each State to extend as far as the area of effective control of "space" by the most powerful State. A variation of this view is that every State can dominate whatever it can effectively control.

SOVEREIGNTY BASED ON A NATION'S "EFFECTIVE CONTROL" ABOVE AIRSPACE ONLY EXTENDS THE WARLIKE RULE OF "MIGHT MAKES RIGHT" INTO OUTER-SPACE.

In 1955 Mr. Cooper advocated a new and distinct theory. He would divide the air into three categories: a) Space; b) Contiguous space; c) Territorial space.
He elaborated as follows:

> "a) Any instrumentalities for air travel would be allowed to fly free of any control in an area designated as "Space" ---300 miles and more above the earth's surface.
> "b) All non-military craft while ascending or descending should be allowed to fly free of any control by the country beneath, from a height of about 10 kilometers (upper portion of the troposphere) to 300 miles (middle portion of the ionosphere).
> "All military ships might be controlled by the nations over which they had to fly and no such flight could under any circumstances take place without permission of the subjacent nation. (This is the area referred to as "Contiguous Space".)
> "c) No ship either commercial or military would be allowed to fly over a nation's "Territorial Space" without first obtaining permission for said flight. This includes the area from the earth's surface to 10 kilometers above (about 6 miles).'"

Apparently this theory is to be based upon no scientific criterion, but rather upon an arbitrary system of classification.

In 1957, Mr. Cooper changed his position to advocate sovereignty to a height sufficient to protect the neutrality of the subjacent State. He later concluded that there is sovereignty in airspace but not in outer-space, but indicated that there was no agreement as to where outer-space began. His next position was that a neutral subjacent State would be held responsible for the passage in space above that sovereign power even though the launching of the missile or rocket occurred in another country over which the first sovereign power had no control or power of opposition. His most recent position is that sovereignty should be limited at the point where "effective atmosphere ends", a point where a satellite could be orbited.

At a meeting of the Aviation Committee of the New York County Lawyers' Association on October 21, 1965, Mr. Cooper indicated his continued criticism of the adherence to the limitations of the Chicago Convention adopted in 1944 and constituting the bulwark of the International Civil Aviation Organization; he indicated agreement with the views of this author on the necessity for establishing a line of demarcation between airspace and outer-space in each of which areas the obligations and rights are different, and also the right of innocent passage. The further question was posed by Mr. Cooper as to whether those using outer-space were guilty of a violation of sovereignty when their missile passed through sovereign territory, airspace, without permission of the sovereign powers---a right claimed by some scholars to be inferentially incidental to the free use of outer-space.

WHERE DOES OUTER-SPACE BEGIN?

This author's position has been reiterated that there is no unilateral right on the part of any nation to trespass upon or invade the sovereign territory of any other nation without consent. The problem must be settled by multilateral agreement by the interested nations.

Turning to the concepts of other law writers, one of them states:

"The stratosphere and the space beyond are incapable of

> being made the subject of dominion and should be classified by lawyers as "res nullius" or "res omnium communis".

That learned author fails to draw a very important distinction between "res nullius" and "res communis". He fails to take cognizance of joint ownership the right held by all nations to use freely an area which is regarded as "res communis". On the other hand, in regard to "res nullius", the right of appropriation by a discoverer with settlement and habitation gives the right to exclude other sovereign powers from that area.

One legal commentator argues that five hundred miles is the maximum height of airspace---sovereign territory---likely to be agreed on internationally. A second legal writer sets one hundred and twenty-four miles to one hundred and eighty-seven miles up as the limit of sovereignty, since there is still sufficient oxygen in this area to properly term it airspace.

All of these concepts are totally obsolete. Let us examine the more modern theories of the third group (c).

Modern theorists offer some kind of specific, consistent answers to the questions of height to which sovereignty extends and the regulatory measures to be adopted in establishing rights and responsibility. Of course, there is still one big problem confronting the members of this group and confronting all students of the subject: how a line of demarcation is to be set up.

One such specific view for control over space travel has been expounded by Delbert M. Draper, Jr., an officer in the United States Naval Reserve, Mr. Draper believes that there must be controlled flight throughout the troposphere and stratosphere, though the ionosphere (25 to 600 miles high) would remain free for any nation's use. This freedom, however, would be subject to control by the subjacent nation for "defensive purposes" (a term which remains undefined).

Mr. Draper gives some mention to another theory, not fully discussed, which would grant control by each nation to that point above its territory where the gravitational force of the earth ceases to exist.

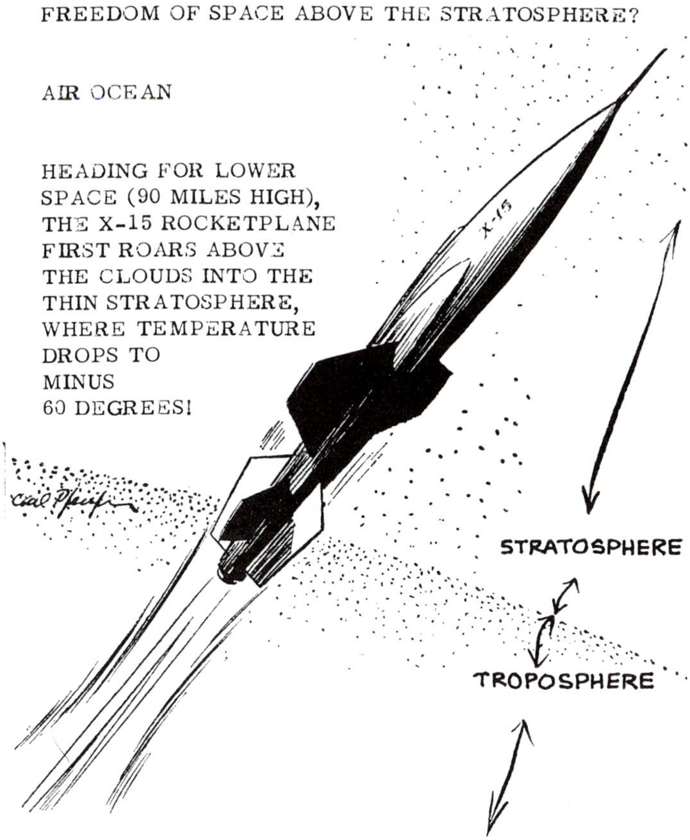

Another naval officer, Rear Admiral Chester Ward, points out that, except for the 3-mile limit which is recognized in international law and is the only limitation recognized by the United States as a restraint upon itself, the high seas are free for any nation to navigate in, and even within the 3-mile zone a right of innocent passage is recognized. He points out that this theory evolved slowly from a theory of sovereign control over as wide an area as can be effectively controlled (undoubtedly by force of arms). He defines "air" as that region of relatively dense air used so extensively for military and commercial purposes, and compares the 300-mile belt suggested by John Cobb Cooper to the 3-mile sea zone. He says that Cooper should be concerned with defense since if a nation can shoot a machine down where it is within or above its territorial space, it will shoot it down if it poses a threat. He is thus advocating a theory with the same manifestations as the theory based upon "might makes right".

Andrew G. Haley, noted authority in the field of rocketry and formerly President of the International Astronautical Federation in 1954-55, believes that sovereignty should extend and in fact does extend beyond the earth's atmosphere. But he believes that this sovereignty was waived by the nonobjection to the International Geophysical Year flights which were carried on for over a year. It must be queried, however, whether or not this waiver is for all time; and it must be asked to what extent and over what areas of space the nations involved in the International Geophysical Year have since waived their control.

More lately, Dr. Haley has urged the von Karman line as a basis for establishing the demarcation between airspace, the area of sovereign jurisdiction, and outer-space, the area that is "res communis". Not to oversimplify the situation, it is sufficient for some guidance toward the understanding of this principle to quote Mr.Haley:

> "The von Karman line is the line at which the component atoms of 'air' dissociate---and, of course, at this point air no longer exists and 'airspace' ends. At this point, also, the lifegiving aspects of air disappear and all functional uses of air are gone, including the aerodynamic lift."

It is not only desirable but indispensable for peaceful determination of this question that we obtain the assistance of scientists, users of space, government administrators and all having an interest in the problems that arise from failure to set forth a boundary line separating airspace from outer-space.

GUIDELINES INTO SPACE

A number of theorists propose to limit sovereignty through some sort of mechanical measurement. Thus, several well-known writers argue that "no state has the right to subject parts of cosmic space to its own legislation, administration or jurisdiction." It is asserted on this score, that any projection of sovereignty into space "would be inconsistent with the basic astronomical facts".

By this is meant, of course, that there is a fluctuating relationship between the subjacent country and transatmospheric space and thus the bounds of subjacent sovereignty can never be computed as mathematical constants. There appears to be general agreement among the scholars that airspace is subject to control by the subjacent sovereign and that the areas above airspace are not subject to such control.

This does not decide, however, the point at which airspace, and sovereignty with it, come to an end.

Some commentators propose to end sovereignty "at a

point in the ocean of air surrounding the earth where aerodynamic lift is gone''. This point is the so-called von Karman Primary Jurisdiction Line located at 275,000 feet up, (about 53 miles altitude), beyond which point a rocketship like the X-15 must switch from useless aircraft controls to a spacecraft's jet-gas reaction system for turning in the almost empty vacuum at that height. But this zero-aerodynamic point is much lower for conventional jet-craft at slower speeds, anywhere from 15 to 25 miles high, and thus is hardly a dependably "fixed" line for all types of aircraft and rocketcraft.

ABOVE 53 MILES (VON KARMAN LINE) AERODYNAMIC CONTROLS ARE USELESS IN THIN UPPER AIR AND ROCKETPLANES SHIFT TO "SPACE STEERING" METHODS.

Another group favors actual height limitations as the

simplest means of setting up the boundary lines. A writer in this field sets fifty miles as the limit on the grounds that the air at this height is not sufficiently dense to permit conventional flight. (He would be more correct to say conventional jet-propulsion as fuel would cease burning).

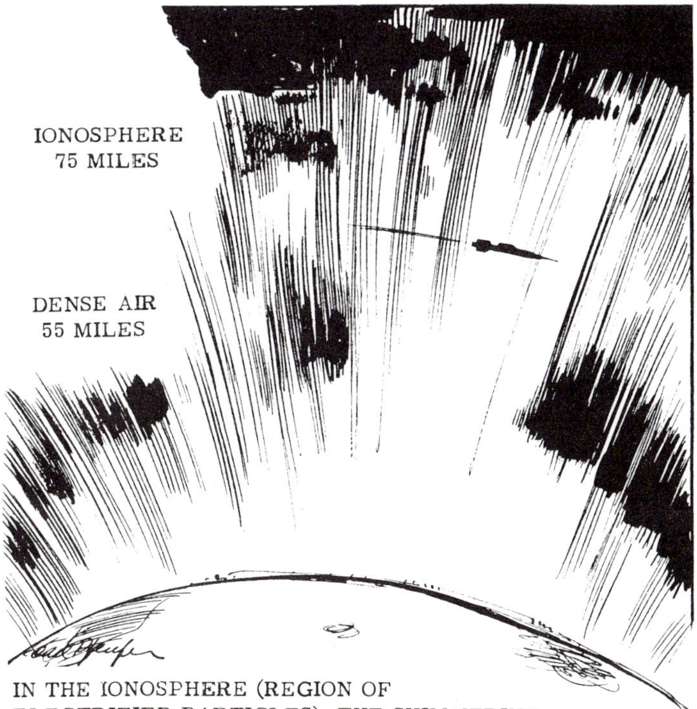

IN THE IONOSPHERE (REGION OF ELECTRIFIED PARTICLES), THE SHIMMERING AURORA BACKLIGHTS THE ROCKETPLANE ON ITS DRIVE TOWARD SPACE!

JET-FUEL WILL NOT BURN AT EXTREME HEIGHTS, WHERE ONLY A ROCKETPLANE CARRYING ITS OWN OXYGEN SUPPLY CAN FLY.

The brilliant physicist, Dr. S. Fred Singer, has suggested that the only "natural" boundary is that between the barosphere and the exosphere. Even there, the exact definition of this "base of the exosphere" is a matter of convention, being defined as the point where barometric air-pressure reaches a "low"---but how low?

It is difficult to find any one of the theorists supporting their sovereignty markers as perfect or precise.

Even on land where boundary lines can be fixed by

physical factors, there occur controversy, tension and even clashes among opposing nations. The instances are too numerous to cite but reference might be made to the Chinese-Indian border dispute, the Israel-Jordan dispute, the Pakistan-Indian controversy, and the numerous conflicts in almost every part of the world concerning the propriety and correctness of a boundary line.

Closer to home, the dispute over the boundary line between Mexico and the United States at the Rio Grande was settled by the Chamizal Treaty after negotiations lasting almost one hundred years.

Instances of violations of sovereign territory are claimed to have occurred in the RB-47 reconnaissance plane incident over the Barents Sea within the limits of Soviet territorial waters; the U-2 observation plane flight over Russia on May 1, 1960; the activity of Soviet trawlers and vessels at, near and allegedly within the three-mile limit of territorial waters off the American coast while naval maneuvers were being conducted; the routine Soviet air flights off the coast of Japan, so frequent as to be called the "Tokyo Express." All of these illustrate the trespass over boundary lines into sovereign territory.

It has been indicated that even the slightest and most innocent violations have led to a bitter clash, as illustrated by the incident several years ago when some Turkish soldiers, while cutting grass, strayed accidently across their boundary line into Soviet territory and were then fired upon.

Therefore, it is clear that where the boundary lines cannot be established by any fixed physical factors such as rivers, mountains, streams and other natural geological conditions, the likelihood of confusion will be that much greater in empty space.

In space, accordingly, the need to set a boundary line between airspace and outer-space is greater and must be met, even if done arbitrarily, to avoid disputes that might lead to bloodshed and use of force. Subsequent experience and analysis might dictate a change in the place where this arbitrary boundary line is set, but this can be done again peacefully through the concerted action of all interested nations.

SPACE LAW MUST SET A DEFINITE BOUNDARY LINE BETWEEN AIRSPACE (SOVEREIGNTY) AND OUTER-SPACE (NON-SOVEREIGNTY) TO AVOID FUTURE ARMED CONFLICT OVER THE UPWARD BOUNDARY OF A SOVEREIGN POWER.

Dealing with space boundaries is admittedly difficult.

There are those who propose limitations in sovereignty based upon non-mechanical means. Several of the writers note the criterion of effective control by the subjacent territory as being of prime importance. Effective control via jets? Guns? Guided missiles? Or what exactly?

It has also been recommended that sovereignty in the skies be limited by means of an international arrangement based on types of spacecraft, probable functions and potential dangers. Such a theory might find difficulty, however, in the flux of a technological situation in which types, functions and dangers are subject to constant change.

Another recommendation is that security is the prime consideration in the determination of limits to national sovereignty. That is to say, sovereignty "reaches an upward limit at the point where whatever happens above that point cannot possibly hurt . . .or affect the lives and safety of the citizens and subjects of the underlying sovereign power". This vague view has the same defects found in the position of those who urge that sovereignty at this time should not be limited.

8

WHERE DOES OUTER SPACE BEGIN?

HAVING discussed the various theories urged by others and the objections to them, it is now in order to suggest a constructive procedure.

First of all, let us try to determine what, or more properly where is "outer-space"? We must agree to define "space" in a specific way in order to proceed further. At present time, however, there is no international agreement on this question since there is no accord as to the point at which airspace ends and outer-space begins. In the author's Report On Space of February 20, 1958, to the American Bar Association meeting at Atlanta, Georgia, he first presented this aerial analysis:

> "At present scientists agree that there are 5 layers which constitute the atmosphere around the earth. They are:
> "a. The troposphere, which is zero to 10 kilometers above the earth's surface (6 miles).
> "b. The stratosphere which is 10 to 40 kilometers above the earth's surface (6 to 25 miles).
> "c. The mesosphere which is 40 to 80 kilometers above the earth's surface (25 to 50 miles).
> "d. The thermosphere which is 80 to 375 kilometers above the earth's surface (50 to 235 miles).
> "e. The exosphere which is above 375 kilometers above the earth's surface (235 miles and beyond).
> "The highest point on the earth therefore lies within the troposphere and it is within the troposphere itself that most of man's travels up to the present time have taken place.
> "The mesosphere, thermosphere and part of the exosphere together combine what is generally referred to by scientists as the ionosphere (definitions vary).
> "The exact outer limits of the ionosphere have not as yet been definitely determined. Scientists have placed this limit between 310 and 620 miles above the earth's surface. Beyond the ionosphere lies what I will refer to as outer-space. This area is sometimes referred to as extraterrestrial

ABOVE 50 MILES IS "THERMOSPHERE" (HIGH TEMPERATURE ZONE) WHERE AIR MOLECULES ARE EXTREMELY TURBULENT,

space, for it lies without the earth's atmosphere. It is with the areas referred to as mesosphere, thermosphere, exosphere and extraterrestrial space that we must now be concerned in a discussion and study of rocketry, missiles and other means of interplanetary travel.

"What makes the problem confronting us most difficult is that the terms referred to above have not been utilized in the formulation of national statutes and international agreements, and thus, there appears to have been no scientific approach to control of air travel prior to this generation."

If the atmospheric definitions are acceptable, the adjustments for determining lines at certain given heights through proper technological means would appear to offer the most easily workable basis for lines of demarcation. Still, however, there is before us the important question as to how we should mark the boundary line between air-space and outer-space.

In order to facilitate the reader's understanding of these

"layers" of the aerospace regions above the surface of the earth, the following chart will be helpful.

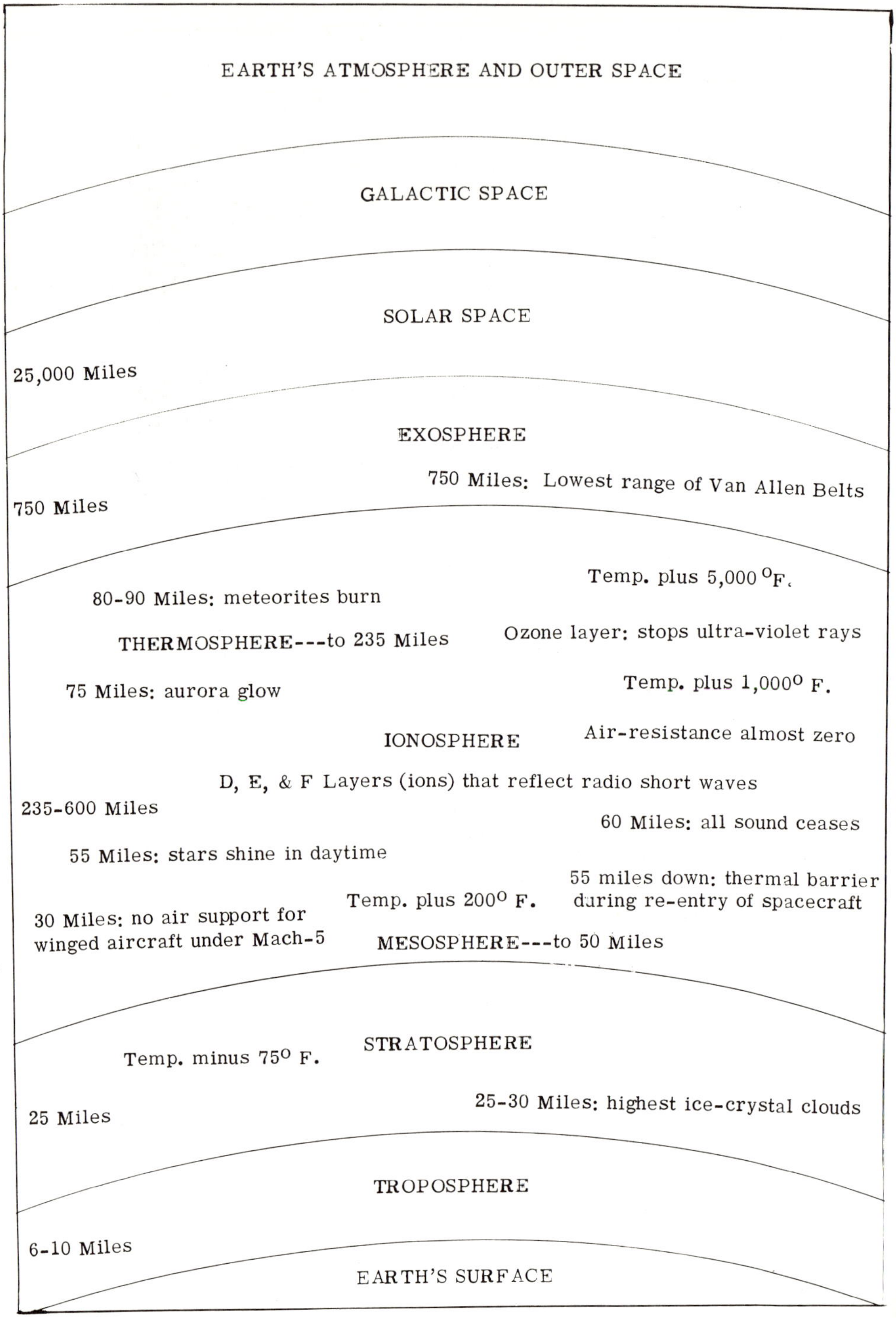

Captain George D. Schraeder (U.S.A.), in a paper titled "National Sovereignty in Space" presented to the Fifth Colloquium on the Law of Outer-Space, of the International Institute of Space Law, September 23-29, 1962, set the highest boundary of all between "airspace" and "outer-space"--- 21,000 miles.

However, few satellites today, and excluding only the Syncom radio relays used by the Comsat network, fly at this extreme height. The "busiest" area of near-earth orbital operations in the future as well as the present, where the most "space traffic" occurs, will be from about 100 miles altitude to 1000 miles high.

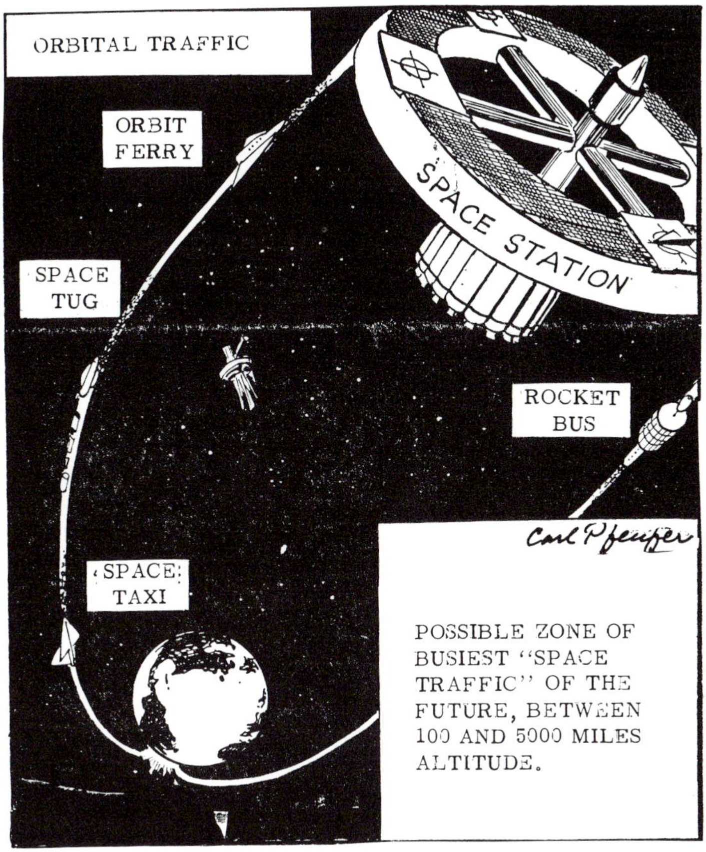

Space-stations, manned laboratories, and other manned vehicles will be set into permanent or semi-permanent orbits within that range, and will start operations before the end of this decade and continue increasing indefinitely. They will become huger and more complex as time goes on, from the early 3-man ventures now planned to gigantic 100-man installations floating above earth like luxurious way-stations in space. They will all, or mostly, hang far below the limit of 21,000 miles.

The author finds several other boundaries---chosen arbitrarily since there is no alternative---to be more practical than Captain Schraeder's line of demarcation. Which line will prove best is not up to this writer, but up to that body---including not only legal minds but scientists, politicians, and government administrators---which will have to someday (hopefully soon) come to grips with the whole problem and set up those standards.

The important thing is to establish some line of demarcation between airspace and outer-space now, as the basic cornerstone of unborn space law.

COVERING THE SPACE FRONT

The author's earliest attempt at narrowing down this intangible boundary line was contained in the report of the Subcommittee on Outer-Space of the Standing Committee on Aeronautical Law, of the American Bar Association, delivered to and accepted by the full Committee in Atlanta, Georgia, in February, 1958. The definition of space set forth therein is as follows:

> "Space is that area existing between the surface of the earth and celestial bodes. It shall comprise two parts. The first, to be known as airspace, shall comprise the troposphere and stratosphere and be under the complete and exclusive sovereignty of the subjacent nation. The second shall comprise the remainder of the area extending to the celestial bodies which shall be termed 'outer-space'. This outer-space shall be free from the claim of sovereignty of any individual nation."

This definition at the time seemed to leave a considerable area for the exercise of subjacent sovereignty. However, in the light of vastly expanding air and space flights since then, the author finds it imperative to extend the boundary upward.

First of all, the height of 25 miles no longer fully contains all air-breathing aircraft. Some recent jetcraft such as the remarkable A-11, can probably range higher. Furthermore, present research into the so-called 'ram-jet'' plane may make them operable up to 50 miles or more. Their powerplants are designed to utilize the i- credibly thin air and oxygen at that height, during high-speed flight.

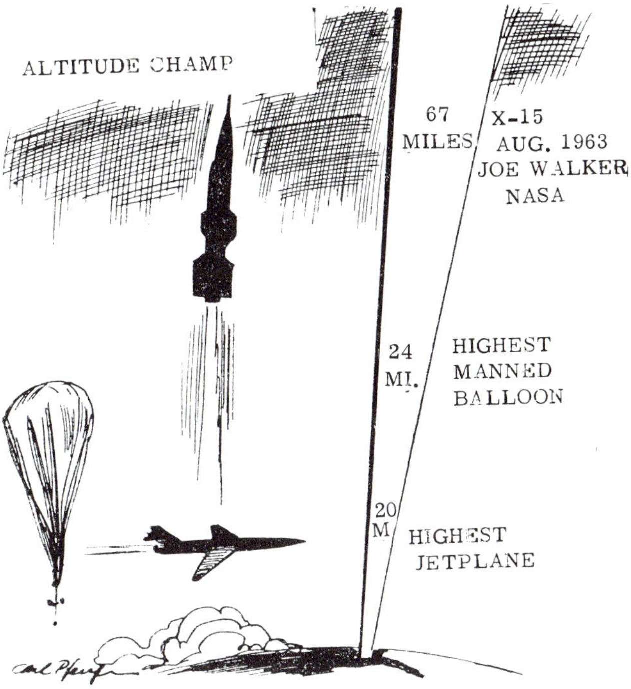

FUTURE RAMJETS MAY OPERATE AROUND 50 MILES HIGH, WHERE ONLY THE X-15 ROCKET PLANE CAN ROAM TODAY.

If we want to be safe, it would be better to extend even this unheard-of range for air-breathing flying craft up to 75 miles, as the Air Force is talking of a combination jet-and-rocket "spaceplane'' which will ramjet its way to 60 or 65 miles and gather in further oxygen gas and liquefy it---all before switching to their rocket engine.

To make all this clear, an air-breathing craft is an

airplane whose engine requires gaseous oxygen, pulled in from the surrounding air, to burn its fuel and produce power. On the other hand, a rocket-craft---like the X-15---carries along its own oxygen (or oxidizer) supply as well as fuel and is thus independent of the atmosphere for motive power. Such craft are the only true "spacecraft".

Hence, in light of this data, the author's first proposed boundary line between airspace and outer-space, based purely on the ranges of air-breathing craft and true spacecraft, is at an altitude of 75 miles above earth's surface at sea-level.

The second proposed line of demarcation would be a height of 100 miles, based on another criterion---the two different areas where non-orbiting and orbiting craft can operate. It is based more specifically on the following scientific points:

> A) Almost all satellites and manned spacecraft are placed in orbit above 100 miles, with a very few perigees temporarily swinging below that figure by a few miles, seldom below 90 miles.
> B) All aircraft and experimental rocketcraft that are non-orbiting, such as the X-15, cruise only below 100 miles altitude.
> C) The density of earth's atmosphere is such, at 100 miles, that any spacecraft venturing much below it will meet enough air-drag to begin de-orbiting by itself. Hence it is truly "airspace" in that real sense.
> D) Only above 100 miles can space vehicles continue circling earth for a length of time without sufficient air-resistance to "fall down" from orbit. Hence this region meets most of the criteria for what the space-launch engineers would consider "outer-space".
> E) Most "spy satellites" of the USA and USSR both are placed in low orbit---the closer the better for their cameras and earth-observations devices---that often dip well below 100 miles. Hence, these possible peace-disturbing vehicles could be placed under "airspace" laws instead of using the umbrella of complete immunity to law under "freedom of space" principles.

Thirdly, we might go by another factor---where will be the heart of earth-orbit space traffic in the future? This is harder to foresee but it would certainly be higher than 100 miles, and a likely figure---again purely arbitrary of course---would be 500 miles altitude.That is, the heaviest concentration of unmanned scientific vehicles, of experimental manned flights, and of big space-stations, will probably center at that height which is completely free of all atmospheric influences yet is reasonably close to earth for back-and-forth ferry and supply service. That altitude, also, is still well beneath the main radiation forces of the Van Allen Belts, thus avoiding any danger to human life in long-term orbital outposts.

Now we have three possible boundary lines between air-space and outer-space from which to choose. All of this leads into what the author believes to be his most unique concept, and the most important new provision of all relating to space law.

This additional proposal was also introduced by the writer to the American Bar Association in February, 1958, where he stipulated that any international agreement on space law should also provide for a neutral zone extending in either direction, above and below the line of demarcation between airspace and outer-space, for the peaceful transit of non-military aircraft, vehicles and objects not likely to represent hazards to person or property. This would not destroy any existing rights of commercial international air transport operations.

Futhermore, even military vehicles going into such a neutral zone should be entitled to a first warning or notification of the invasion of that area, in the same manner in which innocent passage of the seas is termed an excuse for warning and not for attack.

"NEUTRALIA"---BUFFER ZONE OF SPACE

The author proposed, in Article 8 of *The Magna Carta,* to end the impasse over satisfactorily dividing "air" and "space" by establishing an area known as "Neutralia" which will embrace the upper reaches of airspace and the lower extensions of outer-space, in which the right of innocent venture for peaceful purposes shall be recognized in order

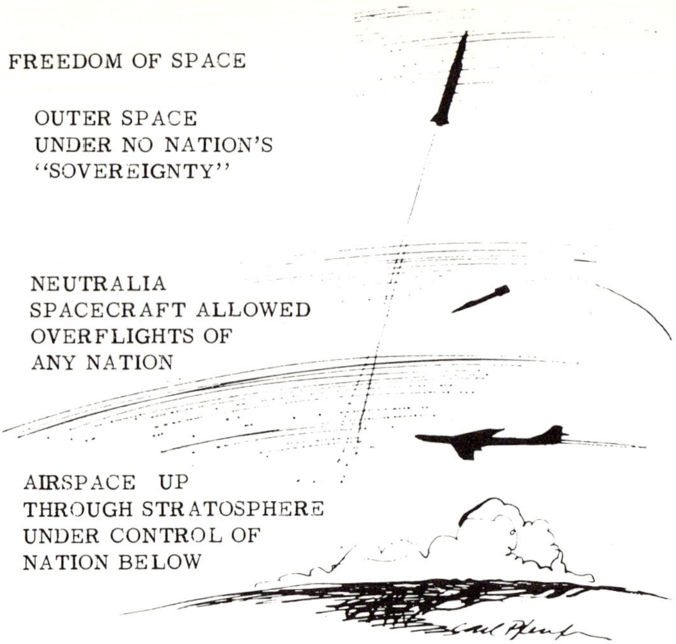

"NEUTRALIA" BUFFER-ZONE AS SPECIFIED IN "MAGNA CARTA OF SPACE" WOULD CLEARLY DEFINE THE LIMITATIONS OF SOVEREIGNTY AND AVOID CONFLICT.

to avoid distorting such incidents into invasions of sovereignty or provocations for international dispute and war.

The earlier controversy concerning the meteorological balloons in 1956; the reversal of decisions of the two leading nations on the questions of upper limits of airspace; the constantly higher altitudes reached by the rocketship X-15; the nearness to earth of the orbits followed by Vostok and Voskhod; the increase in the number of missiles, rockets, satellites in and near this critical area; and the Soviet release of fifteen nuclear bombs in space with fallout dropping into sovereign territory of a number of nations ---give clear indication that this will be the area of origin of serious international controversies which may lead to disastrous consequences.

To a limited extent and certainly with beneficial results to all nations and to all people, nations can agree upon the establishment of this neutral zone with provisions for innocent or accidental passage therein. None could claim this to be an invasion of sovereignty and therefore, a cause for warlike demonstrations and protestations. Likewise, nuclear testing therein may be barred to protect the innocent, helpless people on earth.

Furthermore, if the zone of "Neutralia" is regarded as a counterpart of territorial waters, standing in the same relation to outer-space as territorial waters do to the high-seas, the legal implication follows that the sovereignty of a State would not be violated by the passage through outer-space or the upper regions of airspace above its territory even of a strictly military satellite or space vehicle, if the theory of innocent passage is applied. The nature of the vehicle or object creating such trespass would, of course, bear upon the interpretation of the act.

"NEUTRALIA" WOULD BY LAW DEFINE THE "EDGE OF OUTER-SPACE".

The specific definition of "Neutralia" as given among this writer's provisions in *The Magna Carta* is as follows:

"...that there be established a neutral zone embracing the upper limits of airspace and the lower limits of outer-space to be known as 'Neutralia' in which the right of innocent passage shall be recognized without offense to sovereignty. In this area of 'Neutralia' there shall be the right of innocent passage of all craft, vehicles and objects of transit and movement without any such incident being deemed an invasion of sovereignty. In the event of any such innocent passage no nation shall have the right to attack or destroy such vehicle or object in transit or the nation from which the said vehicle or object was launched or to destroy any occupants thereof without prior, sufficient warning and notice of claim of invasion of sovereignty and without prior opportunity for determination of the merits of such complaints by peaceful methods."

Considering all the factors for and against the establishment of "Neutralia" and weighing the advantages and disadvantages against one another, it appears that more is to be gained than lost by the adoption of this neutral zone. •

EDGE OF OUTER-SPACE

Now, note that in presenting the Neutralia concept, it is nowhere stated just where the boundaries should be placed in fixed figures, but it is only insisted that it must extend from, and include:

a) the upper limits of airspace, and
b) the lower limits of outer-space

This general principle applies to any of the three previous boundary lines between airspace and outer-space that the author suggested. It makes no difference, actually, which line of demarcation is adopted as in each case Neutralia will extend above and below it.

How far above and below it? That, again, is a complex matter whose many factors will have to be taken into consideration---how much "space traffic" it is practical or feasible to include; keeping low-flying spacecraft out of airspace jurisdiction, and high-flying aircraft out of outer-space regulations that might be misfit; how to insure that all or most "spy satellites" and non-orbiting military missiles come under sovereign airspace control for the protection of individual nations; and a host of other considerations that upon analysis might shift the space boundary line up or down, in order to shift the zone of Neutralia up or down to the best and most desirable region.

Taking each line of demarcation separately, for a quick look at the possibilities: A) The 75 mile high boundary line between airspace and outer-space might logically extend Neutralia downward 25 miles and upward 75 miles. Hence, Neutralia would be a zone from 50 miles above earth to 150. This would exclude all air-breathing craft and leave them under established airspace laws and sovereignty principles, which is right and proper. The zone would include, however, all reconnaissance satellites, and many manned and unmanned orbiting vehicles of a purely scientific nature.

This buffer-zone would probably not cover future high-altitude space-stations and other manned outposts set up as "space ports" for interplanetary flight---but then, should such large installations be subject to earthly law, or enjoy complete freedom of space?

"SPACEPORTS" OF THE FUTURE WILL BE IN "FREE SPACE", NOT SUBJECT TO SOVEREIGNTY OF ANY SUBJACENT NATIONS ON EARTH.

B) Dividing airspace and outer-space at 100 miles up might indicate that the Neutralia zone should extend 25 miles below and perhaps 500 miles above---a total range of 75 miles altitude to 600 miles above sea-level. This much broader scope for Neutralia would have to be predicated on the supposition that it is best to have almost all space vehicles under an international innocent-passage code, plus periphery restrictions and rules necessary to keep an orderly "traffic" rocketing above earth at all times, neither unnecessarily hampering scientific and peaceful endeavors, nor allowing potential military devices and systems to escape strict regulations.

Of course, any launch vehicles, interplanetary spaceships, or re-entry craft that merely rocket through Neutralia would also have to be checked in and out, much like air traffic now over any busy airport, to make sure spacecraft and aircraft do not continually collide or interfere with one another.

C) With the 500-mile borderline between airspace and outerspace, Neutralia could then expand, say some 400 miles down and as much as 5000 miles up. Why this high? Because as our technology continues "exploding" and constantly surprising us a few years later, it may well be that manned craft, space-stations, and all sorts of space vehicles will sail with aplomb in orbital paths up to 5000 miles above earth. The densest population of space "hardware" will undoubtedly shift upward year by year, and may reach that height---or higher---sooner than we think. In fact, it may prove within a decade or two that Captain Schraeder's line at 21,000 miles is not so fantastic. Or at least the Zone of Neutralia could extend that far if man pushes back the space frontier that high in the near future.

In fact, it might be most sensible for the authorities who finally sit down to hammer out the fine points of Space Law to set a sliding scale upward for both the boundary line between airspace and outer-space and the overlapping zone of Neutralia. In that way, they could keep up with advancing space progress and not get caught in a few years with an anachronistic law rigidly set for boundaries that have become totally obsolete.

Expanding space technology will send manned rocketcraft and space stations higher and higher above earth.

Too many "fossil" laws of this sort, in all areas of human life, have hampered civilization in the past. Changing the law is admittedly difficult. Therefore, incorporating changing standards within the law is the ideal answer.

SPACE IS A "PLACE"

In summary, merely setting an official boundary line between airspace and outer-space alone is insufficient guarantee that an equitable, peace-keeping Space Code can be promulgated therefrom. Only the additional buffer-zone of Neutralia can encompass the immensely complex system of future space operations and assure solution of most if not all the accumulating problems that space pioneering and exploitation will bring.

Earth's astronauts will eventually explore a hundred worlds, large and small, in our solar system.

SPACE HORDE

SATELLITES AND MANNED SPACE STATIONS WILL BE WEAVING A "COTTONBALL" OF ORBITAL VEHICLES AROUND EARTH IN THE NEAR FUTURE.

Therefore, as a keystone segment of *The Magna Carta* the author most strongly urges that the Zone of Neutralia ---in any of the above-mentioned forms---be incorporated as a vital part of Space Law to come that will carry justice into space and maintain peace on earth below.

As a final commentary on this subject, we should note the reflections of sentiment on these questions, as for example an excerpt from a paper delivered by John E. Stephen, the brilliant General Counsel of the Air Transport Association of America, before the Inter-American Bar Association at San Juan, Puerto Rico, on May 25, 1965:

> "...The Magna Carta of Space by your distinguished Chairman, William A. Hyman, which was approved by the Council and General Assembly of the Inter-American Bar Association at Bogota, Colombia on February 3, 1961, proceeds from the premise that '...it is impossible to set out a boundary line with physical qualities such as characterize boundary lines on land and on the sea...'
>
> "Those conclusions appear to have been adopted more recently by the greater number of writers."

Secondly, this is the comment of Dr. Michel Smirnoff of Yugoslavia, famed international legal authority in an early letter to the author dated April 10, 1961, indicating he was immediately struck by the importance of a buffer-zone of space such as Neutralia:

> "I read with the greatest attention the Magna Carta and I say that I agree with you in almost all the points in it. The difficulty however will always subsist for the point (a) (Article 1) for a technical way of defining and dividing the airspace from (outer) space.
>
> "Now I am not very sure that the principle of sovereignty which you rightly put in the point (b) (Article 2) of the airspace is today absolutely inattachable. I think that the solution of the points (a) (b) and (h) (Article 8) is in a common regime (i.e. Neutralia) which will exist in air-space and in (outer) space and which alone could avoid the conflicts between the norms of the Chicago Convention and the norms of a future Convention on Space Law."

In short, the majority of scholars on this aspect agree that some arbitrary boundary line must be set up as this writer has constantly advocated, so long as it is consistent with one or another set of scientific data. Space is not a thing, but a place.

We must, in all common-sense, deal with space as a "place," but remembering that for the first time in human thought, we must deal with a three-dimensional volume that has no known limits, as airspace does. The range of the rocket and spaceship, in theory, is to infinity. Space Law must absorb and respect this new task of establishing limits within a limitless arena that is the gateway to the entire universe.

To leave the barn door of earth's backyard either completely unguarded, or locked up tight, will painfully handicap all future human endeavors as we try to forge forth into the great wide open reaches of outer-space. A hundred worlds large and small in our own solar system, and millions of possible inhabited planets beyond, are beckoning us. Let us be able to get out to them without being embroiled in a near-earth cabal of space lawlessness that will forever keep us imprisoned in our own pit of folly, futility, fighting, and frustration.

9

MISSING – CELESTIAL COURTS

SUPPOSE a jet airliner containing over one hundred persons and flying over the Atlantic on its way to New York, is struck by a missile or rocket which has either misfired, gone out of control, or strayed from its course. Who will answer for this catastrophe? There is also the question as to who would answer if such a missile or rocket landed in New York City or Moscow or Montreal and destroyed hundreds of lives and millions of dollars worth of property. Who is liable to the injured persons and to the widows and orphans of the dead for damages?

COLLIDING CRAFT

ONLY A NEW KIND OF SPACE INSURANCE WILL COVER FUTURE COLLISIONS OF AIRCRAFT WITH SPACECRAFT.

This is a void in international law. Rocketry has been too fast for global law.

Assume that two vehicles collided in outer-space and that fragmentation results while going through the thermal barrier during atmospheric re-entry, then striking a crowded city. In the opinion of some experts this would deal death to a greater degree than if there were a concentrated attack by gunfire. What protection, what warning, what system would provide the necessary security and safeguard?

Can these victims recover damages? They cannot. There is no law today giving them an absolute legal redress against any offending sovereign party. And what will be the remedy of the sovereign nation whose nationals are the victims? In existing law---none. What if Astronauts White and McDivitt had collided with either of the two satellites they sighted sailing by? The GT-4 flight of June 1965, would have ended in a legal mess.

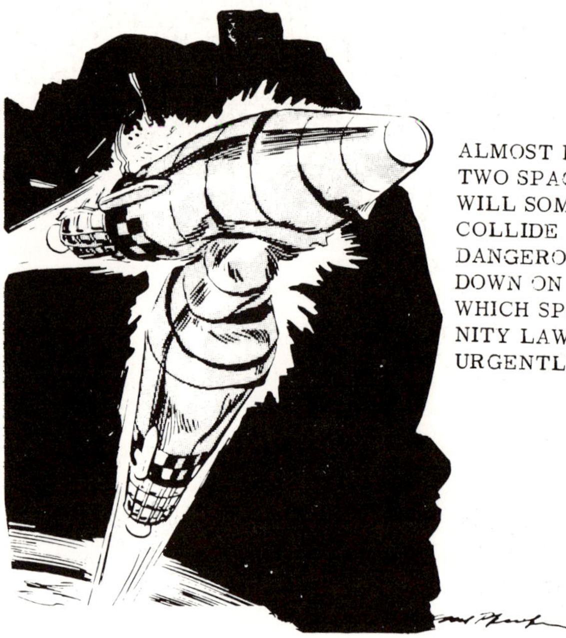

ALMOST INEVITABLY, TWO SPACECRAFT WILL SOMEDAY COLLIDE AND RAIN DANGEROUS DEBRIS DOWN ON EARTH, FOR WHICH SPACE INDEMNITY LAWS ARE URGENTLY NEEDED.

Since October 4, 1957, when Sputnik I heralded the advent of the Space Age, activity in space has been greatly accelerated, with the United States alone now launching over 70 vehicles a year, and other nations also embarking on ambitious programs. Accidents and mishaps will occur, bringing injury and death to innocent persons and tremendous damage to property.

Then---what are the dangers that can be anticipated from nuclear experimentation in outer-space? What contamination may come to the earth as a result of space activity? Shall we wait until a million people have been destroyed before undertaking to act on this question?

And in what courts---celestial or terrestrial---will these questions be determined?

HARDWARE HAZARDS

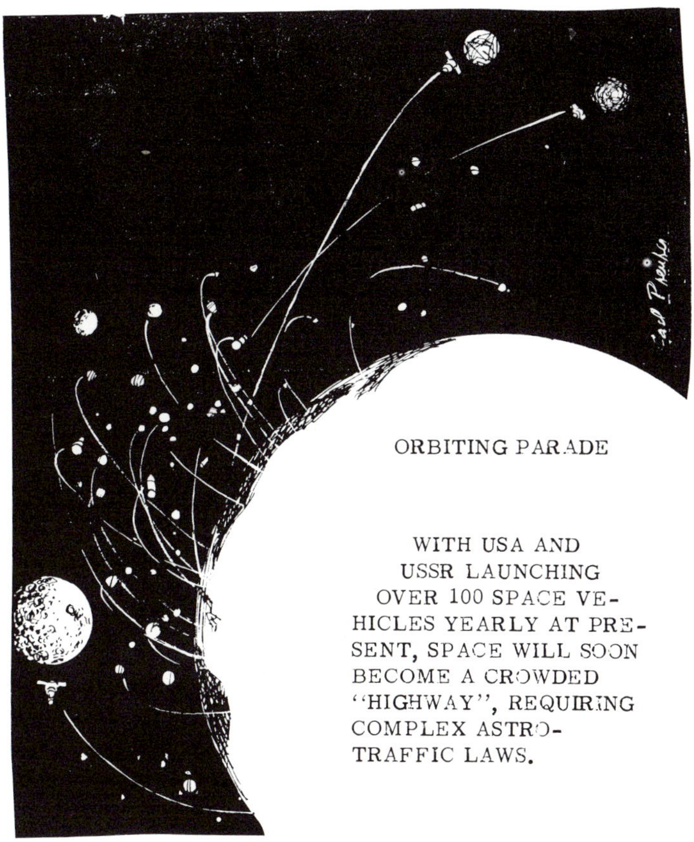

ORBITING PARADE

WITH USA AND USSR LAUNCHING OVER 100 SPACE VEHICLES YEARLY AT PRESENT, SPACE WILL SOON BECOME A CROWDED "HIGHWAY", REQUIRING COMPLEX ASTRO-TRAFFIC LAWS.

Also, there is the question of avoidance of interference between space vehicles and aircraft. Bearing in mind the great number of accidents occurring in aviation, the number of collisions, the great number of near misses ---how much greater will be the danger when missiles and satellites of tremendously greater speed and momentum are launched in areas traversed by aircraft and later re-enter to these congested areas?

The information concerning the structure, launching, operation and control of such spacecraft is a matter of peculiar knowledge to those in the nation charged with that important work. Information is generally classified and confidential. How will the ordinary citizen or even a complaining nation be in a position to prove negligence on the part of the nation launching the space vehicle which caused the damage in question?

This poses the question whether damage should be compensable on a basis of "no fault" or on a basis of res ipsa loquitur or on a basis of established negligence. What principle should govern? Who should answer for the damage? In what manner? These are questions that can be readily determined only by international agreement.

Air law does not help. In the important case of D'Aleman v. Pan American World Airways, Inc., plaintiff's decedent had come to his death as a result of an alleged wrongful act in the airspace over the Atlantic Ocean. The United States Court of Appeals for the Second Circuit, to which this case was taken by the unsuccessful plaintiff, through the very able Judge Leonard Moore, stated:

> "The facts of the case now before the Court make a direct ruling on the question appropriate. To give the passengers on ships protection of the act and deny similar rights to passengers in the air would amount to unjustifiable and highly technical discrimination.
>
> "We, therefore, now hold that the Death on the High Seas Act grants a right of action in admiralty for death caused by wrongful act, negligence or default occurring in the airspace over the high seas and that the trial court properly heard the case in admiralty."

The significant feature in this decision is that a law intended to apply to acts on the high seas was deliberately extended by the Court 30,000 feet into airspace for the purpose of providing some remedy for a claimant who otherwise would have no remedy---because there was no law of airspace to govern such a situation.

How much more complicated will be the situation where death occurs in outer-space!

IF AN ASTRONAUT'S DEATH OCCURED NOW ---PERHAPS THROUGH "RADIATION STORMS" IN SPACE---AIR LAW INDEMNITY WOULD BE TOTALLY INADEQUATE AT PRESENT.

Of course our Government is aware of approaching space-laws problems and is not inactive. It was merely not active enough. It did present to the United Nations its resolution for the creation of an Ad Hoc Committee on the Peaceful Uses of Outer-Space which was established by resolution of the General Assembly adopted on the 13th of December, 1958 at its 792nd plenary meeting. The Committee rendered its final report on June 12, 1959. Its Counsel described the results as "the mountains labored and brought forth a mouse".

First of all, the new body offered no solution. Secondly it posed certain questions and to these questions it established priority for some questions and a secondary position to others.

The report of the Ad Hoc Committee assumed that the Charter of the United Nations and the Statute of the International Code of Justice "which synthesized the idea of co-operation between men and the joint achievement of great projects for the benefit of all mankind" ... "were not limited in their operation to the confines of the earth".

Originally, the first question under the division entitled "Legal Problems Susceptible of Priority Treatment" mentions the question of freedom of outer-space for exploration and use.

However, the problem of exploitation or extension of sovereignty---or of internationalization---was relegated to a non-priority position (in the third question under the division entitled "Other Problems").

Yet it will only be through international law that space principles can be established as acceptable by all interested nations. Without agreement thereon, conflict is inevitable in the light of expected future developments in the exploration of interplanetary space and the planets.

It is necessary to define the limits of sovereignty and to agree that outer-space is "res communis"---jointly owned by all nations---and not "terra nullius" wherein it is not so owned. *The Magna Carta of Space* will provide the necessary law for this.

SPACE INDEMNITIES

Relying both on common sense and legal sense, it is my contention that there must be overall "Space Age insurance", covering all possible phases of this enormously growing field of human endeavor, included under international space law. As an added suggestion for the protection of the people of the nations joining in such an international law, there should be a national insurance program in each particular country, co-ordinated with an international insurance program which would contain either direct international funds or the arrangements for contributing to national funds for payment of monetary damages, of an agreed and stipulated amount, to the victims of the hazards of outer-space: missiles, rockets, satellites, fall-outs, and the like. The methods of payment, premium computation, actuarial data, computation of loss ratios, all could be set forth in such a program. Provision for this protection could well be set forth in the preliminary outline of an international code regulating the use of outer-space and bring to such a code the moral support and public opinion of the world.

Of course, the matter of re-entry and landing of space vehicles commented upon before, and considered by the Ad Hoc Committee of the U.N., presents problems of direct and immediate concern to all humanity. The problem may seem more acute with the unmanned space vehicles than with the manned vehicles of exploration and later on, of transportation.

It is stated that at major airports there is a plane leaving or arriving almost every minute. How much more complicated will air transportation become, ground control be made, and usefulness impaired, if the problems of re-entry and landing of space vehicles are not brought into some skeletal international agreement which will guarantee to the public its maximum protection?

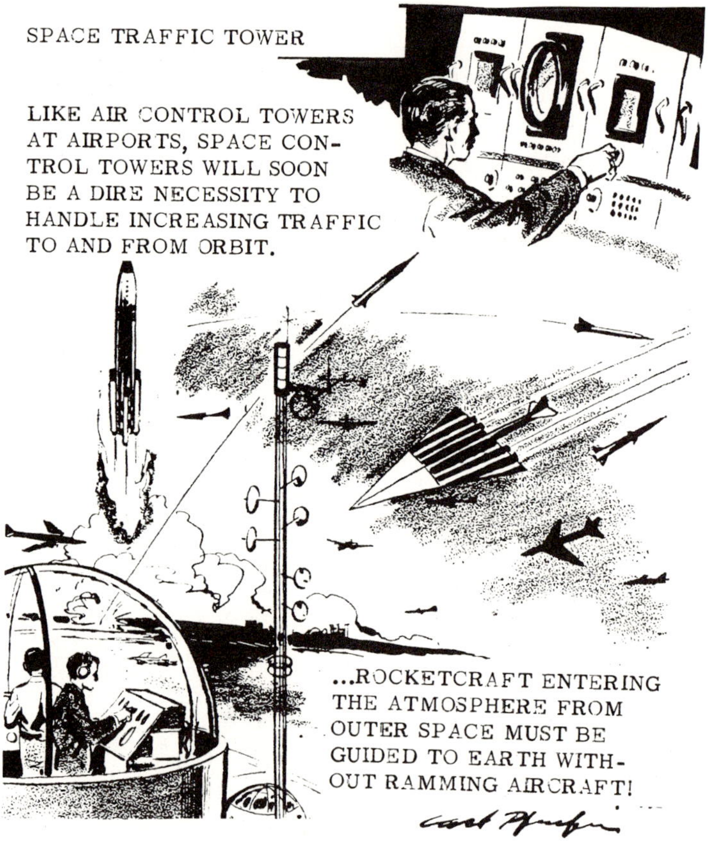

In addition to the priority questions adopted by the Ad Hoc Committee we might add another important matter to be included in such an international agreement, that is, policing of airspace and policing of outer-space. This can be done through tracking devices, inspection on the ground, exchange of information and by systems set up by the experts in the field who would be able to prevent evasions, in as effective a manner as human ingenuity could devise.

Naturally, there can be no question that the matter of identification and registration of space vehicles and coordination of launchings should likewise be included. The methods of identification could be established in the system set up by which, through such identification and registration, there would be coordination of launchings and control of aircraft and spacecraft in the areas to be used by each.

Again, as to the allocation of radio frequencies, which has been discussed at great length by numerous writers, you have another subject properly included in such an international law to avoid the jamming of radio communications.

LEGAL SNARLS OF SPACE

Pursuant to Resolution 1963 (XVIII) of December 13, 1963, the Legal Sub-Committee of the Committee on the Peaceful Uses of Outer Space met in Geneva from March 9 to March 26, 1964. Their objective was to prepare two draft international agreements. The first to deal with assistance and return of astronauts and space vehicles; the second to create an agreement concerning liability for damage caused by objects launched into outer-space (see Chapter XI for the detailed drafts).

During the general debate, it was recognized that a law to govern outer-space was needed, and quickly. The delegate of the USSR felt it imperative that international legal

> "norms to regulate outer-space activities should be codified without delay."

During the specific debate on the two topics, the member nations set forth certain principles they felt must be included in the two agreements. The delegate of the USSR stressed that only vehicles on lawful missions, registered prior to launch, should be returned to the launching nation if it comes down in another country. It was noted by India that the United States proposed the return to the launch nation of all space vehicles which land, due to distress or damage, anywhere else on earth.

LOST ASTRONAUT

U. N. HAS CONSIDERED THE RESCUE OF SPACE CRAFT AND ASTRONAUTS AFTER EARTH RETURN, ON AN INTERNATIONAL BASIS.

A dispute had already arisen among the delegates as to the countries who would be permitted to become a party to this agreement. One faction, headed by the United States, wanted membership open only to members of the United Nations and members of its specialized agencies or parties to the International Court of Justice. The USSR contended that membership must be open to all nations. This initial dispute was never settled.

The Sub-Committees then began their individual discussions. The Rescue and Assistance Committee had three drafts before it: one by the United States, one submitted by the USSR, and a combined effort of Australia and Canada. The key issues under discussion, relative to astronauts returning from space, were:

1. Duty to rescue and render assistance.
2. Rescue on the high seas.
3. Notification (given to whom)?
4. Reimbursement of expenses.
5. Settlement of disputes of interpretation.

The United States, Belgium and Hungary submitted proposed drafts dealing with the liability incurred by countries who launch space vehicles, manned or unmanned. The main areas under discussion included:

1. Statute of limitations.
2. Should liability be absolute?
3. What law determines damages?
4. Who may bring the action?

A subsection had been specifically omitted, to be left open until a provision can be adopted arranging for indemnity to the contracting party who accomplished the return.

In summary, after a full year of work the Sub-Committee adopted the three aforementioned sections to one resolution. The larger problems of dividing space into areas of airspace and outer-space; of distinguishing between "res communis" and "terra nullius"; of proper policing of space and recognizing the rights of peaceful use of space ---all have been avoided. The Sub-Committee was tackling, obviously, the less controversial areas first. *The Magna Carta of Space* answers many of the questions posed at the committee meetings and many of those avoided by the committee. Artcle 13 provides for absolute liability in all cases. It does not exclude nationals of the launching State. Article 14 is the best way to avoid a delay or outright nonpayment by a launching nation (it provides for an international insurance fund).

The Magna Carta also sets forth the broader principles discussed by the Sub-Committee. It states that the countries must make provisions for (a) identification, registration and disclosure of intent of launching; (b) the allocation of radio frequencies; and (c) for unimpaired flight of space vehicles.

It seems that the year of discussions could have been better spent by implementing the clear doctrines set forth in *The Magna Carta* as adopted by the Inter-American Bar Association.

COMSAT---FIRST "SPACE BUSINESS"

Telstar---a microwave satellite launched in July, 1962, a communications triumph for mankind, previewed the Commercial Age in Space.

Launched in July, 1962, famed Telstar satellite opened age of space communications.

The world was astounded. Across the expanse of oceans and continents came television shows that brought closer together the people of different tongues and different cultures. Voices, pictures, messages leaped thousands of miles through space to bring to the natives of the different continents a visual understanding of the lives of people in another country. Syncom and Early Bird comsats then were orbited to carry further the embryo "world radio-TV network."

Syncom radio-relay satellites are in highest orbits, 22,300 miles high, matching earth's rotation and thus remaining stationary in the night sky, like fixed stars.

The United States Senate approved the legislation on August 17, 1962, establishing a Communications Satellite Corporation following the favorable action on this bill by the House of Representatives on May 3, 1962. Final Congressional approval was given by the House of Representatives on August 27, 1962. It established an industrial and profit undertaking in which ownership would be divided between the communications industry and the public under the supervision of the United States Government. Although the Act was dedicated to the purpose of serving the communications needs between the United States and other countries and to contribute to world peace and understanding, it was created and initiated as a national commercial effort in America.

Is there to be any concern over the international direction and control of such a venture? Is there any question of international conflict? Is there a question about invasion of sovereign territory and sovereign rights of other countries? Is its operation in the area which is "res communis" and not "res nullius" a basis for international provocation or misunderstanding?

What will be the cultural controls and how will they be determined? What will be the basic language? The world will enjoy the songs of a great French artist shown on television and the projection of news through our world-famous commentators but what will be the restriction against the projection of the degrading, humiliating and oftentimes vulgar telecasts of the "commercials"? What about the accuracy of the educational telecasts?

These are only some of the questions which as yet, under the present absence of space law, do not have an answer, since the basic principles for space regulation have not yet been properly established.

Here is what has actually been done concerning COMSAT:

On April 2, 1962, there was referred to the Committee on Commerce, pursuant to the order of the United States Senate, the bill introduced by Senator Robert S. Kerr for himself and for Senator Warren G. Magnuson, establishing a commercial communications satellite system. On May 21, 1962, the Senate Commerce Committee unanimously approved a Communications Satellite Corporation Act, establishing a private company to be owned on a fifty-fifty basis by individual investors and United States communications companies.

The Unites States House of Representatives had also passed its bill to provide for the establishment, ownership, operation and regulation of a commercial communications satellite system, and for other purposes on April 24, 1962, at the 87th Congress, Second Session.

This constituted the first definite step towards the commercialization of outer-space, its utilization for private profit---an area not owned by any one nation but logically owned jointly by all nations of the world, and an area where everyone has equal rights.

On March 19, 1962, at the meeting of the Space Committee of the United Nations, Mr. Francis T. P. Plimpton of the United States, speaking for our government, called for international cooperation in various space projects. Among them was the suggestion of the late President John F. Kennedy for a cooperative effort in space communication.

Mr. Plimpton offered the prophecy that "it should be

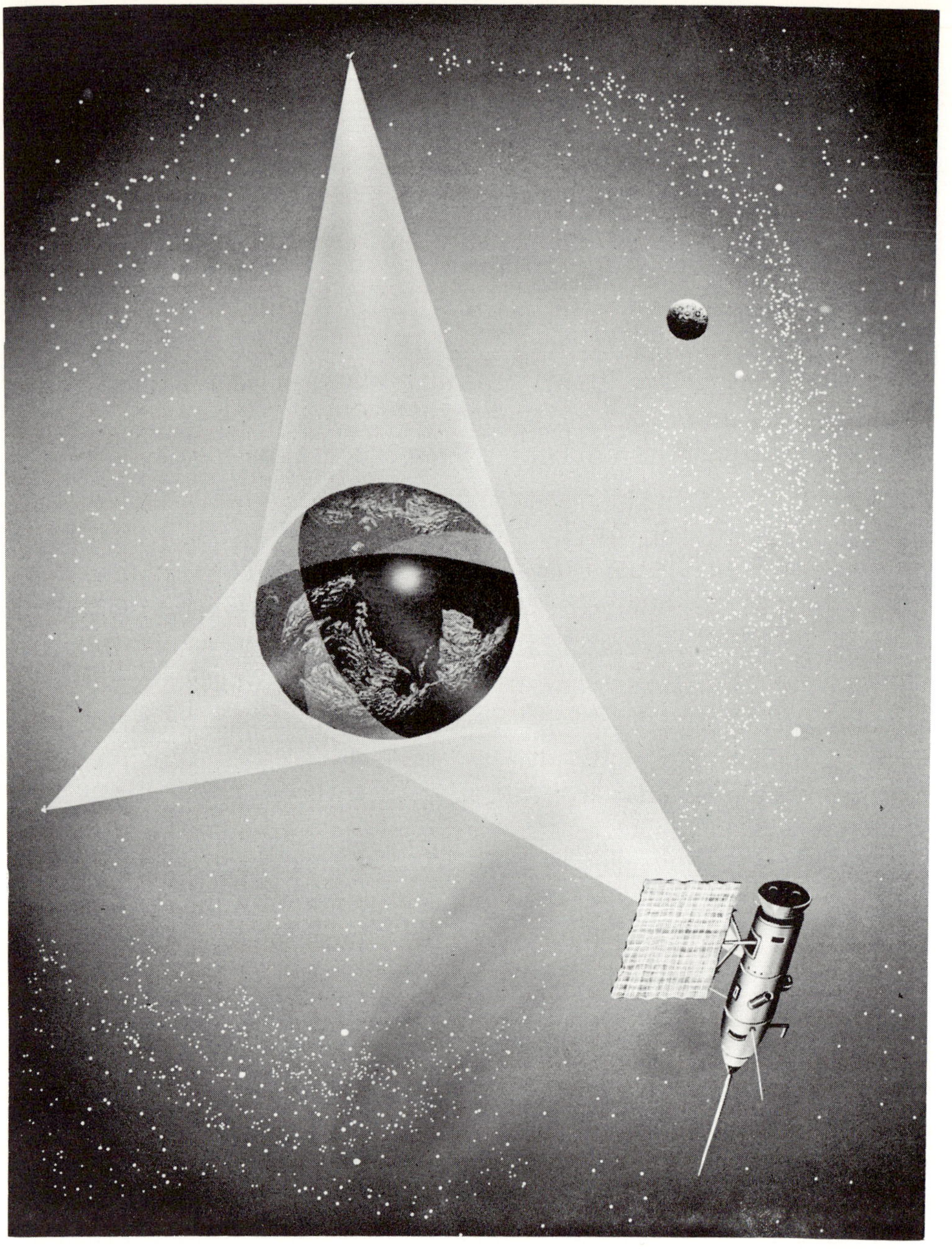

How three equidistant synchronous communications satellites can furnish complete world-wide relay of signals all over earth to every nation.

technically possible by the end of this decade to have in operation a global system of telephone, radio and television communication'' (now scheduled to begin in 1967-68). He made it clear that this communications satellite corporation, created by the United States Congress, was intended to be "the United States participant in a global system---a truly international arrangement with broad ownership and participation.'' However, it should be noted that the Space Committee of the United Nations has failed to give due consideration and take appropriate action on the important questions of sovereignty and security as COMSAT becomes involved in the use of space.

It failed to request the General Assembly of the United Nations and the properly authorized forces therein to make mandatory the application of international law and the United Nations Charter to Outer-Space and the celestial bodies. Up to the present time, this has still not been done.

However, President Kennedy, sensing the importance of immediate action for joining the world in a broad communications system, initiated the plan known as the Communications Satellite Act of 1962. Its policy and purpose is to establish:

> ''in conjunction and in cooperation with other countries, as expeditiously as practicable, a commercial communications system, as part of an improved global communications newwork which will be responsive to public needs and national objectives, which will serve the communications needs of the United States and other countries and which will contribute to world peace and understanding.''

Thus was born the United States Communications Satellite Act of 1962.

SERVICE SATELLITE

The Communications Satellite Act that was enacted into law in the United States Congress at the 87th Congress, 2nd Session, in February 1962, has for its goal:

> ''To provide for the establishment, ownership, operation, and

regulation of a commercial communications satellite system, and for other purposes.''

The launching of the first unmanned Sputnik on October 4, 1957 proclaimed the beginning of the Space Age.

The successful orbiting of the first manned space vehicle on April 12, 1961 with Major Yuri Gagarin initiated the second period in space.

The third great phase of man's space venture was the creation of the Communications Satellite Corporation, known as COMSAT, under the Communications Satellite Act and the successful launching of Early Bird in May 1965. They mark the opening of the commercial stage in the world of space.

Early Bird, now in orbit, can handle 240 two-way telephone calls across the Atlantic.

A Comsat milestone occurred on June 28, 1965, when the Early Bird Satellite---after numerous tests following its May launching---relayed the first "public telephone conversation" across the Atlantic between the shores of the U.S. and Europe.

Participating in the inaugural ceremony was President Lyndon B. Johnson, who first picked up the phone at the White House and sent personal calls through to such European dignitaries as British Prime Minister Harold Wilson, Chancellor Ludwig Erhard of the German Federal Republic, French Minister of State Louis Jacquinot, and officials of several other nations. Various scientific and business personnel connected with COMSAT in America also talked briefly to people across the seas.

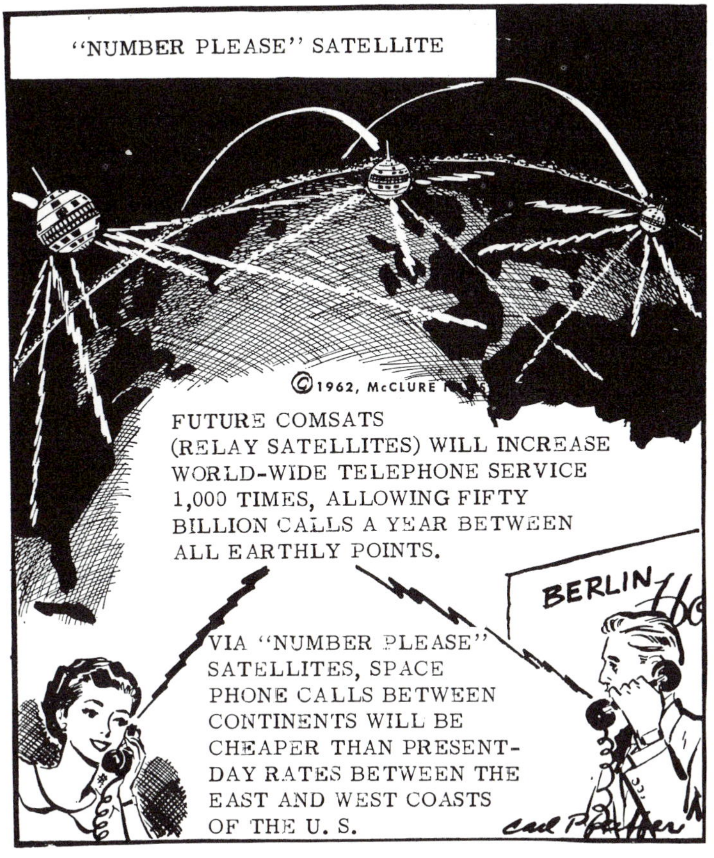

The voices went through with "astounding clarity", it

was reported, bounced thousands of miles across earth by a tiny, invisible satellite hanging in space above Brazil and weighing only 80 pounds. Yet in its intricate electronic mazes and microminiaturized circuits lay the ability to handle 240 telephone connections between the U.S. and Europe, Africa, and South America. The future operational system of "space switchboards" of 1967-68 will be geared to handle thousands of foreign telephone calls, plus hundreds of TV, radio, telegraph and photo-facsimile transmissions.

Space, in one instant of historical time, has created the "world communications network" that has heretofore been impossible or halting at best.

COMSAT, the parent business firm behind space communications, is leasing 114 of Early Bird's voice channels to commercial users, such as AT&T which is renting 74 circuits while RCA, IT&T and Western Union International are utilizing 10 channels each.

Thus, only 93 months since the Space Age opened in October of 1957, man has achived his first commercial goal in the exploitation of space.

Emphasis is laid on the description "commercial" set forth in the Act and in the Articles of Incorporation of Communications Satellite Corporation, in the prospectus issued by the underwriters who sold the stock in June of 1964 and in all public statements made in connection with this venture.

In the forum held under the Auspices of the Federal Bar Association of New York, New Jersey and Connecticut, as far back as May 25, 1962, at the Carnegie International Center in New York City, the views of Hon. Nicholas De B. Katzenbach, then Deputy Attorney General of the United States and now the Attorney General of the United States, and of Hon. George A. Feldman, a member of the United States Delegation to the United Nations, were heard. As the Chairman of that meeting, the author posed certain questions as follows:

> "Who will own it? Is it a private corporation in fact, or a private corporation in name only? Will it be subjected to

complete government supervision, control and operation? What will be the political implications of such a plan? What are the economic problems? What are the sociological consequences? What about the antitrust violations? What about de facto monopoly even if the Bill does provide for competition? What about the labor question?

"Will the employees be required to be affiliated with a labor union or labor unions? Will the right to strike be available or permissible to such labor unions affiliated in such an enterprise? Will there be a repetition of the costly loss of man-days and prejudicial delay like that which occurred in connection with Cape Canaveral (Kennedy) and other missile bases?

"Will there be any restriction on the arbitrary and wilful conduct of any labor organizations which might threaten the survival of such an enterprise?

"What about the question of international participation? Will there be a limitation on the participation in stock ownership by any foreign governments or countries? Will there be representation on the Board of Directors of such a corporation by any representatives of foreign countries?

"Will there be international conflicts arising between the United States and other countries because of the fact that in certain areas there must be necessarily an invasion of sovereign territory by the utilization of the satellites, by the launching of the satellites, by the maintenance of terminal stations on earth, by the necessity for crossing international boundaries?"

MONOPOLY IN SPACE?

One over-riding question comes up---is COMSAT in fact an American monopoly?

Although it is required to offer 50% of its stock to outsiders, yet 50% went to the Communications Carriers such as AT&T Company. The fact is that the public, the owner of fifty per cent of the stock, can elect only six Directors; the public utilities companies, six Directors; and the United States, through the President, appoints three Directors. Thus, the combination of the three Directors appointed by the President and the six nominated by the companies give a majority control of nine out of thirteen and seems to insure control in the United States.

But what are the facts and the extenuating factors?

Following are excerpts from a speech by John A. Johnson, Vice President-International of the Communications Satellite Corporation, delivered before the 14th Conference of the Inter-American Bar Association at San Juan, Puerto Rico, May 27, 1965. He reveals the relatively unknown fact that there are two business organizations involved in running the brand new "radio-relays in space":

"...we cannot fail to be impressed with the speed with which space technology is rushing on. A truly global system of communications satellites, capable of tying the whole world together in a single communications network, will be a reality in less than three more years...

"Although the Communications Satellite Act of 1962 called for the establishment of a global system as expeditiously as practicable and provided that the Communications Satellite Corporation should be the United States participant in it, the Act did not prescribe the nature of the international arrangements which should bring the system into being. This was left to be worked out through negotiations among the international partners in the enterprise.

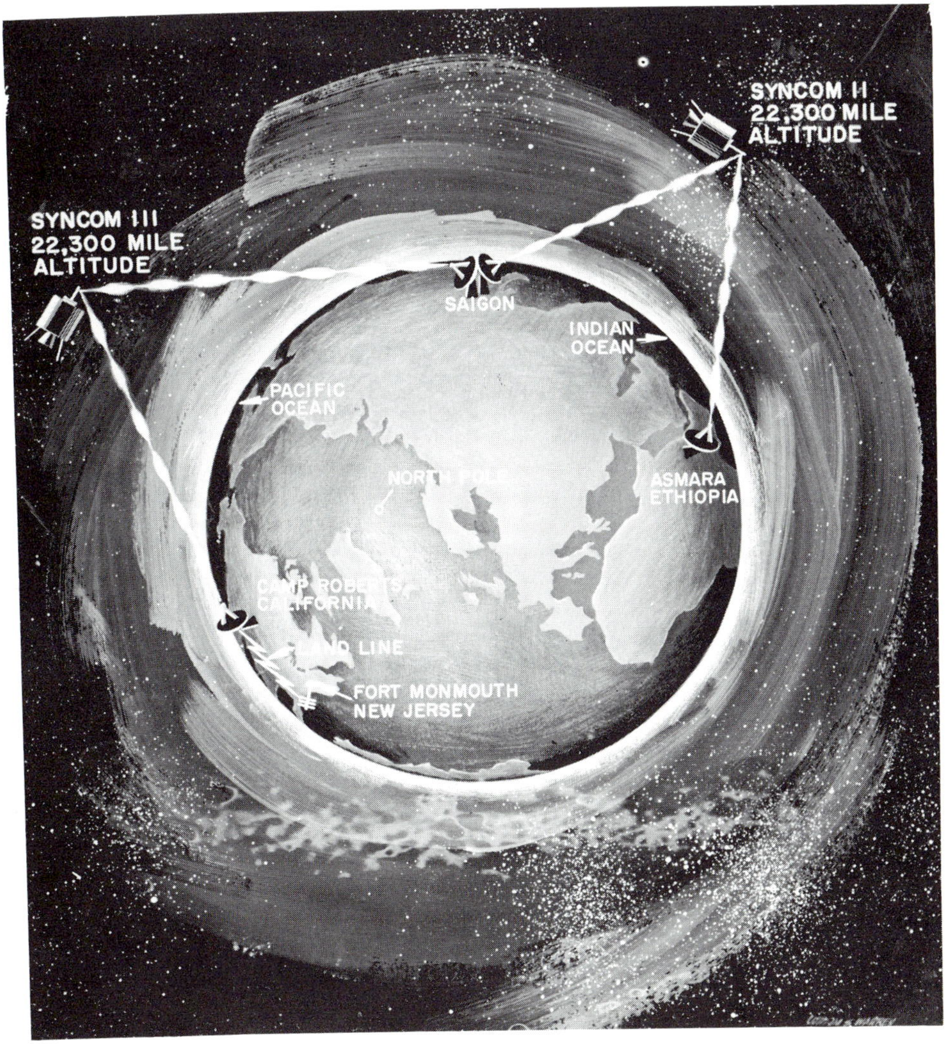

Global system will tie entire world into a single communications network via Syncom-type satellites.

"The negotiations culminated in the conclusion of two interrelated agreements which were opened for signature on August 20 of last year (1964). These two agreements established an international partnership for the financing, ownership and operation of the space segment of the system. The first agreement, entitled Agreement Establishing Interim Arrangements for a Global Commercial Communications Satellite System, is an agreement among governments. The second agreement, called the Special Agreement, is an agreement which may be signed either by the governments themselves or by telecommunications entities, public or private, designated by the governments signing the first Agreement.

"The first of the two interrelated Agreements, the Interim Agreement, establishes certain basic political and economic principles and goals to which all of the signatories are committed, as well as the organizational and financial framework of the partnership. It states the goal of establishing a single global commercial communications satellite system at the earliest practicable date; and it expresses the desire of the signatories that satellite communications should be organized in such a way as to permit all States to have access to the global system on a non-discriminatory basis. It also states the policy of permitting all States wishing to invest in the system to do so, with consequent participation in the establishment, operation, and ownership of the system. The Interim Agreement accordingly provides that it is open for accession to any State which is a member of the International Telecommunication Union.

"On the organizational side, the Interim Agreement established a governing committee, the Interim Communications Satellite Committee, which has overall responsibility for the design, development, construction, establishment, maintenance, and operation of the space segment of the global system. It also provides that COMSAT shall act as the manager in the design, development, construction, establishment, operation and maintenance of the space segment.

"By the terms of the Interim Agreement, the space segment is owned in undivided shares by the signatories to the Special Agreement in proportion to their respective contributions to the costs of the space segment. Arriving at agreement on the investment and ownership quotas to be accorded to each of the participants was, of course, one of the most difficult problems in negotiating the Agreements.

"COMSAT, as the United States participant in this joint venture, was initially obligated by the Agreements to contribute 61% of the capital required for the establishment of the space segment during the interim arrangements, estimated to be approximately $200,000,000.

"With such a disparity of investment and ownership interests, one of the foremost questions to be solved in the negotiations was the composition of the governing committee and the distribution of voting power among its members. It was decided to limit membership on the Interim Communications Satellite Committee to representatives from each of the partners or groups of partners having an ownership interest and a financial commitment of 1.5% or more. Each member of the Committee has voting power in proportion to the ownership share of the organization or organizations he represents. Although COMSAT commands more than a majority of the votes by virtue of its investment quota which is presently about 56.5%, the Agreements specify a number of important subjects on which decisions require the concurrence of a number of parties in addition to COMSAT, the necessary accumulation of votes being such that countries located in several major geographic regions of the world must be in agreement.

"The Agreements obligate the partners to cooperate in the establishment of a system which will achieve basic global coverage in the latter part of 1967, with the first phase consisting of one or more satellites in synchronous orbit in 1965. The first of these, of course, is the Early Bird satellite now in position over the equator just east of Brazil. Early Bird is at this moment owned by 44 international partners, some private, some public, among whom are the four South American countries previously mentioned..."

FIRST SPACE "PAYOFF"

John A. Johnson's resume of his "space firm" continues:

"Is this exciting new medium available only to those currently in the vanguard of achievement in space technology? And, is the participation in this challenging and productive venture limited to those with large amounts of capital?

"The answer to each of these questions can only be a clear and firm No.

"I have tried to indicate that satellite communications provide an immediate opportunity for all countries to participate in a challenging international venture and to derive benefits which are both current and practical. Satellite communications will, for many countries, augment existing facilities as well as proved new services. For others, it offers an opportunity to obtain sophisticated facilities and services in rapid and economical fashion. The Interim Agreement openly invites all to join, whether it be as an owner or only as a user. The present international arrangements embodied in the two Agreements I have described represent the social and legal inventiveness needed to keep abreast of scientific development in what has been termed the race of history."

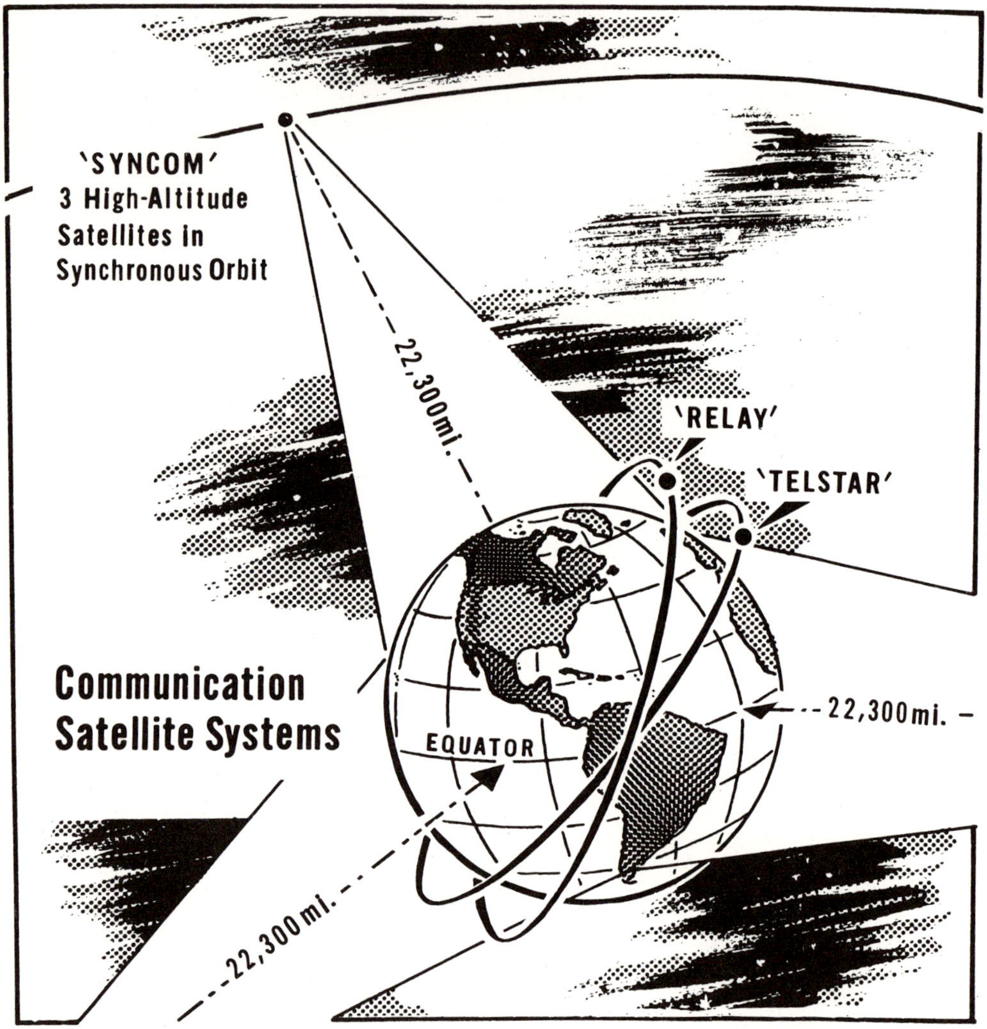

Under the high-flying syncom "switchboards", Telstar and Early Bird type relays will give coverage of worldwide radio, television, telegraph, and photo-facsimile services.

From this heartening resume, it is to be hoped that the organizers of this unique space venture have avoided the pitfalls of monopoly and its retinue of financial evils.

While it is not appropriate here to give credit to any individual engaged in such an undertaking, gross injustice would be done the dreamers of today---who prove to be the realists of tomorrow---if such a rule were followed in this case.

Therefore, commendation and praise are given unqualifiedly to the brilliant management of COMSAT and particularly to Mr. Leo D. Welch, the Chairman and Chief Executive Officer of COMSAT, as well as to his associate officers and directors for the triumphant initiation of the age of commerce in the world of space.

COMSAT has now established itself as an internationally accepted business enterprise. It has been subjected to the ills and controversies attendant upon such ventures. It has already appeared in its own right before various government agencies, exploring the legality and advisability of the acquisition of land stations, expansion into greater areas, the determination of charges, rates and bases of operation, and in numerous other respects, just as if it were any other business corporation brought under the jurisdiction of such an agency as the Federal Communications Commission of the United States.

As further evidence of the commercialization of the Space Age, brief reference might be made to certain conclusive evidence.

Insurability of a project is important in determining whether that project is a freakish or unique experiment, or whether it is an accepted pattern in the new way of life which space has brought to the world.

Proof that COMSAT has been accepted as part of the new life on earth, affiliated with life in space, is furnished by the action of a group of the leading insurance companies who have unhesitatingly issued insurance against certain hazards involved in the activities of COMSAT and have indicated their willingness to give insurance coverage to COMSAT for activities on earth, in the air and in space. This also is a tribute to the advance in the mental and commercial attitude of business today in connection with the world of tomorrow.

The latest information is embodied in a letter to the

author from David J. Melamed, the able Secretary of the Communications Satellite Corporation (commonly known as COMSAT), dated May 25, 1965:

> "Set forth below is a summary of the types of insurance obtained by the Corporation in respect of the launching on April 6, 1965, of the Early Bird Communications satellite, and related activities. The summary should be read against the background of the facts that (a) launching and associated services were furnished to the Corporation by the National Aeronautics and Space Administration (NASA) pursuant to an agreement dated December 17, 1964, between the Corporation and NASA (the NASA Contract), (b) the NASA Contract provides in substance that the Corporation shall pay or reimburse NASA for all identifiable costs incurred by NASA in connection with and properly allocatable to the satellite launching and associated services furnished by NASA pursuant to the Contract, whether or not such launching actually occurs or is successful, except certain specifically excepted such costs.
>
> "(1) Insurance against the risk of liability to NASA for damage to or loss of the launch vehicle, prior to launching. The coverage took effect upon commencement of the assembly of the satellite to the third stage of the launch vehicle and terminated upon intentional ignition of the first stage.
>
> "(2) Insurance against the risks of loss or damage to ground equipment owned or leased by the Corporation for use in connection with the launching.
>
> "(3) Insurance against the risk of liability to NASA for expenses incurred by NASA as the result of launch reschedulings requested by the Corporation, due to loss of or damage to, the satellite while in transit from the place of manufacture to the place of launching (Cape Kennedy) or during the period before launching at Cape Kennedy.
>
> "(4) Public liability insurance for personal injury or physical damage to tangible property, caused by an occurrence arising out of the preparation for launching, launching or orbiting of the launch vehicle, satellite or components thereof and which occurs (1) at Cape Kennedy, prior to, during or after the launching, or (2) elsewhere, during or after the launchings. Under the terms of the insurance, there is not any change in the basis of the insurance when the satellite leaves airspace and enters outer-space.
>
> "As part of planning for future launchings, the Corporation is continuing to study the matter of obtaining insurance against risks associated with launchings and not covered by the types of insurance summarized above."

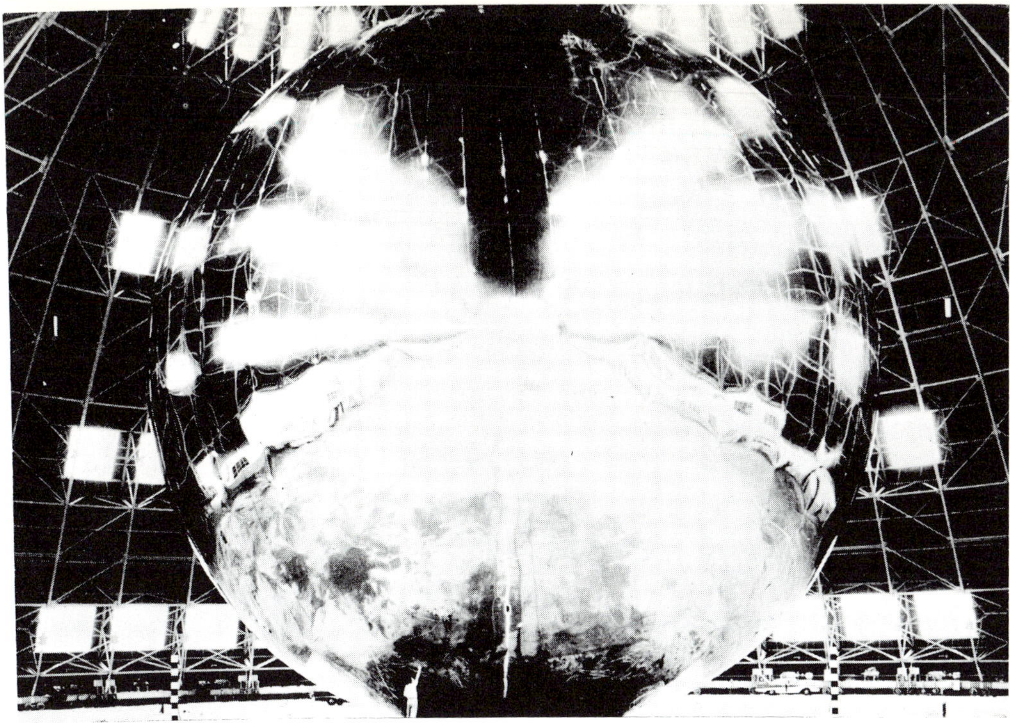

NASA's early experiments in 1960 with giant Echo satellite, bounding radio signals around the world, led to present-day concept of world communications through space.

Significantly, the last paragraph indicates awareness of the many more kinds of "space accidents" that can---and (probably will, in time---occur, with which they will eventually) have to deal.

It is clear that COMSAT will not procrastinate in the face of the onrushing necessity of full space insurance coverage under law and thereby leave themselves open to a Pandora's Box of space liabilities in the future.

Nevertheless, due to inadequate space law today, there are foreseeable difficulties into which COMSAT may run as it begins its operational phase.

COMSAT---CULTURE AND CONFLICT

IT IS recognized that outer-space is distinguishable from airspace. The jurisdiction and authority of the subjacent country extends through airspace. It does not extend into outer-space. All nations have equal rights in outer-space, whether they are big or little, whether they control the arsenal of nuclear warfare or not, whether they are nations which have been recently born or nations which have continued for many decades or centuries. The area has been recognized as "res communis" meaning that it belongs to all nations for peaceful purposes.

How will we meet the charge, if any is made by any other country, that the use of space by any one country for a commercial enterprise invades the common right of ownership of all to that area?

The legislation that created COMSAT is dedicated to competition. The attempt by any one nation to appropriate a new area to its own use for trade or commercial purposes, has often led to war. The days of the Spanish Armada, and the history of the days when Britannia ruled the waves, give us ample illustrations of this danger.

Will there be any invasion into the territory of the communications systems of any government which has government ownership and control, where there are no commercials, where citizens pay for the use of television and radio and where taxes are levied by the government of that nation?

And what about that most important element of modern life---cultural standards? American dignitaries, upon return from a trip to the Orient, frankly and courageously stated that the image of America which they found required a change.

Such is not the intent of COMSAT. Rather, it is free world-wide equality in its use and control.

Will we project across the television channels of the world an image of America which has caused many citizens in this nation to writhe with humiliation and helpless anger? Will this corporation be permitted to project the unfavorable picture of a father suffering tension and headaches and screaming out for some drug, children with dirty clothes, sinks that need scrubbing with some new cleanser, and good looking American women who, nevertheless, need deodorants; and will the world be filled with scenes of violence, murder, with lessons in crime and guidance in vice so often forced upon the helpless viewer by the mad pursuit of operators and sponsors on television trying to stimulate and agitate the jaded nerves and senses of viewers of all ages?

This is a serious concern to all those who believe that the image of America abroad must be improved. Will such supervision be national or international? Will it prohibit that which tends to degrade or reflect upon the dignity and culture of a nation? Will such prohibition be met with the complaint that there is interference with freedom of speech and freedom of expression?

And what about ideological conflicts? Will they be given recognition in any broadcast or telecast made through privately owned communications satellites?

What law should govern interference with operation of multinational communication satellites?

What law should govern space movements of earth-to-earth rocket-borne traffic in persons and goods?

Should private persons be permitted to engage in commerce in space?

Should there be any distinction between earth-to-earth commerce in space and interplanetary movement through space?

Many questions of an economic, legal, political, cultural and ideological nature present themselves. The proper, satisfactory and efficient handling of these problems will mean the difference between a step in the direction of dissension or a step in the direction of peace among the people of the world.

The questions that I have raised are only a small part of the picture. The legal backlashes to come may be a major harassment to the future well-being of the Communications Satellite Corporation.

10

SPACE AND HUMAN RIGHTS

Destruction in one hour! Life expectancy one-half hour! Not materialistic gain, not mere adventure but survival in a world threatened with thermonuclear war compels accelerated exploration of outer-space and the inter-planetary world because through these areas lies the avenue to surprise attack and immediate destruction. Tremendous scientific developments indicate there will be no time for slow or moderate preparation should such a world catastrophe occur. The application of all sciences to the dedicated purposes of survival and health is mandatory. Man himself is about to play a greater part in this drama than ever before---we are passing from the stage of pioneering space exploration to the age of space know-how.

What are the problems to be encountered with increasing manned space flights into orbit, and eventually to the moon and planets? In passing from the stage of experiments on animals to experiments on humans, are there any limitations of law and ethics?

While efforts of government, university research centers, and scientists have been primarily given to the preparation of equipment and space hardware in order to transfer from the earth to upper space man's earthly environment, the question is posed: should the man-machine himself be subjected to change and altered by scientists and physicians to better equip him to survive and even prosper in outer-space and the interplanetary world?

HUMAN "ENGINEERING"

Specifically, how will man in space meet the problems of breathing, eating, elimination, physical and mental performance within a tolerable field of gravitational forces, of survival against the meteoritic and radiation hazards of space?

May human beings be used for experimental purposes and even though consent be given, how far may these experiments be conducted?

No one person has all the answers. Certainly this writer does not, even though he dares to pose some questions on this subject which he does for the purpose of provoking further thought and for the purpose of eventually obtaining some answers.

Numerous instances of successful animal experiments could be cited. It is sufficient, however, to indicate that transition from animal experiments to human experiments became imperative in order to determine man's own ability to meet the hazards to be anticipated in outer-space.

In connection with the use of human beings as "guinea pigs" the important factor of consent of the subject or citizen merits consideration. What about the right of government, of a sovereign power, or even an absolute ruler to force any subject to submit to such experimentation even though held to be for the benefit of the nation or for the benefit of mankind?

Giant centrifuge under construction will house four astronaut "guinea pigs" for 30 days, whirling under high-g stresses to test human endurance.

Ancient absolute monarchies indulged in the practice of imposing experiments on subjects without their consent. Ancient Persia, and Egypt under the Ptolemies, used human beings for scientific experiments without their consent. The other absolute monarchies did likewise and even today in one of the Mideastern countries it is rumored that such experiments are still being secretly performed.

In the British Magna Carta (Issue of 1225, Chapter 29), it is provided:

> "No free man (nullius liber homo) shall be taken or imprisoned or deprived of his freehold or his liberties or free customs, or be outlawed or in any manner destroyed, nor shall we come upon him or send against him except by a legal judgment of his peers (per legem terrae) or by the law of the land".

The Hague Convention of 1907 which prohibited certain methods of waging war included a prohibition, amongst other things, against the "inhuman treatment of prisoners", incorporating what had previously been understood among the nations of the world as crimes punishable as offenses against the laws of the world.

Of course the world knows that the mere statement of a law or the declaration of an obligation under an international treaty does not guarantee its observance.

The atrocious Nazi pseudo-scientific and medical experiments imposed upon victims, civilian as well as military, without their consent, are well known to you.

But aside from these enforced victims, there have also been numerous instances of volunteer human beings in diseases such as yellow fever, cancer research, smallpox, and many others.

The tradition of free-choice volunteers has been carried forward in the Space Age.

Dr. Romny H. Lowry, Medical Doctor and Manager of the Boeing Space Medical Section, entered into a closed chamber and remained there for several hours solely on oxygen supplied by green algae, which was the first test of its kind.

Human tolerance was determined again in tests for acceleration, deceleration, g pressures, impact forces and the forces to be met upon reentry. Body positions and restraints were determined with a view towards lessening the injury to the human system.

Astronaut volunteer in "idiot" machine which dizzily spins him in three axes, simulating spaceflight in three-dimensional space.

In this field of great experiments and training processes for spaceflight, special emphasis must be given to the remarkable work done by Col. John P. Stapp, M.D. and Ph. D., formerly President of the American Rocket Society. He used himself as the "guinea pig" in laboratory impact crash, ascertained the value of lap belts in crash, the problems of the forces to be met on escape; and then finally, he created the "Stapp Sled", to conduct tests at record-breaking speed under rocket power.

Volunteers, of course, have always been accepted by the medical profession under the limitations of necessity, legitimate purpose, proper care, and fitness for the experiments involved.

From such early experimenters came the training program for the original seven Mercury astronauts, who successfully flew two suborbital and four orbital flights, from 1961 through 1963, and for the present Gemini spacemen in their two-man spacecraft.

Reaching a total of 29 members in 1964 and increasing each year, the astronauts are men chosen carefully for their physical, mental, and scientific abilities.

As of this writing, no accident or tragedy has occurred in manned space flights. But if one venture fails---notwithstanding the tremendous preparations made to transfer a portion of earth environment to provide a means of survival in space---what then is the next step?

IF A METEOROID PIERCES AN ORBITING SPACECRAFT, KILLING THE CREW, THIS "ACT OF GOD" WOULD NOT BE INCLUDED IN SPACE INDEMNITY LAWS OF THE "MAGNA CARTA".

TRUE "SPACE" MAN?

In addition to preparing and developing machines and equipment to transport the conditions on earth with the spaceman to outer-space, can the objective be attained by changing man himself?

Experimental work up to the present time has been primarily concentrated on the development of spacecraft, space hardware and equipment by which man, in going into space, will bring along with him oxygen containers, fluid, food and other environmental factors on which he relied on earth in order to live.

Now, can man himself be changed so as to give him the faculties for meeting the problems in outer-space through his own reconstruction, or through accessories to his organism and ultimately by changes in his own biological, physiological and entire body construction?

Of course, all of this is a challenge to the theory offered many years ago by Charles Darwin who enunciated the principle of the extremely slow evolutionary process and also the theory of survival of the fittest. Yet, science has been advancing at so great a rate that the suggestion now made does not seem utterly impossible.

In connection with this proposed means of preparing spaceman, attention is called to the new science of biocybernetics advanced by Dr. Manfred E. Clynes and Dr. Nathan S. Kline at the Air Force School of Aviation Medicine in San Antonio, Texas in May, 1960 at the Symposium on Psychophysiological Aspects of Space Flight.

Can man live in outer-space without breathing? Is inhalation necessary to supply him with oxygen required for his sustenance on earth? These scientists developed a system which says in effect, "Don't breathe!" They urge that automation devices can supply oxygen needed in outer-space for man's survival without this time-honored and much respected function of mankind---breathing.

These visionary scientists have suggested that "altering man's bodily functions to meet the requirements of extraterrestrial environments would be more logical than providing an earthly environment for him in space". Their argument is that "in the past, evolution brought about the altering of bodily functions to suit different environments. Starting as of now, it will be possible to achieve this to some degree without alteration of heredity, by suitable biochemical, physiological, and electronic modifications of man's existing modus vivendi." They predicate their observations on the increased knowledge of homeostatic functioning, "the cybernetic aspects of which are just beginning to be understood and investigated".

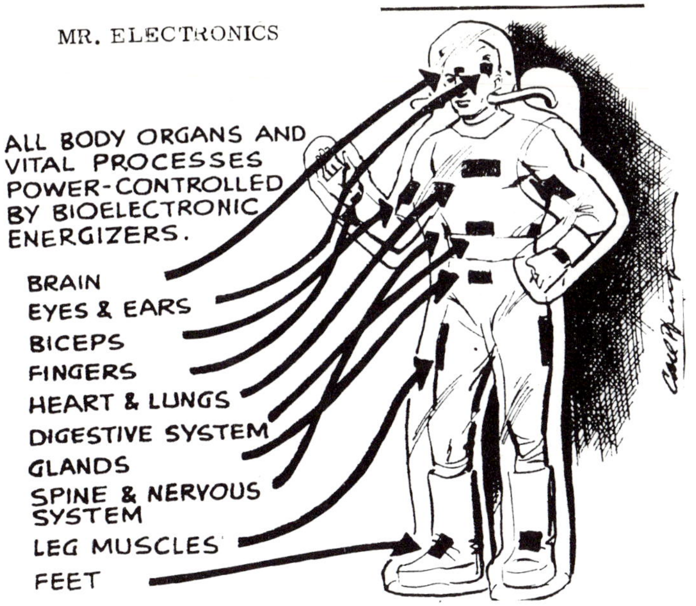

"CYBORG" MAN, ADAPTED BY BIOASTRONAUTICS RESEARCHES TO ENDURE SPACE ENVIRONMENT WITH MINIMUM STRESS.

The problem of respiration, of course, assumes paramount importance. The comparison is made at the present time between an earthman going to the outer regions where oxygen is not presumed to be present or in sufficient quantities to sustain life, and a fish living in water, desiring to live on land and who must bring his water onto land for his activity. On such comparison these learned scientists indicate that the fish itself would accomplish such a purpose, i.e., live on land, only if it were "particularly intelligent and resourceful" and "had studied a good deal of biochemistry and physiology, was a master engineer and cyberneticist, and had excellent lab facilities available to him." In such a case, he might "conceivably have the ability to design an instrument which allowed him to live on land and breathe air quite readily".

The inference here, of course, is that a fish does not possess the intelligence and knowledge of the sciences and the ability to develop as does man, who is presumably the highest form of animal life.

These scientists base their "human engineering" hope

on the ability in the foreseeable future to design instrumental control systems which will make it possible "for our bodies to do things which are less difficult". They cast considerable doubt on the use of artificial atmospheres "encapsulated in some sort of enclosure as a means of maintaining life". They state "that there are much more efficient ways of carrying out the functions of the respiratory system than by breathing, which becomes cumbersome in space".

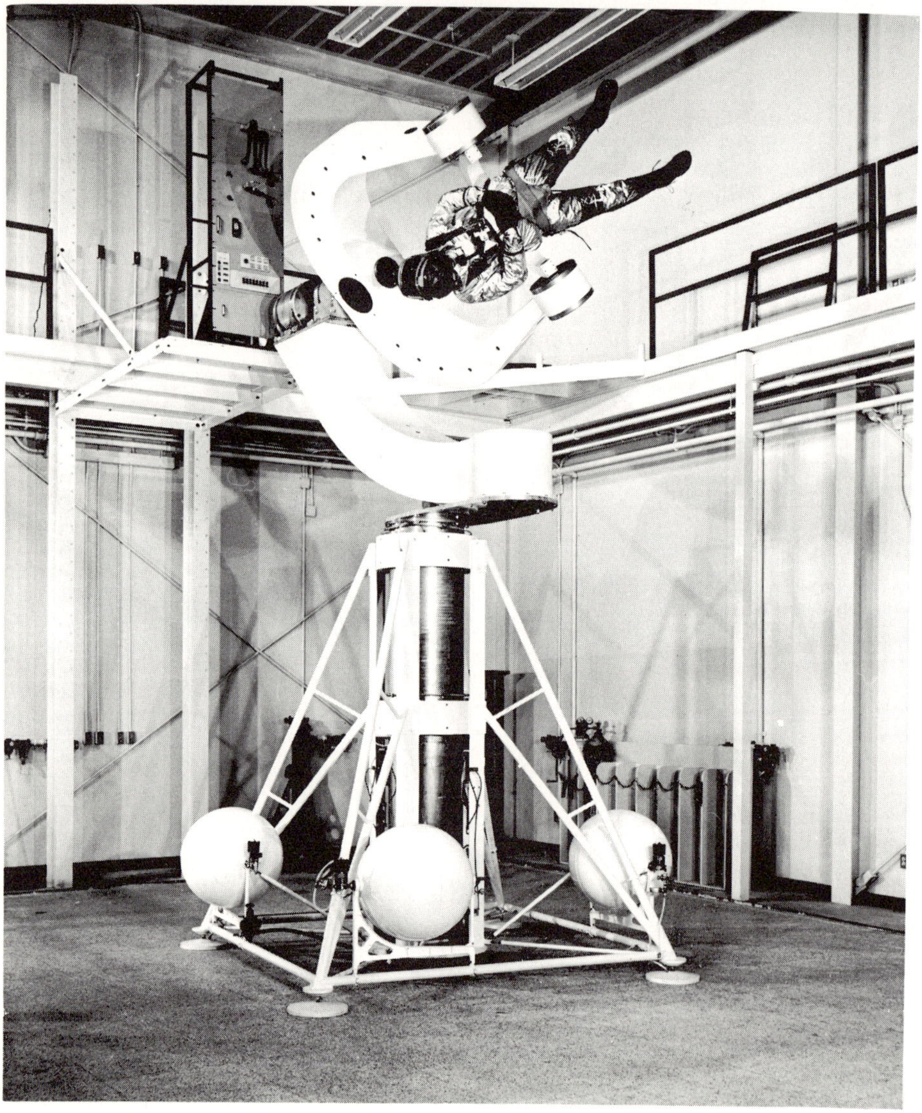

Zero-g (weightlessness) simulator, to test vestibular function of ear-balance mechanism in human body during spaceflight.

The suggestion is made that instead of carrying his whole environment along with him, there should be the "incorporation of integral exogenous devices to bring about biological changes which might be necessary in man's homeostatic mechanisms to allow him to live in space qua natura".

These scientists suggest self-regulating man-machine systems which would function without the benefit of consciousness in order to cooperate with the body's own autonomous homeostatic controls. These they call the "Cyborgs" (from CYBernetics ORGanism).

They argue as follows: "If man in space, in addition to flying his vehicle, must continuously be checking on things and making adjustments merely in order to keep himself alive, he becomes a slave to the machine."

The device suggested by them has already been used in connection with the Rose osmotic pressure pump capsule which permits the continuous injections of chemicals at a slow controlled rate into the organism without any attention on the part of the organism.

With the use of such equipment, controls "can be changed to the desired performance characteristic under various environmental conditions". Reference is made also to the "natural" human physiological and psychological rate of performance as reflected in the demonstrations under controlled conditions of yoga and hypnosis. They give considerable value to hypnosis per se in the world of space travel.

Are these predictions fanciful and unrealistic? Are they incapable of realization?

To some extent exploration along these lines have now been conducted by the Russians, according to the above scientists who said:

> "Thus we find the Russians proposing prior oxygen saturation as a solution to the próblems of respiration during the first few minutes after space vehicle launchings; reporting on alterations of the vestibular function both by drugs and surgery; studying perception and carrying out research on the laws of eye motion in vision; finding that lowering of temperature can aid in solving pressure problems; ..."

In the light of the many technological problems and scientific obstacles, will the better course be to adapt man to his future environment rather than to rest solely on providing him with the mechanical scientific means of transferring earth environment to space environment?

While the scientists who propose the "Cyborg" theory maintain that this will not change man but merely provide him with mechanical systemic controls, nevertheless it is a step forward in the direction of man remaking man to the extent of enabling him to dispense with some of the elements of earthly environment. The sequellae of such experiments are still in the conjectural stage.

It will not be entirely irrelevant to also pose the question "and then what?" Will this new creature produced by man's alterations of himself create a new species of space "monster" which will no longer be subject to the control of the scientists and doctors who create him? Will he develop into a scourge which will destroy earthman while he, the new spaceman, wanders into the interplanetary and interstellar fields for purposes of settlement and habitation?

How far can these experiments go? How far can they be controlled?

What about procreation and heredity? Will the world of science develop embryos in test tubes through appropriate chemical processes? Will future generations of spaceman be controlled by the master scientist through his laboratory procedures? Will the spark of life deemed to be solely of Divine origin be brought within the control of man through his scientific experiments? Will spaceman be devoid of human impulse and emotion?

While this is not a theological discussion, we cannot escape the observation that notwithstanding the great advances of science, man has already made such a mess of affairs on earth as to cause us some fear for the future if man should undertake to usurp the place of the Master Creator in the basic scheme of the life process.

The situation is critical! The nation which controls space controls the world, as emphasized previously.

Space science, proceeding at a most fantastic rate, will affect not only our knowledge and technology as to weather, communications, navigation and our way of life, but also may provide the basis for serious military concern in the light of the philosophy of the military experts who urge "get the high land".

Never before in history has the world witnessed such threats to its welfare as those which now arise from the exploration of outer-space.

Classic military strategy---"Get the high land"---as applied to space warfare was illustrated in Soviet magazine, showing three "space bombers" being launched.

U. S. arsenal of military missiles and launchers will grow into "space weaponry" unless war is outlawed in space.

Meanwhile, back at the bar, law is static. The United Nations has failed to achieve substantial progress in the establishment of a basic law for outer-space although it has made some progress in the resolutions concerning telemetry and weather operations, and in the statement of the Nine Principles enunciated by its Space Committee on the Peaceful Uses of Outer-Space on December 13, 1963.

This, of course, is by no means sufficient since it bypassed the fundamental problems concerned with sovereignty, from which the greater threats to the peace of the world arise. There can be no return to the Fifteenth Century when Spain and Portugal sought to divide the world between themselves. Today there can be no domination by any one nation. There cannot be domination by any two who might want to divide the world between them.

Space belongs to the family of nations.

Nor do the United States and the Soviet any longer have "exclusive" claims on space. Three other nations have orbited their own satellites, designed and tracked by themselves, though they were boosted into orbit by USA rockets through NASA's "free booster" policy on an international scale.

On April 26, 1962, the Union Jack flew into space aboard the Aerial satellite (UK-I) of Great Britain.

September 28, 1962, saw our Canadian neighbor to the north enter the " Space Club " when its Alouette-I curved into orbit (and is still steadily giving telemetry data about the upper ionosphere).

Italy led the forthcoming parade of European nations planning their own satellites, when its San Marco satellite leaped from Wallops Island launch-site in Virginia into the blackness of space on December 15, 1964.

The stake in space is not mere scientific supremacy. It is not an Olympic contest. It is not the advance of empire, nor the extension of sovereignty of any nation into the celestial world.

It is share-and-survive---or else.

The voice of the people of the world and the guidance of learned legal scholars must now break this impasse and force action toward a "Bill of Human Rights" in space which will prevent provocations for catastrophic world war.

For seven long years, the one organization that could have ended this "humanitarian gap" has failed to do so---namely, the United Nations. The proof? We have but to look over the following Resolution---to which it has paid lip service only---which engendered the formation of the U.N. Ad Hoc Committee on the Peaceful Uses of Outer-Space:

> RESOLUTION OF THE GENERAL ASSEMBLY OF THE U. N. OF NOVEMBER 24, 1958.
>
> "The General Assembly,
>
> "Recognizing the common interest in mankind in outer-space and that it is the common aim that it should be used for peaceful purposes only,

AMONG THE "IMPROVEMENTS OF LIFE" IN U. N. SPACE RESOLUTION ARE FOLLOWING FUTURE CONCEPTS:

1) ORBITAL INDUSTRIES.

2) SATELLITE SANITARIUMS AND SPACE HOSPITALS.

3) SPACE LIGHTHOUSES TO WARN OF METEOR SHOWERS.

"Bearing in mind the provision of Article 2, Paragraph 1, of the Charter, which states that 'the organization is based on the principle of the sovereign equality of all its members,'
"Wishing to avoid the extension of present national rivalries into this new field,
"Desiring to promote energetically the fullest exploration and exploitation of outer-space for the benefit of mankind,
"Conscious that recent developments in respect of outer-space have added a new dimension to man's existence and opened new possibilities for the increase of his knowledge and the improvement of his life,
"Noting the success of the scientific cooperative program of the International Geophysical Year in the exploration of outer-space and the decision to continue and expand this type of cooperation,
"Recognizing the great importance of international cooperation in the study and utilization of outer-space for peaceful purposes,
"Considering that such cooperation will promote mutual understanding and the strengthening of friendly relations among peoples,
"Believing that the development of programs of international and scientific cooperation in the peaceful uses of outer-space should be vigorously pursued,
"Believing that progress in the field will materially help to achieve the aim that outer-space should be used for peaceful purposes only,
"Considering that an important contribution can be made by the establishment within the framework of the United Nations of an appropriate international body for cooperation in the study of outer-space before recommending specific programs of international cooperation in this field,

"Establishes an Ad Hoc Committee on the Peaceful Uses of Outer-Space, consisting of the representatives of Argentina, Australia, Belgium, Brazil, Canada, Czechoslovakia, France, India, Iran, Italy, Japan, Mexico, Poland, Sweden, Union of Soviet Socialist Republics, United Arab Republic, United Kingdom of Great Britain and Northern Ireland and the United States of America, and requests it to report to the fourteenth General Assembly on the following:
"(a) The activities and resources of the United Nations, its specialized agencies and of other international bodies relating to the peaceful uses of outer-space;
"(b) The area of international cooperation and programs in the peaceful uses of outer-space which could appropriately be undertaken under United Nations auspices to the benefit of States irrespective of the State of their economic or

scientific development, taking into account the following proposals among others:

"(1) Continuation on a permanent basis of the outer-space research now being carried on within the framework of the International Geophysical year;

"(II) Organization of mutual exchange and dissemination of information on outer-space research; and

"(III) Coordination of national research programs for the study of outer-space, and the rendering of all possible assistance and help toward their realization;

"(c) The future organizational arrangements to facilitate international cooperation in this field within the framework of the United Nations;

"(d) The nature of legal problems which may arise in the carrying out of programs to explore outer-space;

"Requests the Secretary General to render appropriate assistance to the above-named committee and to recommend any other steps that might be taken within the existing United Nations framework to encourage the fullest international cooperation for the peaceful uses of outer-space."

UNLAUNCHED SPACE LAW

Pursuant to a resolution of the United States submitted in November, 1958, this Ad Hoc Committee on the Peaceful Uses of Outer-Space was established in the United Nations. Procedural difficulties delayed action. Boycott by certain nations prevented unanimity or even cooperation between the nations designated to said Committee.

On June 12, 1959, it submitted a report, which failed to do anything other than suggest certain subjects for study but unfortunately, by-passed the important questions of sovereignty and security.

Later, the membership of the Space Committee of the United Nations, after being boycotted for almost a year by the Soviet, was increased in size by the addition of new member-States which satisfied the objections of the Soviet. Pursuant to Resolution of the General Assembly No. 1721 (XVI) (adopted on December 20, 1961) this Committee on Space met on March 19 to 29, 1962. Its report on March 30, 1962 covered features which undoubtedly are of great importance but it failed to give due heed to fundamental principles of sovereignty, security and the like. It failed to meet the demands of the day. It did, however, among other things, recommend the following:

> "1) Emphasize the need and necessity for international cooperation.
> "2) Express satisfaction with the exchange of messages between the Premier of the USSR and the President of the United States in regard to the development of concrete projects in this field.
> "3) Direct the exchange of information and registry of launching objects into orbit.
> "4) Emphasize meteorology and telecommunications."

IN 1962, THE LATE PRESIDENT KENNEDY PROPOSED TO SOVIET EX-PREMIER KRUSHCHEV THAT THE USA AND USSR POOL THEIR SPACE EFFORTS IN A JOINT MANNED VENTURE TO THE MOON.

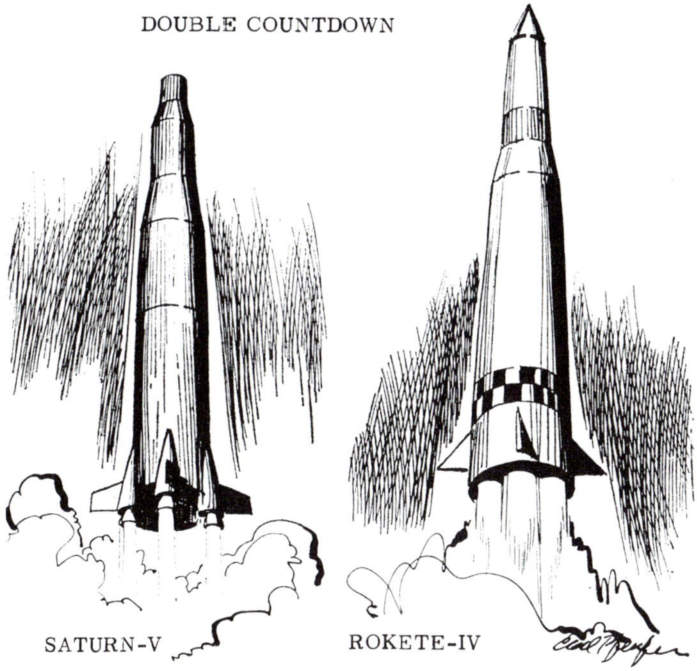

BEFORE 1970, IF A JOINT LUNAR LANDING IS AGREED UPON, TWO MIGHTY BOOSTERS WILL BLAST OFF AT ZERO HOUR...FROM AMERICA AND RUSSIA! DESTINATION...THE MOON!

It must be noted that the Committee on the Peaceful Uses of Outer-Space of the United Nations has now adopted the position that it is desirable to have a statement of basic legal principles rather than await the completion of an extensive code---which has been the author's contention from the very first, and for which reason he formulated *The Magna Carta of Space* (only two pages long) back in 1961.

However, it must be borne in mind that unfortunately, the above U.N. Committee cannot issue any enforceable decree or mandatory directions but can only commend other nations to seriously consider the conclusions reached by this important---and impotent---committee.

The whole question of international law in space must be brought up before the higher bodies of the U.N.---the General Assembly and Security Council. We, the people, have the right to demand this in order to obtain space security.

But before high-level U.N. action can be taken on space law, the Committee on the Peaceful Uses of Outer-Space must forge the proper skeletal code. In the next chapter, we will give a complete analysis and critical review of the Nine Principles of Space Law of this U.N. Committee, showing wherein they must be overhauled to be made truly effective.

11

THE U.N. – GROUNDED IN THE SPACE AGE

A Comparison and Critical Analysis of *The Magna Carta of Space* and Resolution 1962 (XVIII) of the United Nations (The Nine Principles):

THE MAGNA CARTA OF SPACE was adopted by the Inter-American Bar Association at Bogota, Colombia, on February 3, 1961. On December 13, 1963, the General Assembly of the United Nations adopted Resolution 1962 (XVIII) containing the Declaration of Legal Principles Governing the Activities of States in the Exploration and Use of Outer-Space.

Because the scientific exploration of outer-space is still in its infancy, and recognizing that contemporary lawyers cannot conceive of all possible situations which may occur as man invades outer-space, *The Magna Carta* expressly calls for further provisions to be established in the general fields set out in its 19 Articles. *The Magna Carta* is by no means a final determination of the laws of outer-space; to the contrary, it is only a beginning, a "first statement" of what should be the basis for future laws in this field.

On the other hand, Resolution 1962 (XVIII) of the U.N. (especially provisions 5 through 9) tends toward specific situations which may confront sovereign States engaged in space activities. As will be shown in this comparative analysis, each of the specific principles of Resolution 1962 (XVIII) are either set forth in, or are the logical outgrowth of, the 19 Articles of the *Magna Carta* taken individually or implied from this document taken as a whole.

It is also desireable herewith to make critical comments on certain apparent defects in these nine principles of the U.N., to serve as a basis for correction by future action thereon.

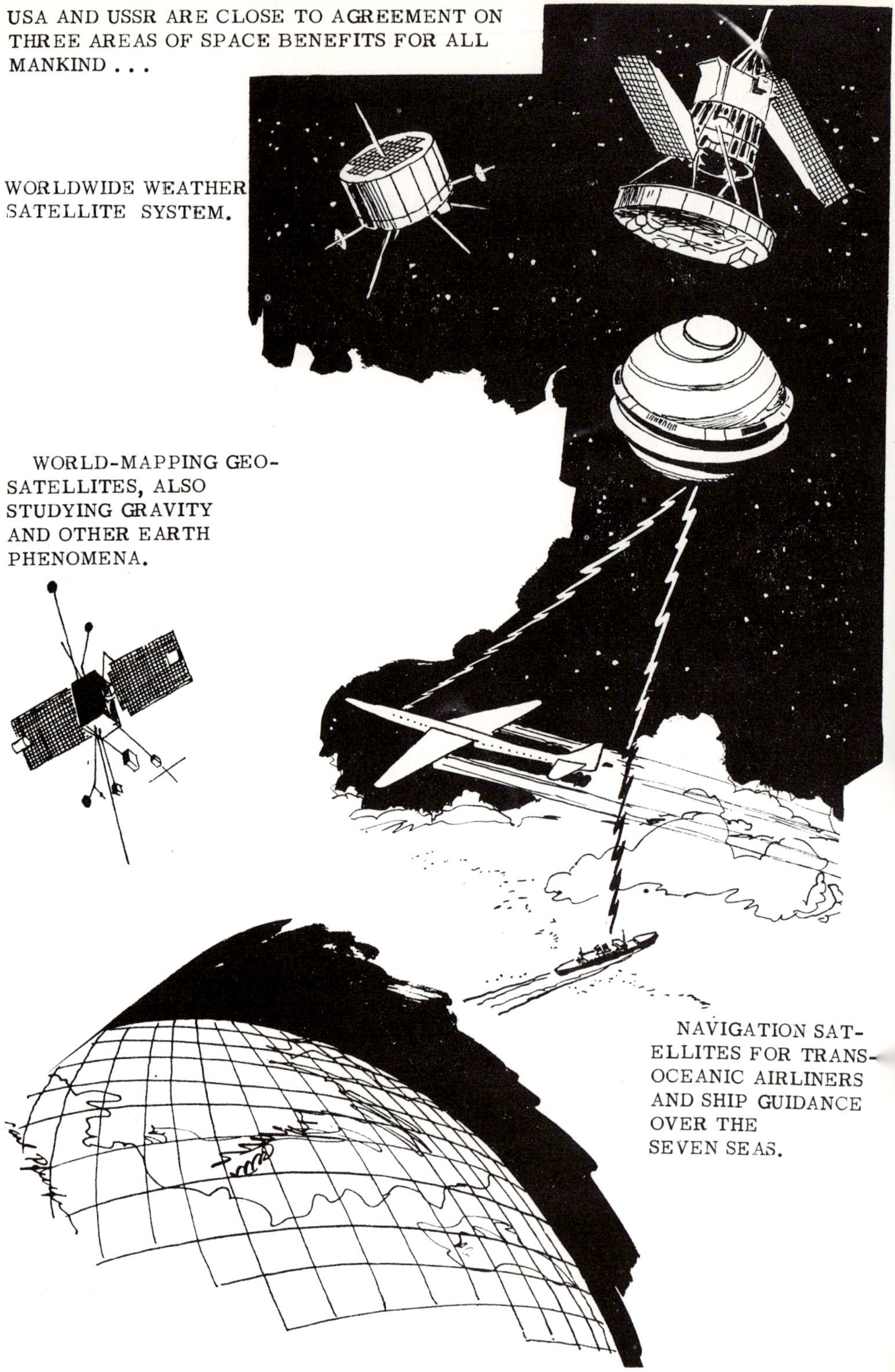
USA AND USSR ARE CLOSE TO AGREEMENT ON THREE AREAS OF SPACE BENEFITS FOR ALL MANKIND . . .
WORLDWIDE WEATHER SATELLITE SYSTEM.
WORLD-MAPPING GEO-SATELLITES, ALSO STUDYING GRAVITY AND OTHER EARTH PHENOMENA.
NAVIGATION SATELLITES FOR TRANS-OCEANIC AIRLINERS AND SHIP GUIDANCE OVER THE SEVEN SEAS.

Referring now to these nine United Nations PRINCIPLES, the COMPARISONS with the author's skeletal code of space law, and his CRITICISMS of the U.N. provisions:

PRINCIPLE 1:

"The exploration and use of outer-space shall be carried on for the benefit and in the interests of all mankind."

COMPARISON:

U.N. Principle 1 uses the phrase "for the benefit and in the interests of all mankind."

The Magna Carta Article 6 provides that---"Outer-Space shall be used solely for peaceful purposes with freedom of exploration and exploitation thereof given to ALL PEOPLES FOR THE BENEFIT OF MANKIND" (emphasis added).

No further discussion is necessary regarding the similarity of these provisions.

CRITICISM:

This U.N. Principle fails to set forth by formula, boundary lines, use and activity, the area encompassed by the phrase "outer-space". This, therefore, avoids the question as to where sovereign airspace ends and where outer-space, the area of "res communis", begins.

PRINCIPLE 2:

"Outer-space and celestial bodies are free for exploration and use by all States on a basis of equality and in accordance with international law."

COMPARISON:

U.N. Principle 2 contains the expression "use BY ALL

STATES on a basis of equality".

The Magna Carta Article 6 provides that "Outer-Space shall be used solely for peaceful purposes with freedom of exploration and exploitation thereof given to ALL PEOPLES for the benefit of mankind" (emphasis added). Furthermore, Articles 9, 10, 11, 12, 14, 15 and 16 provide for the establishment of further provisions to govern various activities and occurrences in outer-space.

Note: Needless to say that if and when the "Provisions" which *The Magna Carta* calls for are established, activities in outer-space shall be carried on in accordance with them.

CONCEPT OF A VENUS STATION IN FUTURE EXPLORATION OF CELESTIAL BODIES.

ASTEROIDS MAY BE "SPACE BONANZAS" OF PRECIOUS METALS, JEWELS, OR RARE MATERIALS

CRITICISM:

The U.N. statement that outer-space shall be "in accordance with international law" fails, of course, to recognize the fact that as yet there is no international law applicable to outer-space (with the exception of the International Treaty to Ban Nuclear Tests, and except for the specific and limited conventions relating to communications and meteorology).

PUBLIC OWNERSHIP OF SPACE?

PRINCIPLE 3:

"Outer-space and celestial bodies are not subject to national appropriation by claim of sovereignty, by means of use or occupation, or by any other means."

COMPARISON:

The Magna Carta Article 3 and Article 4, respectively, pro-

vide that "all outer-space shall be deemed 'res communis' ". Article 6 defines "res communis" (as opposed to "terra nullius") as a denial of the rights of appropriation and exclusive control to any one nation. Article 17 provides that "the landing on any planet containing life, or the occupation thereof, by earthman shall not give to any nation on earth any ownership or control of such other planet."
The similarities here should be obvious.

CRITICISM:

There is no objection, of course, to the assertion by the U.N. that outer-space and the celestial bodies are not subject to national appropriation in any way whatsoever. It fails, however, to affirmatively state that the users of outer-space and the celestial bodies are subject to the principles applicable to "res communis" as specifically stated in the *Magna Carta of Space*

PRINCIPLE 4.

"The activities of States in the exploration and use of outer-space shall be carried on in accordance with international law, including the Charter of the United Nations, in the interest of maintaining international peace and security and promoting international cooperation and understanding."

COMPARISON:

The Magna Carta Article 6 provides that "Outer-space shall be used solely for peaceful purposes....for the benefit of mankind." Also, in this respect, Article 19 bars "war, in, by or through space...forever." Furthermore, as previously noted, other provisions of the *Magna Carta* call for the establishment of further laws to govern future activities in outer-space (see note under Point 2).

AS MILLIONS OF ROCKETCRAFT CARRY ON TRADE AMONG PLANETS, A VAST SPACE TRAFFIC JAM IS PREVENTED BY STELLAR TRAFFIC COPS!

"MAGNA CARTA OF SPACE" PROVIDES FOR LAWS TO GOVERN ALL FUTURE ACTIVITIES IN SPACE, AS THE "THUNDERING HERD" OF INTERPLANETARY ROCKETS SPREADS OUT THROUGH INNUMERABLE PLANETS, MOONS, AND LARGE ASTEROIDS.

CRITICISM:

Again the objection is made to the loose conception of "international law" as herein employed by the United Nations document. Bear in mind also, that at the time of its creation, the Charter of the United Nations did not contemplate supervision of the heavens and the interplanetary regions, which are never named. Again the same objection is made to the use of the words "international law" when clearly the new circumstances and the facts relating to economic, political and international relationships in outer-space find no complete parellel in the Law of the Sea or the Law of the Land. At best, the "existing" law may furnish a limited standard but certainly it does not provide a complete statement of authoritative regulation so necessary in this new field.

INTERNATIONALIZED SPACE?

PRINCIPLE 5.

"States bear international responsibility for national activities in outer-space, whether carried on by governmental agencies or by non-governmental entities, and for assuring that national activities are carried on in conformity with the principles set forth in the present Declaration. The activities of non-governmental entities in outer-space shall require authorization and continuing supervision by the State concerned. When activities are carried on in outer-space by an international organization, responsibility for compliance with the principles set forth in this Declaration shall be borne by the international organization and by the States participating in it."

COMPARISON:

U.N. Principle 5 provides for "international responsibility for national activities in outer-space, whether carried on by governmental agencies or by non-governmental entities." The effect of this provision is to place responsibility for space activities on the State conducting such activities.

The Magna Carta's Article 13 provides that "In the event of injury or death to persons or damage to property by space vehicles...the sovereign power by or through which the same have been launched be responsible and liable for all such damage." This Article also provides that such recovery can be had "without the necessity of showing negligence or fault."

Note: Principle 5 of U.N. Resolution 1962 (XVIII) further calls for State supervision and authorization of activities in space by non-governmental agencies.

Article 13 of the *Magna Carta of Space* makes no distinction between governmental and non-governmental entities or agencies, but places the responsibility for injury or damage caused by space activities entirely on the "sovereign power by or through which the same have been launched."

The practical effect of both provisions is to place responsibility for activities in outer-space upon the State enjoying that activity.

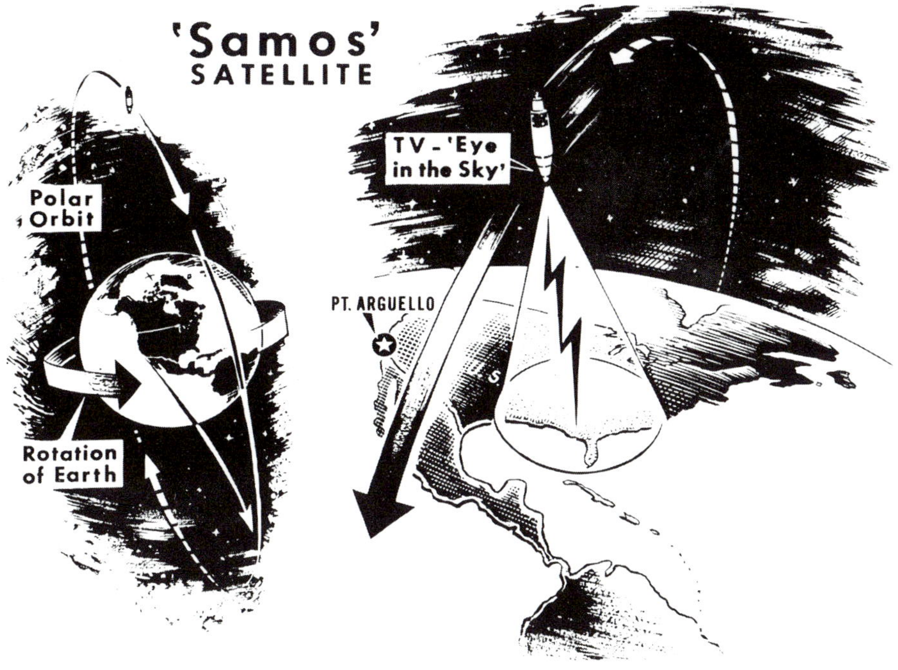

UN Principle 5 fails to mention any regulation of space espionage via satellites---a dangerous omission.

It is significant to point out that Resolution 1962 (XVIII) fails to provide for recovery without the necessity of showing fault. Therefore, under the Nine Principles, the problem of what law to apply in the event that persons or property of one State are injured by the space activities of a foreign State will inevitably arise.

CRITICISM:

There is no prohibition declared by the U.N.'s provision against espionage from outer-space upon the subjacent nation, even though the source of such espionage may be beyond the previously accepted territorial limits of a nation, as in the case of the territorial waters which vary in different parts of the world as to the distances encompassed therein.

On one occasion, one of the Soviet heads boasted that the cosmonauts of his country had photographed every part of the United States as the manned space craft of his nation orbited the earth and passed over America, with the implication that this constituted valuable information for use in any acts of war. Also, the U.S. stated it had photographed all of mainland China, as well as other parts of the world. There is no reference in this principle of the U.N. to restriction against such acts or international responsibility attaching to the offenders. Since it is the consensus of opinion that the strike of an aggressor through space would be aided by the information covered in such espionage, if earthman becomes mad enough to throw the world into another war, this espionage should be prohibited.

PRINCIPLE 6.

"In the exploration and use of outer-space States shall be guided by the principle of cooperation and mutual assistance and shall conduct all their activities in outer-space with due regard for the corresponding interests of other States. If a State has reason to believe that an outer-space activity or experiment planned by it or its nationals would cause potentially harmful interference with activities of other States in the peaceful exploration and use of outer-space, it shall undertake appropriate international consultation before proceeding with any such activity or experiment. A State which has reason to believe that an outer-space activity or experiment planned by another State would cause potentially harmful interference with activities in the peaceful exploration and use of outer-space may request consultation concerning the activity or experiment."

COMPARISON:

U.N. Principle 6 provides for "cooperation and mutual assistance" among the States in "the exploration and use of outer-space" and for "due regard for the corresponding interests of other States." It further provides for "consultation" between States concerning their activities or experiments in situations where the activities of one State may interfere with those of another.

In The Magna Carta of Space, Article 10 provides for "the peaceful recognition of rights and places for re-entry and landing of space vehicles." Article 9 provides for the "identification, registration and disclosure of intent of launching of all space vehicles." Article 12 provides for "the avoidance of interference...by space vehicles with other space vehicles." Article 15 provides for the establishment of "international policing of outer-space and for the protection of peoples and nations against violations of their rights therein."

Note: The provisions of the Sixth Principle of the Res. 1962 (XVIII) relating to space activities or experiments by the States, and their rights to enter into such activities, are similarly provided for in Articles 9, 10, 12 and 15 of the *Magna Carta of Space* both specifically and by the logical implication of these provisions.

CRITICISM:

This U.N. point relies entirely on "cooperation and mutual assistance." There is no reference to the necessary policeman in space who will have enforcement powers. Assume a situation where there are no laws in your city or country and no police to enforce those laws---who would be safe? Perhaps only the criminals making a sneak attack. But not those who believe in law and who idealistically rely upon mutual cooperation. Would you expect that the violator of the peace would come into court and submit himself to its judgement? A violator would not be expected to submit himself for trial on the "honor" system.
Is there any doubt that sudden violations may profit an aggressor seeking world domination? Then this limited principle of "cooperation and mutual assistance" becomes just another piece of paper. Even if there is "cooperation and mutual assistance", what will be the standards of justice to be employed in reaching a proper determination?

PRINCIPLE 7.

"The State on whose registry an object launched into outer-space is carried shall retain jurisdiction and control over such object, and any personnel thereon, while in outer-space. Ownership of objects launched into outer-space, and of their component parts, is not affected by their return to the earth. Such objects or component parts found beyond the limits of the State of registry shall be returned to that State, which shall furnish identifying data upon request prior to return."

COMPARISON:

Principle 7 provides that jurisdiction shall be retained

by the launching State over its vehicle while it is in outer-space, and such ownership is not affected by its passage through outer-space or by its return to earth. This Principle also provides for return of objects to the launching State, which objects have been found beyond its limits.

The Magna Carta's Article 13, which provides for responsibility by the launching State for any injury to persons or damage to property without the necessity of showing negligence or fault, necessarily implies control and ownership of the space vehicle by the sovereign power that launched it. Article 3 and Article 4 declare that outer-space and the interplanetary system, respectively, be deemed "res communis", which in effect denies any nation the right of appropriation, and thus implicitly provides that mere passage of a vehicle through outer-space, an area belonging to no nation, could not affect the ownership of that vehicle.

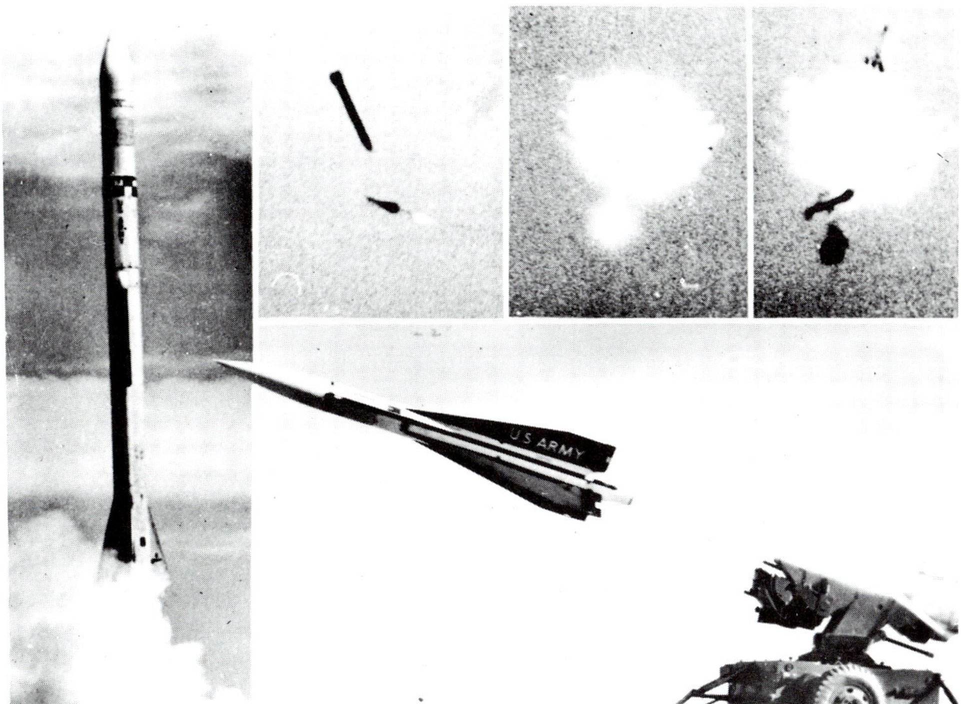

This Army anti-missile missile (Hawk) may be pre-view of "anti-satellite missiles" to come, if space remains lawless.

CRITICISM:

The U.N. principle is acceptable as far as it goes. It disregards, however, the scientific developments to come which surpass all imagination today. The scientists are now exploring the possibility of intercepting meteorites cruising in space. If the fantastic speeds of such objects appear surmountable to the scientists, it is not beyond the realm of probability that missiles may be developed and guided so as to intercept or strike down spacecraft, destroy exploration vehicles, and bar through such tactics the adventure of certain powers into space.

While the launching nation is given the privilege and the right to control the object sent forth from its territory, there should be a reservation of rights to the family of nations, asserted through the United Nations, to ascertain the nature and purpose of the launching and its effects upon the use of outer-space.

SPACE LIABILITY

PRINCIPLE 8.

"Each State which launches or procures the launching of an object into outer-space, and each State from whose territory or facility an object is launched, is internationally liable for damage to a foreign State or to its natural or juridical persons by such object or its component parts on the earth, in airspace, or in outer-space."

COMPARISON:

U.N.Principle 8 provides for liability by the launching State for damage to a "foreign State or its natural juridical persons" caused by the object launched.

The Magna Carta Article 13 provides "In the event of injuries to persons or damage to property caused by space vehicles, rockets, missiles, satellites and the like, the sovereign power by or through which the same have been launched shall be responsible and liable for all such damage, without the requirement of any proof of fault, negligence, carelessness or recklessness.''

Once more, the similarities are obvious. However, it is significant to note that the *Magna Carta* provides also for recovery by persons against their own State in the event of injury to their person or property, while Resolution 1962 (XVIII) fails to so provide.

CRITICISM:

With this U.N. principle, a very serious problem arises. Their wording is strangely silent on the question whether fault should be established by a claimant before that claimant is entitled to recover for damage. The silence is all the more significant since in the deliberations of the Space Committee of the United Nations, some delegates had proposed that it be specifically stated that such right to recovery shall exist without proof of fault.

Furthermore, this provision seems to be limited solely to claimants who live in a State foreign to the State which launched its object. But what about a citizen of the United States who is injured by an object launched in the United States, and who is then relegated to the dubious remedy under the Federal Tort Claims Act? This law does not provide for recovery for damages upon the mere fact of the creation of the damage; it requires proof by the claimant that the United States was reckless, negligent or careless.

Since the evidence bearing on the creation of the launching equipment, its launching procedures, its directional control, and other factors, are within the realm of classified and confidential information, how in the wide wide world will an American claimant ever hope to succeed if he is relegated to the Federal Tort Claims Act?

Take also the citizen of any other nation where the doctrine of sovereign immunity prevails. Will the concept stated in Principle 8 give any rights to such citizen against his own country? Of course not. The illogical result is reached that a citizen of a foreign country may recover against the launching power but a citizen of the country from which the launching emanated cannot recover.

This injustice, of course, should be covered by adequate provision since the launching was intended to be an international project and was destined to traverse the boundaries of the launching nations.

Two regional councils were formally established in February and March of 1964 to provide for international launching. (Note---This will create a problem for the committee on liability since their proposal states that a national of a launching country cannot sue under the international agreement. If both countries A & B join in a launch and a domiciliary of "A" is injured, it is clear that he cannot sue State "A" under the international agreement, but does the agreement prevent him from suing State B? (If, as the Magna Carta provides, liability may be asserted against one's own State under the international agreement then this problem will be eliminated.)

A further provision should be added to this principle, that there shall be liability for such damage by the launching authority without proof of fault, and the right to recover by anyone suffering damages and injury therefrom shall not be barred by any facts relating to citizenship, habitation, domicile or residence.

FREEDOM OF ASTRONAUTS

UNDER U. N. PRINCIPLE 9, ASTRONAUTS LANDING ON FOREIGN SOIL AFTER RE-ENTRY WILL BE PROMPTLY RETURNED TO THEIR COUNTRY.

PRINCIPLE 9.

"States shall regard astronauts as envoys of

mankind in outer-space, and shall render to them all possible assistance in the event of accident, distress, or emergency landing on the territory of a foreign State or on the high seas. Astronauts who make such a landing shall be safely and promptly returned to the State of registry of their space vehicle."

COMPARISON:

U.N. Principle 9 provides for the assistance of astronauts in distress and for their return to the launching State in the event they are forced to land "on the territory of a foreign State or on the high seas."

The Magna Carta Article 9 states that "provision shall be made for identification, registration and disclosure of intent of launchings of all space vehicles", and Article 10 states that "provision shall likewise be made for the peaceful recognition for rights and places for re-entry and landing of space vehicles". Taken together these provisions refer by implication to the "right" of a nation to claim ownership of its space vehicle and astronauts if forced to land on the territory of a foreign State. Assistance to astronauts is merely a logical extension of basic morality.

CRITICISM:

This U.N. principle states correctly a moral obligation upon all to go to the aid of any astronaut in distress. But again, if the activity of such astronaut is related to espionage, the astronaut should then be subject to the responsibilities and liabilities of international law applicable to those who commit espionage on earth.

In brief, the nature of the astronaut's venture---namely, whether peaceful or military---should determine the obligation to return him to his own country summarily.

The following is a further elaboration of one of the Nine Principles of 1963, pursued in March, 1964, by the United Nations:

drafts which were before it. Each of the three drafts denied to persons who were nationals of the State open to suit, the right to sue their own State under the international agreement.

The problem of which theory of liability to apply to suits, brought by persons injured against a foreign State, was not resolved. Hungary proposed that a different theory of liability be used to determine damages which occurred in outer-space (fault liability) and damages occurring in the atmosphere or on the ground (strict liability) unless the launching State proves the damages were caused by a natural disaster or a willful act of the damaged State.

The United States proposed a uniform theory to be applied in outer-space, in the atmosphere and on the ground. Under its proposal, liability would be absolute except where a willful or reckless act on the part of the claimant can be shown.

Belgium suggested that as long as the cause and effect

The Legal Subcommittee on the Committee for Peaceful Uses of Outer-Space at the United Nations, convened in Geneva from March 9 to March 26, 1964. Pursuant to Resolution 1963 (XVIII) of December 13, 1963, this Committee undertook to consider the problems of astronaut rescue and return, and those of damages for liability.

There was considerable discussion but the drafts were not completed. However, Dr. Manfred Lachs of Poland, the learned Chairman of the Committee, stated that good results had been achieved in the discussions that had taken place, and that a foundation had been laid for the next stage of its task.

On October 5, 1964, the Committee reconvened in New York City and continued its sessions to October 23, 1964. Chairman Lachs suggested that efforts first be made to complete the draft on rescue and return, since it was less controversial than that dealing with liability.

During the October session, the Subcommittee on Rescue and Return reached a preliminary agreement on the preamble and three sections of the proposed agreement. The articles agreed upon dealt with:

> "(1) Notification of accident---to be given to the launching State and the Secretary-General of the United Nations.
> "(2) Assistance in the territory of a contracting party---the contracting party shall assist downed spacemen as if they were personnel of its own." Notice of its operations is to be given to the launching State and the Secretary-General. If assistance of the launching State is required, the contracting party shall retain control of the rescue operations.
> "(3) Return of space objects---the contracting party shall return the space object to the launching State as soon as possible and may request proper identification from the launching State. One subsection has been intentionally omitted from this clause. It has been left open until a provision providing for indemnity for expenses, incurred by the contracting party who aided in the return of the space vehicle, is drafted."

The second committee, of the Subcommittee on Liability for Damages, conducted brief hearings to discuss the three can be shown, all liability should be absolute.

All the proposed drafts provided for some statute of limitations, but even on this issue there was no agreement. Belgium suggested two years, the United States proposed one year from discovery or when discovery should have been made, and Hungary submitted a flat one year provision.

CRITICISM:

It is significant again that under the drafts proposed before the Subcommittee on Law of the Space Committee of the U.N., no provision is made for a national to sue his own country. The following hypothetical case points up the injustice of such an exclusion.

IF JOINT USA/USSR LAUNCHINGS OCCUR IN MUTUAL SPACE PROJECTS, BOTH NATIONS MUST ACCEPT LIABILITY FOR DAMAGES IN CASE OF DISASTER CAUSED BY EITHER VEHICLE.

Suppose there is a joint launching by two or more countries. Suppose under ordinary law as prevails on earth, there is joint liability. The injured party is a citizen of one of these countries. If he is barred from suing his own nation and sues only the foreign nation for damages, will the foreign nation have the right to seek a contribution from the citizen's nation as a joint tort feasor?

Will the defense of sovereign immunity, if it exists in the nation of the citizen who is injured, constitute a bar to a contribution by the nation whose subject is the claimant to the other foreign nation?

If the citizen is relegated to a claim against his own government, will his claim be maintainable in the absence of proof of negligence, where the laws of his own nation applicable to national cases require proof of negligence?

And how, if such is the case, would such a claimant ever be able to prove his case when the evidence on which he must rely would clearly be qualified, privileged and confidential, and entirely unavailable for use in any legal proceeding brought by such a claimant?

These problems can all be avoided, and a step in the direction of justice for the common man can only come if the provisions of The Magna Carta of Space are adopted as law everywhere since all such contingencies are covered therein.

It is also relevant here to note the observations of one of the most highly esteemed and currently one of the most respected experts on aerospace law, Mr. John E. Stephens, General Counsel of the Air Transport Association of America. In his speech "The Legal Regulation of Aerospace Transport" delivered at San Juan, Puerto Rico, May 25, 1965 before the Inter-American Bar Association, Mr. Stephens referring to the nine principles declared by the United Nations Space Committee on December 13, 1963, observed:

"As with the earlier U.N. Resolution 1721, the United States' view of Resolution 1962 was that it is declaratory of existing international law. Thus United States Ambassador to the United Nations, the late Adlai Stevenson stated:

> 'We believe these legal principles reflect international law as it is accepted by the members of the United Nations. The United States, for its part, intends to respect these principles.'

"Ambassador Fedorenko of the Soviet Union immediately responded, 'The Soviet Union, for its part, will also respect the principles contained in this declaration.' Notwithstanding this glowing exchange, codification of the declaring principles has not been done.

"Thus, simultaneously with the adoption of Resolution 1962, the General Assembly unanimously adopted Resolution 1963, exhorting the Space Committee to continue to study and report on legal problems and to arrange for codification of the legal principles embodied in Resolution 1962. Subsequent meetings of the Legal Sub-Committee, however, have failed to produce agreement on such codification.

"Two aspects of Resolution 1962 are notable. First, the member States did not find it necessary to locate outer-space in order to enunciate guiding legal principles for activities therein. In fact, outer-space is not defined in the Resolution. At the same time, outer-space is distinguished from airspace which also is neither defined nor located. In similar fashion, the Resolution avoids the legal pitfall of attempting to distinguish aircraft, spacecraft, vehicles, and instrumentatilities, by referring generally to objects. Of course, these omissions are viewed by some as a fatally defective evasion of the issue.

The comments of the learned and eminent scholar, Colonel Morton S. Jaffe, Legal Advisor of the Allied Forces of Southern Europe, are most pertinent:

"But even as the Declaration of Legal Principles was approved by acclamation of the General Assembly, the Assembly cast doubt on its efficacy and force to govern activities in space. On 13 December 1963, the same day that Resolution 1962 (XVIII) was unanimously approved, the Assembly also acclaimed Resolution 1963 (XVIII) with the recommendation 'that consideration should be given to incorporating in international agreement form, in the future as appropriate, legal principles governing the activities of the States in the exploration and use of outer-space.' The Assembly went on to request the Committee on the Peaceful Uses of Outer-Space 'to arrange for the prompt preparation of draft international agreements on liability for damage caused by objects launched into outer-space and on assistance to and return of astronauts and space vehicles.'

"Are we back where we were a year ago? Do we still, notwithstanding the pledges of Ambassadors Stevenson and Fedorenko, need to restate the principles, this time 'in international agreement form', to endow them with dignity and effect? Or are the principles recognized as legally valid, and is it only detailed implementation of the principles affecting liability for damage and assistance to astronauts and vehicles, which is now desired and urged? These questions are especially pertinent when it is recalled that in the meetings in the period preceding the adoption of Resolution 1962, Ambassador Morozov had argued that an international 'declaration' would be binding while a mere 'resolution', such as Number 1721, would not.

"I submit that this is undesirable. The law, even international and spatial, cannot be so frivolous."

12

SPACE WAITS FOR NO MAN

MORE THAN seven years and seven million words later, after the submission of the first resolution of the Ad Hoc Committee on Space to the United Nations in 1958, we are still on a treadmill to nowhere. The declaration of principles of December 13, 1963, with its high-sounding ephemeral phrases does indicate progress perhaps in good fellowship amongst the delegates---but hardly in the establishment of barriers against wrongdoing, invasion of human rights and the destruction of mankind.

Here in the closing years of the first decade of the Age of Space, after the numerous thrusts into space and incredible scientific achievements, this Space Committee has still failed to consider and to adopt basic principles which directly affect the threats to peace and the mainenance of our present society on earth. The Committee's resolutions and reports to date fall far short of answering the plea of the dedicated men who have constantly prayed that "Law must precede man into space".

The U.N. Committee on Space disregarded the pleas, resolutions and views of numerous bar associations, symposia, gatherings of governmental and non-governmental lawyers, sociologists and diplomats who have demanded an immediate law for space.

The Space Committee of the United Nations has failed to request the General Assembly and the proper authorities therein to make mandatory the application of a new international law and the United Nations Charter to outer-space and the celestial bodies. It merely "commends to States for their guidance the application of international law and the Charter of the United Nations." To date, the Charter has not been amended so as to specifically include such application.

During current "space law gap", plans are being conceived for "space troop carrier" rocket, with 18 million pounds thrust.

Advance unit using "paracone" descent devices would be dropped over enemy territory in case of war.

Within 45 minutes, all 1,200 fully-equipped "space soldiers", plus 120 tons of support material, would be landed in battle area, somewhere on earth.

The era of lawlessness in space continues. The era of scientific aggression without regard to the creation of additional dangers for mankind in the absence of law---or a police supervision---proceeds at a faster and faster pace.

Space troop carrier at launch ready attitude.

Space soldiers disembarking from space troop carrier.

Abroad the opinion is predominant that there are real possibilities today for the conclusion of an international convention on outer-space. It appears that the nations of the world are impressed generally with the necessity for further cooperation, even though it means the surrender of some rights of sovereignty.

Science without the control of law is the enemy of mankind. Science under the control of law is the benefactor of mankind. Politics, national and international and beyond the control of law, ethics, and morals, disregarding rights of peoples in the world---is the antagonist of all society.

The void in space is law. This must be filled and it must be filled immediately. The time for its launching is now. Tomorrow may be too late.

GENESIS OF SPACE LAW

To give the history of the author's concept of *The Magna Carta of Space*, the basic principles were stated in various papers and speeches even before (1956) the start of the Space Age. The earliest official presentation, based on studies over a long period of time, was made before the American Bar

Association on February 20, 1958, barely three weeks after the United States had launched its first satellite, Explorer I.

Some of the later provisions of *The Magna Carta* were already formed in the writer's mind then, as shown by his report of February 1958 to the American Bar Association:

> "It is clear that the idea expressed in the major international agreements and in most of the national statutes of the great powers, is that airspace was contemplated by them to be that area lying within that portion of earth's atmosphere which comprises the troposphere and stratosphere, where conventional planes, gliders, balloons and other instrumentalities used for air travel would be able to go. It can hardly be urged that it was contemplated that this area would encompass that portion of space in which missiles, rockets and satellites would fly.
>
> "The Soviet Union in specific legislation similar to others has set forth the claim: To the USSR belongs the complete and exclusive sovereignty in the airspace above the USSR.
>
> "Certain of their scientists have claimed that this signifies without limit. However, since each and every other nation in the world would have the same right to make the same claim as to the space above its own land, the use of space for the transmission of satellites, missiles, rockets and other instrumentalities of travel and flight through space, must result in conflict since each travel must necessarily invade the areas claimed by the individual nations to be their own.
>
> "It is suggested that a realistic, practical, and proper definition of space be stated as follows:
>
> "Space is that area existing between the surface of the earth and the celestial bodies. It shall comprise two parts. The first part shall comprise the troposphere and the stratosphere and be under the complete and exclusive sovereignty of the subjacent nation.
>
> The second part shall comprise the remainder of the area extending to the celestial bodies which shall be termed outer-space. This outer-space shall be free from the claim of sovereignty of any individual nation but shall be subject to multilateral control by all nations.
>
> "All nations should have the right of freedom of use in such outer-space for peaceful international flights subject to control by a competent, duly authorized, international regulatory body.
>
> "This general principle would: 1. Permit the use of space

over any nation's territory (whether or not that space be occupied by the atmosphere) for the non-military, peaceful transit of aircraft, vehicles or objects not likely to constitute any dangerous hazard to persons or property. 2. Condemn the use of space over any nation's territory for the passage of military aircraft, vehicles or objects.

"Security and defense---matters of gravest concern to every nation---make mandatory this course. (1) Sole control of troposphere and stratosphere; (2) multi-lateral control of the remaining portion of space as far as the celestial bodies, i.e., outer-space.

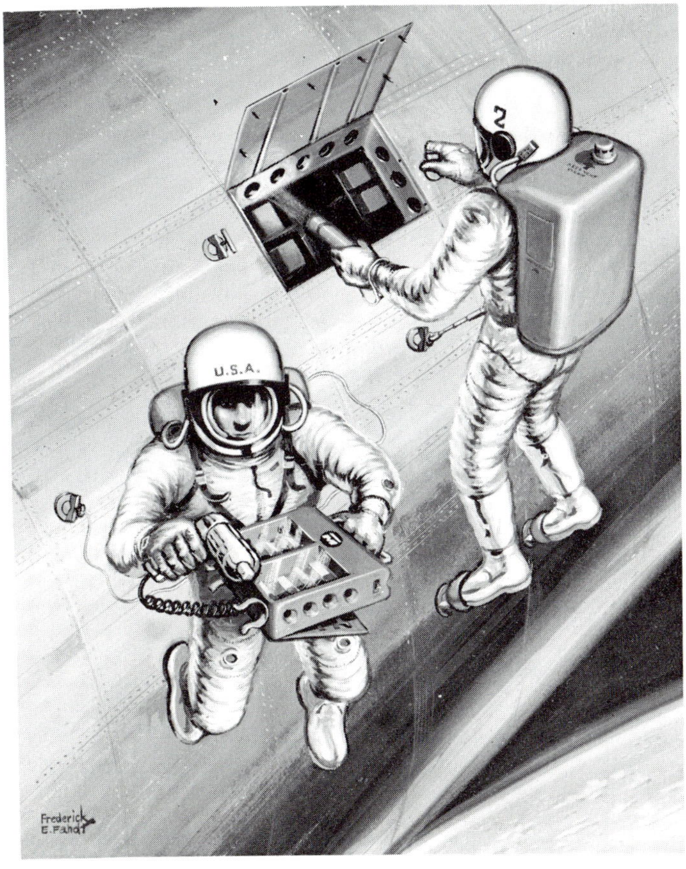

"Freedom of space" is typified by visualization of future "space repairmen" going about their job peaceably, in orbit.

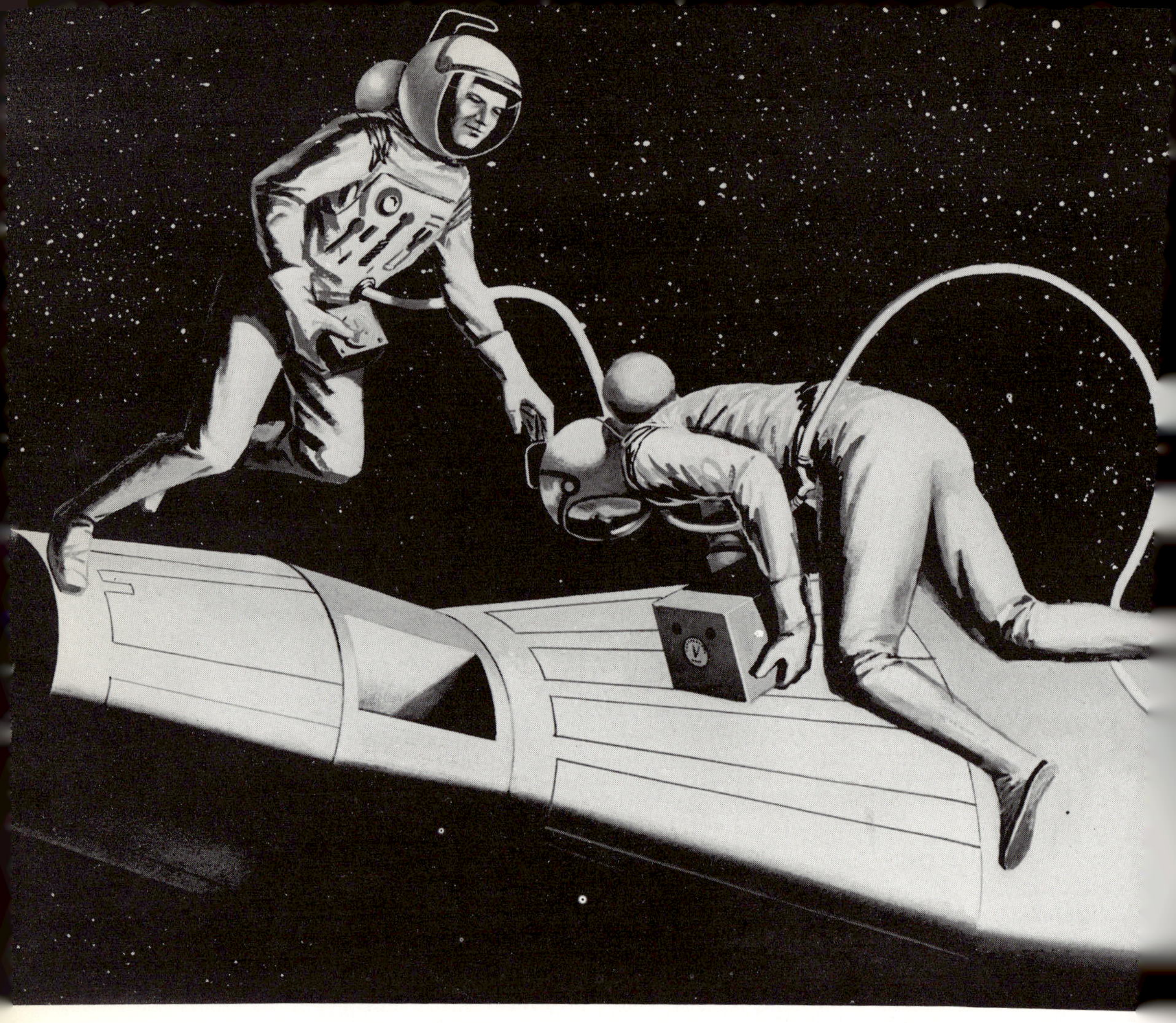

Astronaut-scientists of any nation would be free to conduct space-science researches under MAGNA CARTA OF SPACE.

Long prior to this instance in February 1958, the author was much concerned with the lawlessness in space, which appeared to be a logical conclusion to reasonable men because of the rapid advance in science in the field of rocketry. Prior to the launching of the first Sputnik, the principle was manifestly applicable that reasonable men should take steps to meet problems reasonably to be anticipated, and which, if not properly anticipated and protected by law, would lead to uncontrolled provocations amongst the various explorers into space.

It is inconceivable that men, believed to be most highly trained in the field of law and occupying many high positions in the largest national association of lawyers in the United

States, could so lightly disregard the portents of the future and refuse to give those future problems due attention and action.

This simply demonstrated not merely a lack of proper comprehension of the dangers facing the world, but also the vice of procrastination existing at high levels of the legal profession as well as with high officials in the government. And apathy in the public at large also shares the blame.

As stated in a blurb for this writer's article in Pageant magazine (July, 1965, We Need Space Law Now!, by William A. Hyman, page 87):

> "William A. Hyman, a New York insurance attorney and a pioneer in aeronautical insurance law, warned in 1956 of the importance of formulating some kind of space law. He recalls that he was almost hooted out of the American Bar Association for his 'science fiction' ideas, but when Russia launched the first Sputnik a year later, the legal world quickly acknowledged the validity of his arguments.
> "Since then William Hyman has become a leading authority on space law."

It was in 1956 that the author's actual work on the principles of space law began, and as early as February 1958 ---when the United States had barely managed to orbit one tiny satellite after Russia's two big "spacebusters"---he urged the preparation of a skeletal outline for space law before a large professional organization, the American Bar Association (sic) at its meeting in Atlanta, Georgia, at its conference of October, 1958.

ANTI-SPACE LAW FORCES

When it came to acceptance of the dire need for such space law, neither the American Bar Association nor any government agency made any active moves whatsoever.

In the case of the ABA, there was organized "decapitation" of the writer's committee. The basic principles of *The Magna Carta* met concerted oppositon, and the work of our first Space Committee of the ABA was emasculated by the sinister stratagem of transferring the committee's functions to another committee created subsequently. The hand-picked members were opposed to regulation of space from the start, even to a simple declaration of principles such as set forth in the report of the first Space Committee, of which the author was chairman, as the guidelines only for control of activities in outer-space.

"WASHINGTON IS NOT READY FOR ANY SPACE REGULATIONS"...YET SPACE-CROSSING ROCKET-LINERS ARE ON THE DRAWING BOARDS, WHOSE FLIGHTS WILL "VIOLATE SOVEREIGNTY" OF ANY NATION OVER WHICH THEY FLY, UNDER PRESENT PHASE OF "SPACE ANARCHY".

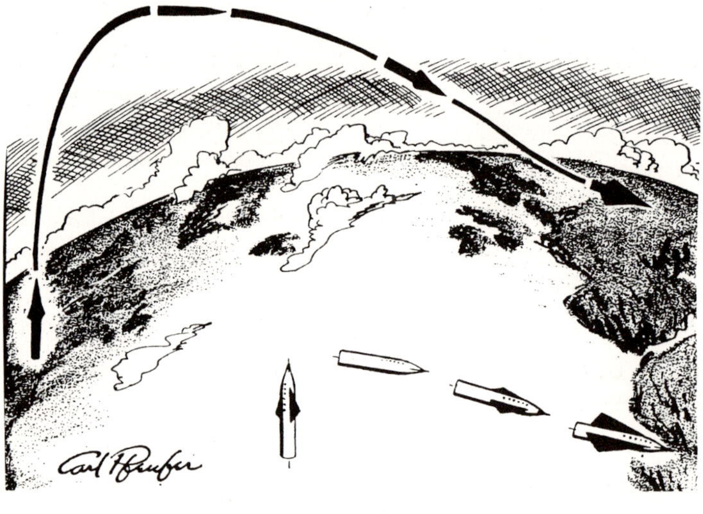

The surprising and lame explanation was given that "Washington was not yet ready for any space regulations at that time." This is borne out by a letter of December 17, 1958, sent to the author by Wilton B. Persons, Assistant to the President (then-President Dwight D. Eisenhower) in which he first gave perfunctory thanks for sending the suggestions for a code to regulate the use of outer-space. Then he went on to say:

"However, the Administration believes that at the present

> time it would be premature to attempt to establish international legal codes to regulate the use of outer-space. Our experience and knowledge of facts are at present insufficient to provide a sound basis for detailed rules of law. We believe we should endeavor to formulate these only as the physical facts of outer-space, as well as problems relating to its exploration and use, are better understood. Of course, we must keep in mind the future development of sound legal rules in this field. For this reason, there was included in our proposal now before the United Nations General Assembly for the creation of a United Nations ad hoc Committee on Peaceful Uses of Outer-Space a provision that one of the duties of this committee should be to study and report on 'The nature of legal problems which may arise in the carrying out of programmes to explore outer-space.' "

The word "lame" was used above not because the ABA's excuse was not true but because it was not a good excuse at all. Instead of tacitly agreeing with the government on their "do-nothing" attitude, it was the duty and responsibility of the American Bar Association to influence the government to change its mind.

After all, it is the body of lawyers in this nation who are the experts and the leaders in law---whether on earth or in space---and not the government which is expert in governing only. For the foremost legal minds in America to supinely accept this short-sighted government view on space law is almost criminal in itself.

Do or do not legal authorities point out where the law is amiss, or where new law is needed? Or do they simply allow the legally lay public---which includes the government right up to and including the President---to decide all about legal matters?

It seems to this writer to be sheer cowardice on the part of the profession to which he belongs that we did not speak forth in a loud voice at the beginning of the Space Age and demand that space law be given immediate attention. Some few of us did and earned only scorn, perhaps of the same unthinking type as that which greeted the first suggestions of Child Labor Laws as something too "radical" and "untraditional" to merit attention.

One would think that no such lack of foresight could

possibly emanate out of the National Aeronautics and Space Administration (NASA), which is the organization charged by Congress and the President to conduct our all-important space program. NASA is to be commended for its highly successful series of manned Mercury flights, and the follow-on Gemini flights that have thrilled the world, not to mention an excellent variety of scientific satellites, and the sensational Mariner-2 and Mariner-4 probes to Venus and Mars, respectively.

Medallion, 2-1/2 feet in diameter, part of Project Mercury Monument at Cape Kennedy, honoring America's first manned spaceflight program.

However, in the early days, even NASA leadership was hesitant to change the legal status quo, as will be seen in the following. On December 7, 1960, the author gave a speech before the American Rocket Society (now the American Institute of Aeronautics and Astronautics) that urged a skeletal code of space law.

In a NASA-financed report (per the Herald Tribune, December 8, 1960) those statements were condemned, or perhaps scorned, as "pious maxims" by a collaborating pair of professors of law.

The author's reply was, in part:

> "The world demands a rule by law and peace---not by lawlessness which inevitably leads to war."

The writer argued further that the absence of space law could lead to incidents between big powers that might trigger nuclear war, the most dread fate earth could suffer.

To it might be added this rebuttal today---if the Nineteen Principles set forth in *The Magna Carta of Space,* and previously given by this author in speeches, are "pious maxims", would the same epithet be applied by the disdainful professors to another nineteen principles known to the human race, divided up between the Ten Commandments and the Nine Principles of the U.N. Space Committee?

Perhaps other brief sets of rules---the Bill of Rights, the Declaration of Independence, and the Constitution of the United States---are also merely "pious maxims" in the eyes of the professors of law in their legal ivory towers. What "impious maxims" would they like to suggest in return as the framework for space law?

To the author, their verdict is all part of the general "anti-space law" spirit that has, from 1957 and Sputnik to the present day, persisted within our nation and internationally, for no better reason seemingly than the anti-suffrage, anti-science, anti-U.N. and all the other anti-progress movements that have constantly tried to hamstring social, economic, and legal change that becomes necessary with the march of time.

IMPASSE AT THE U.N.

This "anti" space law sentiment persisted throughout the nation and the world on into 1959 and further. In 1958 and 1959, the Ad Hoc Committee on the Peaceful Uses of Outer-Space of the United Nations was inactive. It had faced an impasse because the Soviet had boycotted this Committee on the ground that it failed to have sufficient representation thereon from nations in the Soviet's part of the world. To help meet this situation and develop action for immediate attention, various important bar associations took appropriate steps to arouse and alert governments and peoples of the world to the dangers confronting mankind because of the failure to establish a universal law for space.

It was the author's privilege to prepare the report and Resolution adopted by the Inter-American Bar Association in April 1959, for appropriate relief to correct the inactivity in connection with promulgating space law. This Resolution, because of its timelessness and significance, is set forth herein:

> "NOW, THEREFORE, BE IT RESOLVED that the Inter-American Bar Association, through its President, call upon the nations of the world to convene as soon as possible for the purpose of discussing the question of the desirability of establishing an international agreement for the regulation of the use of outer-space for peaceful purposes, and that the respective Governments represented by members of this Association be requested to take steps towards establishing such a convention, and be it
>
> "FURTHER RESOLVED, that such invitations be directed to the nations of the world who are at present undertaking the exploration of space and the interplanetary world and that these nations be requested to convene presently for an ad hoc tentative agreement among the nations of the world for the above-stated purpose to designate an appropriate committee which shall attempt to evolve an international code of law for the benefit of the nations of the world with the avowed purpose to avoid conflict and to preserve peace, and be it
>
> "FURTHER RESOLVED, that the Inter-American Bar Association, whose membership includes men of outstanding

legal and judicial ability of the Americas, cooperate with such convention of nations in such manner as is fit, proper and effective to attain the objectives of peace on earth and good will to men.''

''MAGNA CARTA OF SPACE'' WOULD ENSURE PEACEFUL USES OF OUTER-SPACE, VIA A VARIETY OF SATELLITES AND VEHICLES, FOR THE BENEFIT OF ALL MANKIND.

A copy of this resolution was sent to then-President Dwight D. Eisenhower on April 19, 1959---but nothing of great note was done by the Government.

In 1960 and 1961, at various national and international Conventions and Congresses, the author still drove forward aggressively with constant efforts to secure the recognition of the great need of law in space---for the preservation of people and the avoidance of constant conflicts.

These included lectures, speeches, radio and television appearances in different parts of the world, all the way from Manila in the Philippines to Kyota University in Japan, Hong Kong, Varna (Bulgaria), Warsaw (Poland), Europe and South America, as well as in the United States.

The astro-legal breakthrough was attained on February 3, 1961, in Bogota, Colombia, at the Congress of the Inter-American Bar Association, when with the enlightened help of brilliant colleagues of the author on the Committee on Inter-Planetary Space Law, and the moral and intellectual support as well of the Council and high officials of this distinguished Association, representing the best minds in the Western Hemisphere, *The Magna Carta of Space* as presented herein and as written by the author was approved and duly authenticated, and thereafter was sent to the United Nations and leading scholars, diplomats and government officials who gave it their commendation on an unofficial basis.

LEGAL LODESTAR OF SPACE

The Federal Bar Association of New York, New Jersey and Connecticut, sensing the urgency of the situation, submitted their Resolution, prepared by the author, which was sent to President Dwight D. Eisenhower on April 17, 1959, reading as follows:

> "NOW, THEREFORE, BE IT RESOLVED that the Federal Bar Association of New York, New Jersey and Connecticut, through its President, issue its request to the President of the United States to invite the interested nations of the world to convene as soon as possible either within or without the United Nations for the purpose of discussing the question of the desirability of establishing an international agreement for the regulation of the use of outer-space for peaceful purposes, and be it
> "FURTHER RESOVLED, that the Federal Bar Association of New York, New Jersey and Connecticut offer such assistance as the President of the United States may desire of it in helping to make such meeting a success.

All fine and good. But again, nothing of any importance was done about this by the U.S. Government. The author still had years of efforts and dozens of speeches ahead, in his "one-man crusade"---it almost amounted to that---to extend law from the earth into space.

In the next chapter, we will trace the historical origins

of human rights and see in what degree they lead to this book's aim of "universal human rights" on earth and in space.

13

MAGNA CARTA -OLD

SEVEN hundred and fifty years ago the original Magna Carta was signed by King John at Runnymede which granted to the feudal barons on that June day of 1215 A.D. the protection of the rights demanded by them. That Charter has often been cited as the foundation for the common law, democratic rights, and constitutional law, on which subsequently civil rights were predicated. It is possibly one of the most misunderstood and misquoted documents in all legal history.

It did not represent a fight for the rights of the common man. It was obtained in the fight for rights and privileges for the feudal barons. It represents the first political-constitutional struggle in English history. It resulted from the demands of the feudal barons, who were supported by Archbishop Langton in London, to obtain from King John with national implications, (1) concessions to the barons, (2) rights of summons to the Great Council to be sent individually to the great magnates, (3) some concessions to the agricultural and commercial classes of limitation of royal seizure of private property, (4) reform of the courts and promise of free election, and above all, (5) limitations on arrest and imprisonment, as follows:

> "No free man shall be arrested and imprisoned, or dispossessed, or outlawed, or banished, or in any way molested; nor will we set forth against him, nor send against him, unless by the lawful judgment of his peers and by the law of the land."

The chief significance of the Magna Carta at that time lay in the assertion of the supremacy of law over the King.

Through the centuries, historical legal experiences

transformed the Magna Carta into an accepted formula for constitutional procedure, thus making it the basis of the modern English Constitution. Though rejected by Pope Innocent I, the principles were repeatedly restated by succeeding rulers and became the foundation of law and justice for the common man.

It is significant that the barons, realizing that unwritten law always intended to favor the interest of the crown, sought to define some content of this unwritten law in their "Magna Carta"---for the protection of the feudal barons.

On the 15th day of June, 1215, King John met his barons at Runnymede, a pleasant meadow on the Thames between Windsor and Staines. To quote Professor Colin R. Lovell, Professor of History at the University of Southern California, in his excellent survey entitled "English Constitutional and Legal History":

> "The charter he there granted became one of the most notoriously misinterpreted documents in English history, largely because succeeding generations of Englishmen read into its provisions meanings relevant to their own times. Essentially a manifesto of feudalism, the charter has been termed the 'palladium of English liberties', the foundation of freedom, and the like. Misinterpretation may often have been fruitful but the importance of Magna Carta in English history is to be found in the uses to which it was put in the succeeding centuries and the image it created in the minds of Englishmen.
>
> "The legal form of Magna Carta was that of a charter conveyancing land. This was the most binding and solemn type of a contract, in this instance between the King and certain persons named specifically, together with the community of the realm generally.
>
> "The drafters of the charter hoped that explicit and precise statements of hitherto unwritten feudal law would end royal encroachments on it."

EVOLUTION OF HUMAN RIGHTS

Briefly, the Magna Carta of Runnymede undertook to reduce to writing the feudal demands, practices, privileges and rights of the feudal barons. Through subsequent developments, the rights of the barons were granted to all people, and thus it became the foundation for the universal grant of legal and political rights to all free men, granting to them among other things the approval of the jury system, the designation of qualified justices and the regulation of certain court procedures.

It is noteworthy that its aims were primarily legal and political, rather than humanitarian for the common man.

Another milestone in legal-political history was the formation of the League of Nations and the establishment of its covenant in connection with the treaty of peace following the First World War.

The primary purpose of the League of Nations was the protection of the political status of the victorious signatory nations, believing that in the preservation of the political status, peace would be assured---a step that unfortunately, for reasons which need not be developed now, was not successful. The League of Nations failed after Japan invaded Manchuria and after Italy invaded Ethopia.

Then later a most decisive step for peace was taken. The United States, through its farseeing, fearless and decisive President Harry S Truman, initiated the birth of the United Nations in 1945.

The protection and promotion of human rights was its primary objective. This is clearly indicated in its charter and in the declaration of the "Commission on Human Rights," which Commission was under the chairman of the late, beloved Mrs. Eleanor Roosevelt, and which Commission established the Universal Declaration of Human Rights (see Appendix).

This Declaration was primarily an affirmation of the basic rights due all men in all free countries, though it did lack the status and the force of a written law and a conventional treaty. The policy of "recommendations" in lieu of binding legal obligations was the basis of this procedure.

It is tragic, to say the least, that the Universal Declaration of Human Rights had not been reduced to an enforceable international covenant although it has been accepted and followed for the principles it has advocated chiefly in such matters as the right to life, liberty and property, freedom of speech and assembly, fair trial, religious freedom, the right to participate in government, and the like.

Likewise, another distinguished effort was made to protect human rights and lives by international law through the convention to outlaw Genocide (race murder).

The right to be spared from death because of race, color, creed, religion and genetic origin could not well depend on local good will of governing groups, but for its preservation the principle had to be established in a proper Convention or International Treaty.

The Genocide Convention was brought into being primarily by the efforts of the late Professor Joseph Lempkin of Poland, whom this author subsequently assisted in his committee work. This convention succeeded in getting about seventy national signatories at the United Nations. Unfortunately, though it was signed by the President of the United States, the Convention to Outlaw Genocide has been pigeon-holed by the Committee on Foreign Relations of the United States Senate and, likewise, it has not been signed and ratified by England. The reasons for refusal to ratify this important treaty were never revealed to the public or to the world at large but they were dictated by the force of local racial political problems in the United States and in England.

It has thus become apparent that there are some vital areas in life on earth and in the universe where mere good will, oral commitments and voluntary cooperation cannot and will not prove sufficient.

The force of the written law becomes more apparent when dealing with the need for space regulation and the establishment of world peace through space law.

"UNWRITTEN" WORLD LAW

There is no peace on earth. Racial hatreds, international conflicts, and bloodshed occur everywhere. It is possible, and perhaps even probable, that in a moment of wild, emotional imbalance, striving for greater power and greater self-aggrandizement, an unscrupulous or power-maddened leader of a nation or a group, could readily plunge the whole world into the pit of sudden nuclear destruction.

It is not sufficient that we rest solely on "good will" or the moral force we hope to inculcate. People are swayed by different ambitions and backed by different histories.

Justice Robert Jackson of the Supreme Court of the United States, in his statement as Chief Prosecutor in the Military Trials of the Nazi criminals at Nuremberg, proclaimed one of its purposes to be "Lest we forget."

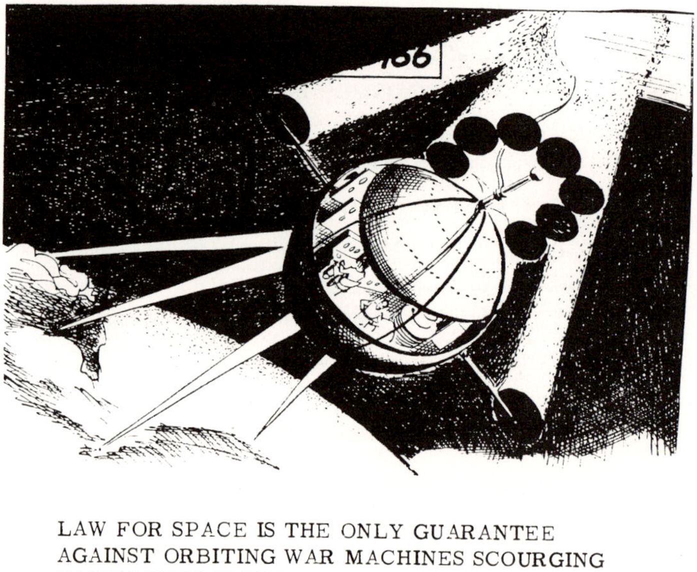

LAW FOR SPACE IS THE ONLY GUARANTEE AGAINST ORBITING WAR MACHINES SCOURGING EARTH WITH FRIGHTFUL NEW WEAPONS.

This forces upon all of us the conclusion that in the new world beyond the horizon where instruments of death fly at incomprehensible speed and where forces of nature can be chained for military attacks, the surest, most reliable, and honest way to help to avoid such a threat to mankind is to reduce to written understanding the law to protect all human beings---a law that is non-political and non-partisan, a law that aims for equal benefits and protections for all.

The Magna Carta of Space meticulously worked out by the author is designed to fill the need for a definite, unequivocal, legal declaration of rights for all people, their children, their grandchildren, their future generations, all over the world. It was written, proposed, and debated by the writer while President of the Section on Interplanetary Space Law at the Convention of the Inter-American Bar Association in February 1961, at Bogota, Colombia, where after a debate of several days in English and in Spanish, it was adopted.

Subsequently, it was duly transmitted to all delegations at the United Nations, to heads of governments and various nongovernmental associations in different parts of the world, where it received almost universal acclaim and approval.

One of the author's basic motivations in devising *The Magna Carta of Space* has recently been most conspicuously echoed, independently, by the Honorable Harlan Cleveland, Assistant Secretary of State for International Organizations Affairs, on December 13, 1964, in an address titled "The Evolution of Rising Responsibility," from which the following excerpts are most pertinent:

> "Nationhood is heady stuff. Every nation, and every national leader, can be expected to overindulge once in a while. But continued overindulgence in nationalist emotion can lead to much senseless killing, and to the death of common sense itself.
>
> "The question about our world, and the question about the U.N. in this International Cooperation Year, is this: Can we all graduate fast enough from the Revolution of Rising Expectations to the Evolution of Rising Responsibility?
>
> "The moment will come, I hope and believe, when the third great issue of the UN's next twenty years is how---and indeed whether---to bring to life the human rights provision of the Charter.
>
> "It is not yet clear that the national leaders in the world, either in the large countries or in the small ones, really mean to promote (as they have agreed in Article 55 of the Charter to promote) the universal respect for an observance of human rights and fundamental freedoms for all without distinction as to race, sex, language, or religion. Nor is it clear that the governments of the members of the UN intend to take (as Article 56 enjoins us to take) joint and separate

action in cooperation with the Organization for the achievement of the purposes set forth in Article 55.

"Part of the trouble, I suppose, is a confusion between nationhood and freedom. Self-determination, that noble goal which brought a billion people out from under foreign rule, was sometimes a racial as well as a national battlecry. Too often in the modern nationalist revolution---let us say it with all honesty---the promise of freedom was a promise of 'separate but equal' status in the world.

"The two most significant issues facing the United States, it appears at present, are the prevention of nuclear proliferation and the promotion of the 1963-64 arms control impetus that had led to the test ban treaty. The detonation of nuclear devices by China and the unfruitful debates of the 18-nation Disarmament Committee at Geneva have both underscored the need for decisive action to halt nuclear spread.

"Since the U.S. would like to bring China into the test ban treaty, the reluctance of China to join the 18-nation Disarmament Committee presents a serious obstacle. The U.S. will continue to explore China's adamant stand on disarmament in informal discussions.

"We who believe in human dignity have hold of a hard reality. We can see the realism of saying a cheerful 'yes' to a world of diversity---and the plain necessity to make common cause with others in the United Nations to save that world from poverty, conformity and war."

Fundamentally, the author's long battle to bring the issue of space law before the world's conscience has not been for the sake of man in space but for the sake of man on earth, to prevent a lawless new frontier from having repercussions in human society that would undermine rather than promote human rights.

This will become apparent in the detailed presentation of *The Magna Carta.* that is set forth in full in the next chapter.

# of Space

B., LL.B., D.H.L.

terplanetary Space Law—
Association

ARTICLE 9.

Provision shall be made for identification, registration and disclosure of intent of launchings of all space ehicles.

ARTICLE 10.

Provision shall likewise be made for the peaceful recognition of rights and places for re-entry and landing of pace vehicles.

ARTICLE 11.

Provision shall be made for the allocation and control of radio frequencies.

ARTICLE 12.

Provision shall be made for the avoidance of interference with aircraft by space vehicles and also by space ehicles with other space vehicles.

ARTICLE 13.

In the event of injuries or death to persons or damage to property caused by space vehicles, rockets, missiles, tellites and the like, the sovereign power by or through which the same have been launched shall be responsible d liable for all such damage without the requirement of any proof of fault, negligence, carelessness or reck-ssness.

ARTICLE 14.

An international insurance fund shall be established through some appropriate international association such the United Nations for the payment of compensation for such damages.

ARTICLE 15.

Proper provision shall be made for the international policing of Outer Space and for the protection of the oples and nations against violations of their rights therein.

ARTICLE 16.

All disputes arising directly and indirectly through the use of Outer Space and the interplanetary regions shall settled and determined solely by arbitration through accepted agency, court or tribunal to be designated by the vereign powers or by the United Nations.

ARTICLE 17.

The landing on any other planet containing life, or the occupation thereof, by earthman shall not give to any ion on earth any right of ownership or control of such other planet.

ARTICLE 18.

The peoples of the earth do hereby declare that they recognize the rights of sovereignty, ownership and con-l of any other planet by the inhabitants thereof.

ARTICLE 19.

War, in, by, or through space is hereby barred forever.

Attested to by:

William Roy Vallance

Secretary General

The entire Magna Carta of Space, with the exception of Article 7 thereof, was duly adopted by the Inter-American Bar Association at Bogota, mbia on February 3, 1961.

Article 7 was duly adopted by the Inter-American Bar Association at San Juan, Puerto Rico, on May 25, 1965.

Magna Ca

by William A. Hyn
President of Committee XV
Inter-America

Preamble

WHEREAS the General Assembly of the United Nations has recognized the common interest of mankind in Outer Space; and

WHEREAS it is the common aim that Outer Space should be used for peaceful purposes; and

WHEREAS Article 2, Paragraph 1, of the United Nations Charter provides that "the organization is based on the principle of the sovereign equality of all its members"; and

WHEREAS it is the aim and purpose of the Inter-American Bar Association to seek agreement to avoid the extension of national rivalries into this field, to promote energetic exploration and exploitation of Outer Space for the benefit of mankind; and

WHEREAS it is our belief that mankind will materially benefit should Outer Space be used for peaceful purposes only,

NOW, THEREFORE, BE IT RESOLVED by this Committee on Interplanetary Space that the Magna Carta of Space set forth herein be accepted and adopted by this Association, for the benefit of mankind, the establishment of peace and the avoidance of war.

Magna Carta of Space

ARTICLE 1.

All space shall be divided into Air Space and Outer Space.

ARTICLE 2.

All Air Space shall be deemed to be part of the sovereign jurisdiction of the subjacent land.

ARTICLE 3.

All Outer Space shall be deemed "res communis" (and not "terra nullius").

ARTICLE 4.

The interplanetary system shall be deemed "res communis" (and not "res nullius").

ARTICLE 5.

Recognition shall be given to the distinction between "res communis" and "terra nullius" (the former deny ing rights of appropriation and exclusive control by any one nation, the latter conceding such rights of appropria tion through the established principles of discovery, habitation and settlement).

ARTICLE 6.

Outer Space shall be used solely for peaceful purposes with freedom of exploration and exploitation thereo given to all peoples for the benefit of mankind.

ARTICLE 7.

There shall be no nuclear experiments in Outer Space.

ARTICLE 8.

Furthermore, since it is impossible to set out a boundary line with physical qualities such as characteri boundary lines on land and on the sea, that there be established a neutral zone embracing the upper limits of A Space and the lower limits of Outer Space to be known as "Neutralia" in which the right of innocent passage sha be recognized without offense to sovereignty. In this area of "Neutralia" there shall be the right of innocent pa sage of all craft, vehicles and objects of transit and movement without any such incident being deemed an invasi of sovereignty. In the event of any such innocent passage no nation shall have the right to attack or destroy su vehicle or object in transit or the nation from which the said vehicle or object was launched or to destroy any occ pants thereof without prior, sufficient warning and notice of claim of invasion of sovereignty and without pri opportunity for determination of the merits of such complaints by peaceful methods.

Magna Carta of Space

by William A. Hyman, A.B., LL.B., D.H.L.
New York City

President of Committee XVI on Interplanetary Space Law
of the Inter-American Bar Association

INTER-AMERICAN BAR ASSOCIATION

Adopted at

Bogota, Colombia on February 3, 1961
San Juan, Puerto Rico on May 25, 1965

14

MAGNA CARTA - NEW

Presented At The Congress of THE INTER-AMERICAN BAR ASSOCIATION, Bogota, Colombia, February 2, 1961

Resolution:

WHEREAS the General Assembly of the United Nations has recognized the common interest of mankind in Outer-Space; and

WHEREAS it is the common aim that Outer-Space should be used for peaceful purposes; and

WHEREAS Article 2, Paragraph 1, of the United Nations Charter, which provides that "the organization is based on the principle of the sovereign equality of all its members"; and

EXPLOITATION OF OUTER-SPACE WILL EVENTUALLY INCLUDE EXPLORATION OF A SATURN MOON THAT IS A UNIQUE "SPACE AMERICA" IN SIZE.

WHEREAS it is the aim and purpose of the Inter-American Bar Association to seek agreement to avoid the extension of national rivalries into this field, to promote energetic exploration and exploitation of Outer-Space for the benefit of mankind; and

SPACE BENEFIT TO COME---PASSENGER ROCKET-PLANES SOARING FROM U. S. TO ANY EARTHLY CITY, ARCHING THROUGH SPACE PART WAY, IN ONE SHORT HOUR.

WHEN BAD WEATHER GROUNDS AIRMAIL PLANES, FUTURE UNMANNED "MISSILE MAIL" WILL BE THE UNFAILING "CARRIER" MAKING THE ROUNDS.

WHEREAS it is our belief that mankind will materially

benefit should Outer-Space be used for peaceful purposes only,

NOW, THEREFORE, BE IT RESOLVED by this Committee on Interplanetary Space that *The Magna Carta* set forth herein be accepted and adopted by this Association, for the benefit of mankind, the establishment of peace and the avoidance of war.

THE MAGNA CARTA OF SPACE

Article 1 All space shall be divided into Air Space and Outer Space;

Article 2 All Air Space shall be deemed to be part of the sovereign jurisdiction of the subjacent land;

Article 3 All Outer-Space shall be deemed "res communis" (and not "terra nullius");

Article 4 The interplanetary system shall be deemed "res communis" (and not "res nullius");

Article 5 Recognition shall be given to the distinction between "res communis" and "terra nullius" (the former denying rights of appropriation and exclusive control by any one nation, the latter conceding such rights of appropriation through the established principles of discovery, habitation and settlement);

Article 6 Outer-Space shall be used solely for peaceful purposes with freedom of exploration and exploitation thereof given to all peoples for the benefit of mankind;

Article 7 There shall be no nuclear experiments in Outer Space; (See ahead for this item first being excluded then later accepted.)

Article 8 Futhermore, since it is impossible to set out a boundary line with physical qualities such as characterize boundary lines on land and on the sea, that there be established a neutral zone embracing the upper limits of Air Space and the lower limits of Outer-Space to be known as "Neutralia" in which the right of innocent passage shall be recognized without offense to sovereignty. In this area of

"Neutralia" there shall be the right of innocent passage of all craft, vehicles and objects of transit and movement without any such incident being deemed an invasion of sovereignty. In the event of any such innocent passage no nation shall have the right to attack or destroy such vehicle or object in transit or the nation from which the said vehicle or object was launched or to destroy any occupants thereof without prior, sufficient warning and notice of claim of invasion of sovereignty and without prior opportunity for determination of the merits of such complaints by peaceful methods;

Article 9 Provision shall be made for identification, registration and disclosure of intent of launchings of all space vehicles;

Article 10 Provision shall likewise be made for the peaceful recognition of rights and places for re-entry and landing of space vehicles;

Article 11 Provision shall be made for the allocation and control of radio frequencies;

Article 12 Provision shall be made for the avoidance of interference with aircraft by space vehicles and also by space vehicles with other space vehicles;

Article 13 In the event of injuries or death to persons or damage to property caused by space vehicles, rockets, missiles, satellites and the like, the sovereign power by or through which the same have been launched shall be responsible and liable for all such damage without the requirement of any proof of fault, negligence, carelessness or recklessness;

Article 14 An international insurance fund shall be established through some appropriate international association such as the United Nations for the payment of compensation for such damages;

Article 15 Proper provision shall be made for the international policing of Outer-Space and for the protection of the peoples and nations against violations of their rights therein;

Article 16 All disputes arising directly and indirectly

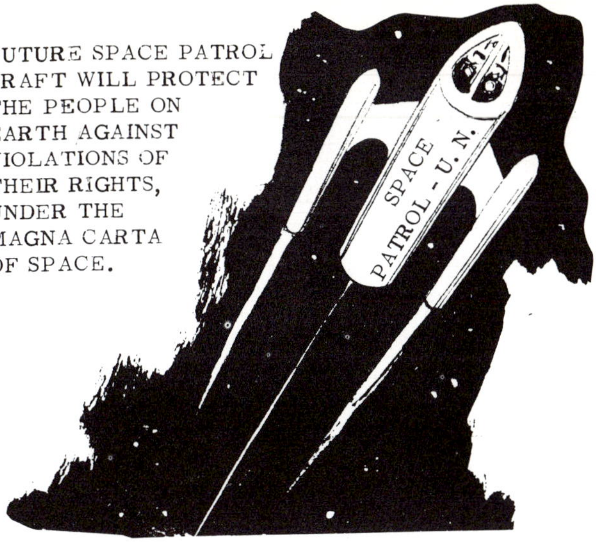

FUTURE SPACE PATROL CRAFT WILL PROTECT THE PEOPLE ON EARTH AGAINST VIOLATIONS OF THEIR RIGHTS, UNDER THE MAGNA CARTA OF SPACE.

through the use of Outer-Space and the interplanetary regions shall be settled and determined solely by arbitration through an accepted agency, court or tribunal to be designated by the sovereign powers or by the United Nations;

Article 17 The landing on any other planet containing life, or the occupation thereof, by earthman shall not give to any nation on earth any right of ownership or control of such other planet;

Article 18 The peoples of the earth do hereby declare that they recognize the rights of sovereignty, ownership and control of any other planet by the inhabitants thereof;

Article 19 War, in, by, or through space is hereby barred forever, and

IT IS FURTHER RESOLVED that the Article VII which reads as follows: "there shall be no nuclear experiments in Outer-Space" be deferred for further study and no action thereon be taken at this time," and

IT IS FURTHER RESOLVED that this *Magna Carta of Space* presented by the President of this Committee be favorably recommended to the General Assembly for acceptance at this session and that copies be sent to the United Nations and to the Governments of the nations interested in this subject.

Respectfully submitted,
William A. Hyman
President Committee XVI
Committee on Interplanetary Space

Nicolas Llinas Pimienta
Reporter

(The above Resolution was fully and duly approved by the Council and then by the General Assembly of the Inter-American Bar Association at Bogota, Colombia on February 3, 1961).

(Copies of the above were sent to all Delegations of the United Nations in May, 1961.)

(The above Resolution was subsequently ratified by the new Council and was duly passed by the Association on May 25, 1961.)

(The Article previously designated (g) in the Bogota version of the Magna Carta of Space was later duly approved as Article VII at the reaffirmation of the Magna Carta of Space at the Congress of the Inter-American Bar Association at San Juan, Puerto Rico on May 25, 1965---see ahead. "The amended Magna Carta of Space now fully approved as to all of its terms reads as follows:"

THE NUCLEAR BAN - A COSTLY FAILURE

Refusal of the Soviet Union and the United States until September 25, 1963, to ban nuclear tests, urged at Bogota, Colombia, in February 1961, has proven harmful.

The sole failure at the Bogota Conference related to clause (g), now designated as Article 7. This Article 7 provided:

> "There shall be no nuclear experiments in outer space."

It lost by one vote before this Committee in its debate at Bogota in February 1961.

Subsequently the Limited Nuclear Test Ban Treaty was signed in Moscow on August 5, 1963 by the United States of America, the United Kingdom of Great Britain and North

Ireland, and the Union of Soviet Socialist Republics.

It was ratified by the United States Senate on September 24, 1963 (U.S. Code & Adm. News, 88th Congress, First Session, 1963, page 1574).

In the period intervening between February 1961 when *The Magna Carta of Space* was adopted (with the exclusion of Article 7) up to the time this nuclear ban treaty was consummated, the fallout from the tremendous experiments conducted by the Soviet and by the United States attained an all-time high record for damage to people, life on earth, vegetation; and even to this day the world still suffers from the quantity of irradiated particles that have been falling upon distant parts of earth.

Last Soviet and American nuclear test series in 1961-62 attained all-time high in fallout, endangering life on earth.

The author's fight for inclusion of Article 7 finally won out. In May, 1965, at the Congress of the Inter-American Bar Association at San Juan, Puerto Rico, the writer's resolution again brought up Article 7 in *The Magna Carta* which would ban nuclear-testing on earth or in space.

The full version of this approval was reported in the Newsletter of the Inter-American Bar Association (Vol. 6, #3, July, 1965) as follows:

> "Committee XVI. Interplanetary Space Law
> "WHEREAS:
> "1. The Magna Carta of Space was duly approved by the XII Conference held in Bogota, Colombia, on February 3, 1961, except as to Article 7 (formerly designated Article g);
> "2. It was likewise duly approved by the new Council on May 25, 1961, in meeting held after the Conference at Bogota, Colombia; and
> "3. Article 7 (formerly Article g) provides 'That there shall be no nuclear experiments in outer-space'; and
> "4. The failure of the governments who possess the greatest nuclear capacity to ban such nuclear tests in outer-space between February 3, 1961, and September 25, 1963, resulted in much damage to the World in great fallout; and
> "5. The United States of America, the Soviet Union, and the United Kingdom of Great Britain, on September 25, 1963, ratified a treaty to ban nuclear tests in outer space,
> "RESOLVES:
> "To give full approval to Article 7 of the Magna Carta of Space which reads as follows: 'There shall be no nuclear experiments in outer-space.'

That provision was again presented to the Council of the Inter-American Bar at San Juan, Puerto Rico, but was "killed" on May 26 through arbitrary action. Certain delegates resented this action. The degree of their anger forced the reopening of the question which then was voted upon favorably on May 27, on which day the Plenary Session reversed itself and then duly ratified the ban against nuclear testing in space, formerly designated as Item (g) and now known as Article VII of *The Magna Carta of Space*. Much credit for this important reversal and ultimate triumph must be given to Mr. Roy Johns of Philadelphia, a brilliant lawyer and member of the Council.

Also, in the report of the American Assembly on Outer Space, in 1962, credit was given to the IABA for the suggestions made in *The Magna Carta* without accreditation to its originator. These suggestions included provisions for an international insurance fund, to provide compensation for victims of space activities, as well as other provisions previously mentioned by this author, who had suggested the creation of an international insurance fund as far back as 1958.

The wisdom and justification for Article 7 is particularly apparent today for the fact that it would prohibit nuclear tests in space, as well as on earth or in the atmosphere. For the testing-grounds of nuclear weapons tomorrow will be up there. Therefore, the task still remains of urging the Powers to sign an ironclad prohibition (rather than the non-enforceable agreement in the Nuclear Test Ban) against extending the atom's horrors into the space realm.

SPACE MAGNA CARTA ACCLAIMED

On May 11, 1961, Honorable John V. Lindsay of New York, one of the most distinguished members of the Congress of the United States recorded in the Congressional Record of 1961 these complimentary remarks concerning *The Magna Carta of Space*:

> "Mr. Speaker, I wish to call to the attention of my colleagues the proposed "Magna Carta of Space" adopted in February by the Inter-American Bar Association and recently submitted to the Secretary General of the United Nations.
>
> "The Magna Carta of Space was originally proposed in a speech by William A. Hyman, chairman of the Inter-American Bar Association's Committee on Interplanetary Space at a conference of the association in Bogota, Colombia, earlier this year.
>
> "Mr. Hyman is a distinguished attorney in New York City and under unanimous consent I include in the record excerpts from his scholarly and farsighted speech"...

Various authors have commented approvingly of various provisions embodied in *The Magna Carta*. One of the recent authors to do so is Mr. James T. Lyon in the chapter on "Space Law" contained in the book "Air Law" compiled by De Forest Billyou, published in 1964.

Referring to the resolution of the Inter-American Bar Association, adopted in its Bogota Conference, February 1961, approving the *Magna Carta.* Mr. Lyon emphasizes certain important features of this document, such as:

> "The division of space into zones of national and extra-national sovereignty; the legal status of outer-space and the interplanetary system (res communis); absolute liability for damage caused by spacecraft, and the creation of an international insurance fund for compensation for losses resulting from such damage; the international policing of outer-space; and the outlawing of war in space." (Erroneously, however, he states "This Resolution also is to be submitted to the United Nations". As a matter of fact, The Magna Carta of Space had already been submitted by the author to the United Nations, as well as to the official bodies, bar associations, scientific congresses and the like, in and before May, 1961)."

It is sufficient furthermore to cite only a few of the many comments made by some leading scholars and lawyers in this new field to indicate the world acceptance of this new space-oriented statement of "Humanitarian Rights", described by some also as a "World Bill of Rights" suitable for the Space Age.

Honorable Arturo A. Alafriz, the scholarly Solicitor General of the Republic of the Philippines and formerly President of the Philippine Lawyers' Association, in a letter to the author, states:

> "Please accept the congratulations of the Philippine Lawyers' Association and my own for having undertaken a selfless tremendous task in an unchartered field of law having as a direct result a Rule of Law where we now find chaos."

From the distinguished author-soldier-officer, Colonel Morton S. Jaffe, Legal Advisor to the Allied Forces of Southern Europe, came the following in a letter of November 20, 1964:

> "Your travels, writings, and speaking engagements over the

decade, I am sure, have played a leading and significant part in bringing about the awakening of the Bar and the public to the serious and challenging problems facing us in the Space Age. Your prodigious efforts, moreover, to advance the rule of law in space, have been marked uniquely by your sensitive appreciation of all mankind's vital interests in a world of peace and progress affecting, not only this planet, but the unplumbed seas beyond.

"All of us who share your interests in the field of space law and your aspirations for a world of peace under law are greatly in your debt. Your splendid efforts have earned our heartiest congratulations and deep gratitude."

Dr. Ernst Fasan of Austria, the eminent President of the Hermann Oberth Society (formerly the Rocket Society) paid the following tribute to the author:

"Your 'Magna Carta of Space' which has been acclaimed loudly all over the world, did receive in the last year the compliment of being in several principles repeated by the U.N. resolutions 1721 (XVI), 1884 (XVIII) and 1962 (XVIII). However, there remains one question unsettled: it is the question of the delimitation between airspace and outer-space."

The International Institute of Space Law at the session held at the Colloquium of Space Law in Paris September 26th through 27th, 1963, under the chairmanship of Dr. Michel Smirnoff, of Yugoslavia, a most highly esteemed international lawyer and scholar, discussed and acted approvingly on various provisions of

SPACE LAW PIONEER

Dr. Michel Smirnoff wrote the author a highly complimentary letter in which he said:

"As I am informed today, in the world space law literature, there are four projects of a new Space Law Convention:

"1. Haber, Wolf: A Draft Convention on International Law of Space, Michigan State Bar Journal, March 1959, vol. XXXVIII, p. 24-28.

"2. Dr. M. Smirnoff: The Role of IAF in the Elaboration of the Norms of Future Space Law, Proceedings of the Second Colloquium on The Law of Outer-Space, London 1959, Springer Verlag, Vienna, 1960, p. 147-155 (with the Draft of the Convention on the p. 151-and 152).

"3. Hyman, William A.: The Magna Carta of Space, XII Conferencia Inter-Americana de abogados, Bogota, Colombia, Enero-Febraio 1961.

"4. Faria, Escobar: Draft to an International Convenant for Outer-Space. Paper prepared to the XIth Congress of IAF in Stockholm, August 1960."

Also, from the late Hon. Adlai E. Stevenson, U.S. Representative to the United Nations, in regard to the author's Resolutions leading to The Magna Carta of Space as adopted by the Inter-American Bar Association:

> "Thank you for...the Resolutions of the committee which you chaired. I am well aware of the importance of the subject of space law and am glad to have the sentiments of the Inter-American Bar Association on this topic..."

In a letter dated February 16, 1965, S. Houston Lay, the able Director of the International Law Program of the American Bar Foundation (as distinguished from the American Bar Association), this request was made of the author:

> "The American Bar Foundation has underway a study of the law of activities in space. A part of this study will of course have to do with the question of space liability. I have known of your interests and activities in this field for a considerable period of time. If you have copies of materials which you have prepared on this subject I would be most pleased to receive them for use in connection with the Bar Foundation's study...
>
> "I would be particularly pleased to receive a copy of The Magna Carta of Space adopted at Bogota, Colombia in 1961 and references to any discussions of the document."

A reply was made to him on the writer's behalf as of

February 20, 1965, by William Roy Vallance, the very capable Secretary General of the Inter-American Bar Association, part of which states:

> "As you know, Mr. William A. Hyman, 111 Fulton Street, New York 38, New York, is the distinguished Chairman of this Committee and presented the important Magna Carta on Space Law that was adopted at our XIIth Conference in Bogota in 1961. Mr. Hyman's Committee includes the following members:
>
> Brazil: Jorge Alberto de Sousa Freitas, Sizinio Rodriguez;
>
> Colombia: Diego Llinas Pimienta, Nicholas Llinas Pimienta, James Raisbeck;
>
> El Salvador: Jose Antonio Rivera, Jr.;
>
> Peru: Augusto Inostroza;
>
> United States: Edward S. Corlett, Matthew J. Corrigan, John O. Dahlgren, Madeline C. Dinu, Leon Dreskin, Luis E. Guillen, Roy W. Johns, Richard C. Peet, Claude Pepper, John E. Stephen."

It would be unduly burdensome to quote further evidence of the recognition of the importance of *The Magna Carta of Space*. However, nothing would be more suitable than to conclude with the reproduction of the award given on November 22, 1964, which reads as follows:

"The Editors of
SPACE WORLD MAGAZINE
are proud to present its 1964 award for the
Most Significant Space Achievement
to
WILLIAM A. HYMAN
for his outstanding concept of
Space Law
as expressed in his
Magna Carta of Space
as an important guideline
to future international cooperation in the field of astronautics
and its impact on
WORLD PEACE".

The Magna Carta of Space, a declaration of World Human Rights or an International Bill of Rights, furnishes the guidelines for all nations and persons to pursue the course to the great goal to which we all aspire so anxiously and perhaps so impatiently at this moment---the protection of mankind against self destruction---the substitution of a rule of law and justice in lieu of a rule of force and fratricide---the rule so aptly stated by Pope Paul VI:

"Force of Right instead of the Right of Force."

To which a voice from the past adds:

"Justice is the great interest of man on earth. It is the ligament which holds civilized nations together.
Daniel Webster"

15

THE ATOM IN SPACE

IN THE adoption of *The Magna Carta* by the Inter-American Bar Association in Bogota, Colombia, in February, 1961, the provision to ban nuclear experiments in outer-space (item g or Article 7) was lost by one vote due to the fact that some delegates left the meeting place before the vote was taken, on the assumption that there would be no objection to this provision.

This provision was to have great significance only shortly afterwards, before the end of the year, when the then-current "moratorium" on nuclear tests was abruptly and shockingly broken by the Soviet Union.

Commencing on September 1, 1961, and continuing on various days thereafter, the Soviet Union detonated seventy-one nuclear bombs in airspace and outer-space (roughly between 10 miles and 350 miles altitude). Fallout occurred over the Western World, increasing radiation as much as thirty-five times in some places and in the Alaskan regions about sixty-five times, with its well-known threat not only to present generations but to future generations.

The high nuclear explosions, which occurred in the lower regions of outer-space, performed by the United States and the USSR, have had consequences which threatened the health of mankind. The fall-out is known to have contaminated vegetation, milk and other items of food. In one of the largest H-bomb experiments of the U.S. the Van Allen Radiation Belt was affected. A new radiation belt was created, causing new hazards of an unknown nature.

Without going into the intricacies of atomic explosions and testing, it is, however, pertinent to our discussion to ascertain whether any nation indulging in this type of experiment in an area that is res communis thereby inter-

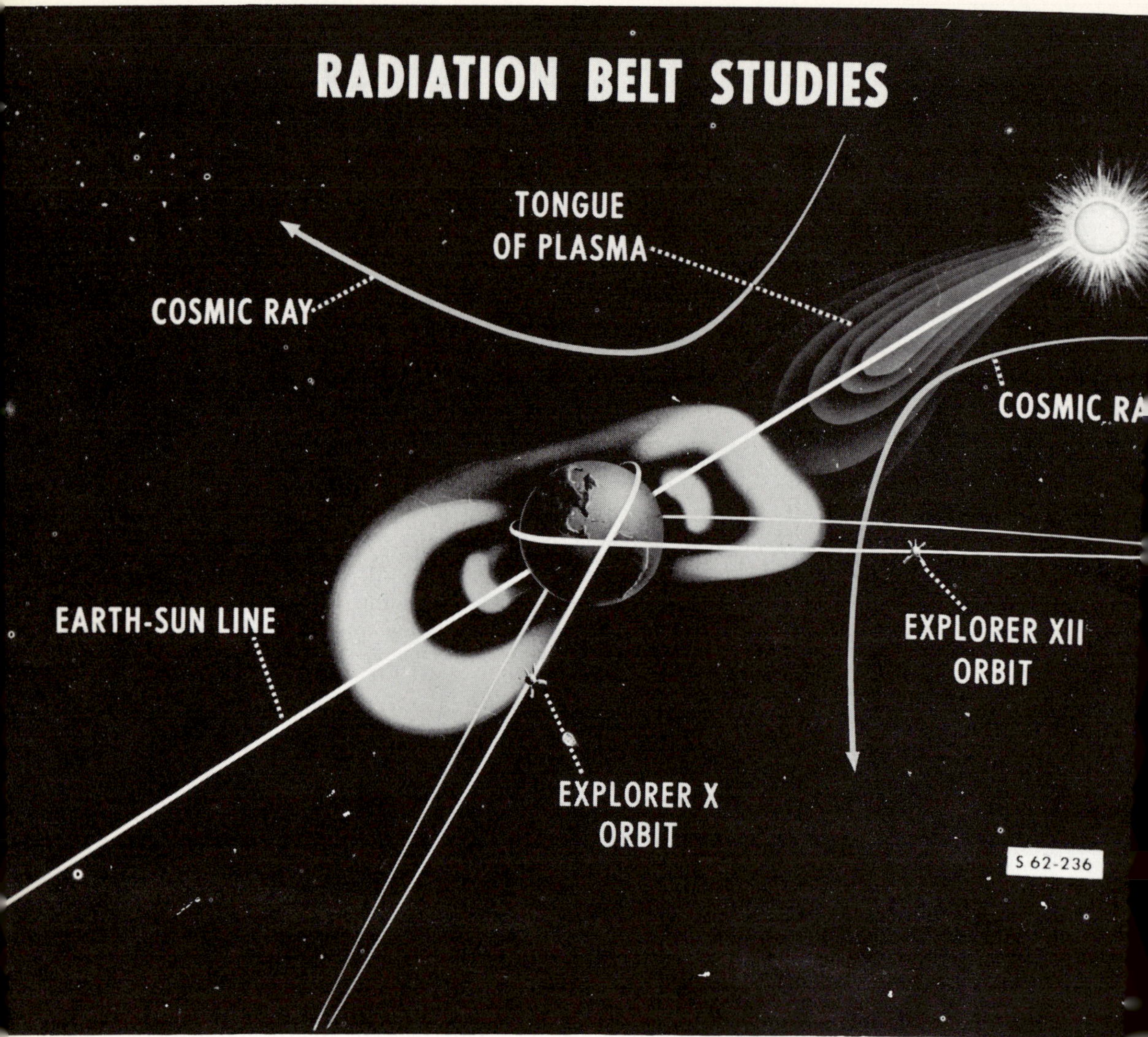

H-bombs exploded in space in 1962 affected the existing Van Allen Belts, created a new radiation belt, and damaged the instrumentation of five satellites.

feres with the rights of all nations as joint owners of space, and particularly the right to be free from injury to their people on earth by reason of such testing and its fall-out. Again, this is a question that can be determined through legal process, and by this is meant agreement through the United Nations or by treaty amongst the nations, to prohibit the use of space for such purposes.

Admittedly, though the Soviet and the United States con-:ol the great arsenals of nuclear weapons---the power to estroy the world---neither one would deliberately set off catastrophic world conflagration. Each knows too well the navoidable consequences of such an undertaking. Yet the hreat comes from an unintentional precipitation, from some ncident not controlled by either side against which neither as taken adequate precautions.

The risk lies in the creation of an unintended war set off by an innocent occurrence which is construed as a warlike ict. It also may readily come from the measures taken by either nation for defensive purposes which spring into action as a result of misinformation by some third party without consultation of either of the two world monopolists of nuclear arsenals. A missile accidentally dropped in New York by the Soviet or an American missile dropped accidentally in Moscow could be construed as such an intentional attack.

SPACE IS HERE TO STAY --- ARE WE?

The two giants who control the nuclear armaments of the world, the United States and Russia, are also striving for superiority in space. Both are spending tremendous sums for tests and exploration which must affect all mankind. Is this merely a race to attain a superior capacity---to destroy the world? This is not to be construed, of course, as disloyalty; but unless the common man speaks out and makes his voice heard through international law, there will be no means of stopping the mad race to space-nuclear death.

The problem is further complicated by the other nations that have achieved atomic-bomb technology, Red China being the most recent and notable. According to the Atomic Energy Commission, the total number of nuclear tests---whether the atomic (fission) or thermonuclear (fusion) types---carried out by these nations up to May 1965 are as follows:

United States	337
Soviet Union	127
Britain	24

France-------------------	5
Red China ---------------	2
	495 . . . Total

The largest known nuclear device exploded by the United States had a yield of 25 megatons (25 million tons of TNT).

In its 1961 tests, Russia announced a final giant blast of 55 to 65 megatons, and intimated that it could easily escalate this to 100 megatons if desired---in one bomb.

Nuclear experts have foretold the fearful results of such a 100 megaton blast. Its fireball alone, at ground-zero, would be seven miles in diameter, or large enough to instantly destroy almost the entire island of Manhattan plus surrounding segments of Long Island and New Jersey, wiping out some 15 million people in one-thousandth of a second.

The later fallout of this 100-megaton bomb would kill any living creature up to 620 miles downwind, and produce severe radiation-sickness upwind for 500 miles.

The estimated effects of a 500-megaton monster-bomb (if such were ever insanely made) are even more nightmarish. Exploded at orbital height about 250 miles high, its radiation flash (gamma rays) alone would instantly wipe out life in an area equal to one-third of the United States.

The following blast of radiant heat (infra-red rays) from that same horrifying bomb would then ignite everything---even steel---and create a "fire-storm" that would literally burn to ashes some 1,000,000 square miles of earthly territory beneath it.

If this 500-megaton terror were exploded over the North Atlantic Ocean, its heat would boil up a vast "geyser" and start off a tidal-wave that would drown every port along the coasts of America and Europe, then rage inland for 250 miles with the fury of a dozen hurricanes.

Another ghastly statistic---even if 1000 miles away, any person who happened to be gazing in the direction of the fireball when it appeared would be blinded for life.

Only twenty of the biggest U.S. nuclear tests combined in one---or eight of the Soviet's largest---would equal one 500-megaton bomb.

Note that this macro-nuclear weapon would be "wasted"

A 500-TON THERMONUCLEAR "MONSTER BOMB" EXPLODED 250 MILES HIGH WOULD WIPE OUT ALL LIFE IN 1/3 OF AMERICA, BURN 1,000,000 MILES OF LAND TO ASHES IN A "FIRE-STORM", AND BLIND ALL PEOPLE OUTDOORS IN A RADIUS OF 1,000 MILES.

near earth and would be most effective in space, at the altitude where USA and USSR spacecraft orbit today, with the capacity to annihilate or maim 100 million people in a populated area, at one stroke. Exploded over the heart of either Russia or the United States, one-third to one-half of the nation below would become a smoking, lifeless ruin, leaving the rest staggering and helpless from the blow.

A stark formula comes out of this by plain mathematics: Nuclear-power plus Space equals National Death.

FATAL FALLOUT

We have already had some sobering, if not frightening, experiences with fallout. In 1953, some 200 miles from the Atomic Energy Commission's proving-grounds in Nevada, ranchers sued the Government for the loss of about a thousand sheep on whom fallout had allegedly descended.

The earliest atom-tests in 1945 also sent swirling clouds of fallout down on a herd of cattle, not fatally harming them but turning their hair grey. Fallout from Nevada's nuclear explosions also went far afield and contaminated cornstalks in Indiana. Before this was discovered, the stalks had been used in the manufacture of paper-boxes, later used by Eastman Kodak in Rochester, N.Y., to ship film---all of which was ruined, being fogged by gamma-radiations (similar to X-rays) that came from the contaminated containers.

An unknown but widespread amount of strontium-90, one of the by-products of the nuclear bombs exploded in 1961-63 by Russia and America, after the Nuclear Test Moratorium was broken, settled down on grazing grounds all over the world. Cows eating this contaminated fodder passed the radioactive strontium-90 into their milk, which caused some degree of bone damage in children since strontium tends to replace calcium in bone-marrow.

The world wants peace not war---hot or cold. It is tired of continued international provocations which constantly threaten the peace of the world.

To maintain and guarantee the sovereignty and security of nations and particularly the security of the people of the world, peace itself does not mean the continuance of the status quo. Peace connotes the right of the common man the world over to live, to survive, to progress, to exercise the fundamental principles of equality, liberty and freedom under law, and in a society under proper supervision.

It may be suggested, further, that an international agreement should condemn the use of space for the passage of military aircraft, vehicles or objects unless prior permission shall have been first obtained. Regulations limiting sovereignty, the classification of space, definitions of "peaceful" and "non-military" and "non-aggressive" purposes could all be included in the framework of a preliminary international code.

Political differences between nations pose no insuperable obstacles to such an agreement. It has been suggested in a number of quarters that differences between East and West are not necessarily applicable in the area of sovereignty in space. It was recently stated that when "the political coating is removed from the heterogeneous mass of commentary, it is found that remarkable agreement exists between the writings of the Soviet Peoples Republic's experts and the view-points of their brother legal experts in other countries of the world."

Although complaint has been made by Russian commentators that the United Nations has not taken a sufficiently active role in promoting space regulation, and the comment has been made that "although we are sure that the initiative of the United Nations in this field is the only offical way of solving this problem", the fact is indisputable that the failure to obtain better results is due to the barrier of fear, of suprise attack, possessing the nuclear giants.

CONTAMINATION CRISIS

Significantly, the treaty to ban nuclear tests was proposed in July, 1963, by the late President John F. Kennedy, after realization of the disastrous fall-out which occurred through the nuclear experiments in space and the harm through radiation fall-out occurring to people in different parts of the world. The agreement was accepted by both the USSR and the United Kingdom. The United States Senate ratified it on September 24, 1963, and it went into effect on October 10, 1963---more than two and one-half years after it had been first proposed by the author at Bogota, Colombia.

During that interim between February 1, 1961 (when the IABA endorsed *The Magna Carta*) and October 10, 1963 (the signing of the Nuclear Test Ban) both the Soviet and America conducted nuclear tests.

The U.S. was keeping the previous unwritten nuclear "moratorium" faithfully, but on September 1, 1961, a Soviet bomb shattered the world quiet as related before.

The world was shocked. After a period of soul-searching and sampling of world-opinion the U.S. finally decided to conduct its own nuclear tests, the unwritten moratorium being completely wrecked. However, no American bomb exceeded the 25-megaton range of power, and there was a conscious attempt by U.S. nuclear scientists to produce relatively "clean" bombs that spead a minimum of fall-out around the world.

But there is no question that the world, and including the USA and USSR, became perturbed at the amount of fall-out from their nuclear tests of 1961-63 that kept settling down long afterward in many densely populated and widely scattotal areas of earth. After their two series of tests, both America and Russia unilaterally cut them off completely. World moral opinion, never a force to be taken lightly, subdued the atom and there was relative quiet again except for underground tests which were confined and scattered no radiation poisons through the atmosphere.

Since Nuclear Test Ban of 1963, America has conducted only relatively safe underground nuclear tests, spreading little fallout into the atmosphere.

But the stark truth is that these two major series of tests by the two nuclear rivals poured far more dangerous fall-out into the air than all previous atomic or hydrogen bomb explosions combined, even including all of Britain's tests. Maps and charts sobered all the people of earth, showing where clouds of radioactive particles had swirled down here and there on earth, blanketing whole countries or half a continent at a time.

Nike-Zeus anti-missiles with atomic warheads---salvos of these in any nuclear war would spread fallout over our own country as they intercepted enemy ICBMs hurtling over the North Pole over Canada, toward the U. S. heartland.

An ineradicable amount of strontium-90, a deadly and long-lasting ingredient of fall-out, was deposited on vegetation, eaten by cattle and thereby transmitted into milk and beef. The statistics on long-range genetic damage to unborn generations, like all statistics, were controversial, but none of the experts denied that some damage had been dealt to the human race as a whole. Fortunately, neither the American nor Russian tests lasted long enough to produce lethal proportions of fall-out that could cause severe radiation sickness or death.

But in effect, most of the three billion inhabitants of earth breathing in the contaminated air after those tests had received a sort of invisible shot of arsenic or cyanide.

All this could have been avoided if *The Magna Carta of Space* (or any similar skeletal code geared to the benefit of mankind) had been adopted in February of 1961, which had been the author's hope. Lost to mankind were two-and-one-half senseless, uncontrolled, scientifically irresponsible years, before the Nuclear Test Ban (still only a partial lame-duck agreement) wiped out some nuclear neuroticism and brought a certain measure of scientific sanity.

But was it worth the price to go that long without space and nuclear law? How much more are we allegedly intelligent creatures on this planet going to pay, unnecessarily, for continued lawlessness in outer-space?

16

WANTED –
A POLICEMAN IN SPACE!

THE BARRIER of millions of words in fruitless discussion over a period of almost five years after the Space Age started was pierced on February 3, 1961 at Bogota, Colombia when the distinguished Inter-American Bar Association accepted and approved *The Magna Carta.*

Subsequently, authenticated copies were duly transmitted to the Secretary General of the United Nations, to all the Missions at the United Nations, and to numerous associations of lawyers, universities and public officials in various parts of the world.

On September 25, 1962, at Varna, Bulgaria, this writer presented to the Congress of the International Astronautical Federation and the International Institute of Space Law, *The Magna Carta* which received the enthusiastic approval of the vast majority of the delegates there assembled.

The next day, on the 26th of September, 1962, when at that Congress the author presided in the Chair over the Section on Space Law and Sociology, Professor Y. A. Korovin, recognized academician and high-ranking member of the Soviet legal profession, took the position that the acceptance of a statement of basic principles, such as are contained in *The Magna Carta* was interwoven with the consummation of a disarmament agreement and that the Soviet could not have one without the other. He indicated, however, that there was acquiescence to the establishment of agreements on such matters of secondary importance as meteorology and telecommunications.

This limited view, however, was not accepted by the other delegates who were present and who believed that such a statement of basic principles (as set forth in *The Magna Carta of Space*) was necessary in order to take up the lag in law.

Controversy also has ensued between the followers of two

schools of thought. The one group believes there should be no statement of basic principles, but that in lieu thereof we should wait until an extensive code can be prepared covering all contingencies and experiences. The trend, however has been in favor of the short, concise statement of general and basic principles immediately rather than to await the passage of more time while further legal explorations are being made to establish an extensive code of regulations. This short statement of basic principles was what the author sought to accomplish in *The Magna Carta of Space.*

WHY THE MAGNA CARTA OF SPACE?

If the space-law vacuum continues and brings war to the space vacuum, this scene might well represent a hostile nuclear missile aimed at destroying an American space-station with 20 astronaut lives lost.

The miracles of science proceed at a rate of speed not commensurate with the comprehension of the world. The scientist, perhaps unwillingly and without intent, has placed the attainment of his scientific objectives ahead of the protection of human rights---simply because law is behind science. We hear of the development of missile might at sea, on the land, in the air and in space---tremendous preparations for destruction and little preparation for consummation and preservation of peace, except by the connotation that increased armaments mean increased assurances for continuance of peace according to political leaders. That this is a fallacy has been demonstrated in the First and Second World Wars by the defeated Germans and the destruction caused by the mad dictator, Adolf Hitler.

Fear or courage---which shall it be?

One takes us on the course to ultimate destruction---the other to the preservation of mankind. The powerful nations today are more powerful, richer and above all, more capable of helping those who need help.

"Help me!", emanating from the different parts of the underprivileged world must, and can be answered now. But help without regard to protection in the future constitutes only a temporary palliative. Never before in the history of mankind has the realization been brought upon us that in the

A FUTURE HITLER MIGHT BE MADMAN ENOUGH TO UTILIZE SPACE MILITARY TECHNOLOGY TO CONQUER THE WORLD, UNLEASHING EARTH-WIDE HOLOCAUST.

heavens---where exists a vast turbulence of winds, cosmic rays, radiation perils, and world-instantaneous communications, and also the path to surprise instantaneous destruction ---there is provided therein the compulsion for joint action through an agency of unity such as the United Nations, for universal involvement in providing help and an ultimate solution against man's mad impulses to destroy man.

Pope Paul VI, in his vibrant appeal for peace made at Castel Gandolfo in Italy on August 26, 1964, said there were new symptoms of the reappearance of divisions among peoples, races and cultures.

"This spirit of division is guided by nationalistic pride, by prestige politics, the armaments race, social and economic antagonisms," he said. This warning, enunciated also by other eminent leaders of the great faiths and world powers and leaders of the common man, must be heeded.

The threat of catastrophic destruction initiated by these moral violations must be averted. It can be averted---by universal adoption of *The Magna Carta* as the law of space, supplementing the general world-wide approval already given to this guideline to rights and obligations in the outer world of the planetary regions.

POLICING OF SPACE

In this book, an objective perspective has been maintained in order to arrive at a fair understanding of the problems arising in space. The guideline herein was simple honesty.

The true vacuum in space is law. *The Magna Carta of Space* will help fill that vacuum.

The common man, the basis of society the world over, wants law in space---the guarantee of peace on earth. Science is based on honesty in its field. Law likewise should be based on honesty of thought and action and not be controlled by expediency.

Most fitting in these troubled times are the words of the poet Yevtushenko:

> "One day posterity will remember
> This strange era, these strange times, when
> Ordinary common honesty was called courage."

The airplane ended the era of multiple worlds and initiated the era of one world. The invasion and conquest of space has made us all in effect, one people---mankind---even though each nation retains its own autonomous government. Any failure, at this time, to recognize this concept of space cooperation will necessarily invite in the near future the unleashing of vicious ambitions and the creation of tremendous means and opportunities for world destruction.

Let it be noted that in this book the author does not purport to cover each and every problem arising now in this great Age of Space. This book does not pretend to cover every legal reference, session of committees, discussion of delegates. It undertakes only to give the highlights of recent developments, to show the trend of past and present thought, and to direct the attention of the reader to the major issues developed by this present situation. If it has succeeded in posing some of the problems current in the Age of Space, then it will have served its purpose.

This constitutes a challenge to men of good will the whole world over. It moreover constitutes a challenge to the lawyers of the world upon whose advice and guidance depend the establishment and maintenance of a society of law and order without which peace cannot prevail.

It poses the problem whether, through the careful guidance of the legal profession, the governments of the world can be persuaded and induced to resolve all these pressing questions by voluntary agreement and not by force of arms---and in this manner bring an end to the cold war and the prevention of a hot war. The writer has abiding faith that the great profession of law can and will rise to meet this tremendous challenge.

A law or treaty which is not enforceable is a nullity. We have discussed the force of public opinion behind international treaties and international law. We have come however, to the realization that it is necessary also to have a competent police authority to implement an international treaty regulating the use of space.

First of all, of course, will be the need to amend the Charter of the United Nations, to extend the jurisdiction of that august and most important international body into space.

It must be freed from its earthbound chains.

This was recognized by the Ad Hoc Committee on Space of the United Nations in its report in June, 1959 when recommendation was made to this effect. The late President John F. Kennedy in his dramatic and effective plea urged that the Charter of the United Nations be made applicable to space. Ex-premier Nikita S. Khrushchev, speaking on behalf of the Soviet, exchanged communications with President Kennedy pledging cooperation in space. Yet up to the present time the U.N. has not followed through.

At international space-law convention in Athens, Greece, September 1965, Cosmonauts Belyayev and "Walk-in-Space" Leonov greet Astronauts Gordon Cooper and Charles Conrad, in sincere wishes for cooperation in space between Soviet Union and United States.

Supplementing this extension of jurisdiction into space, there must be the means of enforcing the law. A traffic regulation without the traffic officer becomes a cause of confusion rather than a step toward order and safety. The history of the United Nations has shown that when the occasion required implementation by proper policing, this helped to prevent a world conflagration and a holocaust which would have meant the destruction of mankind.

Iran, Korea, the Suez, the Congo and the Vietnam events indicate the propriety and the necessity for such police implementation.

This should in the case of space regulation be given immediate attention and supplemented by immediate action.

Such a police power invested in the U.N. would, of course, be just for the purposes indicated, i.e., to police activities in space but not the power to wage aggressive war against any nation or group of nations.

SPACE EMIGRATION?

We come to another aspect of space for which laws will be even more vital. The distinguished scientist, Dr. A. S. Parkes, Mary Marshall Professor of the Physiology of Reproduction, University of Cambridge, one of the world's great physiologists, recently reported that inevitable problems of a most serious nature will be created by the population explosion.

"In 1930", quoting from Dr. Parkes, "the population of the world was about 2000 million. By 1954, it was thought that it was about 2500 million and that it might rush up to 3000 million within the lifetime of many of us". As a matter of fact, it is now over 3000 million. He furthermore added, "Estimates of 10,000 million by the next century, which a few years ago seemed fantastic, seem conservative in the light of present trends".

It is estimated that "with the present rate of increase, it can be calculated that in 600 years the number of human beings on Earth will be such that there will be only one square yard for each to live on"---and yet it has been only about five hundred years since that eventful day in 1492 when America was discovered and the world seemed endless, big and empty.

Also according to a recent report on population growth issued by the United Nations, 2,000,000 new lives are born every seven days---100,000,000 annually.

Where will man go?

The cynics maintain there are three factors which provide the major checks to this tremendous explosion. They are famine, disease and war.

Medical science is devoting itself to eliminating disease. Longevity has already been increased as a result of these studies, thus adding a greater number of older people to the world's population. Reduction of infant mortality due to science contributes to this result.

Governments fearing the political reverberations arising from bitterness of the suffering of the undernourished, have made tremendous efforts to relieve the under-privileged and to limit famine. Reduction of famine also adds to the number of the living. Both, therefore, contribute to the acceleration of the population explosion.

The third factor, war, now raging in various parts of the world and always rearing its ugly head where and when least expected, is being attacked through various agencies of government and appeals to the morals and the reason of world leaders.

Emphasis is laid by government on the creation of greater and more devastating weapons of destruction in the effort to maintain the murderous "balance of terror". If a small amount of the cost of contemplated extermination were devoted to the cause of survival, undoubtedly science, aided by the restraint of law, would give us greater assurance of peace and a better guarantee against extinction.

Today is the day of the irrevocable decision. Once a world-nuclear devastating attack has been made there can be no recalling that blow. There cannot even be sufficient retaliation to avoid world catastrophe.

If war is to become the blind answer to the world's population pressure, then space may come into the picture.

Migrations to the planets fulfilling the mandate, "It is not too late to live a newer life", to areas where life is sustainable and protected against the war ravages of earthman, are not more fantastic than they seemed, in the days of Columbus, the future migrations into the new western world.

And even here the law must precede the space colonists.

It is generally conceded that effective occupation (now considered necessary to ripen the inchoate right of discovery) of outer-space and interplanetary system even by

IN THE WORDS OF OUR BELOVED AND MOURNED PRESIDENT JOHN F. KENNEDY---"TO INVOKE THE WONDERS OF SCIENCE...EXPLORE THE STARS..." ---SPACE MAY YIELD:

ORBIT FARMS TO
END WORLD FAMINE!

MOLTEN METALS
FROM MERCURY!

ASTEROID
"GOLD STRIKES"!

MEDICINES FROM
MARTIAN HERBS!

PETROLEUM
FROM VENUS!

manned satellites is a physical impossiblity or will be of limited degree. Thus, the classification of this area as "terra nullius" becomes quite inapplicable. The more effective formulation would be based on the theory of "res communis". Under such a theory national monopoly of space or the interplanetary bodies would be forbidden. Under this theory nations would be entitled to share equally all the areas of outer-space and the interplanetary bodies.

However, this possible escape from a war-wrecked earth may come too late. A haven out among the planets is too faint a hope for the near future, and it would be far better to make life safe right here on our home planet.

SPACE LAW MEANS EARTH PEACE

In his inaugural address on January 20, 1961, the late President John F. Kennedy made the following plea for peace:

> "Finally, to those nations who would make themselves our adversary, we offer not a pledge but a request: that both sides begin anew the quest for peace, before the dark powers of destruction unleashed by science engulf all humanity in planned or accidental self-destruction."

All sane and sincere peoples the world over subscribe to and join in this plea for peace. War is the dread of mankind. Peace is the proclaimed wish.

There are those cynics who doubt the efficacy of law in outer-space. The following quotations from the "Pages from an Old Volume of Life" should constitute an answer to those negative experts who see such hopelessness:

> "Of relative justice law may know something; of expediency it knows much; with absolute justice it does not concern itself."

However, some law clearly is better than no law. While not perfect and subject in the future to some modification, as experience develops in the problems occurring in space,

The Magna Carta will serve as the necessary guideline for an orderly society in the Universe.

We cannot render any greater service to those desiring peace in the world than to quote another of the resounding and brilliant statements made by the revered President Kennedy in his address to the United Nations on September 25, 1961. He stated on this momentous occasion in connection with this present world crisis:

> "And as we extend the rule of law on earth, so must we also extend it to man's new domain: Outer-Space.
> "All of us salute the brave cosmonauts of the Soviet Union. The new horizons of outer-space must not be riven by the old bitter concepts of imperialism and sovereign claims. The old reaches of the universe must not become the new arena of an even colder war.
> "The events and decisions of the next . . . . months may well decide the fate of man for the next 10,000 years. There will be no avoiding these events. There will be no appeal from these decisions. And we . . . .shall be remembered either as part of the generation that turned this planet into a flaming funeral pyre or the generation that met its vow 'to save succeeding generations from the scourge of war.' "

In his earlier Inaugural Address on January 20, 1961, President Kennedy stated:

> "The world is very different now. For man holds in his mortal hands the power to abolish all forms of human poverty, and all forms of human life".

President Kennedy called upon all sides:

> "To invoke the wonders of science instead of its terrors...to explore the stars, to conquer the deserts, eradicate disease, tap the ocean depths and encourage the arts and commerce".

All sane and sincere peoples subscribe to and join in this plea for peace which has been reiterated and sincerely carried on by his successor---President Lyndon B. Johnson.

On January 30, 1965, President Johnson in a report to

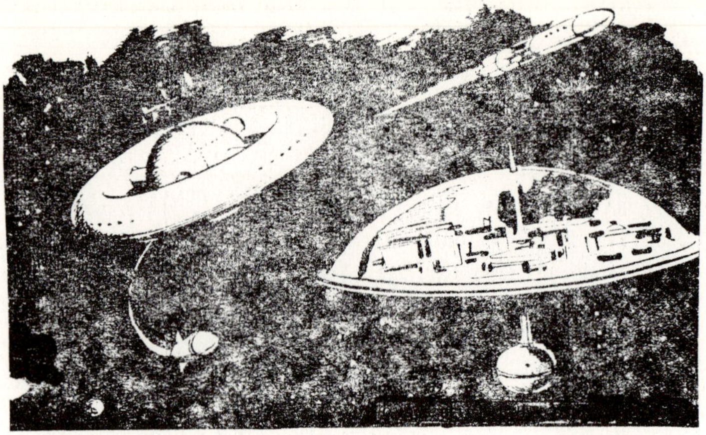

MASS MIGRATIONS OF EARTH PEOPLE TO OTHER PLANETS IS NO WAY TO ESCAPE NUCLEAR HOLOCAUST ON EARTH, UNTIL TOWARD THE END OF THIS CENTURY.

Congress referred to the United States as a "spacefaring" nation. He went on to cite that the:

> "practical uses of the benefits of space technology were almost commonplace around the globe---warning us of gathering storms (Tiros satellites), guiding our ships at sea (Transit), assisting our mapmakers (ANNA and OGO), and serving, most valuably of all, to bring the peoples of many nations closer together in joint peaceful endeavors."

Through NASA, as a matter-of-fact, the United States is engaged in cooperative research rocket programs and space projects with more than 70 nations.

Taking a well-measured glimpse into the future, the President added:

> "We shall expand our earth laboratories into space laboratories, and extend our national strength into the space dimension."
> But his keynote again and again was one overriding issue that all people on earth are most concerned about: "We are determined that space shall be an avenue toward peace, and we both invite and welcome all men to join with us in this great opportunity."

The author spoke before many international law and astronautic conventions, proposing space law since 1956, culminating in the "Magna Carta of Space" as set forth in this book.

"Peace...all men"....President Johnson's message could hardly be more explicit.

It is in accordance with this very same thought and hope that the author has given this "report" on *The Magna Carta* whose official and international adoption he firmly believes will be a sure and certain step in the attainment of peace on earth among all mankind. While no remedy can be perfect, this basic set of space laws can help establish order, not only in space but on earth.

Inevitably, there seems attached to our space venture the whole earthly issue of human rights and mankind's betterment. Not on a local, nationalistic, or even international basis, but on an "earthmen" basis which, like an orbiting satellite, looks down equally and impartially on every land and every person living on this small planet.

There is no special formula or secret principle contained in *The Magna Carta.* It is based on very old and simple verities....

NO MAN IS AN ISLAND ENTIRE OF ITSELF
EVERY MAN IS A PIECE OF THE CONTINENT
A PART OF THE MAIN
IF A CLOD BE WASHED AWAY BY THE SEA
EUROPE IS THE LOSS
AS WELL AS IF A PROMONTORY WERE
AS WELL AS IF A MANOR OF THY FRIENDS
OR OF THINE OWN WERE
ANY MAN'S DEATH DIMINISHES ME
BECAUSE I AM INVOLVED IN MANKIND
AND THEREFORE NEVER SEND TO KNOW
FOR WHOM THE BELLS TOLLS...
IT TOLLS FOR THEE

John Donne

In lawlessness on earth or in space, there is chaos, war, and destruction. In law there is justice. In justice there is peace for all men.

APPENDIX A

BIBLIOGRAPHY

Becker, Loftus, A Symposium on Space Law, United States Foreign Policy and the Development of Law for Outer Space, JAG Journal (February, 1959).

von Behk, Dr. Harald J., The Incidence of Motion Sickness During Exposures to the Weightless State, XIth International Astronautical Congress, (Stockholm, 1960).

Beirne, Francis F., The War of 1812, (1949).

Billingham, J., Control of Microclimate Temperature in Very Hot Environment, XIth International Astronautical Congress (Stockholm, 1960).

Bishop, International Law

von Braun, Dr. Wernher, various speeches, letters, and writings

Bushnell, David, The Impact of Space Technology on Medical Research, Annual Meeting of the American Rocket Society (Washington, D.C.,1959).

Carlson, Loren D., Requirements for Monitoring Physiological Function in Space Flights, XIth International Astronautical Congress (Stockholm, 1960).

Cheng, Bin, International Law and High Altitude Flight: Balloons and Man Made Satellites, International and Comparative Law Quarterly, Vol. 6 (1957).

Coerman, R. R., The Effects of Buffeting on the Human Body, XIth International Astronautical Congress (Stockholm, 1960).

Columbus, Christopher, Christopher Columbus: His Own Book of Privileges (1502).

Commager, Henry S., The Blue and the Gray, Vol. 1.

Cooper, John Cobb, Legal Problems of Upper Space, Journal of Air Law and Commerce, Vol. 23 (1956).
--- Outer Space and the Law, Astronautics (October, 1961).
--- Various articles.

Donworth, Albert B., Why Columbus Sailed (2ND Ed., 1953).

Faria, J. Escobar, L.L.B., Draft of an International Covenant for Outer Space, XIth International Astronautical Congress (Stockholm, 1960).

Feldman, George J., Jurisdiction in Space, Address before the Federal Bar Association of New York, New Jersey and Connecticut (October, 1958).

Fenwick, International Law (3RD Ed., 1948).

Gabrouski, Tudor, Reflections on the Jurisdictional Problems of the Extra-Aeronautical Space And the Reconnaissance-Satellites, Fifth Colloquium on the Law of Outer Space (Varna, Bulgaria, 1962).

Gal, Gyula, Some Legal Aspects of the Uses of Reconnaissance Satellites, Fifth Colloquium on the Law of Outer Space (Varna, Bulgaria, 1962).

Galina, A., On the Question of International Law, Current Digest of the Soviet Press, Vol. X, No. 33 (September 1958).

Graves, William S., America's Siberian Adventure (1931).

Guha, Sujit, Evolution of Pneumatisation of the Tympano-Mastoid and Re-Thinking Into Otological Problems to Prevent Hearing Discord in Space Flights, XIth International Astronautical Congress (Stockholm, 1960)

Guignard, J. C., Human Frequency Response to Vibration, XIth International Astronautical Congress (Stockholm, 1960).

Hackworth, International Law.

Haley, Andrew G., Survey of Opinion on Extraterrestrial Jurisdiction, XIth International Astronautical Congress (Stockholm, 1960).

--- Rocketry and Space Exploration (1958).

--- Space Age Presents Immediate Legal Problems, First Colloquium on the Law of Outer Space (The Hague, 1958).

--- Legal Problems of Space, 1960-1970, Memorial Union (Norman, Oklahoma, 1960).

--- Space Law and Metalaw-Jurisdiction Defined, Journal of Air Law and Commerce, Vol. 23, No. 3, (1957).

--- Space Law - The Development of Jurisdictional Concepts, VIIIth Annual Congress of the International Astronautical Federation (Barcelona, 1957).

Hall, International Law (8th Ed., 1924).

Hanover, H. R. H. Dr. Wolfe Heinrich, Prince of, Die Rechts Probleme de Weltraumes, 4 Weltraumfahst (October, 1953).

Hanrahan, James S., and Bushnell, David, Space Biology, Hazards of Space, The, Air Force (March, 1958).

Hingorani, R. C., Attempt to Determine Sovereignty in Upper Space, University of Kansas Law Review, Vol. 26 (1957).

Hogan, John C., Legal Terminology for the Atmosphere, American Journal of International Law Quarterly, Vol. 51 (1956).

--- Space Law Bibliography, Journal of Air Law and Commerce, Vol. 23 (1956).

Horsford, Cyril E. C., Principles of International Law in Spaceflight, University of Saint Louis Law Journal, Vol. 5 (Spring, 1958).

Hughes, Pathways of Peace, 1925, Canadian Bar Association (Montreal, September, 1923).

Hyde, International Law (2nd Ed., 1945).

Hyman, William A., Magna Carta of Space, Twelfth Conference of the Inter-American Bar Association (Bogota, Columbia, 1961).

--- The Magna Carta of Space, XIIIth International Astronautical Congress and International Institute of Space Law, the Fifth Colloquium on the Law of Outer Space (Varna, Bulgaria, 1962).

--- Magna Carta of Space - A Review of Some Problems, Congress of the Inter-American Bar Association (San Juan, 1965).

--- The Magna Carta of Space - The Legal Lodestar, Thirteenth Conference of the Inter-American Bar Association (Panama, 1963).

--- Outer Space - Some Problems and Solutions, New York State Bar Association Symposium on Outer Space (New York, 1958).

--- Report and Resolution, Inter-American Bar Association, Committee on Interplanetary Space (Miami, Fla. 1959).

--- Report on Space, American Bar Association Committee on Aeronautical Law, Subcommittee on Space Law (Atlanta, Ga., Feb. 1958).

--- Some Terrestrial and Celestial Medical Problems - Impact of the Space Age, The Society of Medical Jurisprudence (New York, 1960).

--- Sovereignty Over Space, Third Colloquium on the Law of Outer Space, XIth International Astronautical Congress (Stockholm, 1960).

--- Space Sovereignty - Analysis of Conflicting Theories and a Suggestion, Fifteenth Annual Meeting of the American Rocket Society (Washington, D.C., 1960).

--- Space - The Lawless Realm of Science, American Rocket Society Space Flight Report to the Nation (New York, 1961).

--- United States Communications Satellite Act of 1962 - Some Questions, Federal Bar Association of New York, New Jersey and Connecticut, Committee on Aeronautics, (New York, 1962). Also appearing in The Antitrust Bulletin, Vol. VII, No. 3 (May-June, 1962).

--- Wanted - A Policeman for Outer Space, American Rocket Society Space Law and Sociology Conference (New York, 1962).

--- Wanted - Law and a Policeman in Space, XVth International Astronautical Congress and the VIIth Colloquium on Space Law of the International Institute of Space Law (Warsaw, 1964). Also appearing in Space World, Vol. A-14, (December, 1964).

--- Who Owns What?, Space World Magazine Vol. 1 #8 (June, 1961).

--- World Peace Through Space Law, Annual Meeting of

the American Rocket Society (Washington, D.C., 1959).

--- World Peace Through Space Law, Ateneo Law Journal Vol. 9 (Centennial Year Volume, Jan. 1960). Publication of the Ateneo Law School, Manila, Philippines.

Jaffe, Morton S.

Article - International Law and Politics of Space - 5 St. Louis University Law Journal, 375, 1959;

Article - International Law and Space Exploration - 6 St. Louis University Law Journal, 68, 1960;

Paper - Reliance upon International Custom and General Principles in the Growth of Space Law - Delivered at XIIIth International Astronautical Congress, Varna, Bulgaria, September 1962. (Published in 7 St. Louis University Law Journal, 125, 1962, and as revised comment, Military Law Review, April 1963.)

Article - Recent Developments in the International Law of Space, 38 Temple University Law Quarterly, 263, 1965 (Based on a paper delivered at the International Astronautical Congress, Warsaw Poland, September 1964).

Jenks, William C., International Law and Activities in Space, International and Comparative Law Quarterly, Vol. 5 (1956).

Jones, Professor Dorsey D., Russia: A Concise History (1955).

Journal of the John Bassett Moore Society of International Law, University of Virginia, Vol. II, No. 2 (1962).

Kahin, The Asian-African Conference (1956).

Knauth, Arnold W., Legal Problems of Outer Space in Relation to the United States, Panel Discussion, American Association for the United Nations (Washington, D.C., 1958).

Kornhauser, J., Structural Resistance of Animals to Inertia Loading of Long Duration, XIth International Astronautical Congress (Stockholm, 1960).

Kovalev, F. N., and Cheprov, I. I., Artificial Satellites and International Law, Soviet Yearbook of International Law (1958).

Legal Problems of Space Exploration, A symposium, U.S. Government Printing Office, Washington, D.C. (1961); by the Committee on Aeronautical & Space Sciences, United State Senate, 87th Congress, 1st Session.

Machowski, Jacek, Certain Aspects of the Right of Innocent Passage of Space Vehicles, XIIIth International Astronautical Congress, Fourth Colloquium on the Law of Outer Space (Washington, D.C., 1961).

--- Selected Problems of National Sovereignty With Reference to the Law of Outer Space, Proceedings of the American Society of International Law (1961).

Melish, John, Travels, Vol. 1.

Morison, Samuel Eliot, Admiral of the Ocean Sea (1942).

Outward Bound, Time Magazine (May 26th, 1958).

Peaceful Cooperation in Space, International Affairs (Moscow, March, 1962).

Proceedings (all) of the Colloquia on the Law of Outer Space, International Institute of Space Law of the International Astronautical Federation.

Ritter, Oskar L., The Sun's Retina Burning Power in Space,

XIth International Astronautical Congress (Stockholm, 1960).

Simsarsian, Acquisition of Legal Title to Terra Nullius, Political Science Quarterly, Vol. 53 (1938).

Smirnoff, Dr. M., The Real Possibilities for the Conclusion of an International Convention on Outer Space, XIth International Astronautical Congress (Stockholm 1960).
--- Various speeches and reports.

Stalin, J. V., Works, Vol. 7 (1954).

St. Korowicz, Marek, Introduction to International Law (1959).

Story, Joseph, Constitution.

Survey of Space Law; Staff Reports of the Select Committee on Astronautics and Space Exploration of the Congress of the United States.

Sztuzki, Jerzy, On the So-Called Upper Limit of National Sovereignty, Fifth Colloquium on the Law of Outer Space (Varna, Bulgaria, 1962).

United Nations, Release of Committee on Peaceful Uses of Outer Space, General Assembly, March 24, 1962. a/AC.105/ INF. 2.

United Nations Resolution 1721 A/XVI adopted on December 20, 1961 at the Sixteenth Session of the General Assembly.

United Nations Resolution 1962 (XVIII), adopted December 13, 1963 at the 1280th Plenary Meeting of the General Assembly, Eighteenth Session.

United Nations Resolution 1963 (XVIII), adopted December 13, 1963 at the 1280th Plenary Meeting of the General Assembly, Eighteenth Session.

United States Senate, Report of the Committee on Aeronautical and Space Sciences (July 15, 1960.)

Verplaetse, Julain G., S.J.D. (Harvard), Dr. Juris (Ghent), Conflicts of Air and Outer Space Law, XIth International Astronautical Congress (Stockholm, 1960).

Wells, H. G., The Outline of History (1961).

Williams, William Appleman, American-Russian Relations, 1781-1947 (1952).

Work Stoppage at Missile Bases, Hearings before the Permanent Subcommittee on Investigations of the Committee on Government Operations, U.S. Senate, 87th Congress, 1st Session (April, May and June, 1961).

World Without Arms, World Without Wars, Book 2 USSR Foreign Language Publishing House (Moscow, August-December, 1959).

Wright, Law and Politics in the World Community (1953).

Zadorozhnyi, Dr. G., The Artificial Satellite and International Law (Rand-78, October 17, 1957).

APPENDIX B

NINE PRINCIPLES OF THE U. N.

U.N. General Assembly Distr. LIMITED
18th Session A/Res/1962 (XVIII)
Agenda Item 28 24 December 1963
RESOLUTION adopted by the General Assembly
(on the report of the First Committee (A/5656)
1662 (XVIII). Declaration of Legal Principles Governing the Activities of States in-the Exploration and Use of Outer-Space.

The General Assembly,

Inspired by the great prospects opening up before mankind as a result of man's entry into outer-space,

Recognizing the common interest of all mankind in the progress of the exploration and use of outer-space for peaceful purposes,

Believing that the exploration and use of outer-space should be carried on for the betterment of mankind and for the benefit of States irrespective of their degree of economic or scientific development,

Desiring to contribute to broad international co-operation in the scientific as well as in the legal aspects of exploration and use of outer-space for peaceful purposes,

Believing that such co-operation will contribute to the development of mutual understanding and to the strengthening of friendly relations between nations and peoples,

Recalling its resolution 110 (II) of 3 November 1947, which condemned propaganda designed or likely to provoke or encourage any threat to the peace, breach of the peace, or act of aggression, and considering that the aforementioned resolution is applicable to outer-space,

Taking into consideration its resolution 1721 (XVI) of 20 December 1961 and 1802 (XVII) of 14 December 1962, adopted unanimously by the States Members of the United Nations,

Solemnly declares that in the exploration and use of outer-space States should be guided by the following principles:

1. The exploration and use of outer-space shall be carried on for the benefit and in the interests of all mankind.

2. Outer-space and celestial bodies are free for exploration and use by all States on a basis of equality and in accordance with international law.

3. Outer-space and celestial bodies are not subject to national appropriation by claim of sovereignty, by means of use or occupation, or by any other means.

4. The activities of States in the exploration and use of outer-space shall be carried on in accordance with international law, including the Charter of the United Nations, in the interest of maintaining international peace and security and promoting international co-operation and understanding.

5. States bear international responsibility for national activities in outer-space, whether carried on by governmental agencies or by non-governmental entities, and for assuring that national activities are carried on in conformity with the principles set forth in the present Declaration. The activities of non-governmental entities in outer-space shall require authorization and continuing supervision by the States concerned. When activities are carried on in outer-space by an international organization, responsibility for compliance with the principles set forth in this Declaration shall be borne by the international organization and by the States participating in it.

6. In the exploration and use of outer-space, States shall be guided by the principles of co-operation and mutual assistance and shall conduct all their activities in outer-space with due regard for the corresponding interests of other States. If a State has reason to believe that an outer-space activity or experiment planned by it or its nationals would cause potentially harmful interference with activities of other States in the peaceful exploration and use of outer-space, it shall undertake appropriate international consultations before proceeding with any such activity or experiment. A State which has reason to believe that an outer-space activity or experiment planned by another State would cause potentially harmful interference with activities in the peaceful exploration and use of outer-space may request

consultation concerning the activity or experiment.

7. The State on whose registry an object launched into outer-space is carried shall retain jurisdiction and control over such object, and any personnel thereon, while in outer-space. Ownership of objects launched into outer-space, and of their component parts, is not affected by their passage through outer-space or by their return to earth. Such objects or component parts found beyond the limits of the State or registry shall be returned to that State, which shall furnish identifying data upon request prior to return.

8. Each State which launches or procures the launching of an object into outer-space, and each State from whose territory or facility an object is launched, is internationally liable for damage to a foreign State or to its natural or juridical persons by such object or its component parts on the earth, in airspace, or in outer-space.

9. States shall regard astronauts as envoys of mankind in outer-space, and shall render to them all possible assistance in the event of accident, distress, or emergency landing on the territory of a foreign State or on the high seas. Astronauts who make such a landing shall be safely and promptly returned to the State of registry of their space vehicle.

1280th plenary meeting,
13 December 1963.

APPENDIX C

Part I - MULTILATERAL TREATIES

Multilateral Treaties (to which the Soviet is a signatory)

Africa - General Act for the repression of slave trade
- Convention re: duties imposed on importation of liquor

The Antarctic Treaty

Atlantic Charter

Statute of the International Atomic Agency

State Treaty for the re-establishment of an independent and democratic Austria

Convention on the regulation of Inter-American automotive traffic

Convention Concerning Customs Facilities For Touring

Customs Convention on the temporary importation of private road vehicles

Convention for the unification of certain rules relating to international transportation by air

UNESCO Constitution

International Convention for the Northwest Atlantic Fisheries: Protocol thereto

Amendments to Articles 24 and 25 of the WHO Constitution

WHO Regulation No. 1 regarding nomenclature re: diseases

and causes of death

International Sanitary Regulations - with respect to the health part of the aircraft general declaration

Instruments for the Amendments of the Constitution of ILO

Convention on the Inter-governmental Maritime Consulting Organization

Convention for the Unification of Certain Rules re: Assistance and Salvage at Sea

Convention on Safety of Life at Sea

Regulations for Preventing Collisions at Sea

United Nations Declaration (1942)

United Nations Charter

Prosecution of War Criminals of the European Axis

Convention re: creation of an international office of weights and measures

International Whaling Convention

Yalta Agreement

ILO Convention fixing the minimum age for the admission of children to employment at sea

Protocol on the Zones of Occupation in Germany and the administration of "Greater Berlin"

Agreement relating to the lifting of restrictions imposed since March 1, 1948 on communications, transportation, and trade with Berlin

International Load Line Convention

Agreement concerning an armistice with Rumania

Armistice Agreement with Bulgaria

Armistice Agreement with Hungary

Act of military surrender---terms between the United States and other Allied Powers and Germany

Communique of the Moscow Conference of Foreign Ministers (1945)

Declaration regarding the defeat of Germany

Protocol on the establishment of a four power naval commission, etc.

Treaty of peace with Italy

Treaty of peace with Rumania

Treaty of peace with Bulgaria

Treaty of peace with Hungary

Interim convention on conservation of North Pacific fur seals

Convention of the World Meteorological Organization

Convention for the Establishment of Right of Protection in Morocco

General Act of the International Conference at Algeciras

Narcotic Drugs Convention of 1931, 1946 and 1948

The Hague Conventions of 1899, 1907

Universal Postal Convention of 1957

Prisoners of War - Geneva Convention of 1949

Agreement for the Suppression of the circulation of obscene publications: Protocol thereto

Convention for the Amelioration of the conditions of the wounded in time of war

Treaty providing for renunciation of war as an instrument of national policy

Convention for the adoption to maritime warfare of the principles of the Geneva Convention of 1864

Convention for the exemption of hospital ships in time of war from the payment of taxes, etc. for the benefit of state

London Naval Treaty (1930)

Convention re: protection of civilians in time of war

Convention to suppress slave trade and slavery

Spitzbergen Treaty

International Sugar Agreement of 1958

Convention for protection of submarine cables

International Telecommunication Conventions: Telegraph Regulations

Convention re: formation of an international union for publication of customs tariffs, etc.

Agreement for the Repression of trade in white women

Part II - BILATERAL TREATIES

Bilateral Treaties (between the United States and USSR)

- Atomic Energy
- Cultural Relations
- Films
- Fisheries
- General Relations
- Judicial Procedure
- Lend-Lease
- Maritime Matters
- Occupied Territory
- Pacific Settlement of Disputes
- Passport Visas
- Prisoners of War
- Rules of Warfare
- Telecommunication
- Territorial Acquisition
- Trade and Commerce

APPENDIX D

INTERNATIONAL MEDICAL CODE OF THE U. N.'s WORLD HEALTH ORGANIZATION

The Constitution of the World Health Organization of the United Nations states that basic to the happiness, harmonious relationships and security of all people are the principles that:

"Health is a state of complete physical, mental and social well being and not merely the absence of disease or infirmity.

"The enjoyment of the highest attainable standard of health is one of the fundamental rights of every human being without distinction of race, religion, political belief, economic or social condition.

"The health of all people is fundamental to the attainment of peace and security and is dependent upon the fullest co-operation of individuals and States.

"The achievement of any State in the promotion and protection of health is a value to all.

"Unequal development of the child is of basic importance; the ability to live harmoniously in a changing total environment is essential to such development.

"The extension to all peoples of the benefits of medical, psychological and related knowledge is essential to the fullest attainment of health.

"Informed opinion and active cooperation on the part of the public are of the utmost importance in the improvement of the health of the people.

"Governments have a responsibility for the health of their peoples which can be fulfilled only by the provision of adequate health and social measures."

Supplementing these purposes, it is suggested that:

1. Opportunities for medical education be increased forthwith.

2. Medical Schools incapable of sustaining themselves be furnished with proper government support.

3. All members of the medical profession be required to undergo further education, study and reorientation to the problems presented on earth and in space by the Space Age.

4. All members of the medical profession be coordinated into one vast army whose members should be subject to call for service in any area of catastrophe and devastation in any part of the world.

APPENDIX E

UNIVERSAL DECLARATION OF HUMAN RIGHTS, OF THE UNITED NATIONS

ON DECEMBER 10, 1948, the General Assembly of the United Nations adopted and proclaimed the Universal Declaration of Human Rights, the full text of which appears in the following pages. Following this historic act the Assembly called upon all Member countries to publicize the text of the Declaration and "to cause it to be disseminated, displayed, read and expounded principally in schools and other educational institutions, without distinction based on the political status of countries or territories."

UNIVERSAL DECLARATION OF HUMAN RIGHTS

PREAMBLE

Whereas recognition of the inherent dignity and of the equal and inalienable rights of all members of the human family is the foundation of freedom, justice and peace in the world,

Whereas disregard and contempt for human rights have resulted in barbarous acts which have outraged the conscience of mankind, and the advent of a world in which human beings shall enjoy freedom of speech and belief and freedom from fear and want has been proclaimed as the highest aspiration of the common people,

Whereas it is essential, if man is not to be compelled to have recourse, as a last resort, to rebellion against tyranny and oppression, that human rights should be protected by the rule of law,

Whereas it is essential to promote the development of friendly relations between nations,

Whereas the peoples of the United Nations have in the Charter reaffirmed their faith in fundamental human rights, the dignity and worth of the human person and in the equal rights of men and women and have determined to promote social progress and better standards of life in larger freedom,

Whereas Member States have pledged themselves to achieve, in co-operation with the United Nations, the promotion of universal respect for and observance of human rights and fundamental freedoms,

Whereas a common understanding of these rights and freedoms is of the greatest importance for the full realization of this pledge,

Now, Therefore,

THE GENERAL ASSEMBLY proclaims

THIS UNIVERSAL DECLARATION OF HUMAN RIGHTS as a common standard of achievement for all peoples and all nations, to the end that every individual and every organ of society, keeping this Declaration constantly in mind, shall strive by teaching and education to promote respect for these rights and freedoms and by progressive measures, national and international, to secure their universal and effective recognition and observance, both among the people of Member States themselves and among the peoples of territories under their jurisdiction.

Article 1. All human beings are born free and equal in dignity and rights. They are endowed with reason and conscience and should act towards one another in a spirit of brotherhood.

Article 2. Everyone is entitled to all the rights and freedoms set forth in this Declaration, without distinction of any kind, such as race, color, sex, language, religion, political or other opinion, national or social origin, property, birth or other status.

Furthermore, no distinction shall be made on the basis of the political, jurisdictional or international status of the country or territory to which a person belongs, whether it be independent, trust, non-self-governing or under any other limitation of sovereignty.

Article 3. Everyone has the right to life, liberty and security of person.

Article 4. No one shall be held in slavery or servitude;

slavery and the slave trade shall be prohibited in all their forms.

Article 5. No one shall be subjected to torture or to cruel, inhuman or degrading treatment or punishment.

Article 6. Everyone has the right to recognition everywhere as a person before the law.

Article 7. All are equal before the law and are entitled without any discrimination to equal protection of the law. All are entitled to equal protection against any discrimination in violation of this Declaration and against any incitement to such discrimination.

Article 8. Everyone has the right to an effective remedy by the competent national tribunals for acts violating the fundamental rights granted him by the constitution or by law.

Article 9. No one shall be subjected to arbitrary arrest, detention or exile.

Article 10. Everyone is entitled in full equality to a fair and public hearing by an independent and impartial tribunal, in the determination of his rights and obligations and of any criminal charge against him.

Article 11. (1) Everyone charged with a penal offence has the right to be presumed innocent until proven guilty according to law in a public trial at which he has had all the guarantees necessary for his defence.

(2) No one shall be held guilty of any penal offence on account of any act or omission which did not constitute a penal offence, under national or international law, at the time when it was committed. Nor shall a heavier penalty be imposed than the one that was applicable at the time the penal offence was committed.

Article 12. No one shall be subjected to arbitrary interference with his privacy, family, home or correspondence, nor to attacks upon his honor and reputation. Everyone has the right to the protection of the law against such interference or attacks.

Article 13. (1) Everyone has the right to freedom of movement and residence within the borders of each State.

(2) Everyone has the right to leave any country, including his own, and to return to his country.

Article 14. (1) Everyone has the right to seek and to enjoy

in other countries asylum from persecution.

(2) This right may not be invoked in the case of prosecutions genuinely arising from non-political crimes or from acts contrary to the purposes and principles of the United Nations.

Article 15. (1) Everyone has the right to a nationality.

(2) No one shall be arbitrarily deprived of his nationality nor denied the right to change his nationality.

Article 16. (1) Men and women of full age, without any limitation due to race, nationality or religion, have the right to marry and to found a family. They are entitled to equal rights as to marriage, during marriage and at its dissolution.

(2)Marriage shall be entered into only with the free and full consent of the intending spouses.

(3) The family is the natural and fundamental group unit of society and is entitled to protection by society and the State.

Article 17. (1) Everyone has the right to own property alone as well as in association with others.

(2) No one shall be arbitrarily deprived of his property.

Article 18. Everyone has the right to freedom of thought, conscience and religion; this right includes freedom to change his religion or belief, and freedom, either alone or in community with others and in public or private, to manifest his religion or belief in teaching, practice, worship and observance.

Article 19. Everyone has the right to freedom of opinion and expression; this right includes freedom to hold opinions without interference and to seek, receive and impart information and ideas through any media and regardless of frontiers.

Article 20. (1) Everyone has the right to freedom of peaceful assembly and association.

(2) No one may be compelled to belong to an association.

Article 21. (1) Everyone has the right to take part in the government of his country, directly or through freely chosen representatives.

(2) Everyone has the right of equal access to public service in his country.

(3) The will of the people shall be the basis of the author-

ity of government; this will shall be expressed in periodic and genuine elections which shall be by universal and equal suffrage and shall be held by secret vote or by equivalent free voting procedures.

Article 22. Everyone, as a member of society, has the right to social security and is entitled to realization, through national effort and international co-operation and in accordance with the organization and resources of each State, of the economic, social and cultural rights indispensable for his dignity and the free development of his personality.

Article 23. (1) Everyone has the right to work, to free choice of employment, to just and favorable conditions of work and to protection against unemployment.

(2) Everyone, without any discrimination, has the right to equal pay for equal work.

(3) Everyone who works has the right to just and favorable remuneration ensuring for himself and his family an existence worthy of human dignity, and supplemented, if necessary, by other means of social protection.

(4) Everyone has the right to form and to join trade unions for the protection of his interests.

Article 24. Everyone has the right to rest and leisure, including reasonable limitation of working hours and periodic holidays with pay.

Article 25. (1) Everyone has the right to a standard of living adequate for the health and well-being of himself and of his family, including food, clothing, housing and medical care and necessary social services, and the right to security in the event of unemployment, sickness, disability, widowhood, old age or other lack of livelihood in circumstances beyond his control.

(2) Motherhood and childhood are entitled to special care and assistance. All children, whether born in or out of wedlock, shall enjoy the same social protection.

Article 26. (1) Everyone has the right to education. Education shall be free, at least in the elementary and fundamental stages. Elementary education shall be compulsory. Technical and professional education shall be made generally available and higher education shall be equally accessible to all on the basis of merit.

(2) Education shall be directed to the full development of the human personality and to the strengthening of respect for human rights and fundamental freedoms. It shall promote understanding, tolerance and friendship among all nations, racial or religious groups, and shall further the activities of the United Nations for the maintenance of peace.

(3) Parents have a prior right to choose the kind of education that shall be given to their children.

Article 27. (1)Everyone has the right freely to participate in the cultural life of the community, to enjoy the arts and to share in scientific advancement and its benefits.

(2) Everyone has the right to the protection of the moral and material interests resulting from any scientific, literary or artistic production of which he is the author.

Article 28. Everyone is entitled to a social and international order in which the rights and freedoms set forth in this Declaration can be fully realized.

Article 29. (1) Everyone has duties to the community in which alone the free and full development of his personality is possible.

(2) In the exercise of his rights and freedoms, everyone shall be subject only to such limitations as are determined by law solely for the purpose of securing due recognition and respect for the rights and freedoms of others and of meeting the just requirements of morality, public order and the general welfare in a democratic society.

(3) These rights and freedoms may in no case be exercised contrary to the purposes and principles of the United Nations.

Article 30. Nothing in this Declaration may be interpreted as implying for any State, group or person any right to engage in any activity or to perform any act aimed at the destruction of any of the rights and freedoms set forth herein.

APPENDIX F

DECLARATION OF INDEPENDENCE (OPENING REMARKS)

In the opening statements of the DECLARATION OF INDEPENDENCE OF THE UNITED STATES OF AMERICA are contained the clear-cut and unequivocal principles which can be summed up as a "Bill of Human Rights" for all peoples, both here on earth and in space ventures to come:

IN CONGRESS, JULY 4, 1776
The unanimous Declaration of the thirteen United States of America, when in the course of human events, it becomes necessary for one people to dissolve the political bonds which have connected them with another, and to assume among the powers of the earth, the separate and equal station to which the Laws of Nature and of Nature's God entitle them, a decent respect to the opinions of mankind requires that they should declare the causes which impel them to the separation.---We hold these truths to be self-evident, that all men are created equal, that they are endowed by their Creator with certain inalienable Rights, that among these are Life, Liberty and the pursuit of Happiness.---That to secure these rights, Governments are instituted among Men, deriving their just powers from the consent of the governed,---That whenever any Form of Government becomes destructive of these ends, it is the Right of the People to alter or to abolish it, and to institute new Government, laying its foundation on such principles and organizing its powers in such form, as to them shall seem most likely to effect their Safety and Happiness.

l Espacio

, LL.B., D.H.L.

ARTICULO 9.

Deberán proveerse maneras de identificación, registro y aviso adelantado de la intención de lanzar cualquier culo al espacio.

ARTICULO 10.

Deberán tomarse disposiciones también para el reconocimiento pacífico de los derechos y de los lugares de trada y aterrizaje de los vehículos del espacio.

ARTICULO 11.

Deberán tomarse disposiciones para la distribución y control de las frecuencias de radio.

ARTICULO 12.

Deberán tomarse disposiciones que eviten la interferencia sobre naves aéras por vehículos interplanetarios y oién la interferencia de vehículos interplanetarios entre sí.

ARTICULO 13.

En caso de lesiones o muerte a las personas o daños y perjuicios a la propiedad, causados por vehículos planetarios, cohetes, proyectiles, satélites y otros objetos similares, la nación que directamente o por medio tros hubiere hecho el lanzamiento será responsable por todos los daños y perjuicios ocasionados, por los cuales ará obligada, sin necesidad de que se le pruebe que ha incurrido en falta, negligencia, descuido o dolo.

ARTICULO 14.

Un fondo de seguro internacional deberá establecerse por medio de una asociación internacional, tal como las ones Unidas, para el pago de daños.

ARTICULO 15.

Deberán insertarse disposiciones apropiadas para la vigilancia internacional del Espacio Interplanetario y la protección de los pueblos y de las naciones, para evitar que se violen su derecho sobre dicho espacio.

ARTICULO 16.

Toda disputa resultante directa o indirecamente del uso del Espacio Interplanetario y de las regiones intertarias deberá resolverse y determinarse solamente por arbitraje por medio de un organismo, corte o tri- aceptado y que designen los poderes soberanos o las Naciones Unidas.

ARTICULO 17.

El desembarque en cualquier otro planeta en donde haya vida o la ocupación del mismo por habitantes te-res no dará el derecho de propiedad o el control de dicho planeta a nación alguna de la Tierra.

ARTICULO 18.

Los pueblos de la Tierra declaran por medio de la Carta Magna que reconocen los derechos de ocupación pro-d y control de cualquier otro planeta en favor de los habitantes del mismo.

ARTICULO 19.

La guerra en el espacio, o por medio, o a través del mismo, se proscribe aquí para siempre.

Atestado por:

WILLIAM ROY VALLANCE
Secretario General

totalidad de la Carta Magna del Espacio, menos su Artículo 7, fué aprobada por la Federación Interamericana de Abogados en Bogotá, Colombia, febrero de 1961.

Artículo 7 fué aprobado por la Federación Interamericana de Abogados en San Juan, Puerto Rico, en 25 de mayo de 1965.

Carta Ma

Por William A

Preámbulo

CONSIDERANDO que la Asamblea General de las Naciones Unidas ha reconocido el interés común que tien humanidad en el Espacio Interplanetario, y

CONSIDERANDO también que es el sentir de todos que dicho espacio se utilice solamente para fines pa cos, y

CONSIDERANDO que el Artículo 2, párrafo 1 de la Carta de las Naciones Unidas estipula que "la org zación se basa en el principio de la igualdad soberana de todos sus miembros", y

CONSIDERANDO que es el propósito y la finalidad de la Federación Interamericana de Abogados busca acuerdo para evitar que se propaguen rivalidades nacionales en este campo y para promover la enérgica explora y explotación del Espacio Interplanetario en beneficio de la humanidad, y

CONSIDERANDO que es nuestra creencia que la humanidad se beneficiará materialmente si el Espacio In planetario se usa solamente con fines pacíficos,

AHORA, POR LO TANTO, RESUELVE este Comité sobre Espacio Interplanetario que la Carta Magna Espacio expuesta aquí sea aceptada y adoptada por esta Asociación para beneficio de la humanidad y el estab miento de la paz y prevención de la guerra.

Carta Magna Del Espacio

ARTICULO 1.

El espacio habrá de dividirse en Espacio Aéreo y Espacio Interplanetario.

ARTICULO 2.

El Espacio Aéreo deberá considerarse constituir una parte del territorio de la soberanía del país tierra qu encuentra bajo el mismo.

ARTICULO 3.

El Espacio Interplanetario deberá considerarse como "res communis" (y no "terra nullius").

ARTICULO 4.

El sistema interplanetario será considerado como "res communis" (y no "res nullius").

ARTICULO 5.

Deberá reconocerse la distinción entre "res communis" y "terra nullius" (la primera expresión siendo n tiva de todo derecho de propiedad y de control exclusivo por parte de nación alguna, y la segunda concediendo t derechos de propiedad mediante los principios establecidos de descubrimiento, habitación y establecimiento).

ARTICULO 6.

El Espacio Interplanetario se deberá usar solamente con fines pacíficos, correspondiendo el derecho de expl ción del mismo a todos los pueblos para beneficio de la humanidad.

ARTICULO 7.

No habrán de hacerse experimentos nucleares en el Espacio Interplanetario.

ARTICULO 8.

Además, puesto que es imposible establecer líneas fronterizas con características físicas tales como las determinan las líneas fronterizas en la tierra y en el mar, deberá establecerse una zona neutral entre los lí superiores del Espacio Aéreo y los límites inferiores del Espacio Interplanetario, la cual se conocerá con el no de "Neutralia", y a través de la cual se reconocería el derecho de paso pacífico, sin ofensa a la soberanía. En zona de "Neutralia" existiría el derecho de tránsito pacífico para toda nave, vehículo u objeto que pueda pa moverse sin producir incidente alguno que pueda considerarse como invasión de la soberanía. Al ejercer derecho de tránsito inocente, ninguna nación tendría el derecho de atacar o destruir el vehículo u objeto en trá ni a la nación que hubiese lanzado dicho vehículo u objeto, ni el derecho de destruir a los ocupantes del mism previo y suficiente aviso y advertencia de que se reclama la existencia de una invasión de soberanía, y sin haya habido una oportunidad previa para que se juzgue la validez de dicho reclamo por medios pacíficos.

APPENDIX G

Carta Magna Del Espacio

Por Willam A. Hyman, A.B., LL.B., D.H.L.

EE. UU. A.

Presidente del XVI Comité sobre la Ley del Espacio Interplanetario

de la Federación Interamericana de Abogados

INTER-AMERICAN BAR ASSOCIATION

Adoptada en

Bogotá, Colombia, en 3 de febrero de 1961

y en

San Juan, Puerto Rico, en 25 de mayo de 1965

APPENDIX H
CONGRESSIONAL RECORD: RE THE MAGNA CARTA OF SPACE

Extension of remarks of Hon. John V. Lindsay of New York in the House of Representatives, Tuesday, June 4, 1963

Mr. LINDSAY. Mr. Speaker, I wish to present to the Members of the House an account of the discussions of the "Magna Carta of Space" at the Congress of the Inter-American Bar Association in Panama in April of this year. The account appears in the Panama American.

The article is primarily devoted to the remarks of William A. Hyman, who originally proposed the "Magna Carta of Space" at a convention of the Inter-American Bar Association held in Bogota, Colombia, in February 1961. Mr. Hyman's comments at this most recent conference afford us an ample and worthwhile discussion of a very timely concern. Through his efforts in regard to the legal problems of space travel he reveals himself to be a forward-looking thinker eminently capable of offering concrete and constructive recommendations.

Mr. Hyman, who was chairman of the Special Committee on Interplanetary Space Law at the Convention, is a trial lawyer of international repute. With the unanimous consent of the House I include this article in the Record:

(From the Panama American, Panama City, Republic of Panama, Apr. 25, 1963)

Bar Convention Hears Noted Lawyer Discuss Sovereignty-In-Space Issue

Legal eyes and ears about this world are turned toward the Republic of Panama and its capital this week where internationally famed attorneys are creating the basis of laws on the control of outer space to submit to the General Assembly of the United Nations and subcommittees pertaining thereto as among principal resolutions on their agenda.

"The Space Committee of the United Nations has failed to give due consideration and take appropriate action on the important question of sovereignty and security as they become involved in the use of space," said William A. Hyman of New York City and an internationally known trial lawyer who spoke yesterday before the 13th Conference of Inter-American Bar Convention now in session in Hotel El Panama Hilton.

Hyman, former chairman of the American Bar Association Subcommittee on Air Space, and former member of the committee on aeronautical law, is author of "The Magna Carta of Space - the Legal Lodestar." He presented a resolution before the Inter-American Bar Association during its convention held in Bogota, Colombia, in February 1961. The resolution was fully approved at that session and ratified by the new council in May of that year.

Yesterday Hyman, chairman of the special committee on interplanetary space law, presented his "Magna Carta of Space."

In pointing out that the U.N. Space Committee has failed to give due consideration to the subject, Chairman Hyman said, "It failed to request the General Assembly of the United Nations and the proper authorities therein to make mandatory the application of international law and the United Nations Charter to outer space and the celestial bodies."

"While regretably the complete and satisfactory statement of basic principles was not established, yet certain other developments provide a basis for hope and encouragement," he continued. "It must be noted that the Committee on Peaceful Uses of Outer Space of the United Nations has now adopted the position that it is desirable to have a statement of basic legal principles rather than await the completion of an extensive code."

"It is clear to all that weapons alone will not provide security," Hyman emphasized as he commented upon the mad dash for superiority in nuclear arsenals as a deterrent to international provocations that may lead to war. The distinguished lawyer declared that a statement of basic principles can be found in specific recommendations by the Space Committee he heads, as contained in the Magna Carta of Space which will provide moral and ethical as well as legal restraints against impulsive, or premeditated military action.

Hyman submitted his Magna Carta of Space yesterday as the basis upon which a declaration might be favorably recommended to the General Assembly of the United Nations.

The noted attorney pointed out that Earl Warren, Chief Justice of the U.S. Supreme Court, in a speech before Georgia Institute of Technology in February of this year, said that a society governed by law will not allow these great scientific discoveries to be used for destructive purposes.

"World without law is hellbent for destruction with or without scientific discoveries", Chairman Hyman quoted the Chief Justice as saying in his speech.

Continuing his description of what he termed a "legal vacuum in space" under his Magna Carta, Hyman reminded his audience that in December 1962 Dr. William Hayward Pickering and his team received messages from Mariner II 36 million miles of space away from Earth and in the vicinity of Venus, which was the first time in history a traveler from Earth was cruising in that range of the heavens and the feat was hailed as the greatest achievement to date in the scientific quest of space.

"If the launching of Lunik IV by the Soviet April 2 of this year to place a robot on the moon, preparatory to placing a man there and, if it had been successful, would prompt the question of whether a claim might be made by USSR of ownership, or exclusive control---political or commercial," Hyman pointed out.

"The Soviet stated that no claim of ownership would be made by it and that 'the moon belonged to the world', yet in the absence of the restraining force of an international agreement declaring that space and the interplanetary void would belong to all; i.e., that it is res communis, there would be no bar to a reversal of the position of the Soviet---except catastrophic war," he continued.

In his "Magna Carta of Space," Hyman gave what he calls a "lesson in history---and a prophecy" this morning and took his fellows back to the time of Christopher Columbus when that farsighted sailor dared to pioneer in uncharted space---of the 15th century, the high seas.

"When Columbus sought a new route to India, going east

by going west, he was subjected to much ridicule,'' Hyman stated. ''In those days not only the average person but leaders and scientists contended the world was flat. Columbus urged that it was round.'' Upon this scientific assumption the rest is history, but Chairman Hyman stressed the fact that his royal backers conveniently forgot some of the terms of their very businesslike contract with Columbus.

''Today, approximately $40 billion is being and will be spent by the United States of America in the race with the Soviet to place a man on the moon,'' the attorney declared. ''Will this happen---will there be a new migration to the moon and will there be need for acceleration of this migration into the interplanetary world?'' he questioned.

Referring to devastating weapons of destruction in an effort to maintain the ''murderous balance of terror'', Hyman said, ''If a small amount of the cost of contemplated extermination were devoted to the cause of survival, undoubtedly science aided by the restraint of law would give us greater assurance of peace and a better guarantee against extinction.''

''Today is the day of the irrovocable decision,'' Hyman concluded. ''Once a world-nuclear devastating attack has been made, there can be no recalling the blow; there cannot even be sufficient retaliation to avoid world catastrophe.''

Hyman stated that, ''The void in space is law---it must be terminated.''

''The apathy of the public is cause for grave concern since government will not often act until made to act by the aroused will of the people,'' the speaker warned. ''The callous indifference may be due to the failure on the part of leaders of nations to correctly, fully, and properly inform the common man as to the implication of the impact on life caused by uncontrolled and lawless science.''

''Law all too frequently awaits the development of a great crisis before it goes into action'' Chairman Hyman said in closing, ''Science without the control of law is the enemy of mankind but science under the control of law is the benefactor of mankind---the time for blastoff is long past---we have been too long on the launching pad. We must now go, go, go.''

APPENDIX I

NUREMBERG CODE OF MEDICAL ETHICS

NUREMBERG CODE of Medical Ethics - (Evolved at the trial of the Nazi medical defendants at Nuremberg)

Nuremberg Rule 1: The voluntary consent of the human subject is absolutely essential.

Nuremberg Rule 2: The experiment should be such as to yield fruitful results for the good of society, unprocurable by other methods or means of study, and not random and unnecessary in nature.

Nuremberg Rule 3: The experiment should be so designed and based on the results of animal experimentation and a knowledge of the natural history of the disease or other problem under study that the anticipated results will justify the performance of the experiment.

Nuremberg Rule 4: The experiment should be so conducted as to avoid all unnecessary physical and mental suffering and injury.

Nuremberg Rule 5: No experiment should be conducted where there is an a priori reason to believe that death or disabling injury will occur; except, perhaps, in those experiments where the experimental physicians also serve as subjects.

Nuremberg Rule 6: The degree of risk to be taken should never exceed that determined by the humanitarian importance of the problem to be solved by the experiment.

Nuremberg Rule 7: Proper preparations should be made and adequate facilities provided to protect the experimental subject against even remote possibilities of injury, disability, or death.

Nuremberg Rule 8: The experiment should be conducted only by scientifically qualified persons. The highest degree of skill and care should be required through all stages of the experiment of those who conduct or engage in the experiment.

Nuremberg Rule 9: During the course of the experiment the human subject should be at liberty to bring the experiment to an end if he has reached the physical or mental state where continuation of the experiment seems to him to be impossible.

Nuremberg Rule 10: During the course of the experiment the scientist in charge must be prepared to terminate the experiment at any stage, if he has probable cause to believe, in the exercise of good faith, superior skill and careful judgment required of him that a continuation of the experiment is likely to result in injury, disability, or death to the experimental subject.

OTHER MEDICAL EXPERIMENT STATEMENTS

On the matter of consent by the subject to the experiment the views of the Roman Catholic Church expressed by Pope Pius XII are illuminating. They are as follows:

"As for the patient, he is not absolute master of himself, of his body or of his soul. He cannot, therefore, freely dispose of himself as he pleases. Even the reason for which he acts is of itself neither sufficient nor determining."

There can no longer be any equivocation on this subject! Part III, Article 7 of the United Nations Draft Covenant of Political and Civil Rights (as adopted by the Commission on Human Rights, 10th Session) states:

"No one shall be subjected to torture or to cruel, inhuman or degrading treatment or punishment. In particular, no one shall be subjected without his free consent to medical or scientific experimentation involving risk, where such is not required by his state of physical or mental health."

APPENDIX J

CHARTER OF THE UNITED NATIONS
(EXCERPTS)

(Nowhere in the entire Charter of the United Nations is there any mention of "space" or "space law", as will be particularly evident in the important sections reprinted herewith:)

CHARTER OF THE UNITED NATIONS
(excerpted portions)

Preamble

We the peoples of the United Nations are determined to save succeeding generations from the scourge of war, which twice in our lifetime has brought untold sorrow to mankind, and

to reaffirm faith in fundamental human rights, in the dignity and worth of the human person, in the equal rights of men and women and of nations large and small, and

to establish conditions under which justice and respect for the obligations arising from treaties and other sources of international law can be maintained, and

to promote social progress and better standards of life in larger freedom,

and for these ends to practice tolerance and live together in peace with one another as good neighbors, and

to unite our strength to maintain international peace and security, and

to ensure, by the acceptance of principles and the institution of methods, that armed force shall not be used save in the common interest, and

to employ international machinery for the promotion of the economic and social advancement of all peoples,

have resolved to combine our efforts to accomplish these aims.

Accordingly, our respective Governments, through representatives assembled in the city of San Francisco, who have exhibited their full powers found to be in good and due form, have agreed to the present Charter of the United Nations and do hereby establish an international organization to be known as the United Nations.

CHAPTER I PURPOSES AND PRINCIPLES

Article 1. The Purposes of the United Nations are:

1. To maintain international peace and security, and to that end: to take effective collective measures for the prevention and removal of threats to the peace, and for the suppression of acts of aggression or other breaches of the peace, and to bring about by peaceful means, and in conformity with the principles of justice and international law, adjustment or settlement of international disputes or situations which might lead to a breach of the peace;

2. To develop friendly relations among nations based on respect for the principle of equal rights and self-determination of peoples, and to take other appropriate measures to strengthen universal peace;

3. To achieve international cooperation in solving international problems of an economic, social, cultural, or humanitarian character, and in promoting and encouraging respect for human rights and for fundamental freedoms for all without distinction as to race, sex, language, or religion; and

4. To be a center for harmonizing the actions of nations in the attainment of these common ends.

Article 2. The Organization and its Members, in pursuit of the Purposes stated in Article 1, shall act in accordance with the following Principles.

1. The Organization is based on the principle of the sovereign equality of all its Members.

2. All Members, in order to ensure to all of them the rights and benefits resulting from membership, shall fulfil in good faith the obligations assumed by them in accordance with the present Charter.

3. All Members shall settle their international disputes

by peaceful means in such a manner that international peace and security, and justice, are not endangered.

4. All Members shall refrain in their international relations from the threat or use of force against the territorial integrity or political independence of any State, or in any other manner inconsistent with the Purposes of the United Nations.

5. All Members shall give the United Nations every assistance in any action it takes in accordance with the present Charter, and shall refrain from giving assistance to any State against which the United Nations is taking preventive or enforcement action.

6. The Organization shall ensure that States which are not Members of the United Nations act in accordance with these Principles so far as may be necessary for the maintenance of international peace and security.

7. Nothing contained in the present Charter shall authorize the United Nations to intervene in matters which are essentially within the domestic jurisdiction of any State or shall require the Members to submit such matters to settlement under the present Charter; but this principle shall not prejudice the application of enforcement measures under Chapter VII.

CHAPTER XIV THE INTERNATIONAL COURT OF JUSTICE

Article 92. The International Court of Justice shall be the principal judicial organ of the United Nations. It shall function in accordance with the annexed Statute, which is based upon the Statute of the Permanent Court of International Justice and forms an integral part of the present Charter.

Article 93. 1. All Members of the United Nations are ipso facto parties to the Statute of the International Court of Justice.

2. A state which is not a Member of the United Nations may become a party to the Statute of the International Court of Justice on conditions to be determined in each case by the General Assembly upon the recommendation of the Security Council.

Article 94. 1. Each Member of the United Nations undertakes to comply with the decision of the International Court of Justice in any case to which it is a party.

2. If any party to a case fails to perform the obligations incumbent upon it under a judgment rendered by the Court the other party may have recourse to the Security Council which may, if it deems necessary, make recommendations or decide upon measures to be taken to give effect to the judgment.

Article 95. Nothing in the present Charter shall prevent Members of the United Nations from entrusting the solution of their differences to other tribunals by virtue of agreements already in existence or which may be concluded in the future.

Article 96. 1. The General Assembly or the Security Council may request the International Court of Justice to give an advisory opinion on any legal question.

2. Other organs of the United Nations and specialized agencies, which may at any time be so authorized by the General Assembly, may also request advisory opinions of the Court on legal questions arising within the scope of their activities.

CHAPTER VI PACIFIC SETTLEMENT OF DISPUTES

Article 33. 1. The parties to any dispute, the continuance of which is likely to endanger the maintenance of international peace and security, shall, first of all, seek a solution by negotiation, enquiry, mediation, conciliation, arbitration, judicial settlement, resort to regional agencies or arrangements, or other peaceful means of their own choice.

2. The Security Council shall, when it deems necessary, call upon the parties to settle their dispute by such means.

Article 34. The Security Council may investigate any dispute, or any situation which might lead to international friction or give rise to a dispute, in order to determine whether the continuance of the dispute or situation is likely to endanger the maintenance of international peace and security.

Article 35. 1. Any Member of the United Nations may

bring any dispute, or any situation of the nature referred to in Article 34, to the attention of the Security Council or of the General Assembly.

2. A state which is not a Member of the United Nations may bring to the attention of the Security Council or of the General Assembly any dispute to which it is a party if it accepts in advance, for the purposes of the dispute, the obligations of pacific settlement provided in the present Charter.

3. The proceedings of the General Assembly in respect of matters brought to its attention under this Article will be subject to the provisions of Articles 11 and 12.

Article 36. 1. The Security Council may, at any stage of a dispute of the nature referred to in Article 33 or of a situation of like nature, recommend appropriate procedures or methods of adjustment.

2. The Security Council should take into consideration any procedures for the settlement of the dispute which have already been adopted by the parties.

3. In making recommendations under this Article the Security Council should also take into consideration that legal disputes should as a general rule be referred by the parties to the International Court of Justice in accordance with the provisions of the Statute of the Court.

Article 37. 1. Should the parties to a dispute of the nature referred to in Article 33 fail to settle it by the means indicated in that Article, they shall refer it to the Security Council.

2. If the Security Council deems that the continuance of the dispute is in fact likely to endanger the maintenance of international peace and security, it shall decide whether to take action under Article 36 or to recommend such terms of settlement as it may consider appropriate.

Article 38. Without prejudice to the provisions of Articles 33 to 37, the Security Council may, if all the parties to any dispute so request, make recommendations to the parties with a view to a pacific settlement of the dispute.

CHAPTER VII ACTION WITH RESPECT TO THREATS TO

THE PEACE, BREACHES OF THE PEACE, AND ACTS OF AGGRESSION

Article 39. The Security Council shall determine the existence of any threat to the peace, or act of aggression and shall make recommendations, or decide what measures shall be taken in accordance with Articles 41 and 42, to maintain or restore international peace and security.

Article 40. In order to prevent an aggravation of the situation, the Security Council may, before making the recommendations or deciding upon the measures provided for in Article 39, call upon the parties concerned to comply with such provisional measures as it deems necessary or desirable. Such provisional measures shall be without prejudice to the rights, claims, or position of the parties concerned. The Security Council shall duly take account of failure to comply with such provisional measures.

Article 41. The Security Council may decide what measures not involving the use of armed force are to be employed to give effect to its decisions, and it may call upon the Members of the United Nations to apply such measures. These may include complete or partial interruption of economic relations and of rail, sea, air, postal, telegraphic, radio, and other means of communication, and the severance of diplomatic relations.

Article 42. Should the Security Council consider that measures provided for in Article 41 would be inadequate or have proved to be inadequate, it may take such action by air, sea, or land forces as may be necessary to maintain or restore international peace and security. Such action may include demonstrations, blockade, and other operations by air, sea, or land forces of Members of the United Nations.

Article 43. 1. All Members of the United Nations, in order to contribute to the maintenance of international peace and security, undertake to make available to the Security Council, on its call and in accordance with a special agreement or agreements, armed forces, assistance, and facilities, including rights of passage, necessary for the purpose of maintaining international peace and security.

2. Such agreement or agreements shall govern the numbers and types of forces, their degree of readiness and general location, and the nature of the facilities and assistance to be provided.

3. The agreement or agreements shall be negotiated as soon as possible on the initiative of the Security Council. They shall be concluded between the Security Council and Members or between the Security Council and groups of Members and shall be subject to ratification by the signatory States in accordance with their respective constitutional processes.

Article 44. When the Security Council has decided to use force it shall, before calling upon a Member not represented on it to provide armed forces in fulfillment of the obligations assumed under Article 43, invite that Member, if the Member so desires, to participate in the decisions of the Security Council concerning the employment of contingents of that Member's armed forces.

Article 45. In order to enable the United Nations to take urgent military measures, Members shall hold immediately available national air-force contingents for combined international enforcement action. The strength and degree of readiness of these contingents and plans for their combined action shall be determined, within the limits laid down in the special agreement or agreements referred to in Article 43, by the Security Council with the assistance of the Military Staff Committee.

Article 46. Plans for the application of armed forces shall be made by the Security Council with the assistance of the Military Staff Committee.

Article 47. 1. There shall be established a Military Staff Committee to advise and assist the Security Council on all questions relating to the Security Council's military requirements for the maintenance of international peace and security, the employment and command of forces placed at its disposal, the regulation of armaments, and possible disarmament.

2. The Military Staff Committee shall consist of the Chiefs of Staff of the permanent members of the Security Council or their representatives. Any Member of the United

Nations not permanently represented on the Committee shall be invited by the Committee to be associated with it when the efficient discharge of the Committee's responsibilities requires the participation of that Member in its work.

3. The Military Staff Committee shall be responsible under the Security Council for the strategic direction of any armed forces placed at the disposal of the Security Council. Questions relating to the command of such forces shall be worked out subsequently.

4. The Military Staff Committee, with the authorization of the Security Council and after consultation with appropriate regional agencies, may establish regional subcommittees.

Article 48. 1. The action required to carry out the decisions of the Security Council for the maintenance of international peace and security shall be taken by all the Members of the United Nations or by some of them, as the Security Council may determine.

2. Such decisions shall be carried out by the Members of the United Nations directly and through their action in the appropriate international agencies of which they are members.

Article 49. The Members of the United Nations shall join in affording mutual assistance in carrying out the measures decided upon by the Security Council.

Article 50. If preventive or enforcement measures against any State are taken by the Security Council, any other State, whether a Member of the United Nations or not, which finds itself confronted with special economic problems arising from the carrying out of those measures shall have the right to consult the Security Council with regard to a solution of those problems.

Article 51. Nothing in the present Charter shall impair the inherent right of individual or collective self-defense if an armed attack occurs against a Member of the United Nations, until the Security Council has taken the measure necessary to maintain international peace and security. Measures taken by Members in the exercise of this right of self-defense shall be immediately reported to the Security Council and shall not in any way affect the authority and responsibility of the Security Council under the present

Charter to take at any time such action as it deems necessary in order to maintain or restore international peace and security.

CHAPTER IX
INTERNATIONAL ECONOMIC AND SOCIAL COOPERATION

Article 55. With a view to the creation of conditions of stability and well-being which are necessary for peaceful and friendly relations among nations based on respect for the principle of equal rights and self-determination of peoples the principle of equal rights and self-determination of peoples, the United Nations shall promote:

a. higher standards of living, full employment, and conditions of economic and social progress and development;

b. solutions of international economic, social, health, and related problems; and international cultural and educational cooperation; and

c. universal respect for, and observance of, human rights and fundamental freedoms for all without distinction as to race, sex, language, or religion.

Article 56. All Members pledge themselves to take joint and separate action in cooperation with the Organization for the achievement of the purposes set forth in Article 55.

APPENDIX K

COMMUNICATIONS GOAL

--- Possible Satellite-to-home-TV Broadcasts in the Future (per testimony from HEARINGS before the COMMITTEE ON AERONAUTICAL & SPACE SCIENCES, U.S. Senate, on NASA AUTHORIZATION FOR FISCAL YEAR 1966, Part1):

COMMUNICATIONS GOAL

Mr. Gehrig. Dr. Newell, in your prepared statement, speaking about communications, you say:

A great deal has already been accomplished and the next goals are to improve the technology of such systems and to make possible direct broadcasting from a satellite to home receivers.

How much power is required for direct broadcasting?

Dr. Newell. For direct broadcasting, simply radio broadcasting, modest powers of the order of a kilowatt are adequate. But when one gets to the television broadcasting, then one has to get to the tens of kilowatt range, and here is where one thinks in terms of such things as nuclear power supplies.

Dr. Gehrig. About how many kilowatts?

Dr. Newell. Well, many people think in terms of 30 kilowatts minimum.

Mr. Gehrig. Do you know of any systems that will give us 30 kilowatts?

Dr. Newell. Well, the SNAP-8 system is in this range.

Mr. Gehrig. When do you estimate that direct broadcasting would be technically feasible?

Dr. Newell. The---

Mr. Gehrig. Outside of the nuclear reactor or the power source equipment?

Dr. Newell. The direct broadcasting of radio, I think, could be feasible in a few years. This, of course, is much simpler than television since it involves less power and because radio receivers are generally standard throughout the world. Television systems involve more power and are not standard throughout the world.

I cannot give you an estimate on the television.

Mr. Gehrig. You cannot?

Dr. Newell. I cannot.

Mr. Gehrig. Dr. Seamans, in his statement, outlined a new four phase project management concept called phased project planning that has been adopted by NASA.

APPENDIX L

ADDRESS BY GREEK KING

Address by H.M. the King of Greece to the 16th International Astronautical Congress September 13, 1965

In the name of the Greek people I welcome you to my country, which is happy and proud to be host to such a distinguished gathering of scientists.

You will permit me to say that it is particularly appropriate that this Congress should be held in this country which, after all, produced the world's first astronaut. I will not weary you with the circumstances in which Icarus took off from Crete, and I must admit that his flight ended somewhat disastrously. He obviously did not give sufficient attention to the Physical Problems of Re-Entry nor to the effects of Solar Energy on his Unconventional Propulsion System. The world has made a few strides since those days, and although there may be some argument as to which country has made the most progress, I hope you will concede that we were the first to try.

In any case, I am sure we all agree that modern science, especially in its philosophical implications, owes much to the ideas of men who lived and taught two-and-a-half thousand years ago not far from where we are sitting here today. The fertile minds of those men provided our modern world with the basic concepts of scientific progress. Their inventive ideas and philosophical thoughts, coupled with the courage of young men and women and the technological facilities which our generation has developed, have made it possible for "Icarus" to fly far into space, and will make it possible for him in the imminent future to reach the stars.

Through their intellectual gifts, the ancient Greeks achieved harmony and balance in human endeavour. Today, perhaps more than at any other time, enlightened men everywhere look upon this harmony of Greek culture as an ideal for our troubled world.

The horizons now opening before us are literally without limits, and the opportunities for the beneficial use of these new discoveries and technological achievements are correspondingly great. But alas, the opportunities for their destructive use are also open to all (note---the author).

Unlike the previous generation, which faced the trials of a world-wide conflict and the problems arising from it, our own generation has had no real test of its moral fibre. At least, not yet. But now a great challenge, a magnificent challenge, a challenge the like of which no other generation has ever faced, looms before us. Political divisions and conflicting ideologies may still separate the countries of the world, but our young generation of people who can soar above the earth in space can also rise above national frontiers and restricting conventions (note---the author).

Ladies and Gentlemen, I am proud to belong to this generation, which is trying to reshape the world and to make it a better place to live in.

I stand before you, the path finders of outer-space, full of admiration for what you are doing and pray to God that your labour will always be to the benefit of humanity as a whole (note---the author).

With all my heart I wish your Congress every success and have much pleasure in declaring the 16th International Astronautical Congress, open.

APPENDIX M
MANNED SPACEFLIGHT CHART, USA

Alan Shepard				
	May 5, 1961	Freedom 7	15 minutes	
Virgil Grissom				
	July 21, 1961	Liberty Bell 7	16 minutes	
John Glenn				
	Feb. 20, 1962	Friendship 7	4 hrs	55 min
Scott Carpenter				
	May 24, 1962	Aurora 7	4 hrs	56 min
Walter Schirra				
	Oct. 3, 1962	Sigma 7	9 hrs	13 min
Gordon Cooper				
	May 15-16, 1963	Faith 7	34 hrs	27 min
Virgil Grissom John Young				
	Mar. 23, 1965	Gemini 3	4 hrs	53 min
James McDivitt Edward White				
	June 3-7,1965	Gemini 4	97 hrs	58 min
Gordon Cooper Charles Conrad				
	Aug. 21-29, 1965	Gemini 5	190 hrs	56 min
Frank Borman James Lovell				
	Dec. 4-18, 1965	Gemini 7	330 hrs	35 min
Walter Schirra Thomas Stafford				
	Dec. 15-16, 1965	Gemini 6	25 hrs	51 min

MANNED SPACEFLIGHT CHART, USSR

Yuri Gagarin Apr. 12, 1961	Vostok I	1 hr	48 min
Gherman Titov Aug. 6, 1961	Vostok II	25 hrs	18 min
Andrian Nikolayev Aug. 11-15, 1962	Vostok III	94 hrs	22 min
Pavel Popovich Aug. 12-15, 1962	Vostok IV	70 hrs	57 min
Valery Bykovsky June 14-19, 1963	Vostok V	119 hrs	6 min
Valentina Tereshkova June 16-19, 1963	Vostok VI	70 hrs	50 min
Konstantin Feoktistov Vladimir Komarov Boris Yegorov Oct. 12-13, 1964	Voskhod I	24 hrs	17 min
Alexei Leonov Pavel Belyayev Mar. 18-19, 1965	Voskhod II	26 hrs	2 min

USSR SPACE RECORDS

Only woman in orbit---Tereshkova, June, 1963.
Only 3-man spaceflight in one craft---Feoktistov, Komarov and Yegorov.
Heaviest spacecraft in orbit---16,000 pounds.

COMPARISON---USA AND USSR MANNED SPACEFLIGHTS

USA

Astronaut	Hrs	Min	Orbits	Mileage
Glenn	4	55	3	81,000
Carpenter	4	56	3	81,000
Schirra	9	13	6	165,000
Cooper	34	27	22	595,000
Grissom	4	53	3	80,000
Young	4	53	3	80,000
McDivitt	97	58	67	1,842,000
White	97	58	67	1,842,000
Cooper	190	56	131	3,330,000
Conrad	190	56	131	3,330,000
Schirra	25	51	19	513,000
Stafford	25	51	19	513,000
Borman	330	35	223	5,716,000
Lovell	330	35	223	5,716,000
TOTALS	1,353	57	920	23,884,000

USSR

Astronaut	Hrs	Min	Orbits	Mileage
Gagarin	1	48	1	25,700
Titov	25	18	17	437,500
Nikolayev	94	22	64	1,663,000
Popovich	70	57	48	1,243,000
Bykovsky	119	6	81	2,070,270
Tereshkova	70	50	48	1,210,500
Feoktistov	24	17	16	416,000
Komarov	24	17	16	416,000
Yegorov	24	17	16	416,000
Keonov	26	2	17	445,400
Belyayev	26	2	17	445,400
TOTALS	507	16	341	8,372,770

	USA	USSR
1-man suborbital flights	2	--
1-man orbital flights	4	6
2-man orbital flights	5	1
3-man orbital flights	--	1
TOTALS	11	8

APPENDIX N

SATELLITE TABLES, USA AND USSR

SPACE LAUNCHINGS

From October, 1957

through November, 1965

Source:

Goddard Space Flight Center

OBJECT	CODE NAME	CATALOGUE NUMBER	SOURCE	LAUNCH
1957 LAUNCHES				
ALPHA 1	ROCKET BODY	001	USSR	4 OCT
ALPHA 2	SPUTNIK 1	002	USSR	4 OCT
BETA 1	SPUTNIK 2	003	USSR	3 NOV
1958 LAUNCHES				
ALPHA 1	EXPLORER 1	004	US	1 FEB
BETA 1	ROCKET BODY	016	US	17 MAR
BETA 2	VANGUARD 1	005	US	17 MAR
GAMMA 1	EXPLORER 3	006	US	26 MAR
DELTA 1	ROCKET BODY	007	USSR	15 MAY
DELTA 2	SPUTNIK 3	008	USSR	15 MAY
EPSILON 1	EXPLORER 4	009	US	26 JUL
ZETA 1	SCORE	010	US	18 DEC
ETA 1	PIONEER 1	110	US	11 OCT
THETA 1	PIONEER 3	111	US	6 DEC
1959 LAUNCHES				
MU 1	LUNIK 1	112	USSR	2 JAN
ALPHA 1	VANGUARD 2	011	US	17 FEB
ALPHA 2	ROCKET BODY	012	US	17 FEB
BETA 1	DISCOVERER 1	013	US	28 FEB
NU 1	PIONEER 4	113	US	3 MAR
GAMMA 1	DISCOVERER 2	014	US	13 APR
DELTA 1	EXPLORER 6	015	US	7 AUG

DELTA 2	ROCKET BODY	017	US	7 AUG
EPSILON 1	DISCOVERER 5	018	US	13 AUG
EPSILON 2	CAPSULE	026	US	13 AUG
ZETA 1	DISCOVERER 6	019	US	19 AUG
XI 1	LUNIK 2	114	USSR	12 SEP
ETA 1	VANGUARD 3	020	US	18 SEP
THETA 1	LUNIK 3	021	USSR	4 OCT
IOTA 1	EXPLORER 7	022	US	13 OCT
IOTA 2	ROCKET BODY	023	US	13 OCT
KAPPA 1	DISCOVERER 7	034	US	7 NOV
LAMBDA 1	DISCOVERER 8	025	US	20 NOV

1960 LAUNCHES

ALPHA 1+	PIONEER 5	027	US	11 MAR
BETA 1	ROCKET BODY	028	US	1 APR
BETA 2	TIROS 1	029	US	1 APR
BETA 3	NONE	101	US	1 APR
BETA 4	NONE	115	US	1 APR
GAMMA 1	ROCKET BODY	030	US	13 APR
GAMMA 2	TRANSIT 1B	031	US	13 APR
GAMMA 3	METAL OBJECT	033	US	13 APR
GAMMA 4	NONE	099	US	13 APR
DELTA 1	DISCOVERER 11	032	US	15 APR
EPSILON 1	SPUTNIK 4	034	USSR	15 MAY
EPSILON 2	ROCKET BODY	035	USSR	15 MAY
EPSILON 3	NONE	036	USSR	15 MAY
EPSILON 4	NONE	037	USSR	15 MAY
EPSILON 5	NONE	038	USSR	15 MAY
EPSILON 6	NONE	039	USSR	15 MAY
EPSILON 7	NONE	040	USSR	15 MAY
EPSILON 8	NONE	041	USSR	15 MAY
EPSILON 9	NONE	042	USSR	15 MAY
ZETA 1	MIDAS 2	043	US	24 MAY
ZETA 2	METAL OBJECT	044	US	24 MAY
ETA 1	TRANSIT 2A	045	US	22 JUN
ETA 2	GREB	046	US	22 JUN
ETA 3	ROCKET BODY	047	US	22 JUN
ETA 4		840	US	22 JUN
ETA 5		841	US	22 JUN
THETA 1	DISCOVERER 13	048	US	10 AUG
THETA 1	CAPSULE	NNA	US	10 AUG
IOTA 1	ECHO I	049	US	12 AUG
IOTA 2	ROCKET BODY	050	US	12 AUG
IOTA 3	METAL OBJECT	051	US	12 AUG
IOTA 4	METAL OBJECT	052	US	12 AUG
IOTA 5	METAL OBJECT	053	US	12 AUG
KAPPA 1	DISCOVERER 14	054	US	18 AUG
KAPPA 1	CAPSULE	NNA	US	18 AUG
LAMBDA 1	SPUTNIK 5	055	USSR	19 AUG
LAMBDA 2	ROCKET BODY	056	USSR	19 AUG
MU 1	DISCOVERER 15	057	US	13 SEP
MU 1	CAPSULE	NNA	US	13 SEP
NU 1	COURIER 1B	058	US	4 OCT
NU 2	ROCKET BODY	059	US	4 OCT
XI 1	EXPLORER 8	060	US	3 NOV
XI 2	ROCKET BODY	062	US	3 NOV
XI 3	NONE	069	US	3 NOV
XI 4	NONE	105	US	3 NOV
OMICRON 1	DISCOVERER 17	061	US	12 NOV
OMICRON 1	CAPSULE	NNA	US	12 NOV
PI 1	TIROS 2	063	US	23 NOV
PI 2	ROCKET BODY	064	US	23 NOV
PI 3	NONE	074	US	23 NOV
PI 4	NONE	075	US	23 NOV
RHO 1	SPUTNIK 6	065	USSR	1 DEC
RHO 2	ROCKET BODY	066	USSR	1 DEC
SIGMA 1	CAPSULE	NNA	US	7 DEC
SIGMA 1	DISCOVERER 18	067	US	7 DEC
TAU 1	DISCOVERER 19	068	US	20 DEC

1961 LAUNCHES

ALPHA 1	SAMOS 2	070	US	31 JAN
ALPHA 2	METAL OBJECT	079	US	31 JAN
BETA 1	SPUTNIK 7	071	USSR	4 FEB
BETA 2	ROCKET BODY	072	USSR	4 FEB
BETA 3	NONE	073	USSR	4 FEB
GAMMA 2	ROCKET BODY	076	USSR	12 FEB
GAMMA 3	SPUTNIK 8	077	USSR	12 FEB
GAMMA 4	NONE	078	USSR	12 FEB
GAMMA 1+	VENUS PROBE	080	USSR	12 FEB
DELTA 1	EXPLORER 9	081	US	16 FEB
DELTA 2	ROCKET BODY	082	US	16 FEB
DELTA 3	NONE	085	US	16 FEB
DELTA 4	NONE	086	US	16 FEB
EPSILON 1	DISCOVERER 20	083	US	17 FEB
EPSILON 2	NONE	088	US	17 FEB
EPSILON 3	NONE	089	US	17 FEB
EPSILON 4	NONE	090	US	17 FEB
ZETA 1	DISCOVERER 21	084	US	18 FEB
ETA 1	TRANSIT 3B & LOFTI	087	US	22 FEB
THETA 1	SPUTNIK 9	091	USSR	9 MAR
THETA 2	NONE	092	USSR	9 MAR
THETA 3	NONE	093	USSR	9 MAR
THETA 4	NONE	094	USSR	9 MAR
IOTA 1	SPUTNIK 10	095	USSR	25 MAR
IOTA 2	ROCKET BODY	096	USSR	25 MAR
IOTA 3	NONE	097	USSR	25 MAR
KAPPA 1	EXPLORER 10	098	US	25 MAR
LAMBDA 1	DISCOVERER 23	100	US	8 APR
LAMBDA 2	CAPSULE	102	US	8 APR
LAMBDA 3	NONE	106	US	8 APR
MU 1	VOSTOK 1	103	USSR	12 APR
MU 2	ROCKET BODY	104	USSR	12 APR
NU 1	EXPLORER 11	107	US	27 APR
XI 1	CAPSULE	NNA	US	16 JUN
XI 1	DISCOVERER 25	108	US	16 JUN
XI 2	NONE	109	US	16 JUN
OMICRON 1	TRANSIT 4A	116	US	29 JUN
OMICRON 2	INJUN-SR-3	117	US	29 JUN
OMICRON 3-206++	METAL OBJECTS		US	29 JUN
OMICRON 25	METAL OBJECT	140	US	29 JUN
OMICRON 28	METAL OBJECT	143	US	29 JUN
OMICRON 46	METAL OBJECT	171	US	29 JUN
PI 1	DISCOVERER 26	160	US	7 JUL
PI 1	CAPSULE	NNA	US	8 JUL
RHO 1	TIROS 3	162	US	12 JUL
SIGMA 2	METAL OBJECT	164	US	12 JUL
RHO 2	ROCKET BODY	165	US	12 JUL
RHO 3	METAL OBJECT	166	US	12 JUL
RHO 4	METAL OBJECT	167	US	12 JUL
SIGMA 1	MIDAS 3	163	US	12 JUL
SIGMA 3	METAL OBJECT	188	US	12 JUL
SIGMA 4	METAL OBJECT	196	US	12 JUL
TAU 1	VOSTOK 2	168	USSR	6 AUG
TAU 2	ROCKET BODY	169	USSR	6 AUG
UPSILON 1	EXPLORER 12	170	US	16 AUG
PHI 1	RANGER 1	173	US	23 AUG
PHI 2	ROCKET BODY	174	US	23 AUG
CHI 1	EXPLORER 13	180	US	25 AUG
PSI 1	DISCOVERER 29	181	US	30 AUG
PSI 1	CAPSULE	NNA	US	30 AUG
OMEGA 1	DISCOVERER 30	182	US	12 SEP
OMEGA 1	CAPSULE	NNA	US	12 SEP
OMEGA 2	METAL OBJECT	185	US	12 SEP
OMEGA 3	METAL OBJECT	187	US	12 SEP
A-ALPHA 1	MA-4	183	US	13 SEP
A-ALPHA 2	ROCKET BODY	184	US	13 SEP
A-BETA 1	DISCOVERER 31	186	US	17 SEP
A-GAMMA 1	DISCOVERER 32	189	US	13 OCT
A-GAMMA 1	CAPSULE	NNA	US	13 OCT
A-GAMMA 2	METAL OBJECT	190	US	13 OCT

A-GAMMA 3	METAL OBJECT	191	US	13 OCT
A DELTA 1	MIDAS 4	192	US	21 OCT
A-DELTA 2		193	US	21 OCT
A DELTA 3	METAL OBJECT	194	US	21 OCT
A DELTA 4	METAL OBJECT	195	US	21 OCT
A-EPSILON 1	DISCOVERER 34	197	US	5 NOV
A-EPSILON 2	METAL OBJECT	198	US	5 NOV
A-EPSILON 3	METAL OBJECT	199	US	5 NOV
A-EPSILON 4	METAL OBJECT	200	US	5 NOV
A ETA 1	TRANSIT 4B	202	US	15 NOV
A-EPSILON 5	METAL OBJECT	203	US	5 NOV
A-ZETA 1	DISCOVERER 35	201	US	15 NOV
A-ZETA 1	CAPSULE	NNA	US	15 NOV
A ETA 2	TRAAC	205	US	15 NOV
A ETA 3	ROCKET BODY	204	US	15 NOV
A-ZETA 2	METAL OBJECT	207	US	15 NOV
A-THETA 1	RANGER 2	206	US	18 NOV
A-IOTA 1	MA-5	208	US	29 NOV
A-IOTA 2	ROCKET BODY	209	US	29 NOV
A-KAPPA 1	DISCOVERER 36	213	US	12 DEC
A-KAPPA 1	CAPSULE	NNA	US	12 DEC
A-KAPPA 2	OSCAR 1	214	US	12 DEC
A-KAPPA 3	MATAL OBJECT	215	US	12 DEC
A-LAMBDA 1		217	US	22 DEC
A-LAMBDA 2		218	US	22 DEC
A-LAMBDA 3		219	US	22 DEC

1962 LAUNCHES

ALPHA 1+	RANGER 3	221	US	26 JAN
ALPHA 2+	ROCKET BODY	222	US	26 JAN
BETA 1	TIROS 4	226	US	8 FEB
BETA 2	ROCKET BODY	227	US	8 FEB
BETA 3	METAL OBJECT	228	US	8 FEB
BETA 4	METAL OBJECT	229	US	8 FEB
GAMMA 1	FRIENDSHIP 7	240	US	20 FEB
GAMMA 2	ROCKET BODY	241	US	20 FEB
DELTA 1		242	US	21 FEB
EPSILON 1	DISCOVERER 38	247	US	27 FEB
EPSILON 1	CAPSULE	NNA	US	27 FEB
EPSILON 2	ROCKET BODY	248	US	27 FEB
EPSILON 3	METAL OBJECT	249	US	27 FEB
EPSILON 4	METAL OBJECT	251	US	27 FEB
ZETA 1	ORB.SOL.OBS. 1	255	US	7 MAR
ETA 1		256	US	7 MAR
ZETA 2	ROCKET BODY	257	US	7 MAR
ETA 2		258	US	7 MAR
ETA 3		259	US	7 MAR
THETA 1	COSMOS 1	266	USSR	16 MAR
THETA 2	ROCKET BODY	267	USSR	16 MAR
IOTA 1	COSMOS 2	269	USSR	6 APR
IOTA 2	ROCKET BODY	270	USSR	6 APR
KAPPA 1		271	US	9 APR
KAPPA 2		272	US	9 APR
KAPPA 3		273	US	9 APR
KAPPA 4		274	US	9 APR
LAMBDA 1		276	US	18 APR
LAMBDA 2		277	US	18 APR
LAMBDA 3		278	US	18 APR
LAMBDA 4		279	US	18 APR
MU 1	RANGER 4	280	US	23 APR
MU 2	ROCKET BODY	282	US	23 APR
NU 1	COSMOS 3	281	USSR	24 APR
NU 2	ROCKET BODY	283	USSR	24 APR
OMICRON 1	ARIEL 1	285	US/UK	26 APR
XI 1	COSMOS 4	287	USSR	26 APR
XI 2	ROCKET BODY	284	USSR	26 APR
XI 3	METAL OBJECT	289	USSR	26 APR
PI 1		286	US	26 APR
OMICRON 2	ROCKET BODY	288	US/UK	26 APR
RHO 1		290	US	29 APR
RHO 2		291	US	29 APR

SIGMA 1		292	US	15 MAY
SIGMA 2		293	US	15 MAY
SIGMA 3		294	US	15 MAY
TAU 1	AURORA 7	295	US	24 MAY
TAU 2	ROCKET BODY	296	US	24 MAY
UPSILON 1	COSMOS 5	297	USSR	28 MAY
UPSILON 2	ROCKET BODY	298	USSR	28 MAY
PHI 1		302	US	30 MAY
PHI 2		303	US	30 MAY
CHI 1		304	US	2 JUN
CHI 2	OSCAR 2	305	US	2 JUN
CHI 3		306	US	2 JUN
PSI 1		307	US	17 JUN
OMEGA 1		308	US	18 JUN
OMEGA 2		310	US	18 JUN
OMEGA 3		314	US	18 JUN
A ALPHA 1	TIROS 5	309	US	19 JUN
A ALPHA 2	ROCKET BODY	311	US	19 JUN
A ALPHA 3	METAL OBJECT	312	US	19 JUN
A ALPHA 4	METAL OBJECT	313	US	19 JUN
A-BETA 1		315	US	23 JUN
A-GAMMA 1		316	US	28 JUN
A-DELTA 1	COSMOS 6	338	USSR	30 JUN
A-DELTA 2	ROCKET BODY	339	USSR	30 JUN
A EPSILON 1	TELSTAR 1	340	US	10 JUL
A EPSILON 2	ROCKET BODY	341	US	10 JUL
A-ZETA 1		342	US	18 JUL
A-ZETA 2		343	US	18 JUL
A-ETA 1		344	US	21 JUL
A-THETA 1		345	US	28 JUL
A-IOTA 1	COSMOS 7	346	USSR	28 JUL
A-IOTA 2	ROCKET BODY	347	USSR	28 JUL
A-IOTA 3	METAL OBJECT	348	USSR	28 JUL
A-IOTA 4	METAL OBJECT	349	USSR	28 JUL
A-KAPPA 1		360	US	2 AUG
A-KAPPA 2		362	US	2 AUG
A-LAMBDA 1		361	US	5 AUG
A-MU 1	VOSTOK 3	363	USSR	11 AUG
A-MU 2	ROCKET BODY	364	USSR	11 AUG
A-NU 1	VOSTOK 4	365	USSR	12 AUG
A-NU 2	ROCKET BODY	366	USSR	12 AUG
A-XI 1	COSMOS 8	367	USSR	18 AUG
A-XI 2	ROCKET BODY	368	USSR	18 AUG
A OMICRON 1		369	US	23 AUG
A OMICRON 2		370	US	23 AUG
A OMICRON 3		378	US	23 AUG
A OMICRON 4		388	US	23 AUG
A-PI 1		371	USSR	25 AUG
A-PI 2		372	USSR	25 AUG
A-PI 3		373	USSR	25 AUG
A-PI 4		379	USSR	25 AUG
A-PI 5		380	USSR	25 AUG
A-PI 6		376	USSR	25 AUG
A-PI 7		386	USSR	25 AUG
A-PI 8		387	USSR	25 AUG
A RHO 1	MARINER	374	US	27 AUG
A RHO 2	ROCKET BODY	375	US	27 AUG
A-SIGMA 1		377	US	29 AUG
A-TAU 1		381	USSR	1 SEP
A-TAU 2		382	USSR	1 SEP
A-TAU 3		383	USSR	1 SEP
A-TAU 4		384	USSR	1 SEP
A UPSILON 1		385	US	1 SEP
A-PHI 1		389	USSR	12 SEP
A-PHI 2		390	USSR	12 SEP
A-PHI 3		391	USSR	12 SEP
A-PHI 4		392	USSR	12 SEP
A-PHI 5		393	USSR	12 SEP
A-PHI 6		394	USSR	12 SEP
A-PHI 7		395	USSR	12 SEP
A-CHI 1		396	US	17 SEP

A PSI 1	TIROS 6	397	US	18 SEP
A PSI 2	ROCKET BODY	398	US	18 SEP
A PSI 3	METAL OBJECT	399	US	18 SEP
A PSI 4	METAL OBJECT	400	US	18 SEP
A-OMEGA 1		422	USSR	27 SEP
A-OMEGA 2		423	USSR	27 SEP
A-OMEGA 3		425	USSR	27 SEP
A-OMEGA 4		428	USSR	27 SEP
A-OMEGA 5		429	USSR	27 SEP
A-OMEGA 6		430	USSR	27 SEP
A-OMEGA 7		431	USSR	27 SEP
A-OMEGA 8		435	USSR	27 SEP
B ALPHA 1	ALOUETTE	424	CANADA	29 SEP
B ALPHA 2	ROCKET BODY	426	US	29 SEP
B-BETA 1		427	US	29 SEP
B ALPHA 3	METAL OBJECT	510	US	29 SEP
B ALPHA 4	METAL OBJECT	511	US	29 SEP
B GAMMA 1	EXPLORER 14	432	US	2 OCT
B GAMMA 2	ROCKET BODY	NNA	US	2 OCT
B-DELTA 1	SIGMA 7	433	US	3 OCT
B-DELTA 2	ROCKET BODY	434	US	3 OCT
B-EPSILON 1		436	US	9 OCT
B-ZETA 1		437	USSR	17 OCT
B-ZETA 2		438	USSR	17 OCT
B ETA 1+	RANGER 5	439	US	18 OCT
B ETA 2+	ROCKET BODY	440	US	18 OCT
B-THETA 1		441	USSR	20 OCT
B-THETA 2		442	USSR	20 OCT
B-IOTA 1		443	USSR	24 OCT
B-IOTA 2		456	USSR	24 OCT
B-IOTA 3		457	USSR	24 OCT
B-IOTA 4		458	USSR	24 OCT
B-IOTA 5		459	USSR	24 OCT
B-IOTA 6		460	USSR	24 OCT
B-IOTA 7		482	USSR	24 OCT
B-IOTA 8		483	USSR	24 OCT
B-IOTA 9		484	USSR	24 OCT
B-IOTA 10		485	USSR	24 OCT
B-IOTA 11		486	USSR	24 OCT
B-IOTA 12		487	USSR	24 OCT
B-IOTA 13		491	USSR	24 OCT
B-IOTA 14		492	USSR	24 OCT
B-IOTA 15		493	USSR	24 OCT
B-IOTA 16		494	USSR	24 OCT
B-IOTA 17		495	USSR	24 OCT
B-IOTA 18		496	USSR	24 OCT
B-IOTA 19		497	USSR	24 OCT
B-IOTA 20		498	USSR	24 OCT
B-IOTA 21		499	USSR	24 OCT
B-IOTA 22		500	USSR	24 OCT
B-IOTA 23		501	USSR	24 OCT
B-IOTA 24		512	USSR	24 OCT
B KAPPA 1		444	US	27 OCT
B LAMBDA 1	EXPLORER 15	445	US	27 OCT
B LAMBDA 2	ROCKET BODY	NNA	US	27 OCT
B MU 1	ANNA 1B	446	US	31 OCT
B MU 2	ROCKET BODY	447	US	31 OCT
B NU 1		448	USSR	1 NOV
B NU 2		449	USSR	1 NOV
B NU 3+		450	USSR	1 NOV
B-XI 1		451	USSR	4 NOV
B-XI 2		452	USSR	4 NOV
B-XI 3		454	USSR	4 NOV
B-XI 4		488	USSR	4 NOV
B-XI 5		489	USSR	4 NOV
B-OMICRON 1		453	US	5 NOV
B-PI 1		455	US	11 NOV
B-RHO 1		481	US	24 NOV
B-SIGMA 1		490	US	4 DEC
B TAU 1		502	US	13 DEC
B TAU 2	INJUN 3	504	US	13 DEC
B TAU 3		507	US	13 DEC

B TAU 4		508	US	13 DEC
B-PHI 1		505	US	14 DEC
B TAU 5		513	US	13 DEC
B TAU 6		520	US	13 DEC
B USPILON 1	RELAY 1	503	US	13 DEC
B UPSILON 2	ROCKET BODY	515	US	13 DEC
B CHI 1	EXPLORER 16	506	US	16 DEC
B PSI 1	TRANSIT 5A	509	US	19 DEC
B PSI 2		514	US	19 DEC
B PSI 3		519	US	19 DEC
B PSI 4		523	US	19 DEC
B-OMEGA 1		517	USSR	22 DEC
B-OMEGA 2		518	USSR	22 DEC

1963 LAUNCHES

1963 1A		521	USSR	4 JAN
1963 1B		522	USSR	4 JAN
1963 1C		524	USSR	4 JAN
1963 2A		525	US	7 JAN
1963 2B		526	US	7 JAN
1963 03A		527	US	16 JAN
1963 3B		528	US	16 JAN
1963 3C		529	US	16 JAN
1963 04A	SYNCOM 1	553	US	14 FEB
1963 04B	ROCKET BODY	532	US	14 FEB
1963 05A		533	US	19 FEB
1963 05B		534	US	19 FEB
1963 05C		535	US	19 FEB
1963 05D		536	US	19 FEB
1963 6A		554	USSR	21 MAR
1963 6B		555	USSR	21 MAR
1963 7A		562	US	1 APR
1963 8A		563	USSR	2 APR
1963 08B		566	USSR	2 APR
1963 09A	EXPLORER 17	564	US	3 APR
1963 9B	ROCKET BODY	565	US	3 APR
1963 10A		567	USSR	13 APR
1963 10B		568	USSR	13 APR
1963 11A		569	USSR	22 APR
1963 11B		570	USSR	22 APR
1963 12A		571	USSR	28 APR
1963 12B		572	USSR	28 APR
1963 13A	TELSTAR 2	573	US	7 MAY
1963 13B	ROCKET BODY	575	US	7 MAY
1963 14A		574	US	9 MAY
1963 14B		579	US	9 MAY
1963 14C		608	US	9 MAY
1963 14D		589	US	9 MAY
1963 14E		602	US	9 MAY
1963 14F		628	US	9 MAY
1963 14G		629	US	9 MAY
1963 14H		702	US	9 MAY
1963 15A	FAITH 7	576	US	15 MAY
1963 15B	ROCKET BODY	577	US	15 MAY
1963 16A		578	US	18 MAY
1963 17A		580	USSR	22 MAY
1963 17B		581	USSR	22 MAY
1963 17C		582	USSR	22 MAY
1963 17D		583	USSR	22 MAY
1963 17E		584	USSR	22 MAY
1963 17F		585	USSR	22 MAY
1963 17G		588	USSR	22 MAY
1963 18A		586	USSR	24 MAY
1963 18B		587	USSR	24 MAY
1963 19A		590	US	12 JUN
1963 20A	VOSTOK 5	591	USSR	14 JUN
1963 20B		592	USSR	14 JUN
1963 21A		593	US	15 JUN
1963 21B	LOFTI 2A	601	US	15 JUN
1963 21C	SOLAR RADIATION	599	US	15 JUN
1963 21D		600	US	15 JUN

1963 21E		598	US	15 JUN
1963 21F		597	US	15 JUN
1963 21G		617	US	15 JUN
1963 22A		594	US	16 JUN
1963 23A	VOSTOK 6	595	USSR	16 JUN
1963 23B		596	USSR	16 JUN
1963 22B		603	US	16 JUN
1963 22C		610	US	16 JUN
1963 22D		611	US	16 JUN
1963 24A	TIROS 7	604	US	19 JUN
1963 24B	ROCKET BODY	605	US	19 JUN
1963 24C	METAL OBJECT	606	US	19 JUN
1963 24D	METAL OBJECT	607	US	19 JUN
1963 25A		609	US	27 JUN
1963 25B		614	US	27 JUN
1963 26A	RESEARCH SATELLITE FOR GEOPHYSICS	612	US	28 JUN
1963 27A		613	US	29 JUN
1963 27B		615	US	29 JUN
1963 27C		616	US	29 JUN
1963 28A		618	US	12 JUL
1963 28B		619	US	12 JUL
1963 28C		620	US	12 JUL
1963 29A		621	US	18 JUL
1963 29B		623	US	18 JUL
1963 30A		622	US	19 JUL
1963 30B		635	US	19 JUL
1963 30C		630	US	19 JUL
1963 30D		624	US	19 JUL
1963 30E		631	US	19 JUL
1963 31A	SYNCOM 2	634	US	26 JUL
1963 31B	ROCKET BODY	625	US	26 JUL
1963 32A		626	US	31 JUL
1963 32B		627	US	31 JUL
1963 33A		632	USSR	6 AUG
1963 33B		633	USSR	6 AUG
1963 34A		636	US	24 AUG
1963 34B		642	US	24 AUG
1963 35A		637	US	29 AUG
1963 35B		638	US	29 AUG
1963 35C		639	US	29 AUG
1963 35D		640	US	29 AUG
1963 36A		641	US	6 SEP
1963 36B		663	US	6 SEP
1963 36C		664	US	6 SEP
1963 36D		665	US	6 SEP
1963 36E		666	US	6 SEP
1963 36F		667	US	6 SEP
1963 37A		668	US	24 SEP
1963 38A		669	US	28 SEP
1963 38B		670	US	28 SEP
1963 38C		671	US	28 SEP
1963 38D		672	US	28 SEP
1963 38E		745	US	28 SEP
1963 39A		674	US	17 OCT
1963 39B		675	US	17 OCT
1963 39C		692	US	17 OCT
1963 40A		673	USSR	18 OCT
1963 40B	COSMOS 20	676	USSR	18 OCT
1963 41A		677	US	25 OCT
1963 41B		678	US	25 OCT
1963 41C		679	US	25 OCT
1963 41D		680	US	25 OCT
1963 42A		681	US	29 OCT
1963 42C		691	US	29 OCT
1963 42B		682	US	29 OCT
1963 43A	POLYOT	683	USSR	1 NOV
1963 43B		684	USSR	1 NOV
1963 43C		685	USSR	1 NOV
1963 43D		686	USSR	1 NOV
1963 44A	COSMOS 21	687	USSR	11 NOV

1963 44B		688	USSR	11 NOV
1963 45A	COSMOS 22	689	USSR	16 NOV
1963 45B		690	USSR	16 NOV
1963 46A	EXPLORER 18	693	US	27 NOV
1963 47A	CENTAUR 2	694	US	27 NOV
1963 48A		695	US	27 NOV
1963 47B		696	US	27 NOV
1963 47C		697	US	27 NOV
1963 47D		698	US	27 NOV
1963 47E		699	US	27 NOV
1963 47F		700	US	27 NOV
1963 47G		701	US	27 NOV
1963 47H		739	US	27 NOV
1963 49A		703	US	5 DEC
1963 49B		704	US	5 DEC
1963 49C		705	US	5 DEC
1963 49D		706	US	5 DEC
1963 49E		715	US	5 DEC
1963 49F		753	US	5 DEC
1963 50A	COSMOS 23	707	USSR	13 DEC
1963 50B		708	USSR	13 DEC
1963 50C		709	USSR	13 DEC
1963 50D		710	USSR	13 DEC
1963 51A		711	US	18 DEC
1963 52A	COSMOS 24	712	USSR	19 DEC
1963 52B		713	USSR	19 DEC
1963 53A	EXPLORER 19	714	US	19 DEC
1963 55A		718	US	21 DEC
1963 53B		721	US	19 DEC
1963 53C		722	US	19 DEC
1963 53D		723	US	19 DEC
1963 53E		724	US	19 DEC
1963 53F		725	US	19 DEC
1963 53G		726	US	19 DEC
1963 53H		732	US	19 DEC
1963 54A	TIROS 8	716	US	21 DEC
1963 54B		717	US	21 DEC
1963 54C		720	US	21 DEC
1963 54D		736	US	21 DEC
1963 55B		719	US	21 DEC

1964 LAUNCHES

1964 1A		727	US	11 JAN
1964 1B	GGSE	728	US	11 JAN
1964 1C	EGRS	729	US	11 JAN
1964 1D	SOLAR RADIATION	730	US	11 JAN
1964 1E		731	US	11 JAN
1964 2A		733	US	19 JAN
1964 2B		734	US	19 JAN
1964 2C		735	US	19 JAN
1963 3A	RELAY 2	737	US	21 JAN
1964 03B		738	US	21 JAN
1964 04A	ECHO 2	740	US	25 JAN
1964 04B		741	US	25 JAN
1964 04C		742	US	25 JAN
1964 04D		743	US	25 JAN
1964 04E		749	US	25 JAN
1964 05A	SATURN 5	744	US	29 JAN
1964 06A	ELEKTRON 1	746	USSR	30 JAN
1964 7A	RANGER 6	747	US	30 JAN
1964 06B	ELEKTRON 2	748	USSR	30 JAN
1964 06C		750	USSR	30 JAN
1964 06D		751	USSR	30 JAN
1964 8A		752	US	15 FEB
1964 8B		755	US	15 FEB
1964 9A		754	US	25 FEB
1964 9B		756	US	25 FEB
1964 10A	COSMOS 25	757	USSR	27 FEB
1964 10B		758	USSR	27 FEB
1964 11A		759	US	28 FEB
1964 11B		760	US	28 FEB

1964 11C		761	US	28 FEB
1964 10C		762	USSR	27 FEB
1964 10D		763	USSR	27 FEB
1964 12A		764	US	11 MAR
1964 12B		765	US	11 MAR
1964 13A	COSMOS 26	766	USSR	18 MAR
1964 13B		767	USSR	18 MAR
1964 13C		768	USSR	18 MAR
1964 13D		769	USSR	18 MAR
1964 14A	COSMOS 27	770	USSR	27 MAR
1964 15A	ARIEL 2	771	US/UK	27 MAR
1964 14B		772	USSR	27 MAR
1964 14C		773	USSR	27 MAR
1964 14D		774	USSR	27 MAR
1964 15B		775	US/UK	27 MAR
1964 16A		776	USSR	2 APR
1964 16B		777	USSR	2 APR
1964 16C		778	USSR	2 APR
1964 16D		785	USSR	2 APR
1964 17A	COSMOS 28	779	USSR	4 APR
1964 17B		780	USSR	4 APR
1964 17C		781	USSR	4 APR
1964 18A	GEMINI 1	782	US	8 APR
1964 19A		783	USSR	12 APR
1964 19B	POLYOT 2	784	USSR	12 APR
1964 20A		786	US	23 APR
1964 20B		787	US	23 APR
1964 20C		788	US	23 APR
1964 20D		789	US	23 APR
1964 20E		790	US	23 APR
1964 21A	COSMOS 29	791	USSR	25 APR
1964 21B		792	USSR	25 APR
1964 21C		793	USSR	25 APR
1964 21D		794	USSR	25 APR
1964 21E		795	USSR	25 APR
1964 22A		796	US	27 APR
1964 23A	COSMOS 30	797	USSR	18 APR
1964 23B		798	USSR	18 APR
1964 24A		799	US	19 APR
1964 25A	SATURN 6	800	US	28 APR
1964 26A		801	US	4 JUN
1964 27A		802	US	4 JUN
1964 26B		805	US	4 JUN
1964 26C		806	US	4 JUN
1964 26D		809	US	4 JUN
1964 28A	COSMOS 31	803	USSR	6 JUN
1964 28B		804	USSR	6 JUN
1964 29A	COSMOS 32	807	USSR	10 JUN
1964 29B		808	USSR	10 JUN
1964 29C		810	USSR	10 JUN
1964 30A		811	US	13 JUN
1964 30B		820	US	13 JUN
1964 31A		812	US	18 JUN
1964 31B		813	US	18 JUN
1964 31C		815	US	18 JUN
1964 32A		814	US	19 JUN
1964 32B		821	US	19 JUN
1964 33A	COSMOS 33	816	USSR	23 JUN
1964 33B		817	USSR	23 JUN
1964 33C		818	USSR	23 JUN
1964 33D		819	USSR	23 JUN
1964 34A	COSMOS 34	822	USSR	1 JUL
1964 34B		823	USSR	1 JUL
1964 35A		824	US	2 JUL
1964 36A		825	US	6 JUL
1964 36B		826	US	6 JUL
1964 36C		827	US	6 JUL
1964 37A		828	US	10 JUL
1964 38A	ELECTRON 3	829	USSR	10 JUL
1964 38B	ELECTRON 4	830	USSR	10 JUL
1964 38C		831	USSR	10 JUL
1964 38D		832	USSR	10 JUL

1964 39A	COSMOS 35	833	USSR	15 JUL
1964 39B		834	USSR	15 JUL
1964 39C		835	USSR	15 JUL
1964 39D		839	USSR	15 JUL
1964 40A		836	US	17 JUL
1964 40B		837	US	17 JUL
1964 40C		838	US	17 JUL
1964 41A	RANGER 7	842	US	28 JUL
1964 41B		843	US	28 JUL
1964 42A	COSMOS 36	844	USSR	30 JUL
1964 42B		845	USSR	30 JUL
1964 43A		846	US	5 AUG
1964 44A	COSMOS 37	848	USSR	14 AUG
1964 44B		849	USSR	14 AUG
1964 45A		850	US	14 AUG
1964 45B		851	US	14 AUG
1964 45C		852	US	14 AUG
1964 46A	COSMOS 38	853	USSR	18 AUG
1964 46B	COSMOS 39	854	USSR	18 AUG
1964 46C	COSMOS 40	855	USSR	18 AUG
1964 46D		856	USSR	18 AUG
1964 46E		857	USSR	18 AUG
1964 46F		859	USSR	18 AUG
1964 46G		860	USSR	18 AUG
1964 47A	SYNCOM 3	858	US	19 AUG
1964 47B		862	US	19 AUG
1964 48A		861	US	21 AUG
1964 49A		863	USSR	22 AUG
1964 49B		865	USSR	22 AUG
1964 49C		868	USSR	22 AUG
1964 49D	COSMOS 41	869	USSR	22 AUG
1964 50A	COSMOS 42	864	USSR	22 AUG
1964 50B		866	USSR	22 AUG
1964 50C	COSMOS 43	867	USSR	22 AUG
1964 51A	EXPLORER 20	870	US	25 AUG
1964 51B		871	US	25 AUG
1964 51C		873	US	25 AUG
1964 51D		874	US	25 AUG
1964 51E		875	US	25 AUG
1964 52A	NIMBUS 1	872	US	28 AUG
1964 53A	COSMOS 44	876	USSR	29 AUG
1964 53B		877	USSR	29 AUG
1964 52B		878	US	28 AUG
1964 54A	OGO I	879	US	5 SEP
1964 55A	COSMOS 45	880	USSR	13 SEP
1964 55B		881	USSR	13 SEP
1964 56A		882	US	14 SEP
1964 57A	SATURN 7	883	US	18 SEP
1964 58A		884	US	23 SEP
1964 58B		887	US	23 SEP
1964 59A	COSMOS 46	885	USSR	24 SEP
1964 59B		886	USSR	24 SEP
1964 60A	EXPLORER 21	889	US	4 OCT
1964 61A		890	US	5 OCT
1964 62A	COSMOS 47	891	USSR	6 OCT
1964 62B		892	USSR	6 OCT
1964 62C		894	USSR	6 OCT
1964 62D		895	USSR	6 OCT
1964 62E		896	USSR	6 OCT
1964 63A		893	US	6 OCT
1964 63B		897	US	6 OCT
1964 63C		900	US	6 OCT
1964 63D		901	US	6 OCT
1964 63E		902	US	6 OCT
1964 63F		903	US	6 OCT
1964 64A	EXPLORER 22	899	US	10 OCT
1964 64B		907	US	10 OCT
1964 65A	VOSKHOD 1	904	USSR	12 OCT
1964 65B		905	USSR	12 OCT
1964 65C		906	USSR	12 OCT

1964 66A	COSMOS 48	908	USSR	14 OCT
1964 66B		909	USSR	14 OCT
1964 66C		910	USSR	14 OCT
1964 67A		911	US	17 OCT
1964 68B		914	US	23 OCT
1964 68C		916	US	23 OCT
1964 69A	COSMOS 49	913	USSR	24 OCT
1964 69B		915	USSR	24 OCT
1964 69C		917	USSR	24 OCT
1964 70A	COSMOS 50	919	USSR	28 OCT
1964 70B		920	USSR	28 OCT
1964 70C		928	USSR	28 OCT
1964 70D		929	USSR	28 OCT
1964 71A		921	US	2 NOV
1964 72A		922	US	4 NOV
1964 72B		925	US	4 NOV
1964 72C		926	US	4 NOV
1964 72D		927	US	4 NOV
1964 73A	MARINER C	923	US	5 NOV
1964 74A	EXPLORER 23	924	US	6 NOV
1964 75A		930	US	18 NOV
1964 76A	EXPLORER 24	931	US	21 NOV
1964 76B	EXPLORER 25	932	US	21 NOV
1964 76C		933	US	21 NOV
1964 77A	MARINER 4	938	US	28 NOV
1964 78A		943	USSR	30 NOV
1964 78B		944	USSR	30 NOV
1964 78C	ZOND 2	945	USSR	30 NOV
1964 79A		946	US	4 DEC
1964 80A	COSMOS 51	947	USSR	9 DEC
1964 80B		948	USSR	9 DEC
1964 80C		950	USSR	9 DEC
1964 80D		952	USSR	9 DEC
1964 80E		954	USSR	9 DEC
1964 80F		955	USSR	9 DEC
1964 81A		949	US	10 DEC
1964 82A	CENTAUR 4	951	US	11 DEC
1964 83A		953	US	13 DEC
1964 83B		956	US	13 DEC
1964 83C		959	US	13 DEC
1964 84A	SAN MARCO	957	ITALY	15 DEC
1964 84B		958	US	15 DEC
1964 84C		962	US	15 DEC
1964 85A		961	US	19 DEC
1964 86A	EXPLORER 26	963	US	21 DEC
1964 87A		964	US	21 DEC
1964 70E		989	USSR	28 OCT
1964 70F		990	USSR	28 OCT
1964 70G		991	USSR	28 OCT
1964 70H		992	USSR	28 OCT
1964 70J		993	USSR	28 OCT
1964 70K		994	USSR	28 OCT
1964 70L		995	USSR	28 OCT
1964 70M		996	USSR	28 OCT
1964 70N		997	USSR	28 OCT
1964 70P		998	USSR	28 OCT
1964 70Q		999	USSR	28 OCT
1964 70R		1003	USSR	28 OCT
1964 70S		1004	USSR	28 OCT
1964 70T		1005	USSR	28 OCT
1964 70U		1006	USSR	28 OCT
1964 70V		1007	USSR	28 OCT
1964 70W		1008	USSR	28 OCT
1964 70X		1009	USSR	28 OCT
1964 70Y		1010	USSR	28 OCT
1964 70Z		1011	USSR	28 OCT
1964 70AA		1012	USSR	28 OCT
1964 70AB		1013	USSR	28 OCT
1964 70AC		1014	USSR	28 OCT
1964 70AD		1015	USSR	28 OCT
1964 70AE		1016	USSR	28 OCT

1964 70AF	1017	USSR	28 OCT
1964 70AG	1018	USSR	28 OCT
1964 70AH	1019	USSR	28 OCT
1964 70AJ	1020	USSR	28 OCT
1964 70AK	1021	USSR	28 OCT
1964 70AL	1022	USSR	28 OCT
1964 70AM	1023	USSR	28 OCT
1964 70AN	1024	USSR	28 OCT
1964 70AP	1025	USSR	28 OCT
1964 70AQ	1026	USSR	28 OCT
1964 70AR	1027	USSR	28 OCT
1964 70AS	1028	USSR	28 OCT
1964 70AT	1029	USSR	28 OCT
1964 70AU	1030	USSR	28 OCT
1964 70AV	1031	USSR	28 OCT
1964 70AW	1032	USSR	28 OCT
1964 70AX	1033	USSR	28 OCT
1964 70AY	1034	USSR	28 OCT
1964 70AZ	1035	USSR	28 OCT
1964 70BA	1036	USSR	28 OCT
1964 70BB	1037	USSR	28 OCT
1964 70BC	1038	USSR	28 OCT
1964 70BD	1039	USSR	28 OCT
1964 70BE	1040	USSR	28 OCT
1964 70BF	1041	USSR	28 OCT
1964 70BG	1042	USSR	28 OCT
1964 70BH	1043	USSR	28 OCT
1964 70BJ	1044	USSR	28 OCT
1964 70BK	1045	USSR	28 OCT
1964 70BL	1046	USSR	28 OCT
1964 70BM	1047	USSR	28 OCT
1964 70BN	1048	USSR	28 OCT
1964 70BP	1049	USSR	28 OCT
1964 70BQ	1050	USSR	28 OCT
1964 70BR	1051	USSR	28 OCT
1964 70BS	1052	USSR	28 OCT
1964 70BT	1053	USSR	28 OCT
1964 70BU	1054	USSR	28 OCT
1964 70BV	1055	USSR	28 OCT
1964 70BW	1056	USSR	28 OCT
1964 70BX	1057	USSR	28 OCT
1964 70BY	1058	USSR	28 OCT
1964 70BZ	1059	USSR	28 OCT
1964 70CA	1060	USSR	28 OCT
1964 70CB	1061	USSR	28 OCT
1964 70CC	1062	USSR	28 OCT
1964 70CD	1063	USSR	28 OCT
1964 70CE	1064	USSR	28 OCT
1964 70CF	1065	USSR	28 OCT
1964 70CG	1066	USSR	28 OCT
1964 70CH	1067	USSR	28 OCT
1964 70CJ	1068	USSR	28 OCT
1964 70CK	1069	USSR	28 OCT
1964 70CL	1070	USSR	28 OCT
1964 70CM	1071	USSR	28 OCT
1964 70CN	1072	USSR	28 OCT
1964 70CP	1073	USSR	28 OCT
1964 70CQ	1074	USSR	28 OCT
1964 70CR	1075	USSR	28 OCT
1964 70CS	1076	USSR	28 OCT
1964 70CT	1077	USSR	28 OCT
1964 70CU	1078	USSR	28 OCT
1964 70CV	1079	USSR	28 OCT
1964 70CW	1080	USSR	28 OCT
1964 70CX	1081	USSR	28 OCT
1964 70CY	1082	USSR	28 OCT
1964 70CZ	1083	USSR	28 OCT
1964 70DA	1084	USSR	28 OCT

1965 LAUNCHES

1965 01A	COSMOS 52	968	USSR	11 JAN
1965 01B		969	USSR	11 JAN
1965 01C		970	USSR	11 JAN
1965 01D		971	USSR	11 JAN
1965 02A		972	US	15 JAN
1965 03A		973	US	19 JAN
1965 03B		974	US	19 JAN
1965 03C		975	US	19 JAN
1965 04A	TIROS 9	978	US	22 JAN
1965 04B		979	US	22 JAN
1965 05A		980	US	23 JAN
1965 05B		981	US	23 JAN
1965 06A	COSMOS 53	983	USSR	30 JAN
1965 06B		984	USSR	30 JAN
1965 06C		985	USSR	30 JAN
1965 06D		986	USSR	30 JAN
1965 07A	ORB.SOL.OBS. 2	987	US	3 FEB
1965 07B		988	US	3 FEB
1965 08A		1000	US	11 FEB
1965 08B		1001	US	11 FEB
1965 08C		1002	US	11 FEB
1965 09A	PEGASUS I	1085	US	16 FEB
1965 09B		1088	US	16 FEB
1965 10A	RANGER 8	1086	US	17 FEB
1965 11A	COSMOS 54	1089	USSR	21 FEB
1965 11B	COSMOS 55	1090	USSR	21 FEB
1965 11C	COSMOS 56	1091	USSR	21 FEB
1965 11D		1092	USSR	21 FEB
1965 11E		1094	USSR	21 FEB
1965 12A	COSMOS 57	1093	USSR	22 FEB
1965 12B		1095	USSR	22 FEB
1965 12C		1100	USSR	22 FEB
1965 12D		1101	USSR	22 FEB
1965 12E		1102	USSR	22 FEB
1965 12F		1103	USSR	22 FEB
1965 12G		1104	USSR	22 FEB
1965 12H		1105	USSR	22 FEB
1965 12J		1106	USSR	22 FEB
1965 12K		1107	USSR	22 FEB
1965 12L		1108	USSR	22 FEB
1965 12M		1109	USSR	22 FEB
1965 12N		1110	USSR	22 FEB
1965 12P		1111	USSR	22 FEB
1965 12Q		1112	USSR	22 FEB
1965 12R		1113	USSR	22 FEB
1965 12S		1114	USSR	22 FEB
1965 12T		1115	USSR	22 FEB
1965 12U		1116	USSR	22 FEB
1965 12V		1117	USSR	22 FEB
1965 12W		1118	USSR	22 FEB
1965 12X		1119	USSR	22 FEB
1965 12Y		1120	USSR	22 FEB
1965 12Z		1121	USSR	22 FEB
1965 12AA		1122	USSR	22 FEB
1965 12AB		1123	USSR	22 FEB
1965 12AC		1124	USSR	22 FEB
1965 12AD		1125	USSR	22 FEB
1965 12AE		1126	USSR	22 FEB
1965 12AF		1127	USSR	22 FEB
1965 12AG		1128	USSR	22 FEB
1965 12AH		1129	USSR	22 FEB
1965 12AJ		1130	USSR	22 FEB
1965 12AK		1131	USSR	22 FEB
1965 12AL		1132	USSR	22 FEB
1965 12AM		1133	USSR	22 FEB
1965 12AN		1134	USSR	22 FEB
1965 12AP		1135	USSR	22 FEB
1965 12AQ		1136	USSR	22 FEB
1965 12AR		1137	USSR	22 FEB
1965 12AS		1138	USSR	22 FEB

1965 12AT	1139	USSR	22 FEB
1965 12AU	1140	USSR	22 FEB
1965 12AV	1141	USSR	22 FEB
1965 12AW	1142	USSR	22 FEB
1965 12AX	1143	USSR	22 FEB
1965 12AY	1144	USSR	22 FEB
1965 12AZ	1145	USSR	22 FEB
1965 12BA	1146	USSR	22 FEB
1965 12BB	1147	USSR	22 FEB
1965 12BC	1148	USSR	22 FEB
1965 12BD	1149	USSR	22 FEB
1965 12BE	1150	USSR	22 FEB
1965 12BF	1151	USSR	22 FEB
1965 12BG	1152	USSR	22 FEB
1965 12BH	1153	USSR	22 FEB
1965 12BJ	1154	USSR	22 FEB
1965 12BK	1155	USSR	22 FEB
1965 12BL	1156	USSR	22 FEB
1965 12BM	1157	USSR	22 FEB
1965 12BN	1158	USSR	22 FEB
1965 12BP	1159	USSR	22 FEB
1965 12BQ	1160	USSR	22 FEB
1965 12BR	1161	USSR	22 FEB
1965 12BS	1162	USSR	22 FEB
1965 12BT	1163	USSR	22 FEB
1965 12BU	1164	USSR	22 FEB
1965 12BV	1165	USSR	22 FEB
1965 12BW	1166	USSR	22 FEB
1965 12BX	1167	USSR	22 FEB
1965 12BY	1168	USSR	22 FEB
1965 12BZ	1169	USSR	22 FEB
1965 12CA	1170	USSR	22 FEB
1965 12CB	1171	USSR	22 FEB
1965 12CC	1172	USSR	22 FEB
1965 12CD	1173	USSR	22 FEB
1965 12CE	1174	USSR	22 FEB
1965 12CF	1175	USSR	22 FEB
1965 12CG	1176	USSR	22 FEB
1965 12CH	1177	USSR	22 FEB
1965 12CJ	1178	USSR	22 FEB
1965 12CK	1179	USSR	22 FEB
1965 12CL	1180	USSR	22 FEB
1965 12CM	1181	USSR	22 FEB
1965 12CN	1182	USSR	22 FEB
1965 12CP	1183	USSR	22 FEB
1965 12CQ	1184	USSR	22 FEB
1965 12CR	1185	USSR	22 FEB
1965 12CS	1186	USSR	22 FEB
1965 12CT	1187	USSR	22 FEB
1965 12CU	1188	USSR	22 FEB
1965 12CV	1189	USSR	22 FEB
1965 12CW	1190	USSR	22 FEB
1965 12CX	1194	USSR	22 FEB
1965 12CY	1195	USSR	22 FEB
1965 12CZ	1196	USSR	22 FEB
1965 12DA	1197	USSR	22 FEB
1965 12DB	1198	USSR	22 FEB
1965 12DC	1199	USSR	22 FEB
1965 12DD	1200	USSR	22 FEB
1965 12DE	1201	USSR	22 FEB
1965 12DF	1202	USSR	22 FEB
1965 12DG	1203	USSR	22 FEB
1965 12DH	1204	USSR	22 FEB
1965 12DJ	1205	USSR	22 FEB
1965 12DK	1206	USSR	22 FEB
1965 12DL	1209	USSR	22 FEB
1965 12DM	1210	USSR	22 FEB
1965 12DN	1211	USSR	22 FEB
1965 12DP	1212	USSR	22 FEB
1965 12DQ	1213	USSR	22 FEB
1965 12DR	1214	USSR	22 FEB

1965 12DS		1215	USSR	22 FEB
1965 12DT		1216	USSR	22 FEB
1965 12DU		1217	USSR	22 FEB
1965 12DV		1218	USSR	22 FEB
1965 12DW		1219	USSR	22 FEB
1965 12DX		1220	USSR	22 FEB
1965 12DY		1221	USSR	22 FEB
1965 12DZ		1222	USSR	22 FEB
1965 12EA		1223	USSR	22 FEB
1965 12EB		1224	USSR	22 FEB
1965 12EC		1225	USSR	22 FEB
1965 12ED		1226	USSR	22 FEB
1965 12EE		1227	USSR	22 FEB
1965 12EG		1230	USSR	22 FEB
1965 12EW		1254	USSR	22 FEB
1965 13A		1096	US	25 FEB
1965 13B		1193	USSR	25 FEB
1965 14A	COSMOS 58	1097	USSR	26 FEB
1965 14B		1098	USSR	26 FEB
1965 15A	COSMOS 59	1191	USSR	7 MAR
1965 15B		1192	USSR	7 MAR
1965 15C		1207	USSR	7 MAR
1965 16A		NNA	US	9 MAR
1965 16B		NNA	US	9 MAR
1965 16C		NNA	US	9 MAR
1965 16D		NNA	US	9 MAR
1965 16E		NNA	US	9 MAR
1965 17A		1228	US	11 MAR
1965 17B		1248	US	11 MAR
1965 17C		1249	US	11 MAR
1965 17D		1250	US	11 MAR
1965 17E		1251	US	11 MAR
1965 18A	COSMOS 60	1246	USSR	12 MAR
1965 18B		1252	USSR	12 MAR
1965 18C		1253	USSR	12 MAR
1965 19A		1247	US	12 MAR
1965 19B		1259	US	12 MAR
1965 19C		1260	US	12 MAR
1965 20A	COSMOS 61	1267	USSR	14 MAR
1965 20B	COSMOS 62	1268	USSR	14 MAR
1965 20C	COSMOS 63	1269	USSR	14 MAR
1965 20D		1270	USSR	14 MAR
1965 16F		NNA	US	9 MAR
1965 16G		NNA	US	9 MAR
1965 16H		NNA	US	9 MAR
1965 17F		1249	US	11 MAR
1965 21A		1273	US	18 MAR
1965 21B		1288	US	18 MAR
1965 21C		1289	US	18 MAR
1965 21D		1290	US	18 MAR
1965 22A	VOSKHOD 2	1274	USSR	18 MAR
1965 22B		1285	USSR	18 MAR
1965 22C		1286	USSR	18 MAR
1965 22D		1287	USSR	18 MAR
1965 23A	RANGER 9	1294	US	21 MAR
1965 23B		1298	US	21 MAR
1965 24A	GT-3	1301	US	23 MAR
1965 24B		1302	US	23 MAR
1965 25A	COSMOS 64	1305	USSR	25 MAR
1965 25B		1306	USSR	25 MAR
1965 25C		1308	USSR	25 MAR
1965 26A		1307	US	25 MAR
1965 27A		1314	US	3 APR
1965 27B	EGRS IV	1315	US	3 APR
1965 27C		1316	US	3 APR
1965 28A	EARLY BIRD	1317	US	6 APR
1965 28B		1318	US	6 APR
1965 30A	MOLNIA 1	1324	USSR	23 APR
1965 30B		1325	USSR	23 APR
1965 30C	ROCKET BODY	1326	USSR	23 APR
1965 31B		1329	US	28 APR

1965 31G		1357	US	28 APR
1965 32A	EXPLORER 27	1328	US	29 APR
1965 32B		1358	US	29 APR
1965 33A		1330	US	29 APR
1965 33B		1367	US	29 APR
1965 34A		1359	US	6 MAY
1965 34B		1360	US	6 MAY
1965 34C		1361	US	6 MAY
1965 35A	COSMOS 66	1362	USSR	7 MAY
1965 35B		1363	USSR	7 MAY
1965 35C		1364	USSR	7 MAY
1965 35D		1365	USSR	7 MAY
1965 36A	LUNIK 5	1366	USSR	9 MAY
1965 36B		1368	USSR	9 MAY
1965 36C		1369	USSR	9 MAY
1965 37A		1374	US	18 MAY
1965 38A		1377	US	20 MAY
1965 38B		1378	US	20 MAY
1965 38C		1379	US	20 MAY
1965 38D		1380	US	20 MAY
1965 39A	PEGASUS 2	1381	US	25 MAY
1965 39B	ROCKET BODY	1385	US	25 MAY
1965 40A	COSMOS 67	1382	USSR	25 MAY
1965 40B	ROCKET BODY	1383	USSR	25 MAY
1965 40C		1384	USSR	25 MAY
1965 40D		1387	USSR	25 MAY
1965 41A		1386	US	27 MAY
1965 42A	EXPLORER 28	1388	US	29 MAY
1965 21E		1376	US	18 MAR
1965 27D		1389	US	3 APR
1965 44A	LUNIK 6	1393	USSR	8 JUN
1965 43A	GT-4	1390	US	3 JUN
1965 43B	ROCKET BODY	1391	US	3 JUN
1965 44B		1394	USSR	8 JUN
1965 44C		1395	USSR	8 JUN
1965 37B		1415	US	18 MAY
1965 45A		1396	US	9 JUN
1965 45B		1414	US	9 JUN
1965 46A	COSMOS 68	1404	USSR	15 JUN
1965 46B		1405	USSR	15 JUN
1965 46C		1406	USSR	15 JUN
1965 46D		1407	USSR	15 JUN
1965 46E		1408	USSR	15 JUN
1965 47A		1412	US	18 JUN
1965 47B		1413	US	18 JUN
1965 48A		1420	US	24 JUN
1965 48B		1425	US	24 JUN
1965 48C		1428	US	24 JUN
1965 49A	COSMOS 69	1421	USSR	25 JUN
1965 49B		1423	USSR	25 JUN
1965 49C		1429	USSR	25 JUN
1965 50A		1422	US	25 JUN
1965 50B		1424	US	25 JUN
1965 50C		1426	US	25 JUN
1965 50D		1427	US	25 JUN
1965 51A	TIROS 10	1430	US	2 JUL
1965 51B		1433	US	2 JUL
1965 52A	COSMOS 70	1431	USSR	2 JUL
1965 52B		1432	USSR	2 JUL
1965 52C		1434	USSR	2 JUL
1965 48D		1435	US	24 JUN
1965 51C		1440	US	2 JUL
1965 53A	COSMOS 71	1441	USSR	16 JUL
1965 53B	COSMOS 72	1442	USSR	16 JUL
1965 53C	COSMOS 73	1443	USSR	16 JUL
1965 53D	COSMOS 74	1444	USSR	16 JUL
1965 53E	COSMOS 75	1445	USSR	16 JUL
1965 53F		1448	USSR	16 JUL
1965 53G		1449	USSR	16 JUL
1965 53H		1473	USSR	16 JUL

1965 54A	PROTON 1	1466	USSR	16 JUL
1965 54B		1451	USSR	16 JUL
1965 54C		1450	USSR	16 JUL
1965 54D		1446	USSR	16 JUL
1965 55A		1447	US	17 JUL
1965 55B		1452	US	17 JUL
1965 55C		1455	US	17 JUL
1965 56A	ZOND 3	1454	USSR	18 JUL
1965 56B		1453	USSR	18 JUL
1965 56C		1456	USSR	18 JUL
1965 57A		1457	US	19 JUL
1965 58A		1458	US	20 JUL
1965 58B		1459	US	20 JUL
1965 58C		1460	US	20 JUL
1965 59A		1464	USSR	23 JUL
1965 59B		1465	USSR	23 JUL
1965 60A	PEGASUS 3	1467	US	30 JUL
1965 60B		1468	US	30 JUL
1965 62B		1472	US	3 AUG
1965 61A	COSMOS 77	1469	USSR	3 AUG
1965 61B		1470	USSR	3 AUG
1965 62A		1471	US	3 AUG
1965 62C		1474	US	3 AUG
1965 63A	EGRS 5	1502	US	10 AUG
1965 64A	CENTAUR 6	1503	US	11 AUG
1965 65A		1504	US	13 AUG
1965 65B		1508	US	13 AUG
1965 65C		1510	US	13 AUG
1965 65D		1511	US	13 AUG
1965 65E		1512	US	13 AUG
1965 66A	COSMOS 78	1505	USSR	14 AUG
1965 66B		1507	USSR	14 AUG
1965 66C		1509	USSR	14 AUG
1965 65F		1514	US	13 AUG
1965 65G		1515	US	13 AUG
1965 65H		1520	US	13 AUG
1965 65J		1521	US	13 AUG
1965 65K		1522	US	13 AUG
1965 67A		1513	US	17 AUG
1965 68A	GT-5	1516	US	21 AUG
1965 68C		1518	US	21 AUG
1965 68D		1519	US	21 AUG
1965 69A	COSMOS 79	1523	USSR	25 AUG
1965 69C		1525	USSR	25 AUG
1965 69D		1526	USSR	25 AUG
1965 69E		1527	USSR	25 AUG
1965 70A	COSMOS 80	1570	USSR	3 SEP
1965 70B	COSMOS 81	1571	USSR	3 SEP
1965 70C	COSMOS 82	1572	USSR	3 SEP
1965 70D	COSMOS 83	1573	USSR	3 SEP
1965 70E	COSMOS 84	1574	USSR	3 SEP
1965 70F		1575	USSR	3 SEP
1965 71A	COSMOS 85	1578	USSR	9 SEP
1965 71B		1579	USSR	9 SEP
1965 72A		1580	US	10 SEP
1965 72B		1581	US	10 SEP
1965 72C		1582	US	10 SEP
1965 72D		1583	US	10 SEP
1965 73A	COSMOS 86	1584	USSR	18 SEP
1965 73B	COSMOS 87	1585	USSR	18 SEP
1965 73C	COSMOS 88	1586	USSR	18 SEP
1965 73D	COSMOS 89	1587	USSR	18 SEP
1965 73E	COSMOS 90	1588	USSR	18 SEP
1965 73F		1589	USSR	18 SEP
1965 73G		1590	USSR	18 SEP
1965 73H		1591	USSR	18 SEP
1965 74A		1602	US	22 SEP
1965 75A	COSMOS 91	1603	USSR	23 SEP
1965 75B		1604	USSR	23 SEP
1965 75C		1605	USSR	23 SEP
1965 75D		1606	USSR	23 SEP
1965 75E		1607	USSR	23 SEP
1965 73J		1617	USSR	18 SEP
1965 73K		1618	USSR	18 SEP
1965 76A		1609	US	30 SEP

1965 76B		1614	US	30 SEP
1965 77A	LUNA 7	1610	USSR	4 OCT
1965 77B		1611	USSR	4 OCT
1965 77C		1612	USSR	4 OCT
1965 79A		1615	US	5 OCT
1965 78A		1613	US	5 OCT
1965 78B		1616	US	5 OCT
1965 80A	MOLNIYA II	1621	USSR	13 OCT
1965 80B		1619	USSR	13 OCT
1965 80C		1622	USSR	13 OCT
1965 80D		1623	USSR	13 OCT
1965 81A	OGO 2	1620	US	14 OCT
1965 81B		1625	US	14 OCT
1965 82A		1624	US	15 OCT
1965 82B-82CG			US	15 OCT
1965 83A	COSMOS 92	1626	USSR	16 OCT
1965 83B		1627	USSR	16 OCT
1965 83C		1628	USSR	16 OCT
1965 84A	COSMOS 93	1629	USSR	19 OCT
1965 84B		1630	USSR	19 OCT
1965 84C		1631	USSR	19 OCT
1965 84D		1632	USSR	19 OCT
1965 85A	COSMOS 94	1636	USSR	28 OCT
1965 85B		1638	USSR	28 OCT
1965 86A		1637	US	28 OCT
1965 86B		1639	US	28 OCT
1965 87A	PROTON 2	1701	USSR	2 NOV
1965 87B		1702	USSR	2 NOV
1965 87C		1703	USSR	2 NOV
1965 87D		1704	USSR	2 NOV
1965 87E		1705	USSR	2 NOV
1965 88A	COSMOS-95	1706	USSR	4 NOV
1965 88B		1707	USSR	4 NOV
1965 88C		1708	USSR	4 NOV
1965 89A	EXPLORER 29	1726	US	6 NOV
1965 89B		1729	US	6 NOV
1965 90A		1727	US	8 NOV
1965 90B		1728	US	8 NOV
1965 91A	VENERA 2	1730	USSR	12 NOV
1965 91B		1731	USSR	12 NOV
1965 91C		1732	USSR	12 NOV
1965 92C		1735	USSR	16 NOV
1965 92A	VENERA 3	1733	USSR	16 NOV
1965 92D		1736	USSR	16 NOV
1965 93A	EXPLORER 30	1738	US	19 NOV
1965 93B		1739	US	19 NOV
1965 94A	COSMOS 96	1742	USSR	23 NOV
1965 94B		1743	USSR	23 NOV
1965 94G		1775	USSR	23 NOV
1965 94H		1776	USSR	23 NOV
1965 95A	COSMOS 97	1777	USSR	26 NOV
1965 95B		1779	USSR	26 NOV
1965 95C		1782	USSR	26 NOV
1965 95D		1783	USSR	26 NOV
1965 96A	A-1	1778	FRENCH	26 NOV
1965 96B		1805	FRENCH	26 NOV
1965 97A	COSMOS 98	1780	USSR	27 NOV
1965 97C		1803	USSR	27 NOV
1965 97B		1781	USSR	27 NOV
1965 98A	ALOUETTE 2	1804	CANADA	29 NOV
1965 98B	EXPLORER 31	1806	US	29 NOV
1965 98C		1807	US	29 NOV
1965 98D		1808	US	29 NOV
1965 99A	LUNA 8	1810	USSR	3 DEC
1965 99B		1809	USSR	3 DEC
1965 99C		1811	USSR	3 DEC
1965 100B		1813	US	4 DEC
1965 100A	GT-7	1812	US	4 DEC
1965 101A	FR-1	1814	FRENCH	6 DEC
1965 101B		1815	US	6 DEC
1965 102A		1816	US	9 DEC
1965 102B		1838	US	9 DEC
1965 103A	COSMOS 99	1817	USSR	10 DEC
1965 103B		1818	USSR	10 DEC

INDEX

A

B

D

E

F

G

H

I

J

K

L

M

Mc

N

O

P

R

T

W

Y

PICTURE CREDITS

AEC - 311, 326, 326
Aerojet General Corporation - 157
AT & T - 234
Atomic Energy Commission, Yucca Test Site, Nev. - 46
Bell McClure Syndicate (Drawings by Carl Pfeufer) 40, 41, 42, 50, 56, 80, 88, 89, 94, 128, 136, 139, 147, 150, 151, 154, 158, 160, 162, 163, 165, 169, 181, 183, 185, 186, 188, 189, 191, 193, 195, 197, 200, 201, 203, 206, 209, 210, 211, 213, 215, 216, 218, 222, 227, 229, 240, 245, 247, 254, 257, 260, 262, 263, 265, 274, 276, 278, 290, 295, 302, 305, 306, 309, 323, 331, 337
British News Service - 109
Douglas Aircraft Company - 138, 220, 283, 283, 284, 284, 285, 330
Garrett Aireach Corporation - 92
General Dynamics Astronautics - 38
General Dynamics Convair - 248, 292
General Electric - 206, 288
Goodyear Aircraft - 205
Hughes Aircraft - 221, 226, 231
IT & T - 224
Martin Company - 148, 149, 287
NASA - 66, 114, 115, 125, 132, 133, 237, 244, 320
North American Aviation, Inc. - 242
Ryan Electronics, Division, Ryan Aeronautic Company - 57
Soviet News Agency, Tass Soviet News Agency, Tass - 103, 104, 131, 132, 251
U. S. Air Force - 143, 146, 172, 175, 252, 267
U. S. Army - 108, 111, 118, 119, 271, 327
U. S. Information Service, Athens - 112, 334, 341